Syriac Christian Culture

Syriac Christian Culture

❖ *Beginnings to Renaissance* ❖

Aaron Michael Butts and Robin Darling Young, Editors

The Catholic University
of America Press
Washington, D.C.

The paper used in this publication meets the minimum
requirements of American National Standards for Information
Science Permanence of Paper for Printed Library Materials,
ANSI Z39.48-1984.
∞

Cataloging-in-Publication Data available from the Library of Congress
ISBN 978-0-8132-3368-0

Introduction

Many scholars and students in North America cultivate an interest in Syriac studies, even though there is only a small number of university programs or faculty positions dedicated to the Syriac language or the history, culture, and religion of the historically Syriac-speaking communities. Scholars of early Christianity continue to investigate the distinctive culture of the Syriac-speaking regions in Syria and Mesopotamia expressed in biblical translations and subsequent compositions, while historians of late antiquity or early Islam trace the connections between this region and culture and their neighboring or competitor cultures, such as those of Sassanian Persia or the realm of Islam. The growing number of digitized collections of Syriac manuscripts and Syriac scholarship expresses this continuing interest, as do the essays published here. They are just a small part of the scholarly work on Syriac studies being pursued in North America.

The articles published in this volume represent a selection of the papers presented at the Seventh North American Syriac Symposium (NASS VII), which was convened at The Catholic University of America, Washington, D.C. on June 21-24, 2015. Held every four years, the North American Syriac Symposium brings together university professors, graduate students, and scholars from the United States and Canada as well as from Europe, the Middle East, and India, in particular from the State of Kerala. The Symposium offers a unique opportunity for exchange and discussion on a wide variety of topics related to the language, literature, and cultural history of Syriac Christianity, which extends chronologically from the first centuries CE to the present day and geographically from

Syriac Christianity's homeland in the Middle East to South India, China, and the worldwide diaspora. The first North American Syriac Symposium met at Brown University in 1991. It was followed by symposia at the Catholic University of America (1995), the University of Notre Dame (1999), Princeton Theological Seminary (2003), the University of Toronto (2007), and Duke University (2011).[1] With the 2015 symposium, the Catholic University of America became the first university to host this prestigious event for a second time.

The theme for NASS VII was *Ad Fontes*, or literally, 'to the sources'. This Latin phrase is found in the Latin vulgate version of Ps 42:1: 'As a deer longs for sources (*ad fontes*) of water, so my soul longs for you, God'.[2] The phrase *ad fontes* is, however, better known as an epitomization of the renewed study of Greek and Latin classics during the Renaissance. It was, for instance, used by Erasmus of Rotterdam, who stressed that 'above all, one must hasten to the sources themselves (*ad fontes ipsos*)'.[3] For Erasmus, these sources were in Greek and Latin, but we wanted to extend this to Syriac as well. Thus, one of our goals with NASS VII was to celebrate the rich and varied sources on which the field of Syriac studies is built, from manuscripts and inscriptions to architecture, from objects of art to oral tradition. Symposium participants were encouraged to re-evaluate well-known sources, investigate lesser-known sources, and bring to light entirely new sources. The symposium was also a time to reflect on disciplinary, theoretical, and methodological approaches to these sources.

We have included in this volume those papers that explore or reflect this theme of *Ad Fontes*. In order to make a coherent volume, we selected papers that focused on *texts* as sources and especially literary texts. We are grateful to the contributors, and to all who attended and supported the conference, for their participation.

Aaron Michael Butts
Robin Darling Young

1. For the history of the North American Syriac Symposium, see S. P. Brock and A. M. Butts, "Syriac Conferences," in *GEDSH*, 389–390.

2. This is *ʿal pṣidā* in the Syriac Peshiṭta translation.

3. Erasmus, *De ratione studii ac legendi interpretandique auctores* (Paris: G. Biermant, 1511), edited in *Desiderii Erasmi Roterodami Opera omnia*, vol. 1.2, 120.11 (Amsterdam: North-Holland, 1969).

Table of Contents

Introduction v

Abbreviations ix

Aphrahaṭ and Ephrem: From Context to Reception 1

1. Making Ephrem One of Us 3

❖ Joseph Amar, University of Notre Dame

2. The Significance of Astronomical and Calendrical Theories for Ephrem's Interpretation of the Three Days of Jesus' Death 37

❖ Blake Hartung, Arizona State University

3. Reconsidering the Compositional Unity of Aphrahaṭ's *Demonstrations* 50

❖ J. Edward Walters, Hill Museum and Manuscript Library

4. From Sketches to Portraits 66

The Canaanite Woman within Late Antique Syriac Poetry

❖ Erin Galgay Walsh, University of Chicago Divinity School

Translation 83

5. The Syriac Reception of Plato's *Republic* 85

❖ Yury Arzhanov, Ruhr University, Bochum

6. Did the Dying Jacob Gather His Feet into His Bed (MT) or Stretch Them Out (Peshiṭta)? 97

Describing the Unique Character of the Peshiṭta

❖ Craig Morrison, Pontifical Biblical Institute

Hagiography: Formation and Transmission 111

7. The Invention of the *Persian Martyr Acts* 113

❖ Adam Becker, New York University

8. The Sources of the *History of ʿAbdā damšiḥā* 149

The Creation of a Persian Martyr Act

❖ Simcha Gross, University of Pennsylvania

9. Stories, Saints, and Sanctity between Christianity and Islam 174

The Conversion of Najrān to Christianity in the Sīra of Muhammad

❖ Reyhan Durmaz, University of Pennsylvania

Christians in the Islamic World 199

10. Syriac in the Polyglot Medieval Middle East 201

Digital Tools and the Dissemination of Scholarship Across Linguistic Boundaries

❖ Thomas A. Carlson, Oklahoma State University

11. Christian Arabic Historiography at the Crossroads between the Byzantine, the Syriac, and the Islamic Traditions 212

❖ Maria Conterno, Ghent University

12. Seeing to be Seen 226

Mirrors and Angels in John of Dalyatha

❖ Zachary Ugolnik, Stanford University

13. On Sources for the Social and Cultural History of Christians during the Syriac Renaissance 251

❖ Dorothea Weltecke, Goethe Universität

Epilogue 277

14. Syriac Studies in the Contemporary Academy 279

Some Reflections

❖ Kristian Heal, Brigham Young University

Bibliography 287

Index 343

Abbreviations

General Abbreviations

ca.	*circa*, approximately
ms(s).	manuscript(s)
PMA	*Persian Martyr Acts*, or *Acts of the Persian Martyrs*

Journals, Serials, and Reference Works

AB	*Analecta Bollandiana*
AJSLL	*American Journal of Semitic Languages and Literature*
AKM	Abhandlungen für die Kunde des Morgenlandes
BF	*Byzantinische Forschungen*
BHG	*Bibliotheca Hagiographica Graeca*
BHO	*Bibliotheca Hagiographica Orientalis*, SH 10, edited by Socii Bollandiani. Brussels: Societe des Bollandistes, 1910.
BZ	*Byzantinische Zeitschrift*
CCSG	Corpus Christianorum Series Graeca
CH	*Church History*
CRINT	Compendia Rerum Iudaicarum ad Novum Testamentum
CSCO	Corpus Scriptorum Christianorum Orientalium
DOP	*Dumbarton Oaks Papers*
ECA	*Eastern Christian Art*
ECS	Eastern Christian Studies
ECS	*Eastern Christian Studies*

*EI*²	*Encyclopaedia of Islam*, 2nd ed. Leiden: Brill, 1960–2005.
*EI*³	*Encyclopaedia of Islam*, 3rd ed. Leiden: Brill, 2007–.
EIr	*Encyclopaedia Iranica*. London: Routledge, 1982–.
ÉS	Études syriaques
EVO	*Egitto e Vicino Oriente*
FOC	Fathers of the Church
GCS	Griechischen christlichen Schriftsteller
GEDSH	Sebastian P. Brock, Aaron M. Butts, George A. Kiraz, and Lucas Van Rompay, eds., *Gorgias Encyclopedic Dictionary of the Syriac Heritage*. Piscataway: Gorgias Press, 2011.
GNO	Gregorii Nysseni Opera
GRBS	*Greek, Roman and Byzantine Studies*
HTR	*Harvard Theological Review*
Hugoye	*Hugoye: Journal of Syriac Studies*
HZ	*Historische Zeitschrift*
ICMR	*Islam and Christian-Muslim Relations*
IJMES	*International Journal of Middle East Studies*
JA	*Journal asiatique*
JAAS	*Journal of the Assyrian Academic Studies*
JAOS	*Journal of the American Oriental Society*
JBL	*Journal of Biblical Literature*
JCSSS	*Journal of the Canadian Society for Syriac Studies*
JECS	*Journal of Early Christian Studies*
JESHO	*Journal of the Economic and Social History of the Orient*
JJS	*Journal of Jewish Studies*
JLA	*Journal of Late Antiquity*
JNES	*Journal of Near Eastern Studies*
JRAS	*Journal of the Royal Asiatic Society*
JRS	*Journal of Roman Studies*
JSP	*Journal for the Study of the Pseudepigrapha*
JSS	*Journal of Semitic Studies*
JSS Supplement	Journal of Semitic Studies Supplement
JTS	*Journal of Theological Studies*
LCL	Loeb Classical Library

Image 1. Participants at the Seventh North American Syriac Symposium, The Catholic University of America, June 21-24, 2015.

Image 2. Keynote Speakers: Adam Becker, Dorothea Weltecke, Bas ter Haar Romeny, Joseph Amar (from left to right).

Aphrahaṭ and Ephrem

From Context to Reception

1. Making Ephrem One of Us

❖ Joseph P. Amar

It is a pleasure to be asked to share my thoughts on *Mor Aphrem*, and I thank the members of the local steering committee for their kind invitation. The theme of our conference, *Ad Fontes*, has particular meaning for me since it was here, at The Catholic University of America, that my formal training in Syriac and Arabic began. My ruminations today began to take shape in reading groups directed first by Prof. Patrick Skehan, and later by Prof. Sidney Griffith.

Prof. Skehan's reading group was making its way through Brockelmann's *Chrestomathie*. My graduate students, several of whom are here today, know it well. I still use it for the range of periods and genres it offers, and for the fact that you are forced to read slowly and confront the Syriac. That struggle is necessary training for reading Ephrem, who demands struggle, not because of the esoteric content of his thought—Ephrem is no mystic—but because of the way he coils his writing like a spring. It is only when he lets loose the energy in bursts of insight that we realize that he has been teaching us every step of the way.

Conventional wisdom has it that so little Syriac survives from the fourth century and earlier because monastic scribes charged with preserving the legacy of the past copied only those authors they considered to be orthodox. Even if this argument from silence can be demonstrated, it does not take into account what is self-evident to anyone reading Ephrem in Syriac: He is one-of-a-kind. He impressed a vision on the collective consciousness of Syriac-speaking Christians that was so unique and original, so masterfully unlike anything that had come before, that it obliterated the competition.

There were certainly other high-profile poets working at the time, but we have no record of conversations that may have taken place among them. Ephrem referred to a pompous windbag infatuated with the sound of his own voice; Ephrem had no patience for the man: "He drones on and on like a drunk." We wish Ephrem had mentioned the fellow's name, but doing so would have only contributed to the celebrity the man craved; in any event, Ephrem's audience would have recognized who he was referring to. The point was, the man needed to get over himself—"shake off his inflated self-regard."[1] Ephrem would be equally pained by later, lesser, more timid minds: His monastic editors found his writing woefully out of step with contemporary tastes. They took it upon themselves to update someone who had railed against the obfuscating theological jargon they were perfecting. In the process, they invented someone who never existed.

I begin from the premise that Ephrem was a prodigy and a genius. If the word genius does not convey much beyond extravagant admiration, we get closer to the truth with Jacob of Serugh's description of Ephrem as "New wine ... who made men and women drunk."[2] The Seventh North American Syriac Sympoisum is testimony to the fact that he is still doing it.

As a graduate student, I developed an interest in Syriac hagiography, particularly the *Life of Ephrem*, which, in contrast to Ephrem's authentic writings, is easy to read. The *Life* is written in discursive prose, most of it originating in Greek, either in reports of ecclesiastical historians, or in anonymous documents falsely attributed to high-profile Greek authors like Gregory of Nyssa and Basil of Caesarea. These latter narratives belong to a category of writing referred to in academic circles as "pseudepigraphy"—literally, "false ascription"—which tactfully avoids the less flattering label of "forgeries."

At the time, I was translating Maronite liturgical books: the *Rish Quryān*—a lectionary which includes remnants of liturgical poetry;

1. E. Beck, *Des Heiligen Ephraem des Syrers Hymnen de Fide*, CSCO 154–155 (Louvain: Peeters, 1955), 22:12. Hereafter, *Hymnen de Fide*. Throughout this paper, references to Beck's editions are to the Syriac text. Although the insights of previous translators have greatly benefited me throughout this paper, unless otherwise indicated, all translations are my own.

2. Joseph P. Amar, *A Metrical Homily on Holy Mar Ephrem by Mar Jacob of Sarug*, PO 47.1 (Turnhout: Brepols, 1995), 113. Hereafter, *A Metrical Homily on Holy Mar Ephrem*.

and the *Synksar,* the Syriac version of the *Synaxarion*, which exists only in manuscript form.[3] The *Synksar* provides background commentary, most of it apocryphal, for major feasts and commemorations. The *Synksar* entry on Ephrem recounted an episode found in several Syriac and Greek recensions of his life, but which never made it into the Syriac *Life*.[4]

The episode involves Ephrem's encounter with the sister of Bardaiṣan. The anonymous author of the account was either unaware, or chose to overlook the fact that Bardaiṣan died in the first quarter of the third century—222 is the date usually cited—making it quite impossible that a sister of his would have survived into the fourth century. Conflations of this sort are commonplace in Syriac hagiography. They belong to the same category of quasi-historical belief held by some even today that dinosaurs and humans inhabited the earth simultaneously. The *Life of Ephrem*, as I was to discover, contained numerous examples of this phenomenon. They are early instances of what Harold Bloom calls the "anxiety of influence": the persistent and recurring pattern by which a new age finds cause to "upgrade," according to its own standards, the timeless influences produced by the age that went before.[5]

As the *Synksar* entry had it, Bardaiṣan's sister was in possession of a heretical Gospel written by her brother which Ephrem was intent on destroying. Bardaiṣan is not known to have crafted a Gospel of his own, but that detail did not constitute an impediment to the author of this episode. Mani and Marcion had written alternative Gospels, and since Ephrem included them, along with Bardaiṣan, in his *Prose Refutations*, it may have seemed to the author of our account that the creation of a heretical Gospel could be alleged of Bardaiṣan as well. Which brings us to another feature of Syriac hagiography: its propensity to borrow freely from unrelated narratives which it reshapes and tailors to accommodate a destination for which they were never intended. The process is what specialists refer to, far too benignly, as

3. Joseph P. Amar, "An Unpublished *Karšûnî* Arabic Life of Ephrem the Syrian," *Le Muséon* 106 (1993): 119–144.

4. Joseph P. Amar, *The Syriac Vita Tradition of Ephrem the Syrian*, CSCO 629 (Louvain: Peeters, 2011). Hereafter, *The Syriac Vita Tradition*. All references are to the Syriac text.

5. Harold Bloom, *The Anxiety of Influence: A Theory of Poetry* (New York: Oxford University Press, 1997).

"the motility of folk material." The Syriac *Life of Ephrem* is a classic example of this phenomenon.

The *Life* is an extended exercise in cutting and pasting material from other accounts to create a narrative purporting to describe the circumstances of Ephrem's life.[6] The appropriated material typically signals developments that took place well after Ephrem's time but which the compilers of the *Life* called upon him to legitimate. The fiction that brought together Bardaiṣan's sister and Ephrem may have been encouraged by a law enacted by the Emperor Theodosius II (408–450) in 409 targeting heretical books: "If someone should be convicted of having hidden any of these books... and of having failed to deliver them (for burning), he shall know that he himself shall suffer capital punishment as a retainer of noxious books and writings."[7] The episode preserved in the *Synksar* casts Ephrem as a zealous agent of Byzantine orthodoxy who dutifully seeks out and destroys hidden repositories of heresy.

Bardaiṣan's sister—we never learn her name—agrees to hand over her brother's heretical text on the condition that Ephrem have sex with her. The ancient audience for which the account was crafted would have gasped in disbelief when they heard Ephrem agree to her condition.[8] When the woman hands over the heretical Gospel, Ephrem informs her of a condition of his own: He will accede to her demand only if the act takes place in public for all to see. As Ephrem explains, there is no point in hiding the deed, since God sees everything, even things done in private. When the woman hears Ephrem's condition, she has an abrupt change of heart and retreats into the shadows. The episode concludes with Ephrem destroying the heretical Gospel, his virtue intact.

Although, as I have said, what would eventually emerge as the Syriac *Life of Ephrem* does not include this episode, the *Life* preserves other no less contrived tales suggestive of sexual impropriety initiated

---

6. The sources of the Syriac *Life* are reviewed in Bernard Outtier, "Saint Éphrem d'après ses biographies et ses oeuvres," *PdO* 4 (1973): 11–34. For a fuller treatment including Arabic and Armenian versions of the *Life*, see *The Syriac Vita Tradition*, Vol. 630, XVI–XXIX.

7. Caroline Humfress, "Roman Law, Forensic Argument and the Formation of Christian Orthodoxy," in *Orthodoxie, christianisme, histoire*, edited by S. Elm, E. Rebillard, and A. Romano, 125–147 (Rome: École Française de Rome, 2000), 140.

8. The *Life* combines drama with pathos. See, for example, *The Syriac Vita Tradition* ch. 4, where Ephrem is accused of fathering a child but is vindicated when the newborn miraculously speaks, makes known the identity of his father, and dies as soon as the words leave his mouth.

MPI	Monographs of the Peshitta Institute
NAS	*New Arabian Studies*
NPNF	Philip Schaff, ed., *A Select Library of Nicene and Post-Nicene Fathers of the Christian Church.* New York: Scribner, 1898-1909.
OC	*Oriens Christianus*
OCA	Orientalia Christiana Analecta
OCP	*Orientalia Christiana Periodica*
OLA	Orientalia Lovaniensia Analecta
PdO	*Parole de l'Orient*
PEQ	*Palestine Exploration Quarterly*
PG	J.-P. Migne, *Patrologia cursus completes, Series Graeca.* Paris: Bibliothecae cleri universae, 1857–1866.
PO	Patrologia Orientalis
PS	Patrologia Syriaca
PTS	Patristische Texte und Studien
RLMCMS	Religion and Law in Medieval Christian and Muslim Societies
ROC	*Revue de l'orient chrétienne*
RSO	*Rivista degli Studi Orientali*
SC	Sources chrétiennes
SFOC	Selections from the Fathers of the Church
SH	Subsidia Hagiographica
SKCO	Sprachen und Kulturen des Christlichen Orients
SOK	Studien zur Orientalischen Kirche
SP	*Studia Patristica*
SymSyr III	R. Lavenant, ed., *III*° *Symposium Syriacum 1980: Les contacts du monde syriaque avec les autres cultures (Goslar 7–11 Septembre 1980)*, OCA 221. Rome: Pontificium Institutum Studiorum Orientalium, 1983.
SymSyr IV	Han J. W. Drijvers, René Lavenant, Corrie Molenberg, and Gerrit J. Reinink, eds., *IV Symposium Syriacum, 1984: Literary Genres in Syriac Literature (Groningen – Oosterhesselen 10–12 September)*, OCA 229. Rome: Pontificium Institutum Studiorum Orientalium, 1987.

SymSyr V	R. Lavenant, ed., *V Symposium Syriacum 1988*, OCA 236. Rome: Pontificium Institutum Studiorum Orientalium, 1990.
SymSyr VI	R. Lavenant, ed., *VI Symposium Syriacum 1992*, OCA 247. Rome: Pontificium Institutum Studiorum Orientalium, 1994.
SymSyr VII	R. Lavenant, ed., *Symposium Syriacum VII. 1996*, OCA 256. Rome: Pontificium Institutum Studiorum Orientalium, 1998.
TEG	Traditio Exegetica Graeca
TSAJ	Texts and Studies in Ancient Judaism
TTH	Translated Texts for Historians
TU	Texte und Untersuchungen
TUCL	Texte und Untersuchungen zur der altchristlichen Literatur
VC	*Vigiliae Christianae*
VT	*Vetus Testamentum*

by dark female figures intent on deflowering Ephrem.[9] These episodes, which would become a leitmotif in the expanding mythology of Ephrem, say far more about the monastic compilers of his Syriac *Life* than they do about the historical Ephrem. The monks' discomfort with their own sexuality seamlessly morphed into the belief that the women who excited their passions were the source of their disease: In a world where Eve is always the problem, men are inevitably portrayed as hapless victims.

If Ephrem's monastic biographers were unnerved by his high regard for women, Jacob of Serugh praised him for it. He quoted from a work of Ephrem's that has not survived—we cannot rule out the possibility that it was actively suppressed and ended up on the monastery's cutting room floor. Jacob quotes Ephrem as saying: "Uncover your faces; sing out without shame / to the One who let you speak freely by His birth."[10] Although Jacob is traditionally numbered among a small circle of Ephrem's continuators, his writing never achieved the cultural currency that Ephrem's did. This may have worked in Jacob's favor: By flying under the radar of later monastic censors, he was able to preserve words of Ephrem's that would otherwise have been lost.

At the next meeting of our reading group, I asked Prof. Skehan how it was that Ephrem had become a magnet for so many lurid caricatures. How was someone of Ephrem's stature reduced to a two-dimensional stick-figure of a man who spent his days foiling the advances of "wicked city women"? Prof. Skehan was as much a gentleman as he was a scholar, but he did not pull punches. He looked me straight in the eye and said: "People who feel the need to cut Ephrem down to size inevitably cut him down to their own size." It was only later that I realized that Skehan's words came very close to what Ephrem himself had said about *boʿuyē* and *dorušē* —today we call them dogmatic theologians: "Someone who can investigate [God] / becomes the container of what he investigates."[11] In a sense, the words apply to Ephrem as well. They serve as a cautionary note to

9. The Syriac *Life* fits a pattern of much earlier episodic texts from Christian antiquity—the apocryphal Gospels and Acts are obvious parallels—in which individual episodes that circulated independently were brought together to form discrete works. See the examples adduced in Christine M. Thomas, *The Acts of Peter, Gospel Literature, and the Ancient Novel: Rewriting the Past* (Oxford: Oxford University Press, 2003).

10. *A Metrical Homily on Holy Mar Ephrem*, 113.

11. *Hymnen de Fide* 9:16.

anyone bold, or foolish, enough to put Ephrem under a microscope: You have to be very careful about the lens you choose to look through. Analyzing people with exceptional spiritual gifts is best left to people with exceptional spiritual gifts.

Syriac studies have come a long way since the days of that reading group, when Syriac was still largely an appendage to biblical studies. Interest in Ephrem has grown as well, as translations of his works into modern languages have made the rich legacy of Syriac's most gifted writer available to a wider reading public. The growing interest in Syriac Christianity, and in Ephrem in particular, is welcome and to be encouraged. At the same time, however, the early influence of the Syriac *Life* established a precedent that is still very much with us. So it is there, with the *Life of Mor Ephrem the Syrian*, that our story must begin. This means cutting through the layers of pseudo-biography that form the core of the *Life* and which continue to influence our views of Ephrem. In what follows, I do not propose to advance a new understanding of Ephrem; my aim is to show why the original remains the only one that matters.

❖ ❖ ❖ ❖

In the early decades of the fifth century, monks in the city of Edessa were hard at work dismantling the works of Syria's most revered writer. If "dismantling" suggests a haphazard exercise in cutting and pasting, then it accurately describes the process that was underway. Ephrem had been dead for less than a century, but his writings were uncomfortably old-fashioned. They belonged to an earlier form of discourse, the survival of a creative ferment that left traces of itself in the Mishnah and the *Acts of Thomas*. We no longer have a clear picture of the communities that produced these texts. They were replaced by a new technology, a specialized language which defined the Great Church of the Byzantine Empire and was married to imperial necessity. The monks gathered what they saw as the usable fragments of Ephrem's *madrošē* which they cobbled together to accommodate the emerging cycle of liturgical prayers that punctuated monastic life.[12]

12. What has come down to us of Ephrem's authentic writings represents a pitiful fragment of a much larger archive. See Dom B. Outtier, OSB, "Contribution à l'étude de la préhistoire des collections

Their more challenging project was to create a portrait of Ephrem as the ideal monk who legitimated their way of life. Drawing from purportedly biographical accounts circulating among Greek-speaking churchmen who were themselves proponents of the monastic lifestyle, the monks laid down the broad strokes of an image which they supplemented with vividly implausible tales of their own creation intended to depict Ephrem as the paragon of monastic virtue.[13]

Crafting Ephrem in the image of the ideal ascetic was only one element in a far more ambitious project. The monks formed the vanguard in a process that would take definitive shape early in the sixth century under the inspiration of Philoxenos, the ascetical-minded bishop of Mabbog, and Severus, the patriarch he supported and endorsed. Their goal was to craft a literary and ecclesiastical culture to meet the challenges from Byzantine Chalcedonians to the West, and Dyophysite Persians to the East. The *Life of Ephrem* would serve as the centerpiece of their project.

In his own way, Ephrem encouraged the creation of the anachronistic and wildly contradictory image which the monks depicted in the *Life*. Everything about Ephrem resists biography. Not only was he frustratingly tight-lipped about the details of his life, but on the rare occasion when he alluded to himself he did so in language that was so vague that it invited speculation. This, however, was no impediment to his monastic handlers: They were not interested in the historical accuracy of their account; their purpose was to elicit the renown of Syria's most celebrated author in support of their own project.

In his own time, Ephrem's authority was that of a prophet and a visionary: The earliest Arabic *Life of Ephrem* calls him "The Syriac Prophet."[14] That image would be subsumed by a Syriac church in the process of crafting a new literary identity for itself. The *Life*, which depicts Ephrem as a hermit and monk, distanced him from active participation in everyday life and secured his place in the emerging circle of Edessan ecclesiastical culture.

---

d'hymnes d'Ephrem," *PdO* 6–7 (1975–1976): 49–61. Also S. P. Brock, "St. Ephrem in the Eyes of Later Syriac Liturgical Tradition," *Hugoye* 2 (1999): 5–25; *idem*, "The Transmission of Ephrem's *madrashe* in the Syriac Liturgical Tradition," *SP* 33 (1997): 490–505.

13. On the monastic appropriation of Ephrem, see Joseph P. Amar, "Byzantine Ascetic Monachism and Greek Bias in the *Vita* Tradition of Ephrem the Syrian," *OCP* 58 (1992): 123–156.

14. Addai Scher, *Histoire nestorienne inédite (Chronique de Séert)*, PO 4.3, 5.2, 7.2, 13.4 (Paris: Firmin-Didot, 1907–1919), vol. 5.2, 291.

By the time the monks set about appropriating Ephrem's reputation in support of their cause, a sea change had swept across Syria. Ephrem's hometown of Nisibis, the city he boasted had been "the herald of the truth of its Savior," was in Persian hands.[15] In 363, the Roman Emperor Jovian had ceded Nisibis to Persia in exchange for safe passage of a Roman army in humiliating retreat. In 489, the onus of heresy further complicated the city's suspect affiliations. In that year, the Emperor Zeno closed the School of the Persians in Edessa for its association with the anathematized teachings of Theodore of Mopsuestia. The school relocated to Nisibis where, in the decades to come, it would emerge as the intellectual powerhouse of East Syriac Christianity.

In light of these traumatic events, the Edessan churchmen charged with updating Ephrem's image saw fit to distance him from a city that was now both politically and theologically suspect, and in the process, to transfer his allegiances to their own beloved Edessa. They did this, in part, by creating the fiction that Ephrem arrived in Edessa, not as an old man of sixty-plus years, but as a teenager, an eighteen-year-old by one account, who, in the words of the *Life*, when he first caught sight of city, "could not wait to get there, and made up his mind to spend the rest of his life in Edessa." The *Life* bathes Edessa in an other-worldly glow; it is a gleaming Emerald City, "its hillsides crowned all about with monasteries and hermits' cells."[16] Here, again, we find evidence that the Syriac *Life* was a key element in a much larger program to secure the status of Edessa as an emerging bastion of Syriac orthodoxy.

The project to distance Ephrem from his Nisibean roots and claim him as an Edessan required written evidence which the monks produced by way of a *mimro*, a metrical praise-song, *On Edessa* which they claimed Ephrem had composed.[17] Not surprisingly, the anonymous author of the *mimro* exhibits detailed familiarity with the legend preserved in the *Teaching of Addai* purporting to establish the apostolic origins of the church of Edessa; the *mimro*, like the

15. E. Beck, *Des Heiligen Ephraem des Syrers Hymnen de Paradiso und Contra Julianum*, CSCO 174–175 (Louvain: Peeters, 1957), 2:19. Hereafter, *de Paradiso* und *Contra Julianum.*

16. *The Syriac Vita Tradition*, ch. 10.

17. Joseph P. Amar, "An Encomium on Edessa attributed to Ephrem the Syrian," *Orientalia Christiana Analecta* 58 (2008): 120–162. See also *The Syriac Vita Tradition*, ch. 38.

Syriac *Life*, emerged from the same monastic circles that produced the Addai legend.[18] The *mimro* exploits every opportunity to remind its hearers of Edessa's preeminence: "Edessa, adorned with glory; / her boast is in the name of Jesus. // And again, she is glorified by her emissary, / by Addai the blessed apostle."[19]

The *mimro* brought together two tendentious claims: the first, that Christianity reached Edessa in the lifetime of the apostles; and second, that Syriac Christianity's most celebrated writer had immortalized the city in verse. At the same time, of course, the *mimro* counterbalanced the devotion Ephrem expressed for his native city in his authentic collection of *Madrošē on Nisibis*.[20]

Chapter 10 of the Syriac *Life* contends that Ephrem left Nisibis immediately following its handover to the Persians, but that he went first to Amid before continuing on to Edessa. As with so much else in the *Life*, there is good reason to question the veracity of the report. The most serious issue for reconstructing Ephrem's transition from Nisibis to Edessa is the loss of verses 22–24 of the *Madrošē on Nisibis*. The missing verses occur at precisely the point in the narrative where the handover of Nisibis takes place; as such, they may well have preserved details related not only to Ephrem's continued presence in Nisibis, but to the circumstances surrounding his eventual departure. We cannot overlook the possibility that Ephrem's monastic editors suppressed the missing verses, especially if they contradicted when, according to the Syriac *Life*, Ephrem arrived in Edessa. Ephrem's own version of events only deepens the mystery.

In his *Madrošē against Julian*, Ephrem praises Shapur, the Persian Shah, for the leniency he showed to Nisibean Christians by reopening the churches which Julian had closed: "The Magus who entered our place regarded it as holy... He neglected his [own] fire temple and honored [our] sanctuary...".[21] Other details relating to Shapur's take-

---

18. For a comprehensive treatment of the *Teaching of Addai* in its historical and cultural setting, see S. P. Brock, "Eusebius and Syriac Christianity," in *Eusebius, Christianity, and Judaism*, edited by Harold W. Attridge and Gohei Hata, 212–234 (Detroit: Wayne State University Press, 1992).

19. *The Syriac Vita Tradition*, 89 (ms. Vatican Syriac 117, fol. 193r).

20. Edmund Beck, *Des Heiligen Ephraem des Syrers Carmina Nisibena*, I-II, CSCO 218, 219 and 240, 241 (Louvain: Peeters, 1961 and 1963). Hereafter, *Carmina Nisibena*.

21. Also, "The [Roman] king [Julian] became a [pagan] priest and dishonored our churches; but the Magian king honored the sanctuary. His honoring the sanctuary increased our consolation." *Contra Julianum* 2:22, 27.

over of the city add to the ambiguity: "The city [of Nisibis] was not dealt with as other [cities]... / The Just One whose anger is mighty, mixed love with His anger. / Rather than leading us away as captives into exile, He let us dwell in our country."[22]

The ambiguity of the lines has generated a flurry of scholarly speculation: While some take the evidence of the *Life* at face value, and place Ephrem in Edessa soon after 363, others, like Addai Scher, insist that Ephrem could not have arrived in Edessa before 369, a mere four years before his death.[23] The question of when Ephrem left Nisibis remains entirely unresolved, as does the possibility that, at some point after leaving, he returned.

The greater challenge the creators of the Syriac *Life* faced was to find a way of bringing a complex, multi-faceted creative genius, a cultural icon who fired the imagination of Syriac Christians, within safe and controllable boundaries. They would guarantee this, not simply by making Ephrem an Edessan and a monk, but by making him a deacon. This would begin the long and contorted effort to re-make Ephrem in the image of *homo ecclesiasticus*. It was Jerome, who, with no first-hand knowledge of Ephrem—he did not even know of Ephrem's Nisibean origins—identified him exclusively as "deacon of Edessa."[24]

Ephrem uses two words, *mšamšonē* and *šamošē*, to refer to deacons, but he never uses either word in reference to himself. Nor is his self-identification as *ʿallono*—a word that is as rare as it is ambiguous—of much help. Ephrem uses it to speak of priests and bishops—unless, of course, we accept the testimony of the Greek text of Pseudo-Amphilochios of Iconium which claims that Basil ordained Ephrem to the priesthood and his translator to the diaconate![25] Identifying Ephrem as a deacon is harmless enough, so long as we keep in mind that whatever function he had in the church of Nisibis has no analogue to anything we know today.

Robert Murray, who set out to map the ecclesiology of early Syriac Christianity, concluded that, in the formative period, Syriac

---

22. *Contra Julianum* 2:26.

23. Scholarly opinions on the handover of Nisibis are summarized in Kathleen E. McVey, *Ephrem the Syrian: Hymns* (New York: Paulist Press, 1989), 241 fn. 104.

24. E. C. Richardson, *Hieronymous. Liber de Viris Inlustirbus*, Texte und Untersuchungen 14 (Leipzig: J. C. Hinrichs, 1896), 87.

25. *The Syriac Vita Tradition*, vol. 630, xxiii–xxv.

Christianity lacked a well-defined sense of itself. This judgement by an acknowledged specialist in the field serves as a reminder that, although we know significantly more about Nisibis beginning in the fifth century, we know little about how the church was structured, or its precise lines of authority in Ephrem's day. This, however, was no impediment to Ephrem's monastic editors who felt the need to burnish his image even as they blunted his message. In the words of Luk Van Rompay's subtitle to his study of Ephrem's fading influence, the monks found a way that combined both "Respect and Distance."[26]

In the end, they settled on a strategy guaranteed to make the Ephrem of history irrelevant: They made him a saint. Like Christ himself, the Ephrem they created calmed raging seas, cured paralytics, and even raised the dead![27] Elevating Ephrem to saintly status insured that he would be fervently invoked in the public prayer of the church as a model of piety and submission to ecclesiastical authority. Absent from their profile was any evidence of the man who challenged authority and took serious exception to the direction the church was taking. Ephrem was on his way to being effectively neutered.

The monks supported the fictional image they created by producing an archive of texts which they attributed to Ephrem. Their project was part *hommage*, part propagandistic tool. Known collectively as *Ephraem Graecus*, the pseudo-Ephrem archive of writings is the second largest collection of its kind to survive from late antiquity. It is surpassed only by works falsely attributed to John Chrysostom. The strategy allowed Greek-speaking churchmen, no less than their Syrian admirers, to point to Ephrem as evidence that the church was, in fact, a worldwide *oikoumene*, with Greek language and culture its highest, divinely-sanctioned, expression. By attaching the name of Ephrem to a way of life he never lived, and to doctrines he never espoused, the monks laid claim to the prestige and authority of Syriac Christianity's brightest light.

The two projects—the first, to forge an image of Ephrem that comported with monastic values; and the second, to use Ephrem's name and reputation to support a way of life he never lived—were mutually complicit. Ephrem was on his way to becoming the iconic

26. Lucas Van Rompay, "*Mallpânâ dilan Suryâyâ*: Ephrem in the Works of Philoxenus of Mabbog: Respect and Distance," *Hugoye* 7 (2004): 83–105.

27. *The Syriac Vita Tradition*, ch. 21, 33, and 29 respectively.

homo ecclesiasticus, the "Father of the Church" whom we know him as today. The transformation was necessary if Ephrem was to take his place in the pantheon of approved ecclesiastical writers. The irony, of course, is that as far as educated Greeks and Romans were concerned, Syrians were loathsome creatures, the dark shadow of the West.

Romans inherited their low regard for Syrians from Greeks. Roman preeminence may have been served by the notion that all roads led to Rome, but the first-century satirist, Juvenal, had something quite different in mind when he complained:

> The Syrian Orontes has been disgorging into the Tiber for some time now... It has brought us the language and customs of Syria: female flute-players, slanting harps, exotic tambourines, and young girls with instructions to loiter near the Circus. Go to them if you love barbarian she-wolves in gaudy head-dresses.[28]

When the Roman historian, Tacitus, described Rome as "the cesspool of the world" he was referring to the influx of easterners whose faces, ways of dressing, language, and customs had contributed to the city's seething, motley life.[29]

But it was Libanius, a contemporary of Ephrem's, who found a way to ridicule both the Syriac language and Syrian ethnicity in a swipe at Sabinianus, a member of the Roman Senate whom he despised. Libanius compared him to low-life tradesmen who hawked their wares in the streets: "Someone like [Sabinianus] is a greater disgrace to the senate than all those who yell out in Syriac for customers who need them for mending bowls."[30] Ephrem's appeal to Greek-speaking ecclesiastics was due, in no small measure, to the fact that here was a Syrian who was almost as good as they were.

Knowledge of Ephrem trickled into Europe through Latin translations of *Ephraem Graecus* circulating in Roman Catholic monastic

28. Juvenal, *Satire* III, 62–66. For edition and translation, see S. M. Braund, *Juvenal and Persius*, LCL 91 (Cambridge: Harvard University Press, 2004).

29. Tacitus, *Annals*, 15: 20–23, 33–45. For edition and translation, see J. Jackson, *Tacitus. Annals 13–16*, LCL 322 (Cambridge: Harvard University Press, 1937).

30. Libanius, *Oration 42 "For Thallasius."* For translation, see A. F. Norman, *Antioch as a Centre of Hellenic Culture as Observed by Libanius*, TTH 34 (Liverpool: Liverpool University Press, 2000), 158–159.

circles. Ephrem's formal debut in the West would await the arrival of Joseph Simon Assemani who came to study at the Maronite College in Rome in the first half of the eighteenth century.[31] Assemani's purported linguistic skills attracted the attention of Pope Clement XII who, in 1717, commissioned him to travel throughout the Middle East and collect manuscripts for the Oriental section of the Vatican Library. Assemani returned to Rome with a treasure trove of texts, most notably, from the famed Monastery of Our Lady of the Syrians in the Nitrian Desert of Egypt. Two years later, we find him serving as Prefect of the Vatican Library where, between 1719 and 1728, he produced the nine enormous folio volumes of the *Bibliotheca Orientalis Clementino-Vaticana*—we know it today as the *Editio Romana*. The *Editio* made available Syriac texts by major writers under the headings of Orthodox (by which Assemani meant "Chalcedonian"), Monophysite, and Nestorian.[32] Between 1732 and 1746, Joseph Simon, in collaboration with relatives, Butros Mubarak (Petrus Benedictus) and Estefan ʿAwwad (Stephanus Evodius), produced the six-volume *Sancti Patris Nostri Ephraem Syri Opera Omnia*. While we cannot expect these early efforts to conform to modern critical standards, they raise serious questions that continue to baffle scholars.

The first of these concerns the Syriac texts which the Assemanis reproduced: In a large number of cases, the printed versions of the manuscripts which appear in the *Opera Omnia* do not faithfully represent the Syriac originals.[33] The second problem concerns the Latin translations of the manuscripts which appear in parallel columns. Not only are these translations periphrastic; in a large number of cases, they bear little relationship to the Syriac texts they purport to translate.[34]

A full study of Simon Joseph Assemani and his relatives would take us very far afield, but such a study would be enormously helpful in understanding what motivated them and their project. The

31. A detailed treatment of the Assemani family is not of immediate concern to us here. However, Assemani's personal history, as well as the history of the Maronite Church during this period, are key to understanding the texts that the Assemanis produced and the interpretations they imposed on them.

32. J. Melki, "S. Ephrem le Syrien, un bilan de l'édition critique," *PdO* 11 (1983): 3–88, at 16–17.

33. See, for example, T. Jansma, "The Provenance of the Last Sections in the Roman Edition of Ephrem's Commentary on Exodus," *Le Muséon* 85 (1972): 155–169.

34. T. Jansma, "Ephrem's Commentary on Exodus: Some Remarks on the Syriac Text and the Latin Translation," *JSS* 17 (1972): 203–212.

Assemanis were not only leading orientalists of their day, they were ideologues. In the *Praefatio Altera* to the *Opera Omnia*, Butrus Mubarak invoked Ephrem as a witness to the unchanging truth of the See of Rome ("Romanae Cathedrae Doctrina"); he went on to make the tendentious claim that Ephrem supported Roman Catholic dogma against the "perfidious influences of Jansenism, Lutheranism, and Calvinism."[35]

Dom Edmund Beck was one of the first western scholars to be appalled by Joseph Simon Assemani's poor grasp of Syriac.[36] More recently, Joseph Melki judged translations made by the Assemanis to be not only periphrastic, but, in some cases, entirely invented.[37] Melki observed that "corrections" the Assemanis made to passages in Ephrem which they found difficult or unsettling were dictated by "purely dogmatic considerations."[38] Joseph Simon's questionable methods, in particular, begin to make sense when we consider the full scope of his career. In 1736, Pope Clement delegated him in the role of Apostolic Visitator to the Synod of Mount Lebanon. The synod institutionalized Latinizations in the Maronite Church that had accumulated over centuries.

The Catholicizing tendency continued with Pope Benedict XV's encyclical *Principi Apostolorum Petro* (Oct. 5, 1920) declaring Ephrem a Doctor of the Universal Church.[39] No one would question Ephrem's worthiness of the accolade, but many have wondered at the timing of the encyclical, pointing to its obvious weaknesses. The encyclical, which was written before Ephrem's authentic writings were separated from the tangle of monastic writings circulating under his name, based its image of Ephrem on a spurious Greek *Life* falsely attributed to Gregory of Nyssa. The problem, however, went much deeper than Benedict's reliance on Pseudo-Gregory.[40] The encyclical

35. *Sancti Patris Nostri Ephraem Syri Opera Omnia, Praefatio Altera,* xiv–xv.

36. Beck, "Ephrem le Syrien," *Dictionnaire de Spiritualité*, t. 4 (1960) col. 790; *idem*, *Die Theologie des hl. Ephräm in seinen Hymnen über den Glauben*, Studia Anselmiana 21 (Rome: Libreria Vaticana, 1949), 2.

37. Melki, "Un bilan," 24.

38. Melki, "Un bilan," 25.

39. *Acta Apostolicae Sedis* 12 (1920), 457–471.

40. As Sebastian Brock has noted: "It would be interesting to know what had led Pope Benedict to make the declaration at that particular time when there was only imperfect and incomplete editions of [Ephrem's] works available, and very few translations into modern European languages." S. P. Brock,

summonses the authority of Ephrem in defense of "the perfect harmony of Catholic teaching modulated by one and the same spirit."[41]

Making sense of the encyclical's claims and context requires that we read it in light of Vatican I's dogmatic constitution, *Pastor Aeternus* (July 18, 1870) which, in its triumphant final paragraph, asserted papal infallibility. As the anonymous crafters of *Ephraem Graecus* sought to make Ephrem one of their own, the encyclical proclaiming him Doctor of the Universal Church called upon him to support Catholic universality and papal infallibility.

Between 1955 and 1975 Dom Edmund Beck produced the first critical editions of Ephrem's works. The importance of Beck's work would be difficult to overestimate. In addition to giving us access for the first time to Ephrem's own words, Beck's project drew attention to early efforts to manipulate Ephrem and his writings for purposes they were never intended. However, as Jeffrey Wickes has noted, in 1949, before Beck produced his first edition of Ephrem's works, he published a study of the *Madrošē on Faith* in which he declared unambiguously "[t]he major theme of all...[the] *Hymns on Faith* is the defense of the church's teaching against the innovation of Arianism." As Wickes perceptively concludes, Beck's statement, like the encyclical proclaiming Ephrem "Doctor of the Church," assumes "a monolithic church with a single defense against a recently conceived Arianism."[42]

The Luminous Eye: The Spiritual World Vision of Saint Ephrem (Kalamazoo: Cistercian Publications, 1992), 159. See also E. Mathews, "The Vita Tradition of Ephrem the Syrian, the Deacon of Edessa," *Diakonia* 22 (1988–1989): 15–42, at 24. In fact, the opening lines of *Pastor Aeternus* suggest the motivation for naming Ephrem Doctor of the Church.

41. The text deserves to be quoted in full: "We, who embrace the Eastern Church with no less solicitude and charity than our predecessors, truly rejoice, now that the frightful war is ended. We rejoice that many in the Eastern community have achieved liberty and *wrested their holy things from the control of the laity* (emphasis added). They are now striving to set the nation in order, consistent with the character of its people and the established customs of their ancestors. We propose, appropriately, a splendid example of sanctity, learning, and paternal love for them to diligently imitate and nurture. We speak of St. Ephrem the Syrian, whom Gregory of Nyssa compared to the River Euphrates because he 'irrigated by his waters the Christian community to bring forth fruits of faith a hundred-fold.'[13] We speak of Ephrem, whom all the inspired orthodox Fathers and Doctors, including Basil, Chrysostom, Jerome, Francis of Sales, and Alphonsus Liguori, praise. We are pleased to join these heralds of truth, who though separated from each other in talent, in time and place, nevertheless perfect a harmony modulated by one and the same spirit." (*Principi Apostolorum Petro*, Para. 4).

42. Jeffrey T. Wickes, "'Borrowed' Speech and the Scriptural Poetics of Ephrem's *Hymns on Faith*," unpublished paper given at the 38th Annual Byzantine Studies Conference, Holy Cross Greek Orthodox Theological Seminary, Boston, MA, Nov. 2012. Cited here with the author's permission.

Beck's categorical judgement of the *Madrošē,* and later, the *Mimrē on Faith,* as "anti-Arian" has had staying power: It is echoed in most treatments of Ephrem ever since, and it has fostered the textbook presentation of Ephrem as staunchly Nicene and inflexibly anti-Arian. Again, however, as Wickes has shown, Ephrem's Christology, to the extent that it can be discerned, leans in the *homoian* direction.[43] Nowhere in his writings does Ephrem employ the phrase *bar ituto,* the Syriac equivalent of *homo-ousios.* In its place, he asserts more boldly, and controversially: "Blessed is the one who discerns that Adonai is the One who begot You."[44] Casting Ephrem as a staunch Nicene has the obvious virtue of aligning him with fourth-century Greek defenders of Nicaean orthodoxy. At the same time, however, it overlooks just how Jewish he could be.

Ephrem has gone from being depicted as a Greek, a Byzantine Father of the church, a monk, a deacon, and a witness to a monolithic orthodoxy that never existed, to being called upon as an apologist for the newly promulgated doctrine of papal infallibility. More recently, it is not unusual to see Ephrem promoted as a feminist, an environmentalist, as virulently anti-Jewish, and, depending on the church one identifies with, as an upholder of orthodoxy—a saint, in other words, for all seasons.[45] These well-intentioned efforts are rooted in a romanticized view of Ephrem that takes selective account of the historical record and overlooks how vitally linked he was to his own time and place. So it is time to ask how things looked from the other side of the Euphrates. What was the view from where Ephrem stood?

When Ephrem looked out at his native Nisibis, he saw more than a military outpost teetering between two warring empires—a blip on the map of late antique Rome. He saw a place of vital culture and self-awareness. When he surveyed the biblical landscape of Eden in his *Commentary on Genesis,* he noted: "The four rivers [of Paradise], then, are these: the *Pishon,* which is the Danube; the *Gihon,* which is the Nile." But at this point in the narrative he makes a strategic shift in perspective—from "out there" to "right here". He continues "then [there

43. See now, Jeffrey T. Wickes, *St. Ephrem the Syrian. The Hymns on Faith,* FC 130 (Washington: The Catholic University of America Press, 2015).

44. *Hymnen de Fide* 3:8

45. See, for example, Sidney H. Griffith, "A Spiritual Father for the Whole Church: The Universal Appeal of St. Ephrem the Syrian," *Hugoye* 1 (1998): 1–33.

are] the *Deklat* (Tigris) and the *Prat* (Euphrates)."[46] Ephrem did not need to identify the *Deklat* and the *Prat* for his hearers as he had the *Pishon* and *Gihon*. Rather, after mentioning the *Deklat* and the *Prat*, he interrupts himself with an aside: "'Look (*hā*)'—he says—'between them we live."[47] The words are designed to get our attention. After identifying the *Pishon* and the *Gihon*, Ephrem turns to address his audience with what seems to be a casual aside. But there is nothing casual about it. The words are consciously crafted for their insider appeal. We hear Ephrem, a local, commenting to other locals, not just on a land inscribed by the rivers of Paradise, but on a shared identity—"between them *we live*." There is more at work here than simple pride of place.

For Ephrem, scripture was a palimpsest on which he recorded his own life and times, but without erasing the underlying text. His story, the story of Nisibis, was the continuation of a biblical story. The Genesis account of the rivers of Paradise formed the subtext that gave shape to his own story and suffused it with meaning.[48]

Identification with the Genesis narrative imparted a blessedness to Nisibis and the ancestral lands that surrounded it. Ephrem's treatment of the biblical text is a labor of ancestral devotion—a laying claim, yes, to a place, but also to an identity, and beyond that, to forbears stretching back to biblical times who shaped and defined a people, his people. He celebrated that land and its ancestry in lines that soar with a sense of pride and communal identity: "Let ten thousand tongues give thanks for our land / where Abraham and his son Jacob walked, / Sarah, Rebecca, Leah, and Rachel, too; / Even the twelve heads of the tribes [of Israel]. / From your treasury Sion enriched herself with sons of Jacob."[49]

The lines play into the popular image of Ephrem as choir-master, but go well beyond the Ephrem whom Jacob of Serugh

46. Alessandro Scafi, *Mapping Paradise. A History of Heaven and Earth* (Chicago: The University of Chicago Press, 2006), 33–36.

47. R.-M. Tonneau, *Sancti Ephraem Syri, In Genesim et in Exodum Commentarii*, CSCO 152-153 (Louvain: Peeters, 1955), 29.4–5.

48. The point is developed by Averil Cameron, *Christianity and the Rhetoric of Empire: The Development of Christian Discourse* (Berkeley: University of California Press, 1991), 6ff.

49. Edmund Beck, *Des Heiligen Ephraem des Syrers Hymnen auf Abraham Kidunaya und Julianos Saba*, CSCO 322 (Louvain: Peeters, 1972), 46. Hereafter, *Hymnen auf Abraham Kidunaya und Julianos Saba*. Melki ("Un bilan," 56–58) places this collection of *madrošē* as a whole in the category of "oeuvres contestées," but notes Beck's judgement that, while the collection as a whole does not reflect Ephrem's thought, *madrošē* 1–6 represent his vision, and may have been composed by a disciple.

described as "stirring chaste women to sing melodies of praise."[50] Here, we glimpse Ephrem in the act of summoning a cosmic choir—ten thousand voices strong—to sing the praises of "our land." The thread of communal identity is strung in words that are so simple that we are tempted to push past them, but we do so at our own peril. Ephrem is tracing what is contemporary and familiar, *Aram*—Nisibis and lands surrounding it—to its foundations in scripture: to "our land" blessed by the Hebrew patriarchs. But not just the patriarchs. Ephrem interrupts the succession of male heirs to fill out the ancestral record with "Sarah, Rebecca, Leah, and Rachel, too." The litany of female names pays homage to the women of scripture who were Ephrem's personal heroines. And not just to the women of scripture, but to the church of Nisibis, "that one mother who was in the city with daughters in all regions."[51]

Ephrem's devotion to *Aram* leads him to make a claim that is unique for a Christian writer of his, or any other time and place:

> The name of our land is greater than that of her companion.
> For in her Levi, the chief priest, was born;
> And Judah, head of the kingdom,
> And Joseph, the boy who went on to become
> Lord of Egypt. With the light that came from you, the whole world has lit up!
>
> The new Sun which spread its rays throughout creation
> From Judah, who was born in our land,
> Dawned in our country, and sent its rays to shine from Bethlehem.[52]

The words are not just bold, which we come to expect from Ephrem, they are staggering: Bethlehem basked in borrowed light. The star that led the Magi to Jesus arose in the East, in "our land."[53] The boldness of Ephrem's vision is exceeded only by the prophetic conclusion he

50. *A Metrical Homily on Holy Mar Ephrem*, 98.

51. *Carmina Nisibena* 14:1.

52. *Hymnen auf Abraham Kidunaya und Julianos Saba* 4:9–10.

53. "...Magi from the east arrived in Jerusalem, saying: 'saw his star at its rising and have come to do him homage'" (Mt 2:1–2).

addresses to the land itself: "Because the beginning appeared from you / By you, too, will the end be enriched."[54]

Ephrem traced an unbroken continuity between the birth of Christ and the origins of Christianity in Nisibis, to their Abrahamic roots in Mesopotamia. From these, he crafted a paean to his native *Aram* that conferred not only honor, but preeminence on the land of his birth. Even in *madrošē* extolling the virtues of chastity, he found occasion to sing the glories of his native land: "That dove [which Noah sent out] found and eagerly desired [us]; that bird sought out the land where we live."[55] In Ephrem's vision, *Aram*—Syria—is at the center of the three great events of human history: the primordial act of creation, the re-creation of the earth following the Great Flood, and the birth of the Messiah. In all of these, "the land where we live" was the undisputed place of honor.

Ephrem's vision of his Mesopotamian homeland in the divine plan for the world directly challenges Greco-Roman narratives of preeminence. The New Testament mapped a trajectory that made Christianity's rendezvous with Rome seem all but inevitable. For the scholar-bishop, Eusebius of Caesarea (ca. 260–ca. 339), this convergence fulfilled a plan divinely pre-ordained from the beginning of human history.[56] Ephrem entirely upends this view. His reading of scripture placed his Mesopotamian homeland at the beginning and end of history: It was there that Eden was planted, there that God reconstituted life after the Flood, there that "the end will be enriched." Mesopotamia was the land of salvation. It was there that the light dawned, and from there, sent its rays to the distant regions of the earth. His choice of verbs maps the progression:

> The East lit up (*nehrat*) ... / the West became bright (*neṣḥat*) ...
> the North rose up (*qāmat*) ..., / the South learned (*ilpat*) ... [57]

54. *Hymnen auf Abraham Kidunaya und Julianos Saba* 4:9–10.

55. Edmund Beck, *Des heiligen Ephraem des Syrers Hymnen de Virginitate*, CSCO 222-223 (Louvain: Peeters, 1962), 2:3.

56. *Pace* Sidney Griffith who, in his "Ephrem, the Deacon of Edessa, and the Church of the Empire," in *Diakonia. Studies in Honor of Robert T. Meyer*, edited by T. Halton and J. P. Williman, 22–52 (Washington: The Catholic University of America Press, 1986), presents Ephrem as a representative of "Eusebian Christianity," concluding "In the fourth century Ephraem was the casebook example of a conservative Christian who in a certain sense refused to accept modernity" (p. 46).

57. *Hymnen de Paradiso* 6:22.

Eusebius traced a path that led inexorably to Rome; Ephrem traced a path that began and ended in *Aram*, Syria.

When Ephrem looked at the church of Nisibis he was no less bold. He saw foundations laid by Thomas, "the Apostle who betrothed me to You."[58] By the fourth century, that church had grown beyond the confines of Nisibis and had "daughters in all regions."[59] Ephrem does not relate the details that led to their dispersal, he tells us only that the outlying congregations were in disarray: "My daughters who are outside of me, their walls are broken down, their children scattered."[60] He communicated the pain of loss and separation through Nisibis, "mother of the church," which grieved for her homeless children: "Bring my far-off ones home to me; let my near ones rejoice."[61]

The church in Nisibis had apostolic origins of its own; there was no need to legitimate its authority by linking it to "more prominent" apostolic sees. This stands in marked contrast to Edessan churchmen of later generations. They expanded the legendary *Teaching of Addai* to include the contrived death of Aggai, Addai's Edessan successor, who, they contended, had been martyred before he could consecrate Paluṭ as his replacement. As a result, Paluṭ set out for Antioch to receive ordination from Serapion who had been ordained by Zephyrinus, bishop of Rome.[62] But as many have noted, the entire sequence is invented; the connection of Serapion to Zephyrinus is "a patent anachronism."[63] For Ephrem, there was no need to create elaborate fictions to legitimize the church of Nisibis: Not only was Nisibis the church, it was the "mother of churches."

As a Syriac-speaking Aramean living on the far eastern fringes of the empire, Ephrem was culturally and geographically attuned to Persia. Of the three bishops of Nisibis during his time, the first had a Jewish name: Jacob; the two others—Walgesh and Babu—had emphatically Persian names. Artifacts in the possession of the

58. *Carmina Nisibena* 6:13.

59. *Carmina Nisibena* 14:1.

60. *Carmina Nisibena* 10:1.

61. *Carmina Nisibena* 6:33.

62. George Howard, *The Teaching of Addai*, The Society of Biblical Literature (Chico: Scholars Press, 1981), 105.

63. Brock, "Eusebius and Syriac Christianity," 228.

Catholic University of America's Institute for Christian Oriental Research (ICOR) attest to a vital borderland culture that looked east. Among them are late antique seals, amulets, and jewelry that feature fire temples, scorpions, the sun, and Ishtar, known to Greeks as Astarte. Ephrem knew Nisibeans who wore these amulets, consulted "Chaldean conjurors," and warded off evil with incantation bowls; and he railed against them.[64]

But while he was an outsider to Greco-Roman culture, as a Christian, Ephrem knew the benefits that came with submission to imperial power. Emperors kept the peace; they also exacted brutal retribution on subject populations that failed to submit to their authority. Ephrem acknowledged both functions of empire when he asked: "Lord, make peace between priests and kings, so that in one church priests may pray for kings, and kings may show mercy to their own cities..."[65]

Ephrem depended on the emperor to maintain order by bringing warring factions in line and establishing harmony in the church.[66] The apostate emperor Julian—"that miscreant" —had reversed the imperial mandate: "The opposite was true of the king who apostatized." Rather than fulfilling his role as "shepherd of humanity," Julian encouraged "wolves, lions, and leopards" to attack his own subjects.[67] He failed to deliver the one thing Ephrem looked to emperors to do: keep the peace.

Bishops were a part of the equation; it was their duty to pray for the emperor to maintain order, which included keeping order in the church. Praying for the emperor would favorably predispose him toward the church. But like Julian who turned against the church, bishops had betrayed their responsibility. Rather than encouraging harmony in the church, they tied the emperor's hands by feeding the flames of controversy for their own purpose: "Bishops who consecrate crowns set traps for kings. Instead of praying for kings to bring conflicts among people to an end, / Bishops incite conflicts that set

64. See, for example, *Carmina Nisibena* 40:7; 41:1, 7; 55:14.

65. *Hymnen de Fide* 87: 23. By referring to bishops as "priests," Ephrem reflects common fourth-century usage. His views on imperial authority, at least in this instance, seem to agree with Paul's (Rom 13:1–7).

66. He mentioned the following groups by name: "Arians, Aëtians, Paulinians, Sabellians, Photinians, Borborians, Cathars, Audians, Messallians" before concluding "May the Good One lead them back to his flock" (*Contra Heresies* 22:2–5).

67. *Contra Julianum* 1:1.

kings in opposition to those around them."[68] Bishops, not the emperor, were responsible for the chaos that engulfed the church: "The crown is absolved because bishops have put obstacles in the way of kings."[69] In lines that vent his frustration, Ephrem decries the dereliction of episcopal duty: "One bishop argues with another, / a chief shepherd with his counterpart. / And while bishops bicker, / the flock and the community waste away."[70]

Ephrem did not mince words when it came to reminding bishops of where they should direct their energies: "Do not argue with the mighty... lower your voices!... Equip yourselves with ten thousand remedies and set forth. Offer cures to the sick to heal them, and to the healthy to keep them well."[71] Ephrem's vision is closer to Pope Francis' definition of the church as a "field hospital" than to imperial manipulation by high-ranking churchmen. In a statement that is exceptional, even by Ephrem's standards, for its bluntness, he reminded bishops: "Our Lord spoke humbly so that leaders of his church would speak humbly."[72]

Chasing after imperial recognition brought bishops enormous material benefits in the form of patronage, but it wreaked havoc on the church. Ephrem demanded they put aside aspirations of upward mobility. He reminded them of a different kind of wealth—the economy of God: "Put an end to evil customs: The church should not possess wealth; it should be satisfied with souls."[73] It is all too easy to understand Ephrem's disappointment and frustration with highly placed "insider factions" (*gawwoyyē*) vying with each other for influence and control. He saw something very different when he looked out at the Jewish community in Nisibis.

---

68. *Contra Julianum* 7:7.

69. *Hymnen de Fide* 87:21. The ideally complimentary roles of emperor and bishops are spelled out by Griffith, "Ephraem, the Deacon of Edessa."

70. Edmund Beck, *Des Heiligen Ephraem des Syrers Sermones de Fide*, CSCO 212 (Louvain : Peeters, 1961), 6:13–16.

71. *Carmina Nisibena* 29:10–11. Earlier in this collection of *madrošē*, Ephrem gives similar advice to bishop Abraham of Nisibis: "Guard the sheep that are whole, and visit those that are sick. Bind up the broken, and seek out the lost; feed them in the pastures of Scripture, and let them drink at the spring of teaching" (19:4).

72. Edmund Beck, *Des Heiligen Ephraem des Syrers Sermo de Domino Nostro*, CSCO 270 (Louvain: Peeters, 1966), 25.

73. *Carmina Nisibena* 21:8.

Judaism was well-established and boasted a world-renowned rabbinic academy in Nisibis long before Christianity made its first appearance in the city.[74] And while it is unclear when or in what form Christianity arrived there, the two communities shared a language, a culture, and family ties that made them brothers, neighbors, and bitter rivals. What set the two groups radically apart was that, even in captivity—or perhaps because of it—Jews knew how to be a "people," an *'ammo*. Christians, with their high profile public brawling and competing for imperial attention, were hopelessly divided. Ephrem trusted that the emperor would bring the warring factions together, but it was a naïve hope: It was Jovian, after all, "a right believing Christian emperor," who committed the ultimate betrayal by handing Nisibis over to Persia.

We know something of the local response to the imperial order to vacate the city: In a final, desperate attempt to save their families, their way of life, and their city, the *limitanae*, the local militia, defied imperial orders and refused to abandon the barricades.[75] Protecting Nisibis was a matter of family pride, a sacred trust passed down through generations of defenders who had fought, and even fallen, to preserve a way of life. Along the ever-shifting borders of empire, family and clan took precedence over imperial politics. Nisibean Jews would not have mourned Jovian's about face. [76]

Jews had good reason to despise Rome; they referred it to as Edom, the land of Esau's disinherited descendants.[77] Jews would fare far better outside a Christian empire that had become increasingly draconian in its drive to suppress Judaism. The Babylonian Talmud interpreted a cryptic passage in the Book of Daniel as evidence of Rome's arbitrariness: "Three ribs were in his mouth between his teeth" (Dan 7:5). Rabbi Yohanan said: "This refers to Helzon, Adiabene, and Nisibis, which [Rome] sometimes swallows whole, and

74. For the significance of Nisibis as a center of Jewish learning, see Aharon Oppenheimer, Benjamin H. Isaac, and Michael Lecker, *Babylonia Judaica in the Talmudic Period* (Wiesbaden: L. Reichert, 1983), 328–331.

75. Benjamin Isaac, "The Meaning of the Terms *Limes* and *Limitanei*," *JRS* 78 (1988): 125–147. Also, D. L. Kennedy, "The Garrisoning of Mesopotamia in the Late Antonine and Early Severan Periods," *Antichthon* 21 (1987): 57–66.

76. Isaiah Gafni, "Babylonian Rabbinic Culture," in *Cultures of the Jews*, edited by David Bialle, Vol. 1, 23–265 (New York: Schocken Books, 2002).

77. Gen 25:22–28.

sometimes spits out."[78] Nisibean Christians were hardly prepared to see things so clearly. When Rome did the unthinkable, and "spit out" Nisibis, Ephrem could only ask in stunned disbelief: "Who can fathom the enormity of the dishonor?"[79]

What did Ephrem see when he considered mainstream Greco-Roman culture? The question has special meaning in light of a provocative statement of Ephrem's that those who study him have struggled to interpret: "Blessed is the one who has not tasted / the bitterness of the wisdom of the Greeks. // Blessed is the one who has not / relinquished the simplicity of the apostles."[80] Sebastian Brock has commented: "Ephrem's disparagement of the 'wisdom of the Greeks' should not, however, be taken as active opposition to Greek culture and learning as a whole, seeing that *hekmta d-yawnaye* ["wisdom of the Greeks"] is the exact equivalent of Athanasius' *hē sophia tōn Hellēnōn*, and so should properly be translated "pagan wisdom."[81] Prof. Brock is, and has been, a tireless promoter of Syriac studies; I am personally indebted to him for his many kindnesses and his generous collaboration. However, his judgement regarding Ephrem's reference to "the wisdom of the Greeks" as "the exact equivalent of Athanasius' ἡ σοφία τῶν Ἑλλήνων" is open to challenge.

Ephrem and Athanasius came from entirely different worlds. Athanasius was metropolitan bishop of a major Greek-speaking city. Ephrem's ethnicity, language, and culture placed him outside the circles of influence that men like Athanasius took for granted. Ephrem, in fact, enjoyed emphasizing his distance from such men: "I am an uneducated, simple man, unacquainted with books."[82] The hyperbole was part of a strategy to distance himself from the pedigree and privilege that destined men like Athanasius for high office in the church. Ephrem belonged to an ethnic minority that Greeks had conquered and which they, like their Roman successors, did not think much of.

78. Babylonian Talmud, Qiddushin 72a. Cited in Aharon Oppenheimer, *Between Rome and Babylon. Studies in Jewish Leadership and Society*, TSAJ 108 (Tübingen: Mohr Siebeck, 2005), 426.

79. *Hymnen contra Julianum* 2:25.

80. *Hymnen de Fide* 2:24.

81. Brock, "From Antagonism to Assimilation: Syriac Attitudes to Greek Learning," in *East of Byzantium: Syria and Armenia in the Formative Period*, ed. Nina Garsoian, Thomas Mathews, and Robert Thompson, 17–34 (Washington: Dumbarton Oaks, 1982). Reprinted in his *Syriac Perspectives on Late Antiquity* (London: Variorum, 1984), V.

82. *Hymnen de Fide* 1:19.

Ephrem and Athanasius may have used the same words, but they meant very different things.

Glen Bowersock has shown that Ephrem's reference to "the wisdom of the Greeks" cannot be "the exact equivalent of Athanasius' *hē sophia tōn Hellēnōn*." Bowersock begins by pointing out that Syriac had an overarching advantage over Greek: It had distinct words to distinguish "Greeks" (*yawnoyē*) from "pagans" (*ḥanpē*). If Ephrem had wanted to, he could have made a clear distinction between Greeks and pagans, but he did not: He wrote *ḥekmat yawnoyē*, "wisdom of the Greeks," not *hekmat ḥanpē*, "pagan wisdom."

Bowersock acknowledges the parallels between Ephrem's *ḥekmat yawnoyē* and Athanasius' *hē sophia tōn Hellēnōn*, but it is what he goes on to point out that deserves to be quoted in full:

> That marvelous poet, whose control of the Syriac language and whose subtle use of metaphor has justly led to comparisons with Pindar and Dante, notoriously did not trust Greeks or their culture. What is more important still is that he had no need of Greek. His own language was a more than adequate instrument for expounding his Christian theology. In this respect, accordingly, he was far removed from the tribulations that afflicted his contemporaries, Gregory of Nazianzus and Basil of Caesarea.[83]

Bowersock goes on to assert:

> ...there is little reason to believe that Ephraem could have made (or would have made) a distinction between Greeks as cultural carriers and Greeks as pagans. If Ephraem's principal targets were paganism and the logic-chopping ways of philosophers, as they undoubtedly were, he could not conceal an evident satisfaction that he and his Syrian coreligionists had no need to rub shoulders with pagans by communicating in the same language as they do.[84]

83. G. W. Bowersock, *Hellenism in Late Antiquity* (Ann Arbor: University of Michigan Press, 1990), 33.

84. Bowersock, *Hellenism in Late Antiquity*, 34.

Ephrem was quite clear when it came to what he thought of churchmen trained in what Bowersock refers to "the logic-chopping ways" of Greek philosophers and rhetoricians. He even ridiculed them for their displays of schoolroom erudition: "Why is your speech so muddled, you profitless professor?"[85] High-ranking churchmen locked in struggles for intellectual one-upmanship and imperial attention belonged to another place entirely; in contrast to the hometown bishops Ephrem knew, they offered a starvation diet of shallow certitudes: "The land of the debaters, the field of their words, / is parched by a hot wind of errors that starves the soul."[86] The divisiveness that was tearing the church apart was due to "foreign" influence: "Great was the terror that came out of nowhere and engulfed the sons of Aaron. They dared to introduce foreign fire and were consumed by it (cf. Lev 10:1–3). / Who, then, will escape this great firestorm—foreign investigation—which has made its way into the church?"[87]

Moulie Vidas is the most recent scholar of Jewish studies to note attitudes to what Ephrem referred to as *hekmat yawnoye*, "the wisdom of the Greeks," and its precise Hebrew cognate, *hokhmat yevanit*, in the Babylonian Talmud. Opposition to philosophical Hellenism among Mesopotamian Jews ran in distinctly parallel lines to Ephrem's thought. As Vidas explains: "In serving God, human beings could help the divine will prevail in history. Such a conception was at odds not only with prevailing Near Eastern mythology but also with Greek philosophy, which viewed the world as an entity made intelligible by the use of reason..."[88] This formulation brings us strikingly close to Ephrem's own views on the matter: Reason is essential to human life, but knowing when its exercise was appropriate was a choice. For reason to serve its purpose, it had to be balanced with the discerning use of human will.

85. *Hymnen de Fide* 52:5.

86. *Carmina Nisibena I*, 29:34.

87. *Hymnen de Fide* 8:9.

88. Moulie Vidas, in *Cultures of the Jews*, edited by David Bialle, vol. 1, 143 (New York: Schocken Books, 2002); also Moulie Vidas, "Greek Wisdom in Babylonia," in *Envisioning Judaism*, edited by R. S. Boustan et al., vol. 1, 287–305 (Tübingen: Mohr Siebeck, 2013). More recently, Daniel Boyarin "hypothesizes—a cultural relationship between the Greek Christian West and the Babylonian Talmud." See his "An Unimagined Community. Against The Legends of the Jews," in *Louis Ginzberg's Legends of the Jews*, edited by Galit Hasan-Rokem and Ithamar Gruenwald, 49–63 (Detroit: Wayne State University Press, 2014).

Finally, when we ask what Ephrem saw when he looked at the consecrated life, we arrive at an essential key to knowing him. Under the influence of Greek ascetical thought, Syrian monks had crafted a legend intended to invest their adopted way of life with a proper Greek pedigree. By tracing their origins to one Eugenius, *Mor Awgen* in Syriac, they recast their native history of the consecrated life to conform to western models. It was *Mor Awgen*, they insisted, who had transplanted the consecrated life to the Syriac East from Egypt where he had apprenticed, so the legend goes, under no less a master than Pachomius, the reputed founder of coenobitic monasticism.[89] This process of subverting the history of the consecrated life in Syria with a consciously created fiction has been called, rather too benignly, a case of "cultural amnesia." However, what the monks were encouraging was not a passive act of forgetting: It was a carefully crafted element in a larger program to distance Syriac Christianity from its organic development and to align it with emerging western models. Syrian monks actively forgot the impulse that had arisen from within their tradition and was embodied by the *Bnay wa-Bnot Qyomo*, "The Sons and Daughters of the Covenant." It would be difficult to overestimate the success of their efforts: Writing in the middle of the ninth century, Isho'dad of Merv, a bishop and renowned exegete in East Syriac tradition, identified Ephrem as a Greek Father of the church![90]

The trend toward conflating the native Syriac understanding of the consecrated life with western models is still very much with us. Contemporary scholarship reinforces it by referring to the *Bnay wa-Bnot Qyomo* as *pre-* or *proto*-monastic.[91] This view relegates the Syriac practice of the consecrated life to an intermediate step, a precursor to institutionalized monasticism—an import from the Greco-Roman West—in which it found its full and legitimate

89. The most comprehensive work on the origin and spread of the legend of Mar Awgen remains that of J. M. Fiey, "Aônès, Awun et Awgin," *AB* 80 (1962): 52–81; see also Fiey's, *Jalons pour une histoire de l'église en Iraq*, CSCO 310 (Louvain: Peeters, 1970), 100–112.

90. Melki, "Un bilan," 2.

91. Brock acknowledges that associating Ephrem with the monastic movement is, "misleading, for two reasons. First, anachronistic, and secondly (and fundamentally more important) because it ignores and neglects the existence of a native Syrian tradition of the consecrated life which may be termed 'proto-monasticism.'" The ambiguity is compounded by the statement that: "...Ephrem was never formally a monk, as later tradition portrayed him." See Brock, *Luminous Eye*, 131, 17.

expression. In addition, the effort to recreate the *Bnay wa-Bnot Qyomo* as the forerunner of institutionalized monasticism invests the monastic movement with a historical inevitability that is by no means the case. More seriously, it obscures a defining characteristic of the *Qyomo* as a movement rooted in Syrian family life.[92] The *Bnay wa-Bnot Qyomo* were not an early version of monks and nuns; nor did they constitute a pseudo-clerical culture that defined itself apart from the lives of everyday Christians. Everything we know about the *Qyomo* places it squarely in the context of a domestic, not an institutional, church.

Turning specifically to the *Bnot Qyomo*, the "Daughters of the Covenant," Ephrem gives us no reason to think that, apart from their vow to remain unmarried, they were in any way different from other women living in multi-generational, Syrian households of the time. They spent their days doing what women did: preparing meals, looking after younger siblings, nieces and nephews; assisting during child birth; attending to elderly family members; growing and preparing herbs to ease pain and treat sickness; and preparing the dead for burial. And like women in traditional societies everywhere, they recited poetry handed down by mothers and grandmothers as they worked. But in addition to undermining their rootedness in Syrian family life, labelling the *Bnot Qyomo* "pre-monastic" obscures the central role they played in Ephrem's work and, indeed, in his life.

In his *mimro* on Ephrem, Jacob of Serugh addresses Ephrem in his role as an innovator who shattered taboos: "Our sisters were encouraged by you to sing praises; / for women had not been allowed to speak in church."[93] Jacob stopped short of identifying the source of the prohibition against women speaking in church; his audience knew who he was referring to. If Ephrem's writings tell us anything, it is that most Syriac-speaking Christians had a well-developed ear

92. A similar impulse was at work in efforts by P. Nagel to make *qyomo* mean "resurrection" rather than "covenant." By imposing a meaning on *qyomo* which it never had, Nagel strove to make *qyomo* conform to the teaching of Jesus on the afterlife: "At the resurrection of the dead (*b-qyomto ger d-mitē*) people will neither marry nor be given in marriage; they will be like the angels in heaven" (Mt 22:30). This is not to deny an understanding of sexual renunciation as a participation in the "angelic life." Rather, it sounds a cautionary note to scholars quick to arrive at predetermined conclusions. Nagel's interpretation obscured the obvious origins of *qyomo* in Judaism. See P. Nagel, *Die Motivierung der Askese in der alten Kirche und der Ursprung des Mönchtums*, TUCL 95 (Berlin: Akademie-Verlag, 1966).

93. *A Metrical Homily on Holy Mar Ephrem*, 40.

for scripture. They would have immediately recognized that Jacob was referring to Paul who famously decreed: "A woman must receive instruction silently and under complete control. I do not permit a woman to teach or to have authority over a man; she should be quiet." (I Tm 2:11–12). And further on: "As in all the churches of the holy ones, women should keep quiet in the churches; they are not allowed to speak, but should be subordinate, as even the law says." (1 Cor 14:33–35). Paul follows this command with a defense intended to silence his opposition: "If anyone thinks that he is a prophet or a spiritual person, he should recognize that what I am writing to you is a commandment of the Lord. If anyone does not acknowledge this, he is not acknowledged." (1 Cor 14:37). The coda suggests that Paul's ruling faced challenges from the start.

Paul's stern warning notwithstanding, in his *mimro* on Ephrem, Jacob of Serugh unambiguously declares that Ephrem, after surveying his local situation, decided that it was time for a change: "Blessed [Ephrem] observed that women were silent from praise; / and this wise man judged that it was right for them to give praise."[94] Jacob follows this by emphasizing Ephrem's role as innovator: "[This is] a new sight—women uttering proclamation; / and see, they are called teachers among the congregations."[95] For Jacob, Ephrem's collaboration with the *Bnot Qyomo* prophetically anticipated the full realization of the Gospel. Addressing Ephrem, he says: "Your teaching marks an entirely new age / for there, in the kingdom, men and women are equal."[96] Ephrem's dedication to the *Bnot Qyomo* cannot be separated from another defining feature of his writing, namely, the devotion he lavishes on the women of scripture.

Ephrem's life-long devotion to the *Bnot Qyomo* was an expression of a deeply-held sensibility that also manifested itself in the exceptional attention he paid to women in scripture—Jewish and Gentile—who, impelled by their own initiative, seized opportunities to take matters into their own hands: They were risk-takers who defied custom. One woman, in particular, whom the Gospel identifies as a Syro-Phoenician (Mk 7:24–30, Mt 15:21–28), captured Ephrem's imagination. Although

94. *A Metrical Homily on Holy Mar Ephrem*, 40.

95. *A Metrical Homily on Holy Mar Ephrem*, 42.

96. *A Metrical Homily on Holy Mar Ephrem*, 43.

Jesus' followers had tried to shoo her away like a pesky fly or a troublesome dog nipping at their heels, the woman refused to give up. When Jesus rebuffed her request to heal a sick child with what amounts to an ethnic slur ("it is not right to take the food of the children and throw it to dogs"), the woman shot back: "But even dogs eat the crumbs that fall from their masters' tables." In the highly compressed diction of his poetry, Ephrem had only to use the word "crumbs" to evoke the entire episode in his writing, and with it, his admiration for the woman's persistence and boldness.

What makes Ephrem's choice of women as personal and communal models of behavior so exceptional is that it came at a time when the celibate lifestyle—and the disparagement of women that accompanied it—was becoming the norm for churchmen in both East and West. Ephrem expressed unambiguous preference for the "single life." But in spite of the growing trend toward celibacy, and his personal preference to remain unmarried, women were his preferred models of courage in the face of social and religious marginalization.

Ephrem's identification with female, and specifically maternal, sensibilities is nowhere more poignantly portrayed than in *Madrošē on the Nativity* where he inhabits the body of Mary to sing a lullaby to the infant Jesus: "I am the earth and You are the farmer... Since I have learned by You a new way of conceiving, let my mouth learn from You a new [way of] giving birth to songs of praise."[97] Mary's request that her mouth "learn...a new [way of] giving birth to songs of praise," makes her a sister in the sisterhood of the Covenant which Ephrem taught to "sing a new song of praise."[98]

The subtle shift from Mary's birth-giving to the praise-giving of the *Bnot Qyomo* is exceptional even by Ephrem's standards. Given his lifetime of dedication to the *Bnot Qyomo* and the regard he showed for women in scripture, we are left to consider if there was not perhaps an element of biography in his preoccupation. Understanding how women came to occupy so central a place, not only in Ephrem's thought, but in his life as a teacher, must take into account his upbringing and early experience. The question, simply put, is this: Did the centrality of women in Ephrem's life and thought reflect

97. Edmund Beck, *Des heiligen Ephraem des Syrers Hymnen de nativitate (Epiphania)*, CSCO 82-83 (Louvain: Peeters, 1959), 15:1, 5.

98. *A Metrical Homily on Holy Mar Ephrem*, 102.

the love and affection he experienced from the women in his life? It would have been women, after all, who first sang to him, recited rhymes to comfort him, rocked him to sleep, and impressed him with the power of words.

It is unlikely that, from this remove, we will learn the specific circumstances that contributed to the early formation of Ephrem's poetic sensibilities. But it would be exceptional if the emotional acuity and powers of observation that mark him as a poet were somehow consciously acquired. What is more likely is that they point to a habit of mind that took shape in infancy when bonds between mother and child are formed. What I am suggesting is that the gravitational pull of strong female figures on Ephrem was rooted in his early experience of a caring woman who affirmed him and sanctioned his imagination. She may have been his mother, but she need not have been: In the multi-generational households that were, and remain the norm in traditional Middle Eastern families, she might just as well have been a grandmother, an older sister, or an aunt whose caressing voice and admiring smile delighted and encouraged him. The early experience of a nurturing, affirming woman remained a sustaining presence in his life, predisposing him for an aspect of his work for which, thankfully, we possess abundant evidence: his lifelong dedication to the *Bnot Qyomo*. The affection and encouragement which he heard as a young child echoed in their voices and continued to nurture his creative genius. As he himself admitted: "The wombs of our ears are filled with the songs of pure women."[99]

The image takes us a step beyond the consistently positive view Ephrem had of the human body—a view he often expressed in maternal terms: "The very breath [of Paradise], was like a mother's breast, / nourishing [Adam]."[100] By using the gender-specific "wombs," in reference to "our ears," Ephrem expressed a poetic sensibility that reaches its conclusion in a no less complex image in which he describes his labor as a poet as the product of "a marvelous conception," a giving birth "from the womb of my mouth."[101] Scripture, as

99. *De Resurrectione* 2:8, as edited in Edmund Beck, *Des Heiligen Ephraem des Syrers Paschahymnen (De Azymis, De Crucifixone, De Resurrectione*, CSCO 248-249 (Louvain: Peeters, 1964).

100. *Hymnen de Paradiso* 11:1.

101. *Hymnen de Fide* 2:7. Elsewhere, he confides that, for him, the creation of poetry was a force of nature. He could no more restrain it than a woman could defer giving birth: "If the womb holds back

we know, was Ephrem's constant inspiration. But here, he makes a more personal admission: The voices of the *Bnot Qyomo* stirred his creative sensibilities. No less than the women of his youth who loved him and doted on him, the voices of the *Bnot Qyomo* were sources of his empowerment.

The tendency of modern scholarship to view the Sons and Daughters of the Covenant as forerunners of institutionalized monasticism also obscures the essential role of the covenant in the ongoing rivalry between Syriac-speaking Christians and Jews. Syriac Christianity, which had its origins in Jewish Christianity, was, in Ephrem's day, still organically linked to its Jewish matrix.[102] The shared histories of Nisibean Jews and Christians made rivalries between the two communities all the more intense and vitriolic. Ephrem's insistence that "The treasury [of scripture] is the common property of humanity,"[103] challenges Jewish claims of proprietary ownership of scripture and its interpretation. The context of Ephrem's declaration of "common property" predates even that contest by several centuries.[104]

The Syriac *Odes of Solomon* preserves a window onto a time when converts to Christianity were in the process of actively separating from Judaism. The *Odes* never refers to *ʿēdto* ("church"), while *knušto* ("synagogue") appears only once. Aphrahaṭ, Ephrem's older contemporary, uses *ʿēdto* and *knušto* interchangeably, although he shows the beginning of a trend to use *ʿēdto* to distinguish "church" from "synagogue." Over time, Christians adapted the text of the Syriac Bible by substituting *ʿēdto*, "church," where the original Jewish translators had used *knušto.*[105] This begins to explain the note of defensiveness in Ephrem's assertion that "[scripture] is the common property of humanity." Jews claimed, and with good reason, that Christians had tampered with the text of

the child, both [mother and child] will perish. The tree that holds back its buds withers. Birth pangs accompanying the wind beget tender buds" (*Hymnen de Fide* 20:2–3).

102. See the seminal work of Michael P. Weitzman, *From Judaism to Christianity. Studies in the Hebrew and Syriac Bibles*, JSS Supplement 8 (Oxford: Oxford University Press, 1999).

103. Edmund Beck, *Des Heiligen Ephraem des Syrers Hymnen de Ieiunio*, CSCO 246–247 (Louvain: Peeters, 1964), 6:3.

104. See now Jaroslav Pelikan, *Whose Bible Is It? The History of the Scriptures Through the Ages* (New York: Viking, 2005).

105. R. Murray, *Symbols of Church and Kingdom: A Study in Early Syriac Tradition*, Rev. Ed. (London: T&T Clark International, 2004), 17–18.

2. The Significance of Astronomical and Calendrical Theories for Ephrem's Interpretation of the Three Days of Jesus' Death

❖ Blake Hartung

Introduction

From the beginning, Christian writers have struggled to reconcile the New Testament's varied accounts of the chronology of Jesus' death and resurrection. In this paper, I will focus upon one chronological issue that drew the attention of Ephrem in his sixth *Hymn on the Crucifixion*[1]—what I call the "three day problem." The New Testament describes Jesus' resurrection as occurring "on the third day,"[2] "in three days,"[3] "after three days,"[4] and most notoriously, "three days and three nights," found in Matthew's first account of the "sign of Jonah" (Mt 12:40). Here we read: "For as Jonah was three days and three nights in the belly of the whale, so will the Son of Man be three days and three nights in the heart of the earth." This saying is particularly difficult to

* I would like to express my thanks to the other panel participants and attendees of NASS VII for their helpful questions and comments.

1. Edmund Beck, *Des heiligen Ephraem des Syrers Paschahymnen (de azymnis, de crucifixione, de resurrectione)*, CSCO 248–249 (Louvain: Peeters, 1964). Hereafter referenced as *De crucifixione*. All translations are my own, unless otherwise indicated. I am grateful to Prof. Jeffrey Wickes for his helpful feedback on my translation of this difficult text.

2. E.g. Mt 16:21, 17:23, 20:19, 26:61; Lk 13:32, 18:33, 24:7; 1 Cor 15:4.

3. E.g. Mt 26:61; Mk 14:58; Jn 2:19.

4. E.g. Mk 9:31, 10:34.

reconcile with the chronology of the resurrection accounts; if Jesus died on Friday afternoon and was raised on Sunday morning, how can that possibly add up to three days and three nights?

In *De crucifixione* 6, Ephrem offers an answer. He draws upon his knowledge of astronomy and his convictions that the created universe symbolically bears witness to its Creator and argues that the three hours of darkness (followed by three hours of light) that occurred on the Friday of Jesus' crucifixion actually constituted an additional day (and night). Consequently, he posits three days (Friday, the added day, and Saturday) before the resurrection. Ephrem takes this argument a step further, claiming that both the solar and the lunar calendars symbolically reflect the addition of this extra night and day into the calendar through their excess hours and need for regular intercalation. As a result, a considerable knowledge of ancient calendars and timekeeping is essential to make sense of this hymn.

This essay will first provide background to the three-day problem itself by comparing Ephrem's answer with those of other early Christian writers, particularly in the Syriac tradition. Next, this essay will examine Ephrem's chronology of the three days by situating it within the context of late ancient calendars and astronomy. Finally, this essay will offer some conclusions about the significance of this issue for Ephremic studies.

The Three-Day Problem

Before we examine *De crucifixione* 6 more closely, I will provide a brief sketch of early Christian attempts to address the three-day problem, with a particular focus on Syriac literature. First of all, we should note that many early Christians do not seem to have been concerned with addressing these chronological discrepancies. For example, one of the earliest Christian reflections on the "sign of Jonah" saying comes from Justin Martyr's *Dialogue with Trypho*. Justin, however, glosses over the chronological difficulty: "Though these words were veiled in mystery, his listeners could understand that he would arise from the dead on the third day after his crucifixion."[5] Similarly, Origen, in

5. Justin, *Dialogue with Trypho* 107.1 (edited in Miroslav Marcovitch, *Iustini Martyris Dialogus cum Tryphone*, PTS 47 [Berlin: Walter de Gruyter, 1997], 472; English translation in Thomas B. Falls and Thomas P. Halton, *Dialogue with Trypho*, SFOC 3 [Washington, D.C.: The Catholic University of

his *Commentary on Matthew,* does not address how "three days and three nights" could be reconciled with other passages, but instead takes the "sign of Jonah" saying as an opportunity to expound a model for reading the Old Testament in light of the New.[6] These examples reflect the typical approach to the three-day problem in early Greek-speaking Christianity.

Gregory of Nyssa is an exception to this general rule. In a paschal homily (*De tridui spatio*), he acknowledges the chronological problems posed by "three days and three nights" and explains them as follows: The three days and three nights began on Thursday at the Last Supper, and the second day and night were the period of darkness and light on the Friday of the crucifixion.[7] This explanation is strikingly similar to that provided by Ephrem in *De crucifixione* 6. Indeed, Gregory's solution has an impressive pedigree in early Syriac literature.[8]

Aphrahaṭ, in the twelfth *Demonstration,* similarly suggests that the three days began at the Last Supper, when Jesus broke his body and poured out his blood. Like Ephrem, Aphrahaṭ is familiar with a tradition of reckoning the three hours of darkness on the Friday of the crucifixion as a night, and the subsequent three hours of light before sundown as a day. We may summarize Aphrahaṭ's chronology

America Press, 2003], 161).

6. Origen, *Commentary on Matthew* 12.3; edited in Erwin Preuschen, *Origenes Werke,* vol. 4. *Commentarius in Iohannem,* GCS 10 (Leipzig: Hinrichs, 1903), 73.7.

7. Gregory of Nyssa, *De tridui spatio* edited in G. Heil, A. van Heck, E. Gebhardt, and A. Spira, *Sermones, Pars I,* GNO 9 (Leiden: Brill, 1992), 286–90. See Hans Boersma, "Overcoming Time and Space: Gregory of Nyssa's Anagogical Theology," *JECS* 20 (2012): 575–612, 594–595.

8. Gregory's divergence from other early Greek interpretations raises questions. Had Gregory heard of this interpretation through the transmission of earlier traditions, or did he arrive at his conclusion independently? If Gregory drew upon a source, the Greek version of the *Didascalia* seems the most likely candidate. Most scholars agree that the *Didascalia* was originally composed in Greek (although the extant Greek text is fragmentary) and later translated into Syriac (likely in the fourth century), Latin, and other languages. For the fragments of the Greek text, see J. Vernon Bartlet, "Fragments of the Didascalia Apostolorum in Greek," *JTS* 18, no. 72 (1917): 301–309.
For the question of the original language of composition, see R. Hugh Connolly, *Didascalia Apostolorum: The Syriac version translated and accompanied by the Verona Latin fragments* (Oxford: Oxford University Press, 1929), xi; Arthur Vööbus, *The Didascalia Apostolorum in Syriac,* CSCO 407–408 (Louvain: Peeters, 1979), 26–8; Alistair Stewart-Sykes, *The Didascalia Apostolorum: An English Version with Introduction and Annotation,* Studia Traditionis Theologiae: Explorations in Early and Medieval Theology 1 (Turnhout: Brepols, 2009), 89–90. However, because the Greek text is so fragmentary (only fragments of ch. 15 are extant), we cannot be certain whether the paschal chronology was included in the Greek version, or whether it was the product of Syriac redactors.

as follows: The first day and night began Thursday night and ran through noon (the "sixth hour") on Friday. The second day and night consisted of the three hours of darkness and subsequent three hours of light on Friday until sundown. The third day and night were made up of the night of Friday night (the night of the Sabbath) and the full Sabbath day.[9]

The Syriac version of the *Didascalia,* ch. 21, begins its chronology on the Friday of the crucifixion and numbers the three hours of darkness and three hours of light as a night and day, respectively. As its justification, the *Didascalia* cites Psalm 39:6: "Behold you have set out my days with a measure."[10] The Syriac *Commentary on the Diatessaron*—attributed to Ephrem but of disputed authorship—mentions beginning the chronology at the Last Supper and counting the period of darkness and light as a day and night as two distinct options for reconciling the chronological question.[11]

What is Ephrem's relation to these traditions? If we accept Ephrem's authorship of the *Commentary on the Diatessaron,* then it seems he was aware of traditions beginning the three-day chronology on Thursday *and* Friday. Nevertheless, *De crucifixione* 6 alone is sufficient evidence to show that the *Didascalia* and Ephrem, and with some modification, Aphrahaṭ, knew a common tradition of measuring the darkness and light on the Friday of the crucifixion as a day. Given the layers of redaction and interpolation in a document such as the *Didascalia,* I am unwilling to argue that it is the source upon which Ephrem and Aphrahaṭ drew.[12]

9. Aphrahaṭ, *Demonstration* 12.7, edited in D. Ioannes Parisot, *Aphraatis Sapientis Persae Demonstrationes I–XXII*, PS 1.1 (Paris: Firmin-Didot, 1894), 520–21.

10. *Didascalia Apostolorum* 21; Arthur Vööbus, *The Didascalia apostolorum in Syriac*, CSCO 407–408 (Louvain: Peeters, 1979), 5.14.9–13 (text).

11. Unfortunately, this passage survives only in Armenian. Ephrem, *Commentary on the Diatessaron* XIX.4: "From the moment when *he broke* his body for his disciples *and gave it* to his apostles, three days are numbered during which he was counted among the dead, like Adam... Or [alternatively], the sixth day must be counted as two and the Sabbath as one." (edited with French translation in Louis Leloir, *Saint Ephrem. Commentaire de l'Évangile concordant. Version arménienne*, CSCO 137, 145 [Louvain: Peeters, 1953–1954], 270 (texte); English translation in Carmel McCarthy, *Saint Ephrem's Commentary on Tatian's Diatessaron: An English Translation of Chester Beatty Syriac MS 709* [Oxford: Oxford University Press on behalf of the University of Manchester, 1993], 284).

12. As I noted above, the likely Greek origins of the *Didascalia* could explain the transmission of this paschal chronology to Gregory of Nyssa. Indeed, its translation into Syriac (or the transmission of earlier traditions upon which it drew) could have been the source for the spread of the paschal chronology to Ephrem and Aphrahaṭ. However, the Syriac text of chapter 21 of the *Didascalia* appears to be

There has been very little scholarly consideration of these Syriac traditions. In his study of the Paschal hymns, G. A. M. Rouwhorst contends that the common argument for a full three days and three nights, found in Aphrahaṭ, the *Didascalia,* and *De crucifixione* 6 was an attempt to refute the earlier, Quartodeciman, one-night paschal celebration.[13] While the tradition may have had its origins as a polemic against a Quartodeciman Pasch, it is a considerable stretch to claim that this is a concern of Ephrem's in *De crucifixione* 6, due to his utter silence on the matter. He makes no mention here of any alternative views to refute. Rather, I believe Ephrem's impetus is to provide an answer to a scriptural problem and support that interpretation with symbols from the natural world.

In a brief article in the *Journal of Jewish Studies,* Burton Visotzky cites the relevant passages from the *Didascalia* and Aphrahaṭ and considers how these texts could justify counting shorter periods of time as a "day."[14] The answer, he argues, lies in the Babylonian Talmud, in the so-called "partial day" principle.[15] However, these examples of shorter "days" seem to flow from different impetuses. The rabbinic "partial day" addresses potential difficulties for ritual practice, while Ephrem and the Syriac tradition attempt to solve an exegetical question. Unfortunately, however, Visotzky does not deal with *De crucifixione* 6, which devotes the most attention to this problem. Visotzky fails to take into account the most fundamental difference in timekeeping between the ancient and modern worlds. For modern people, a day is 24 equal hours, while for ancient people, a day was a variable amount of time beginning with the sunrise and ending with

heavily redacted: Rouwhorst attributes the paschal chronology to an anti-Quartodeciman revision of a Quartodeciman original, while Stewart-Sykes sees it as the work of an anti-Jewish "apostolic redactor" (G. A. M. Rouwhorst, *Les hymnes pascales d'Ephrem de Nisibe. Analyse théologique et recherche sur l'evolution de la fête pascale chrétienne à Nisibis et à Edesse et dans quelques églises voisines au qautrième siècle*, vol. 1, Supplements to Vigiliae Christianae 7 [Leiden: Brill, 1989], 181–2; Stewart-Sykes, *The Didascalia Apostolorum,* 43). Unfortunately, neither the Greek nor Latin versions of this passage are extant. Therefore, we cannot know with any certainty whether the chronology of chapter 21 originated with the Greek *Didascalia* or whether it was a later addition to the Syriac text of the *Didascalia.*

13. G. A. M. Rouwhorst, *Les hymnes pascales d'Ephrem de Nisibe*, 196.

14. Burton L. Visotzky, "Three Syriac Cruxes," *JSS* 42 (1991): 167–175.

15. At several points in the Talmud, the rabbis argue that part of a day can in fact be considered as a "day" for the sake of certain ritual requirements. For instance, the Talmud allows a man to shave on the seventh day of mourning—rather than the customary eighth day—if the following day is the Sabbath or a holy day. (Visotzky, "Three Syriac Cruxes," 170. See Babylonian Talmud, Moed Katan 17b, 19b, 20b; Pesachim 4a).

sunset. In other words, the duration of the "day" was entirely subject to the movements of the heavenly bodies. Therefore, the parallels between the Syriac writers and the rabbis are interesting, but only insofar as they reveal the general temporal flexibility of antiquity. It is unsurprising that Ephrem closely ties the justification for his three-day chronology to astronomical and calendrical considerations.

De crucifixione 6: Analysis

Let us now consider Ephrem's argument in *De crucifixione* 6 more closely. The hymn begins with a single reference to Jonah and Christ: "Three days were numbered for the Messiah, just as for Jonah" (st. 1). Although Ephrem does not mention Jonah again in the hymn, the reference is fundamentally important. It alludes to Matthew 12:40 and sets up the chief problem with which the hymn is concerned: the chronology of the passion and resurrection. Almost immediately after this reference to Jonah and Christ, Ephrem states his solution:

> That One who brings darkness and light
> reckoned the duration and time when it darkened [as] a day.
> (*De crucifixione* 6.1)

At first glance, the basis for Ephrem's claim remains unclear: How could three hours of darkness and three hours of light constitute a day? One key, I believe, can be found in stanza 3, where Ephrem compares the "glorious symbol" of Joshua and the sun standing still with the events of the crucifixion. In this stanza, he explains that Joshua's miracle produced a day that spanned two days according to the normal measure of the calendar but remained a single day in the sense that the sun did not set. The crucifixion, he posits, was the reverse of this: one day according to the normal calendar measure but two days because of the sun's movements. Thus Ephrem establishes that the rising and setting of the sun form an acceptable basis for marking a day, regardless of how long that day is "by measurement" (*bgaw kaylā*). However, Ephrem cannot ignore the calendar, given that it is based upon the sun. Thus, it is no surprise that the hymn turns to a discussion of the calendar in stanza six, where Ephrem writes:

> Every four years an entire day is intercalated (*etkbeš*).
> It is a great symbol which has revealed beforehand the three hours
> That were prepared in order to darken at his death. (*De crucifixione* 6.6)

How could the addition of an extra day every four years qualify as a symbol of the three hours of darkness at the crucifixion? As is typical in his poetic writings, Ephrem does not provide every detail. However, he does develop the symbol to the point that we may unpack the basic logic of the symbolism. First, we must recall that the ancient "day" consisted of twelve hours, as Ephrem says explicitly in his *Second Discourse to Hypatius.*[16] In fact, because the "day" began at sunrise and ended at sunset, its length could vary considerably depending upon the season.[17] The notion of a significantly shorter or longer "day" was thus not as foreign to an ancient person as it would be to us.

In his reference to the calendar, Ephrem mentions the practice of *intercalation*, the addition of extra time to the calendar for the purposes of keeping it on track. Although intercalation is a necessity for both lunar and solar calendars, Ephrem is describing the regular intercalation of the solar calendar.[18] Ephrem's solar calendar appears to have been an adapted version of the Julian calendar, likely what scholars call the Syro-Antiochene calendar.[19] Like our modern calendar (itself a revision of the Julian calendar), Ephrem's solar year featured 365 ¼ days. If a day was intercalated every four years to account for the extra ¼ of a day, that ¼ of a day would equal 3 hours. According to Ephrem, the annual addition of three hours is not a corrective measure for a defective calendar.[20] Indeed, he rebuts unnamed

16. He writes: "But if the day consists of twelve hours, and the sun moves through a course of twelve hours, it is clear that the sun is the fount of days." (edited with English translation in C. W. Mitchell, *S. Ephraim's Prose Refutations of Mani, Marcion, and Bardaisan,* vol. 1 [London: Williams and Norgate, 1912], 23 [Syriac], xxxix [translation]).

17. Robert Hannah, *Time in Antiquity*, Sciences of Antiquity (Abingdon: Routledge, 2008), 74.

18. See *De crucifixione* 6.9 and 6.15.

19. Sacha Stern, *Calendars in Antiquity: Empires, States, and Societies* (Oxford: Oxford University Press, 2012), 255–57.

20. However, as Dr. Trevor Lipscombe reminded me in an email correspondence, these extra three hours are present in the calendar each year, regardless of whether or not the calendar was intercalated, and would thus serve (in Ephrem's thinking) as a perpetual reminder of the crucifixion.

"learned ones" who claimed that the excess hours in the solar year somehow made up for the waning of the moon (*De crucifixione* 6.8). Rather, he repeatedly contends that the three extra hours were present in the calendar from the beginning, in order to attest to the three hours of darkness on the Friday of the crucifixion. He thus argues that his hearers should not imagine that there were "six" extra hours in the year of the crucifixion (*De crucifixione* 6.11). Although he does not develop this point further, he seems to say that in the year of the crucifixion the hours of darkness *were* the extra hours to which the annual intercalary hours were designed to point.

The symbolic witness of these additional hours functions on several levels. Ephrem notes that the three extra hours in the year are not visible to the eye, but can only be perceived by the intellect through the use of a device such as a "water clock" (*De crucifixione* 6.10).[21] Further, like the three symbolic hours in the solar calendar, the three hours of darkness at the crucifixion were also hidden to the eye, shrouded in darkness. "The symbol," Ephrem writes, "is like / the reality, both being hidden" (*Hymnen de crucifixione* 6.10). Indeed, both the sun hidden by darkness and the added hours attest to a further level of symbolism to which Ephrem alludes in stanza 9: The hiddenness of God made known in revealed things.

In the course of the hymn, Ephrem returns to astronomical and calendrical considerations, arguing that the moon also bears witness to the extra "day" on the Friday of the crucifixion:

> You, O glorious Jesus, whom even the moon, behold, proclaims,
> because half a day in an entire month has lost its measure.
> And how much greater is the full measure
> of the hours of the year; thus they have lost their measure of months. (*De crucifixione* 6.12)

Ephrem's statements here require some knowledge of the lunar calendar. The lunar calendar in question was likely a derivative of the

21. The Syriac literally reads "staircase of water" (*ḥawqā d-mayyā*). There were numerous forms of the device known in Greek as the κλεψύδρα (lit. "water thief) in use in antiquity. Such devices measured time by controlling a steady flow of water either in or out of a large basin. A water clock large enough to measure out the twelve hours of the day could then show the passage of time through indications of the hours inscribed within. See Hannah, *Time in Antiquity*, 100–115.

Babylonian calendar, which was in wide use throughout the eastern Mediterranean until the spread of the solar Julian calendar.[22] This calendar, to which Ephrem attests in the *Second Discourse to Hypatius,* consisted of 12 months, each with 29 ½ days—thus "a half day every month has lost its measure." In total, the lunar calendar was made up of 354 days. Therefore, due to the discrepancy between the lunar and solar calendars, the lunar calendar will "drift" significantly if it is not regularly intercalated. The shifting location of the Islamic month of Ramadan in relation to the seasons of the year is an instructive example of this "drift."[23] In stanza 17, Ephrem elaborates further on this "deficiency" of the lunar calendar:

> For behold: eleven days are lacking from its year,
> From the 365 days,
> The reckoning of the full solar year. (*De crucifixione* 6.17)[24]

The lunar calendar's missing half-day and loss of eleven days provides Ephrem with further opportunities to develop the symbolic testimony of the calendars. He writes that just as the sun bears witness to the Son through its three extra hours, so the moon also attests through its six hours (or half a day, which if we recall, is how much the lunar month "loses" each year).[25] In the course of the hymn, the missing hours of the moon and excess hours of the sun provide fertile ground for further symbolic interpretation. Ephrem depicts the sun's excess hours and the moon's missing hours as symbols of Jesus' divinity and humanity (*De crucifixione* 6.14); and of the blessing, and subsequent diminishment of the Jewish People (*De crucifixione* 6.16).

Ephrem's final remarks on the calendar turn to Moses as an example.

22. Stern, *Calendars in Antiquity,* 72.

23. Hannah, *Time in Antiquity*, 18–21.

24. Cf. Ephrem, *Commentary on Genesis*, I.25.3 (edited in R. Tonneau, *Sancti Ephraem Syri in Genesim et in Exodum commentarii*, CSCO 152–153 [Louvain: Peeters, 1955]; English translation in Joseph Amar and Edward G. Mathews, Jr., *Ephrem the Syrian: Selected Prose Works,* FOC 91 [Washington: The Catholic University of America Press, 1994]).

25. See *De crucifixione* 6.13.

Moses mixed and mingled the reckoning of the year and the calculation of the Moon.
He ordered, constructed, and fixed the number of the year.
The year of the house of Noah [had] two reckonings.
Of both luminaries, the skillful scribe[26]
Made one reckoning. (*De crucifixione* 6.18)

Ephrem's references here are somewhat obscure. In the *Second Discourse to Hypatius* he similarly offers Moses as an example for demonstrating the true purpose of the sun and moon. In that text too, he explains that God has arranged both the sun and moon as markers for time.[27] But what do we make of Ephrem's references to Moses in this hymn? When we consider both of these passages in light of Ephrem's exegesis of Genesis 1:14 in the *Commentary on Genesis,* it seems likely that Ephrem is referring to that passage, of which Moses was the presumed author.[28] There, "Moses" describes the sun and the moon as timekeepers. The reference to the "house of Noah" is also obscure, but probably refers to the muddled chronology of Genesis 8, in which two different dates are given on which the earth became dry.[29] For this passage, too, Moses was the supposed author. Regardless of Ephrem's specific allusions, however, it is clear that he believes that Moses' accounts in scripture provide a model to demonstrate the importance of the sun and the moon to mark the time.

Let us now briefly summarize Ephrem's answer to the three-day problem as given in *De crucifixione* 6. The first day occurred on Friday morning and lasted until midday. Then, for three hours, from midday until the ninth hour there was a period of "night." This "night of the daytime" was followed by three hours of light.

26. I.e. Moses.

27. *Prose Refutations* I, 21–23. There, Ephrem argues that though God has ordained the sun to count days and the moon to mark months, the inaccuracy of both solar and lunar calendars shows their insufficiency as objects of worship.

28. *Commentary on Genesis* I.23.2: "That [God] said: 'Let them be for signs', [refers to] measures of time, and 'let them be for seasons', clearly indicates summer and winter. 'Let them be for days', are measured by the rising and setting of the sun, and 'let them be for years', are comprised of the daily cycles of the sun and the monthly cycles of the moon."

29. In *Commentary on Genesis* VI.12, Ephrem argues on the basis of the dates given in Genesis 8 that Noah had been in the ark for 365 days. This is evidence for Ephrem that even "the generation of the house of Noah" had used a 365-day calendar, and thus it was clearly not the creation of the Chaldeans or Egyptians. (Tonneau, *Commentarii,* 61).

At this point, then, two days and one night had elapsed. The second night was Friday night (the night of the Sabbath), and it was succeeded by the Sabbath day (the third day). By the evening after the Sabbath, three days and two nights elapsed, so the final night was completed in the first six hours of the night, after which—at midnight—Ephrem speculates that Jesus was raised from the dead (*De crucifixione* 6.19).[30] His preoccupation with the solar and lunar calendars reflects, I believe, the underlying assumptions of this odd chronology of the Passion week—that "day" and "night" are subject more to the movements of the heavenly bodies than to fixed lengths of time.

As I noted above, Ephrem shared aspects of this chronology with other Syriac Christian writers. However, Ephrem's elaboration of the calendrical and symbolic significance of the extra "day" that occurred on the Friday of the crucifixion is unique. This preoccupation reflects Ephrem's attempts throughout his writings to demonstrate the fundamental agreement between scripture and nature: The two speak with one voice. In this case, both speak to the centrality of the crucifixion of Jesus. At that moment, the heavenly bodies themselves bore witness to their Lord, to such a degree that the measuring of time itself points to the event.

Conclusions

What, therefore, is the significance of this hymn? First, there are a number of parallels between this hymn and Ephrem's prose works, particularly the critiques of Manichean cosmology in the *Second Discourse to Hypatius* and the interpretation of the creation of the sun and moon in the *Commentary on Genesis*. These correlations are particularly notable, since in my experience, examination of the *Prose Refutations*, the commentaries, and the poetic works can lead to the question: Is this really the same author?

Given the diversity within Ephrem's corpus, many studies focus on one portrait of Ephrem in particular: either Ephrem the

30. "But perhaps on the sixth hour of that blessed night / Our Lord and our God was raised." Rouwhorst (*Les hymnes pascales*, vol. 1, 196) believes this conjecture has a liturgical background, stemming from Ephrem's church's celebration of the resurrection on the midnight between the Saturday and Sunday of the Pasch.

poet-theologian of symbols (*mēmrē and madrāšē*); Ephrem the philosophically-inclined polemicist (*Prose Refutations*); or Ephrem the interpreter of the "plain sense" of scripture and heir of Jewish interpretation (commentaries). *De crucifixione* 6 challenges such categorizations. Here, we find Ephrem resolving a scriptural difficulty (the three-day problem), with the support of his knowledge of astronomy and the calendar, and finding therein great symbols which God has embedded into the created universe. Indeed, Ephrem's reliance upon the Roman Julian calendar in this hymn—which led French translator François Cassingena-Trévedy to describe him as "the Westerner"[31]—is another reminder that Ephrem was not so distant from the mainstream of Greco-Roman thought as we sometimes assume.[32]

Finally, the level of sophistication in the development of the symbolism in this hymn is quite notable. A considerable amount of background study is necessary simply to understand Ephrem's reasoning. This complexity begs the question: In what context might a *madrāšā* like this one have been performed? Indeed, though we might typically assume a public liturgical setting, a hymn such as this seems more suited to the schoolroom than the *bema,* especially given the close parallels in subject matter with one of the sophisticated *Discourses to Hypatius* and the *Commentary on Genesis.* Perhaps Ephrem's language might provide some hints. Consider, for instance, Ephrem's self-identification throughout many of his *madrāšē.* He often calls himself *a harp.* Furthermore, he frequently characterizes his hymnic actions as *singing, playing,* etc. In this hymn, however, Ephrem refers to himself as a "scribe of secrets" (*sāpar stirātā*) (18) and asks God to help him "write" (*ktab*) (17) and "translate" (*targem*) (18). These examples certainly call to mind a more "scholastic" image than we often encounter in the *madrāšē.*

While the ancient biographical traditions' portrayals of Ephrem as a hymnist and liturgical song leader have seen increased attention in recent scholarship (with the growing interest in performance and audiences), we should not forget another common ancient image of Ephrem—as a teacher. Indeed, perhaps these two portraits

31. François Cassingena-Trévedy, *Éphrem de Nisibe: Hymnes pascales,* SC 502 (Paris: Cerf, 2006), 243.

32. See Ute Possekel, *Evidence of Greek Philosophical Concepts in the Writings of Ephrem the Syrian,* CSCO 580 (Louvain: Peeters, 1999).

should not be separated. In an unpublished conference paper, Jeffrey Wickes has recently suggested that some of Ephrem's *madrāšē* might have been composed for a sort of hybrid space: as hymns not for public liturgy, but for a "school" setting.[33] This hymn may well be that sort of composition.

33. Jeffrey Wickes, "In Search of Ephrem's Audience" (Paper presented at the Sacred Song in the Late Antique & Byzantine East: Comparative Explorations Workshop, Providence, RI, May 2015). I would like to express my thanks to Prof. Wickes for sharing an unpublished draft of this paper.

3. Reconsidering the Compositional Unity of Aphrahaṭ's *Demonstrations*

❖ J. Edward Walters

The collection of writings known as the *Demonstrations* was first published, and thus first became known to Western scholars, in an Armenian translation.[1] Over a century later, it was discovered that two Syriac manuscripts that had been brought to the British Museum in the early nineteenth century from the monastery of Dayr al-Suryān in Egypt—Brit. Libr. Add. 14,619 and Brit. Libr. Add. 17,182 contained the Syriac *Vorlage* of this work. Upon the discovery of the Syriac text, scholars noted some differences between the Syriac and Armenian versions, namely: The Armenian corpus contained only nineteen demonstrations, whereas the Syriac version contained twenty-three; the order of the texts in the two traditions differed slightly, and the Armenian text was attributed to Jacob of Nisibis, while the Syriac manuscripts lacked this ascription. Following the publication of the Syriac text,[2] it was indisputable that the Syriac version was

1. Nicholas Antonelli, *Sancti patris nostril Jacobi Episcopi Nisibeni Sermones cum praefatione, notis, & differatione de Ascetis* (Rome: Sacrae Congregationis de Propoganda Fide, 1756). The Armenian version has since been re-edited as a critical edition with a French translation in Guy Lafontaine, *La version arménienne des œuvres d'Aphraate le Syrien*, CSCO 382–383, 405–406, 432–424 (Louvain: Peeters, 1977, 1979, 1980).

2. There are two publications of the Syriac text of the *Demonstrations*: William Wright, *The Homilies of Aphraates, the Persian Sage, edited from Syriac Manuscripts of the fifth and sixth Century in the British Museum,* vol. 1. *The Syriac Text* (London: Williams and Norgate, 1869) [note: this was intended as a two volume set with an English translation in the second volume, but the second volume was never completed]; and D. Ioannes Parisot, *Aphraatis Sapientis Persae Demonstrationes I–XXI*, PS 1.1 (Paris:

more ancient than the Armenian version, not only because of the antiquity of the Syriac manuscripts, but also because the twenty-three individual *Demonstrations* were organized as an acrostic of the Syriac alphabet. As such, the work must have been composed in Syriac and only later translated into Armenian. Based on this conclusion, the differences between the Syriac and Armenian versions could be resolved in favor of the original Syriac edition.

Once the primacy of the Syriac version was established, and given the relatively stable transmission of the Syriac text witnessed by two manuscripts, there was very little reason to question the unity or integrity of the corpus. After all, the corpus forms an acrostic; any challenge to a single piece in the corpus represents a challenge to the entire work. Thus, when J. M. Fiey argued that *Demonstration* 14 was not originally part of the corpus,[3] his argument was not well received. Indeed, not only did Fiey's argument fail to gain much traction, it even spawned a published rebuttal.[4] Even Fiey, though, who was willing to challenge the integrity of the corpus as a whole by questioning the originality of *Demonstration* 14, did not challenge the overall organization of the *Demonstrations.* To my knowledge, no one since Fiey has attempted to question the integrity of the *Demonstrations* corpus.

In the present article, I will argue, based on a combination of newly discovered evidence and a re-consideration of some old evidence, that the *Demonstrations* as they are preserved in Syriac represent the end product of a two-stage composition: The twenty-three *Demonstrations* as we have them are the creation of a redactor who compiled and edited pre-existing writings into the two-volume, acrostic work that is preserved in the two ancient Syriac manuscripts.

Firmin-Didot, 1894), and D. Ioannes Parisot, *Aphraatis Sapientis Persae Demonstrationes XXIII*, PS 1.2 (Paris: Firmin-Didot, 1907), columns 1–150. Citations from the *Demonstrations* in this article come from Parisot's edition.

3. J. M. Fiey, "Notulae de littérature syriaque: La Démonstration XIV d'Aphraate," *Le Muséon* 81 (1968): 449–454.

4. George Nedungatt, "The Authenticity of Aphrahat's Synodal Letter," *OCP* 46 (1980): 62–88. See also Marie-Joseph Pierre, "Un synode contestataire à l'époque d'Aphraate le sage Persan," in *La controverse religieuse et ses formes*, edited by Alain Le Boulluec, 243–279 (Paris: Cerf, 1995).

Re-Considering Old Evidence: Gennadius' List

Sometime near the end of the fifth century, Gennadius of Marseilles completed his continuation of Jerome's *De viris illustribus*.[5] The very first author in Gennadius' volume is Jacob of Nisibis, to whom Gennadius attributes twenty-six books and a short chronicle. More importantly, Gennadius goes on to list the specific titles of the works attributed to Jacob, and these titles bear a striking resemblance to many of the titles of the individual *Demonstrations* of Aphrahaṭ. This is, of course, not new evidence. In the introduction to his edition of the *Demonstrations*, Ioannes Parisot pointed out these similarities and even provided a table for comparison, which I have reproduced below in Figure 1.

FIGURE 1: Gennadius' List of the Writings of Jacob of Nisibis compared with titles of Aphrahaṭ's individual *Demonstrations*[6]

Gennadius' Title	**Parisot's Corresponding *Demonstration***
De fide, Adversus omnes haereses	*Dem.* 1: De fide
De caritate generali	*Dem.* 2: De caritate
De ieiunio	*Dem.* 3: De ieiunio
De oratione	*Dem.* 4: De oratione
De dilectione erga proximum speciali	*Dem.* 2 *bis*
De resurrectione	*Dem.* 8: De resurrectione mortuorum
De vita post mortem	*Dem.* 8 *bis*
De humilitate	*Dem.* 9: De humilitate
De paenitentia	*Dem.* 7: De paenitentibus
De satisfactione	*Dem.* 7 *bis*
De virginitate	*Dem.* 18: De virginitate
De sensu animae	*Dem.* 6 ?
De circumcisione	*Dem.* 11: De circumcisione

5. For an edition and German translation, see Claudia Barthold, *De viris illustribus = Berühmte Männer / Hieronymus, mit umfassender Werkstudie herausgegeben, übersetzt und kommentiert* (Mülheim: Carthusianus, 2010).

6. I have used the Latin titles provided by Parisot in his table for easy comparison. Parisot, *Demonstrations*, xxxiii–xxxiv.

De acino benedictionis	*Dem.* 23: De acino
De Christo quod filius Dei sit et consubstantialis patri	*Dem.* 17: De Christo Dei filio
De castitate	*Dem.* 18 *bis*
Adversum gentes	*Dem.* 16 ?
De constructione tabernaculi	*Dem.* 19: De Iudaeis non congregandis
De gentium conversatione	*Dem.* 16: De gentium electione
De regno Persarum	*Dem.* 5: De bellis
De persecution Christianorum	*Dem.* 21: De persecutione
χρονικόν	*Dem.* 23 *bis*

Unfortunately, we do not know anything about Gennadius' source for this material. There is no specific indication that he himself had access to the texts or if he relies on an intermediary. So, what does this list tell us? At best, this list provides evidence that before the end of the fifth century—roughly contemporary with the composition of the earliest Syriac manuscript of the *Demonstrations*—Gennadius knew of a set of writings attributed to Jacob of Nisibis with titles that correspond strikingly with individual *Demonstrations*. In comparison with the manuscript evidence, Gennadius' list does not count for much against the antiquity of Brit. Libr. Add. 17,182. That is, it is difficult to use the existence of Gennadius' list alone as evidence for an alternative composition and reception history of the *Demonstrations*.

However, if we look carefully at Gennadius' list and then consider the text of the *Demonstrations* closely, I contend that there are good reasons to believe that this list may very well represent a distinct set of writings that was subsequently edited and shaped into the *Demonstrations* as we know them. In what follows, I will present evidence from two case studies for comparing Gennadius' list with the *Demonstrations*: *Dem.* 2 and *Dem.* 6.

Dem. 2: On Love

There are two titles from Gennadius' list (lines 3 and 6 in Figure 1) that deal with the topic of love: *De caritate generali* and *De dilectione erga proximum speciali*, which may be translated "On love in general" and "On Particular Love for One's Neighbor." However, there is only one title in the Syriac *Demonstrations* on the topic of love: *Dem.* 2 "On Love" (*taḥwitā d-ḥubbā*). It is thus worth considering whether *Dem.* 2 as preserved in the *Demonstrations* might represent either or both of these titles.

When reading the text of *Dem.* 2 carefully, the reader is struck by a rather abrupt transition between the sections designated in Parisot's edition as 2.11 and 2.12. The text and translation of these passages are included below in Figure 2.

FIGURE 2: *Dem.* 2.11–12[7]

Dem. 2.11

ܗܠܝܢ ܕܝܢ ܟܠܗܝܢ ܕܟܬܒܬ ܠܟ ܚܒܝܒܝ ܡܛܠ
ܕܡܢ ܩܕܝܡ ܒܡܐܡܪܐ ܗܘ ܩܕܡܝܐ ܕܥܠ ܫܪܪܐ
ܕܗܝܡܢܘܬܐ ܚܘܝܬܟ ܕܒܗܝܡܢܘܬܐ ܡܫܟܚܐ
ܡܬܬܣܡܟܐ ܫܬܐܣܬܐ ܕܗܢܐ ܩܝܡܐ ܕܩܝܡܝܢ
ܚܢܢ ܒܗ. ܘܒܗܢܐ ܡܐܡܪܐ ܕܬܪܝܢ ܟܬܒܬ ܠܟ
ܘܐܥܗܕܬܟ ܕܟܠܗ ܢܡܘܣܐ ܘܢܒܝܐ ܒܬܪܬܝܢ
ܦܘܩܕܢܝܢ ܬܠܝܢ: ܗܢܘܢ ܕܐܡܪ ܥܠܝܗܘܢ ܦܪܘܩܢ
ܘܒܗܘܢ ܒܗܠܝܢ ܬܪܬܝܢ ܦܘܩܕܢܝܢ ܚܒܝܫ ܟܠܗ
ܢܡܘܣܐ ܘܢܒܝܐ. ܘܒܗ ܒܢܡܘܣܐ ܚܒܝܫܐ
ܗܝܡܢܘܬܐ: ܘܒܗܝܡܢܘܬܐ ܡܬܬܩܝܡ ܚܘܒܐ
ܫܪܝܪܐ: ܗܘ ܕܐܫܬܘܗܝ، ܡܢ ܗܠܝܢ ܬܪܬܝܢ ܦܘܩܕܢܝܢ
ܕܡܢ ܒܬܪ ܕܠܡܪܝܐ ܐܠܗܗ ܢܪܚܡ ܒܪ ܐܢܫܐ ܐܦ
ܠܩܪܝܒܗ ܢܚܒ ܐܟܘܬ ܢܦܫܗ.

I have written all of these things to you, my friend, because previously in the first *mēmrā* on the subject of faith I showed you that the foundation of this covenant in which we stand can be established through faith. And in this second *mēmrā* I have written to remind you that all the law and the prophets hang on two commands—those about which our savior spoke. All the law and prophets are held together in these two commands. Faith is contained within the law, and true love is established through faith. This [true love] comes from these two commands: After someone loves the Lord his God, he should also love his neighbor as himself.

Dem. 2.12

ܡܛܠ ܫܡܥ ܚܒܝܒܝ ܥܠܘܗܝ، ܥܠ ܚܘܒܐ
ܕܐܫܬܘܗܝ، ܡܢ ܗܠܝܢ ܬܪܬܝܢ ܦܘܩܕܢܝܢ. ܟܕ ܐܬܐ
ܓܝܪ ܡܚܝܢܢ ܗܘ، ܫܦܝܠܬܗ ܕܚܘܒܐ...

Now, my friend, listen concerning the love that comes from these two commands. For when our lifegiver came, he explained the significance of love...

7. Parisot, *Aphraatis Sapientis Persae Demonstrationes,* I.72.7–25.

This text reads like the conclusion of one work with a seamless transition to the beginning of a new work. I am not the first person to take note of this awkward transition. Indeed, Parisot provides a footnote in his critical text here claiming that section 2.12 begins Gennadius' second title on love: "Hic videtur incipere sermo a Gennadio dictus: De dilectione speciali erga proximum."[8] Parisot's claim here seems to suggest that Gennadius' list simply represents *Dem.* 2 as we now know it and separated it into two titles because of this transition. However, this is not necessarily the case; it is at least possible that Gennadius knew of two distinct titles on love, and that *Dem.* 2 as we know it combines these two under a single overarching title.

It is worth noting that in Gennadius' list, the two titles on love do not appear in successive order. That is, the title "On particular love for one's neighbor" does not appear immediately following "On love in general." This suggests that Gennadius' list does not represent the format of *Dem.* 2 or the order of the *Demonstrations* as we know them. In addition, and more importantly, the internal rhetorical evidence of these passages suggest that *Dem.* 2.11 was originally the conclusion of a stand-alone *mēmrā*, and 2.12 was originally the introduction to a different—yet of course related—*mēmrā.*

The text of *Dem.* 2.11 begins as follows: "I have written all these things to you, my friend, because previously, in the first discourse on the subject of faith, I showed you that…."[9] This particular wording is important for the present argument because the rhetorical summary phrase "I have written [all these things…]" appears (in the same or very similar form[10]) in the conclusions of *Demonstrations* 1, 4, 5, 6, 7, 9, 10, 12, 13, and 15–23.[11] On some occasions, this rhetorical device does occur in the middle of a *Demonstration* rather than at the end,[12]

8. Parisot, *Aphraatis Sapientis Persae Demonstrationes,* I.71–71, fn. 3.

9. *Dem.* 6.11 (Parisot, *Aphraatis Sapientis Persae Demonstrationes,* I.72.7–10).

10. This formula does not always say "all these things;" sometimes, it says "this argument" or "this reminder." However, despite this variation, the rhetorical purpose of concluding the argument is the same.

11. This phrase often appears in the final paragraph or section (according to the section numbering provided by Parisot). In some cases, though (such as *Dem.* 7 and 12) it is not in the final section, but still close to the end. Indeed, regardless of the numbering of the section, it is clear that this line frequently serves as a rhetorical signal for the beginning of the conclusion of a *Demonstration.*

12. See, for example, *Dem.* 4.13, 13.3, 19.2, 21.5, 21.8, and several times throughout *Dem.* 23.

but it occurs most frequently as an indication of conclusion. Thus, the frequency of this rhetorical pattern to indicate the conclusion of a written unit, in this case a *mēmrā*, suggests that the transition between *Dem.* 2.11 and 2.12 at least plausibly represents a "break" between two originally separate *mēmrē*.

Furthermore, the opening line of *Dem.* 2.11 refers to the "first *mēmrā* on the subject of faith," and in the lines that follow, it continues: "In this second *mēmrā*, I have written to you."[13] In this case, in juxtaposition with the previous *mēmrā* "On Faith," the literary unit of this *mēmrā* clearly refers to what immediately precedes the conclusion in *Dem.* 2.11. Thus, it is logical to conclude that this paragraph represents the conclusion of a self-standing *mēmrā* that corresponds to *Dem.* 2.1–11.

The following section, 2.12, begins as follows: "Now, my friend, listen concerning the love that comes from these two commands." This rhetorical device of addressing the "friend" who serves as the anonymous recipient of these writings appears in the first section (in several cases in the very first line) of *Dem.* 1, 3, 4, 5, 13, 15, and 18. To be sure, this is a very frequent rhetorical device throughout the *Demonstrations*, and not just in the opening sections. Thus, not every occurrence of this rhetorical address suggests a new *mēmrā* or a break in continuity. However, it is at least noteworthy that this rhetorical device does appear in the opening lines of several other *Demonstrations* and particularly notable that it occurs in the introduction for each of the first five *Demonstrations*.

This brief textual analysis of the transition between 2.11 and 2.12 does not necessarily prove that 2.1–11 and 2.12–20 represent two originally distinct *mēmrē*, especially given the frequency with which Aphrahaṭ uses the "listen, my friend" rhetorical device. However, the combination of this identifiable transition within *Dem.* 2 that splits it into two parts with Gennadius' indication of two separate titles that deal with the topic of love provides at least some level of suspicion regarding the original unity of this *Demonstration*.

Moreover, it is worth pointing out that Gennadius' titles "On love in general" and "On the particular love for neighbor" do actually correspond quite well with the contents of these respective sections.

13. Parisot, *Aphraatis Sapientis Persae Demonstrationes*, I.72.12–13.

That is, *Dem.* 2.1–11 provides a more generic exegetical treatment of the "love commandment" from Mt 23:37–40, whereas *Dem.* 2.12–20 is more specifically focused on the love of one's neighbor. In fact, it seems that sections 1–11 are a treatment of the "first command" to love God, and that 12–20 are a treatment of the "second command" to love one's neighbor. As such, these two titles clearly belong together and overlap in content. However, that does not mean that they were necessarily originally written as one seamless argument. In fact, given the continuity of these two arguments, it makes perfect sense why an editor might combine them as a single work.

In summary, I have argued here that there is a literary seam in *Dem.* 2 between sections 11 and 12. Moreover, I have argued that this literary seam may be indicative of two originally separate writings, which were subsequently joined together. If accepted, this argument provides an explanation for why there are two separate titles on the topic of love in Gennadius' list. Moreover, it would suggest that Gennadius' list actually represents the earliest stage of composition of the writings that comprise the *Demonstrations* before they were edited into the form found in the earliest extant manuscripts. Now we will consider a second case study: *Dem.* 6.

Dem. 6: On the bnay qyāmā

Returning to the table in Figure 1, Parisot is unsure of his association of *Dem.* 6 with Gennadius' title *De sensu animae* (line 14), as signified by the question mark. Scholars familiar with Aphrahaṭ's oeuvre will be most familiar with *Dem.* 6 for its treatment of the *bnay qyāmā*, the "covenanters." However, *Dem.* 6 also includes a somewhat lengthy excursus on the soul and the bodily resurrection (6.14–18), which explains Parisot's choice to link it with this title. Beyond Parisot's uncertainty, there is another anomaly in Gennadius' list that demands explanation. Immediately preceding *De sensu animae* we see the title *De virginitate*, which Parisot assumes must correspond with the anti-Jewish *Dem.* 18, which does deal with the topic of virginity. Parisot also correlates *Dem.* 18 to another title in Gennadius' list: *De castitate* (row 19 of the table). I propose that there is a simpler explanation than splitting up *Dem.* 18 to cover two titles. It is more likely that Gennadius' titles *De virginitate* and *De sensu animae* actually represent two originally distinct works that have been combined to form what is now *Dem.* 6.

A literary and rhetorical analysis of *Dem.* 6 supports this hypothesis. First, it should be noted that the treatment of the soul in *Dem.* 6 is a relatively small portion of the *Demonstration* as a whole. It appears as an excursus within a broader argument about the requirements placed upon the covenanters. Second, neither the introduction nor the conclusion of the *Demonstration* says anything about the soul or the body/soul relationship. But the introduction and conclusion of *Dem.* 6 *do* talk about virginity. For example, the introduction of *Dem.* 6 reads, "Whoever loves virginity (*btulutā*) should be like Elijah. Whoever takes up the yoke of the holy ones should sit and be silent. Whoever loves silence should look to his Lord as the hope of life."[14] Likewise, the conclusion of *Dem.* 6 also refers to virginity: "I have written these things as a reminder for myself and for you, my friend. Therefore, love virginity (*btulutā*), the heavenly portion, the fellowship of the watchers of heaven, for nothing compares to it. Christ dwells in those who maintain it... Read what I have written to you, as well as the brothers, the *bnay qyāmā*, those who love virginity (*btulutā*)..."[15]

The closing lines of *Dem.* 6.1, quoted above, offer a concise introduction to the topic at hand. This brief statement contains two explicit references to the concept of virginity, including a specific word for virginity (*btulutā*) and a metaphor that Aphrahaṭ often applies to virginity: the "yoke of the holy ones."[16] And, as seen in the second quote, the vocabulary of virginity is also prominent in the concluding paragraphs of *Dem.* 6. Thus, it is quite clear that virginity is a significant theme in the framing of this *Demonstration*.

Turning to a closer analysis of the text of the *Demonstration* beyond the introduction and conclusion, we may observe that the various words and metaphors for virginity are ubiquitous in significant portions of this *Demonstration*, but not all the way through. There are at least 25 explicit references to "virginity" in this *Demonstration* (i.e.

14. *Dem.* 6.1 (Parisot, *Aphraatis Sapientis Persae Demonstrationes*, I.253.9–13).

15. *Dem.* 6.19–20 (Parisot, *Aphraatis Sapientis Persae Demonstrationes*, I.309.21–24, 312.6–8).

16. See Naomi Koltun-Fromm's treatment of this metaphor in *Dem.* 6: "Yokes of the Holy Ones: The Embodiment of a Christian Vocation," *HTR* 94 (2001): 205–218.

words for virgins, virginity, holy ones, holiness,[17] singleness, yokes of the holy ones)—*not* including occurrences of *bnay qyāmā*. But all 25 of these references occur in select parts of the *Demonstration*, namely 6.1–8 and 19–20. From 6.9 to 6.18, there is not a single instance of one of the words or metaphors for virginity. Thus, in the section of the *Demonstration* that contains the treatment of the body/soul relationship (6.14–18), there is not even a mention of virginity. So, even though the wording of the transition here is not as abrupt as the case with *Dem.* 2, the thematic shift from 6.8 to 6.9 could indicate that two originally distinct writings, one on virginity and the other on the body/soul relationship, were combined.

Taken alone, this analysis of *Dem.* 6 may be suggestive that two originally separate writings have been edited together, but it is probably not entirely persuasive. It is, however, dramatically confirmed by a newly discovered piece of evidence, which originates from the reception history of the *Demonstrations* in the later Syriac tradition, to which we now turn.

Considering New Evidence: The Reception History of the *Demonstrations*

Compared with other authors of early Syriac literature, most notably the near-contemporary Ephrem the Syrian, the *Demonstrations* did not fare well in transmission and reception in the later Syriac tradition. The *Demonstrations* survive in full in Syriac in only two ancient manuscripts, those described above. Of course, it is difficult to judge the popularity of a work based on manuscript evidence alone. If Moses of Nisibis (and perhaps others) had not collected manuscripts and brought them to Dayr al-Suryān, then we would have even less surviving evidence for this period.[18]

---

17. Regarding the use of "holiness" as synonymous with "virginity," see Naomi Koltun-Fromm, *Hermeneutics of Holiness: Ancient Jewish and Christian Notions of Sexuality and Religious Community* (Oxford: Oxford University Press, 2010).

18. Sebastian P. Brock, "Without Mushē of Nisibis, Where Would We Be? Some Reflections on the Transmission of Syriac Literature," *Journal of Eastern Christian Studies* 56 (2004): 15–24; see also Monica Blanchard, "Moses of Nisibis (fl. 906–943) and the Library of Deir Suriani," in *Studies in the Christian East in Memory of Mirrit Boutros Ghali*, edited by L. S. B. MacCoull, vol. 1, 13–24 (Washington: The Society for Coptic Archaeology, 1995).

Looking beyond manuscript attestation, George, bishop of the Arabs, denounced the writings of the anonymous "Persian Sage," and this testimony stands as one of precious few surviving historical references to the *Demonstrations*. Recently Lucas Van Rompay has surveyed the reception history of the *Demonstrations* in East Syriac exegetical works and shown that at least some portions of the *Demonstrations* were known and transmitted under the name "Aphrahaṭ" or "Persian Sage" in the eighth and ninth centuries.[19] Outside these citations and the manuscript evidence mentioned above, the text of the *Demonstrations* do not seem to have circulated widely.

However, it has recently been discovered that some portions of the *Demonstrations* were preserved in Syriac, not under the name Aphrahaṭ, but attributed to Abraham of Nathpar.[20] There are at least two manuscripts that include such citations: Brit. Libr. Orient 6714 and Mingana Syr. 601. Sebastian Brock is responsible for identifying these citations as belonging to the *Demonstrations*,[21] but until now there has been no further attention paid to the content of these citations.[22] The two manuscripts contain different amounts and different selections of text from the *Demonstrations*, but it is significant for the purposes of the present article that they both contain extracts from *Dem.* 6, including the text of *Dem.* 6.8, the portion of the text mentioned above where we might expect a potential literary seam between two different texts.

In Figure 3 below, I have re-produced the text in question for comparison. The text in the column on the right comes from the Abraham of Nathpar citations in both Brit. Libr. Orient 6714 (f. 98r) and Mingana Syr. 601 (f. 57a). The column on the left contains the corresponding texts from *Dem.* 6 as transmitted in the *Demonstrations*.

19. Lucas Van Rompay, "Aphrahat, 'A Student of the Holy Scriptures', The Reception of His Biblical Interpretation in Later Syriac Tradition," in *Storia e Pensiero Religioso nel Vicino Oriente: L'età Bagratide – Maimonide – Afraate*, edited by Carmela Baffioni, Rosa Bianca Finazzi, Anna Passoni Dell'Acqua, and Emidio Vergani, 256–270 (Bulzoni: Biblioteca Ambrosiana, 2014).

20. Although very little is known about Abraham of Nathpar, his name frequently appears in monastic miscellany manuscripts. For a brief entry, see J. W. Childers, "Abraham of Nathpar," in *GEDSH*, 9.

21. Brock, "Without Mushē of Nisibis," 19 fn. 14.

22. Grigory Kessel mentioned these citations, along with several others, in a 2006 article, and he noted that this area of research "is still waiting for investigation" (Grigory Kessel, "A Note on One Borrowing from Aphrahat," *PdO* 31 [2006]: 301).

FIGURE 3: Citations from the *Demonstrations* attributed to Abraham of Nathpar compared with the text of *Dem.* 6

	Dem. 6 according to Parisot's Edition	Dem. 6 according to Brit. Libr. Orient 6714 (f. 98r) and Mingana Syr. 601 (f. 57a)
6.8 end	... ܘܟܕ ܠܝܬ ܠܗ ܠܐ ܬܒܪܐ ܠܗ. ܘܟܡ ܒܪܢܫܐ ܒܢܫܐ ܠܐ ܢܗܘܐ ܠܗ ܚܢܝܢܐ ܘܟܡ ܓܒܪܐ ܡܢ ܒܢܬܐ ܠܐ ܢܬܠܠ ܕܠܐ ܢܬܠ ܢܦܫܗ ܠܝ ܒܪܐ: ܘܟܡ ܓܒܪܐ ܡܓܕܦܢܐ ܠܐ ܢܕܘܫ ܕܠܡܐ ܠܝ ܢܦܫܐ ܡܢܗ ܡܬܠܠܬܗ. ܘܡܢ ܡܟܚܠ ܡܢܝ ܐ ܢܗܘܐ ܐܣܝܗ: ܘܠܐ ܢܬܬܦܪ ܠܒܪܢܫܐ ܟܕ ܐܢܫܐ ܒܡܦܪܢܘܬܐ ܕܝܠܗ. ܗܠܝܢ ܟܐܐ ܠܡܫܝܚܐ ܐܝܠܝܢ ܕܡܟܠܝܢ ܚܢܢܐ ܡܫܝܚܐ ܘܗܘܘܢ ܬܠܡܝܕܐ ܠܡܫܝܚܐ. ܗܟܢܐ ܓܒܪ ܟܐܐ ܠܗܘܢ ܠܬܠܡܝܕܘܗܝ ܕܡܫܝܚܐ. ܕܠܒܪܗܘܢ ܡܫܝܚܐ ܢܬܕܪܟܘܢ.	... ܘܟܕ ܠܝܬ ܠܗ ܠܐ ܬܒܪܐ ܠܗ. ܘܟܡ ܒܪܢܫܐ ܒܢܫܐ ܠܐ ܢܗܘܐ ܚܢܝܢܗ. ܘܟܡ ܓܒܪܐ ܡܢ ܒܢܬܐ ܠܐ ܢܬܠܠ. ܕܠܐ ܢܬܠ ܢܦܫܗ ܠܝ ܒܪܐ. ܘܟܡ ܓܒܪܐ ܡܓܕܦܢܐ ܠܐ ܢܕܘܫ. ܕܠܡܐ ܠܝ ܢܦܫܐ ܡܢܗ ܡܬܠܠܬܗ. ܘܡܢ ܡܟܚܠ ܡܢܝ ܐ ܢܗܘܐ ܐܣܝܗ. ܘܠܐ ܢܬܬܦܪ ܠܒܪܢܫܐ ܒܡܦܪܢܘܬܐ ܕܝܠܗ. ܗܠܝܢ ܟܐܐ ܠܡܫܝܚܐ: ܐܝܠܝܢ ܕܡܟܠܝܢ ܚܢܢܐ ܕܡܫܝܚܐ ܘܗܘܘܢ ܬܠܡܝ̈ܕܐ: ܗܟܢܐ ܕܝܢ ܟܐܐ ܠܗܘܢ ܕܢܬܕܪܟܘܢ ܠܒܪܗܘܢ.
6.9	ܢܣܒ ܠܟ ܕܡܘܬܐ ܣܓܝܐܐ ܡܢ ܡܟܣܝܢ: ܕܟܕ ܟܠܬܪܐ ܗܘܐ ܡܗܝܡܢ ܢܦܫܗ: ܘܟܕ ܪܘܚܐ ܗܘܐ ܐܡܝܢ ܪܚܘܬܗ: ܘܟܕ ܡܟܡܟܪܗ ܒܡܪܘܡܐ ܗܘܐ ܠܝܬ ܗܘܐ ܠܗ ܐܬܪ ܕܢܣܡܘܟ ܪܫܗ: ܘܟܕ ܚܠ...	ܘܟܕ ܕܠܗ ܫܡܝܐ ܘܐܪܥܐ. ܠܝܬ ܗܘܐ ܠܗ ܐܝܟܐ ܕܢܣܡܘܟ ܪܫܗ. ܐܝܟ ܢܦܫܝ ܣܓܝܐܐ ܢܦܫܝ.
6.19	ܗܠܝܢ ܟܬܒܬ ܒܗܕܬ ܠܢܦܫܝ ܘܐܦ ܠܟ ܚܒܝܒܝ. ܡܟܝܠ ܐܣܝܪ ܒܬܘܠܘܬܐ ܡܢܬܐ ܫܡܝܢܬܐ ܣܠܝܩܘܬܐ ܕܒܢ̈ܝ ܫܡܝܐ. ܠܝܬ ܓܒܪ ܡܕܡ ܕܦܣܩ ܠܗ̇. ܘܒܐܝܠܝܢ ܕܗܒܝܢ ܐܢܘܢ ܒܗܘܢ ܒܒܪ ܡܫܝܚܐ. ܘܒܝܢ ܕܡܣܩܢܐ ܩܪܒ ܠܗ ܘܬܬܐ ܐܦܪܥܬ ܘܢܦܩܘ ܦܐܪ̈ܘܗ̇: ܐܬܘ̈ܬܐ ܕܢܗܒ ܦܘܪܩܢ ܥܪ̈ܝ ܥ̈ܠܡܝܢ. ܐܡܪ ܓܒܪ: ܕܢܩܘܡ ܒܒܟܐ ܒܠ ܒܒܟܐ ܘܡܠܟܐ ܒܠ ܡܠܟܐ: ܘܢܗܘܘܢ ܒܩ̈ܢܝܐ ܘܡܬܘ̈ܬܢܐ ܘܕܫ̈ܠܬܐ ܡܢ ܫܡܝܐ. ܘܗܠܝܢ ܟܠܗܝܢ ܒܢܘ̈ܡܣܝ ܗܐ ܫܠܝܢ.	ܐܣܝܪ ܒܬܘܠܘܬܐ ܡܢܬܐ ܫܡܝܢܬܐ ܣܠܝܩܘܬܐ ܕܒܢ ܒܢ̈ܝ ܪܘܡܐ. ܠܝܬ ܓܒܪ ܡܕܡ ܕܦܣܩ ܠܗ̇. ܒܐܝܠܝܢ ܕܗܒܝܢ ܐܢܘܢ: ܒܗܘܢ ܒܒܪ ܡܫܝܚܐ. ܘܒܝܢ ܕܡܣܩܢܐ ܩܪܒ ܠܗ. ܬܬܐ ܐܦܪܥܬ ܘܢܦܩܘ ܦܐܪ̈ܘܗ̇. ܐܬܘ̈ܬܐ ܕܢܗܒ ܦܘܪܩܢ ܥܪ̈ܝ ܥ̈ܠܡܝܢ. ܐܡܪ ܓܒܪ ܕܢܩܘܡ ܒܒܟܐ ܒܠ ܒܒܟܐ ܘܡܠܟܐ ܒܠ ܡܠܟܐ. ܘܢܗܘܘܢ ܒܩ̈ܢܝܐ ܘܕܫ̈ܠܬܐ ܘܡܬܘ̈ܬܢܐ ܒܪܘܡܐ ܕܘܟܐ. ܘܗܠܝܢ ܟܠܗܝܢ ܒܢܘ̈ܡܣܝ ܗܐ ܫܠܝܢ.

6.8 end	...and if he does not have [anything to give], he should not be sad. He should not associate with an evil person, nor speak with a shameful person, so that he might not give himself over to shame. He should not dispute with a blasphemer, lest his Lord should be maligned because of him. He should stay away from a slanderer, and he should not attempt to make one person acceptable to another person with pleasing words. These things are proper for the single ones, those who have received the heavenly yoke and who have become disciples of the Messiah. It is fitting that disciples of the Messiah should be like their teacher, the Messiah.	...and if he does not have [anything to give], he should not be sad. He should not associate with an evil person, nor speak with a shameful person, so that he might not give himself over to shame. He should not dispute with a blasphemer, so that his Lord might not be maligned because of him. He should stay away from a slanderer, and he should not attempt to make one person acceptable to another person with pleasing words. These things are proper for the single ones, those who have received the yoke of the Messiah and who have become penitent. It is fitting that they should be like their teacher.
6.9	My friend, let us accept the example of our lifegiver: Although he was rich, he made himself poor; although he was exalted, he humbled his greatness; although his dwelling place was in the highest places, he had no place to lay his head; although he will come...	Although heaven and earth belonged to him, he had no place to lay his head. Be vigilant for yourself, my friend, [and] for me.
6.19	I have written these things as a reminder to myself and also to you, my friend. Therefore, love virginity—the heavenly portion, the communion of the watchers of heaven—for there is nothing comparable to it. Christ dwells in those who do thus. Summer has come; the fig tree has blossomed, and its leaves have appeared. The signs that our Savior gave are beginning to be fulfilled, for he said, "People will rise against people, and kingdom against kingdom. There will be famines, plagues, and terrors from heaven. All these things will be fulfilled in our days."	Love virginity—the heavenly portion, communion with the watchers on high—for there is nothing comparable to it. Christ dwells in those who do thus. Summer has come; the fig tree has blossomed, and its leaves have appeared. The signs that our Savior gave are beginning to be fulfilled, for he said, "People will rise against people, and kingdom against kingdom. There will be famines, earthquakes, and plagues in many places. All these things will be fulfilled in our days."

The significant feature of these citations for the purposes of the present argument is that, following the text that corresponds with 6.8, there is one sentence that corresponds with the beginning of 6.9 and then a seamless transition to the text of 6.19. Moreover, it is noteworthy that both versions of the citation (i.e. Brit. Libr. Orient 6714 and Mingana Syr. 601) provide exactly the same transition from 6.8/9 to 6.19, even though they both preserve different amounts of the overall text of *Dem.* 6. Thus, these citations preserve a version of *Dem.* 6 that completely lacks 6.9–6.18 (except for one sentence from 6.9), the precise sections that correspond to the discussion of the body/soul relationship.

Based on this evidence, it seems likely that the source text of the citations attributed to Abraham represents an alternate version of the text in *Dem.* 6 and one which transitions directly from 6.8/9 to 6.19, omitting the long section of *Dem.* 6 that is not concerned with the topic of virginity/*bnay qyāmā*. In other words, these citations would seem to provide external proof of Gennadius' distinction between two originally separate titles, *De virginitate* and *De sensu animae*. If this is the case, then the text of *Dem.* 6 as it was transmitted in the *Demonstrations* represents a later combination of what was earlier two distinct texts, one on virginity and the other on the body/soul relationship, both of which correspond to titles listed in Gennadius' list.

To be certain, there are some significant issues with using these citations as corroboration for this point; namely, the later date of these manuscripts and the editorial activity of re-purposing texts in ascetic miscellany manuscripts.[23] Despite these objections, though, there is still good reason to think that *Dem.* 6 represents two originally distinct texts. It would explain the appearance of an otherwise inexplicable title in Gennadius' list, *De sensu animae*, as well as the existence of the alternate version of the text that appears in two later extracted citations attributed to Abraham of Nathpar. Most importantly, though, this theory would provide a reason for the significant shift in topic from 6.8 to 6.9. The preponderance of virginity/celibacy terminology in 6.1–8, 19–20 and the complete lack of such language in 6.9–18 is striking, and this theory provides a plausible explanation.

23. For a very brief overview of such manuscripts, see Grigory Kessel, "Syriac monastic miscellanies," in *Comparative Oriental Manuscript Studies: An Introduction*, edited by Alessandro Bausi (general editor) et al., 439–443 (Hamburg: COMSt, 2015).

Conclusion

The likely date of composition of Gennadius' list in the late fifth century makes it a potentially significant witness to the textual history of the *Demonstrations*. That is, the list is contemporaneous with the earliest Syriac manuscripts of the *Demonstrations*, which means it is at least possible that Gennadius was aware of a collection of texts that represent an earlier version of texts that came to make up the *Demonstrations* as we know them. The theory presented here that the *Demonstrations* represent, at least in part, a collected and edited version of pre-existing writings is the best explanation for the version of the titles that Gennadius provides.

Of all the evidence presented in this article, no single piece is persuasive when taken alone. However, when taken collectively, the evidence presented here builds a compelling case. Rather than thinking of this evidence as "proof" of the theory, I tend to think of the theory as the best possible explanation for the evidence. The early manuscript attestation of the *Demonstrations* in Syriac provides a sense of confidence that allows us to overlook the potential historical value of Gennadius' list. So, I suggest that if we take Gennadius' list more seriously as a witness to the reception history of the *Demonstrations*, we may actually find it to be more reliable than previously imagined.

Concluding Excursus: Authorship of the *Demonstrations*

The theory presented in this article may also indirectly provide the answer to another problem in the reception history of the *Demonstrations*: the thorny issue of authorship. Gennadius attributes these texts to Jacob of Nisibis. The name "Aphrahaṭ" is not associated with the *Demonstrations* until at least the seventh or eighth century, and our earliest external witness to the text, George, bishop of the Arabs, does not know the identity of the author. Ms. Brit. Libr. Add. 14,619 attributes the text to an anonymous "Persian Sage," as does the colophon of the first part of ms. Brit. Libr. Add. 17,182. The second half of ms. Brit. Libr. Add. 17,182, however, names "Mar Jacob" as the Persian Sage. Likewise, the very early tradition of the *Demonstrations* in Armenian—as early as the fifth century—attributes this work to Jacob of Nisibis. Thus, if it is plausible to postulate a multi-stage compositional theory including an editor/redactor, then it is also plausible that Gennadius' tradition of authorship is correct. That is, it is possible that Jacob of Nisibis authored a set of writings—those writings represented by Gennadius' list—that were subsequently edited into the form of the *Demonstrations* as we know them, perhaps even by someone named Aphrahaṭ, the Persian Sage.

4. From Sketches to Portraits

The Canaanite Woman within Late Antique Syriac Poetry

❖ Erin Galgay Walsh

Introduction

Among the female characters of the Gospel narratives, the Canaanite Woman in Matthew 15:21–28 intrigued and challenged early Christian interpreters.[1] As a female and a non-Israelite, the Canaanite Woman pursues Jesus with an audacity sustained by maternal love for her demon-possessed daughter. Initially Jesus dismisses the woman, claiming that his commission was limited to gathering the lost sheep of Israel (15:24). Undeterred, the Canaanite Woman persists, and in the confrontation that unfolds, her powers of persuasion demonstrate the potential for Jesus' salvific power to operate beyond the boundaries of Israel.[2] Ephrem, the fourth-century poet and exegete, invoked her

1. Within modern New Testament scholarship, this pericope is often read in light of Mark's Syro-phoenician woman (7:24–30). Historical and redaction critical approaches have yielded much interpretative insight into how the author of Matthew recast his source material from Mark in light of his christological themes. Our interpreters primarily focus on the text of Matthew. For a thorough treatment of this narrative, see Nancy Klancher, *The Taming of the Canaanite Woman: Constructions of Christian Identity in the Afterlife of Matthew 15:21–28* (Berlin: De Gruyter, 2013).

2. The debates around Matthew are revealing of how scholars approach questions of the setting of the Gospel through textual clues such as the inclusion of the Gentile centurion (Mt 8:5–13) and the Canaanite Woman (15:21–28) who are praised for their extraordinary faith. See Daniel J. Harrington, *The Gospel of Matthew* (Collegeville: Liturgical Press, 1991), 141–143; John Nolland, *The Gospel of Matthew* (Grand Rapids: Eerdmans, 2005), 17; W. D. Davies and Dale C. Allison, *Matthew: A Shorter Commentary* (New York: T&T Clark, 2004), xxix; Amy Jill-Levine, *The Social and Ethnic Dimensions of Matthean Salvation History* (Lewiston: Edwin Mellen Press, 1988), 3. Levine argues that the

story sporadically, often focusing on her penitent posture as a model for Christians. In the late-fifth and early-sixth centuries, this Matthean pericope inspired both Narsai and Jacob of Serugh to compose sustained re-narrations of her story through vivid dialogue and characterization.

In the process of contextualizing the compositions of fifth- and sixth-century Syriac poets such as Jacob and Narsai, one must query the extent to which their literary forebear, Ephrem, set the exegetical trajectories for later poets to follow. Against these earlier exegetical traditions, the compositions of Narsai and his younger contemporary, Jacob, stand as distinct expressions of their theological and poetic sensibilities. The Canaanite woman's narrative is among a handful of biblical texts for which we have *mēmrē* from both Jacob and Narsai, offering the opportunity to compare their poetic style and exegetical approaches. Despite their conflicting Christological views and fierce disagreement over the writings of Theodore of Mopsuestia, Narsai and Jacob use imagery and themes in common with Ephrem as well as one another, underscoring the presence of shared features in their literary environments.[3] In the case of the Canaanite Woman, the tradition of interpretation builds from mere allusions in Ephrem's poetry to portraits of philosophical and psychological depth in the compositions of his inheritors. While Ephrem's rare invocations of the Canaanite woman attend to her faith and lowliness within the encounter with Jesus, later Syriac treatments of her tale draw greater attention to her extraordinary speech act, shifting the interpretative focus to her powers of discernment and tenacity.

The Poetry of Ephrem

Throughout his poetic corpus, Ephrem returns time and again to harvest spiritual insights and moral instruction from the biblical

"commission" described in the final chapter of the Gospel creates a space for Gentiles and suggests equality between Jews and Gentiles. Other scholars have challenged the assumption that such statements regarding Gentiles should be read positively. See J. Andrew Overman, *Matthew's Gospel and Formative Judaism: The Social World of the Matthean Community* (Minneapolis: Fortress Press, 1990), 156–158; Anthony J. Saldarini, *Matthew's Christian-Jewish Community* (Chicago: University of Chicago Press, 1994), 157. For a complete overview, see D. N. Gullotta, "Among Dogs and Disciples: An Examination of the Story of the Canaanite Woman (Matthew 15:21–28) and the Question of the Gentile Mission within the Matthean Community," *Neotestamentica* 48 (2014): 327–329.

3. Lucas Van Rompay, "Humanity's Sin in Paradise: Ephrem, Jacob of Sarug, and Narsai in Conversation," in *Jacob of Serugh and His Times: Studies in Sixth-Century Syriac Christianity*, ed. George Anton Kiraz, 199–217 (Piscataway: Gorgias Press, 2010), 216–217.

accounts of Eve, the Virgin Mary, and the Sinful Woman.[4] In contrast, the Canaanite Woman exists in the periphery of Ephrem's biblical imagination. In analyzing specific references to Matthew 15:21–28, three questions guide the present inquiry: How does Ephrem allude to her story? Who are the biblical characters that frequently appear alongside her? And lastly, how does he embed the Canaanite Woman within the larger biblical narrative? Instead of treating Ephrem in isolation, I will weave into my treatment of Ephrem examples from Jacob and Narsai that show resonances between these three authors.

Often Ephrem evokes this story through referencing the imagery of crumbs and dogs, relying on the listener to recall the Gospel narrative. The *Hymns on Paradise* contain a cluster of such citations which center on the theme of the topography of Paradise and the search for sustenance after the expulsion of Adam and Eve from the garden. A prime example of this is found in the seventh hymn when Ephrem praises the promise of the eschatological existence which awaits the faithful. Unwilling to posit his own future status among the blessed, Ephrem assumes the posture of the Canaanite Woman to express his hope that even those relegated to the margins of Paradise enjoy the blessings of divine nourishment:

> And if no one defiled is able
> to enter that place,
> then allow me [to live] by its fence,
> dwelling in its shade.
> Since Paradise resembles that table (*b-ṭupsā d-pātorā*),
> let me, through Your grace,
> eat the fallen (bits) of its fruit
> which (lay) outside,
> that (I might be as) the dogs sated with the crumbs of their masters.[5]

4. An excellent overview may be found in Susan Ashbrook Harvey, *Song and Memory: Biblical Women in Syriac Tradition* (Milwaukee: Marquette University Press, 2010).

5. Ephrem, *Hymns on Paradise*, VII.26. The Syriac is edited with a German translation in Edmund Beck, *Des Heiligen Ephraem des Syrers Hymnen de Paradiso und Contra Julianum*, CSCO 174 (Louvain: Peeters, 1957); an English translation is available in Sebastian Brock, *Hymns on Paradise* (Crestwood: St. Vladimir's Seminary Press, 1990). I have substantially modified Brock's beautiful translation to emphasize the sparseness of the references to Mt 15:21–28.

The references to crumbs and dogs anchor Ephrem's verses in the Gospel text while allowing the poet's theological aims to take precedence. While modern New Testament interpreters have focused on the implications of the text for understanding the boundaries and scope of salvation envisioned by the Gospel writer, Ephrem accentuates the universal message of the story as a foreshadowing of divine abundance.[6] Jeffrey Wickes observes that Ephrem fashions his self-presentation as a poet through his use of the narratives of the Canaanite Woman, the Hemorrhaging Woman, and the Sinful Woman.[7] Focusing on the *Hymns on Faith*, Wickes identified three levels at which the narratives of these women operate for Ephrem: as an example of proper posture for receiving the Eucharist, a dramatic image for the poet's own reception of divine inspiration, and lastly the experience of God's loftiness and beneficence.[8] Ephrem deploys this narrative imagery in both the *Hymns on Faith* and the *Hymns on Paradise*, providing deep theological and biblical resonances between the two bodies of poetry. Ephrem pivots between these biblical texts as he crafts his identity as a speaker, modeling a posture of humility and abject dependence on divine aid. In his hands, the figure of the Canaanite Woman personifies the lowliness of the human condition that nevertheless finds respite in the presence of Paradise. This representative example of Ephrem's treatment of the Canaanite woman from the *Hymns on Paradise* demonstrates the often fragmentary and fleeting nature of references to her story within his poetry. To use a favored image of Ephrem, Scripture was a "treasury" of images which could be separated and reassembled as the tesserae in a mosaic.

A common thread that unites Ephrem's invocation of her tale is his penchant for the Eucharistic image of a morsel of bread. The image of the crumb is relatively uncommon in Scripture. The Greek term for crumb in Mt 15:27, ψιχίον, appears in only two other places

6. Ulrich Luz, *Matthew: A Commentary 8–20,* trans. James E. Crouch and ed. Helmut Koester, Hermeneia: A Critical and Historical Commentary on the Bible (Minneapolis: Fortress Press, 2001), 336–342.

7. Jeffrey Wickes, "The Poetics of Self-Presentation in Ephrem's *Hymns on Faith* 10," in *Syriac Encounters: Papers from the Sixth North American Syriac Symposium at Duke University, 26–29 June 2011,* ECS 20, edited by Maria Doerfler, Kyle Smith, and Emanuel Fiano, 51–64 (Louvain: Peeters, 2015), 57–58.

8. Wickes, "The Poetics of Self-Presentation in Ephrem's *Hymns on Faith* 10," 57–58.

within the New Testament: the Syro-Phoenician woman's tale in Mark (7:28) and the parable of the Rich Man and Lazarus in Luke (16:21). The Lukan text includes a reference to dogs as well: "And (Lazarus) desired to fill his belly with the crumbs which fell from the table of that rich man. And also the dogs came and licked his wounds" (Lk 16:20–21).[9] The Syriac Peshiṭta employs the same word for all three instances: *partutā*. Codex Sinaiticus and Codex Curetonianus do not use this term for the image in Luke.[10] Likewise Codex Sinaiticus omits the term for the Matthean verse but uses it for the corresponding verse in Mark (7:28).[11] Ephrem uses the term *parkukā*, and this variant is consistently used for all three biblical instances in the Ḥarklean translation.[12] Editors and translators of Ephrem's poetry consistently identify the imagery of crumbs and dogs as references to the Canaanite Woman, but as one follows these images—a veritable "trail of bread crumbs"—the logic of Ephrem's biblical reasoning comes to light. Ephrem's exegetical dexterity weaves together the Gospel narratives of this woman with the parable of the Rich Man and Lazarus, further crafting a model for the religious self as impoverished and dependent on divine nourishment.

9. François Bovon, *Luke 2: A Commentary on the Gospel of Luke 9:51–19:27*, trans. Donald S. Deer and ed. Helmut Koestler (Minneapolis: Fortress Press, 2013), 480–481. As Bovon notes, Erich Klostermann made the connection between the Syro-Phoenician woman and the parable earlier, citing sources external to the New Testament which relate breaking bread at table with the presence of dogs (*Das Markusevangelium*, Handbuch zum Neuen Testament 3, 4th ed. [Tübingen: Mohr Siebeck, 1950], 72–73). Klostermann further surmises that the images of crumbs and dogs were connected in reference to the plight of the poor (*Das Lukansevangelium*, Handbuch zum Neuen Testament 5, 3rd ed. [Tübingen: Mohr Siebeck, 1975], 167–168). See also Glenna Jackson, *Have Mercy on Me: The Story of the Canaanite Woman in Matthew 15:21–28* (London: Sheffield Academic Press, 2002), 124–125.

10. George Anton Kiraz, *Comparative Edition of the Syriac Gospels: Aligning the Sinaiticus, Curetonianus, Peshîṭtâ and Ḥarklean Versions*, vol. 3 (Leiden: Brill, 1996), 335. Instead of *partutā* these manuscripts render the Greek with the generic word for "something" or "few," *meddem*; the Syriac of the Ḥarklean version contains the same variation of the term as Ephrem: *parkukā*. Whereas *parkukā* recalls the verb *prkk* "to crumble," *partutā* is connected to the verb *prty* "tear up" (Michael Sokoloff, *A Syriac Lexicon: A translation from the Latin; correction, expansion, and update of C. Brockelmann's Lexicon Syriacum* [Winona Lake: Eisenbrauns, 2012], 1241 and 1256). As Beck notes in his critical apparatus, manuscripts of Ephrem's *Hymns on Paradise* do substitute *partutā* for *parkukā*, perhaps aligning the text more closely with the Peshiṭta as well as providing evidence for the interchangeable nature of the two words. See Kiraz, *Comparative Edition of the Syriac Gospels*, 2.99–100 (on Mark); 1.227–228 (on Matthew).

11. Kiraz, *Comparative Edition of the Syriac Gospels*, 1.227–228.

12. Kiraz, *Comparative Edition of the Syriac Gospels*, 1.227–228 (Matthew); 3.335 (Luke); 2.227–228 (Mark).

The question of how Ephrem evokes the story of the Canaanite woman dovetails with the question of what figures he associates with her. The parallels between the parable of the Rich Man and Lazarus and the Canaanite Woman—table, crumbs, and canines—suggest that Ephrem layers multiple allusions through a sparing use of images. Within this same poem in the *Hymns on Paradise,* Ephrem follows the verse we examined with an explicit reference to the Lukan parable: "And may I learn how much I will then have received from the parable of the Rich man," underscoring the intertextual link.[13] Of the two further instances that "crumbs" appear in the *Hymns on Paradise,* one includes an explicit reference to both the Canaanite woman and Lazarus, and the other may be read as an oblique reference to either narrative.[14] One wonders if such loose intertextual links undermine claims to scriptural references, but our poet provides sufficient details for detecting the scriptural echoes.[15] In *Hymns on Paradise* VII.26, Ephrem beseeches the Lord not only to eat from the crumbs, but he also aspires to the rank of the dogs, providing sufficient warrant for identifying this as an allusion to the Matthean story of the Canaanite Woman as well as the Lukan text. I have not yet found this intertextual connection in Greek and Latin authors despite the strong lexical link, and neither Jacob nor Narsai seem to make the same association.[16]

While Ephrem invokes the example of Canaanite woman in the *Hymns on Paradise* to reflect on divine provision for those in need of sustenance, he shifts his focus to other exegetical possibilities of the Gospel text elsewhere in his corpus. In the *Homily on our Lord,* Ephrem turns his attention to the scope of Jesus's mission and employs the Canaanite woman to build a contrast between Israel and the

13. Ephrem, *Hymns on Paradise,* VII.27 (Beck, *Des Heiligen Ephraem des Syrers Hymnen de Paradiso,* VII.27; Brock, *Hymns on Paradise,* 129).

14. See Beck, *Des Heiligen Ephraem des Syrers Hymnen de Paridiso,* I.12–16 and V.15.

15. Ephrem, *Hymns on the Nativity,* IV. 83. The Syriac is edited with a German translation in Edmund Beck, *Des Heiligen Ephraem des Syrers Hymnen de Nativite,* CSCO 186 (Louvain: Peeters, 1959), IV.83; an English translation is available in Kathleen E. McVey, *Ephrem the Syrian: Hymns* (New York: Paulist Press, 1989). In Ephrem's *Hymns on the Nativity* IV. 83, our poet exhorts Christians on the Lord's feast day to "cast away, as is right, the crumb of bread." Embedded within the broader thematic context of the poem, namely the Eucharist, this usage seems to be less exact than the examples we have cited from the *Hymns on Paradise.*

16. One could also argue that Ephrem might be casting himself as Lazarus or the Canaanite woman with these scriptural references, but it is less clear what these parallels say about the character of God. I am grateful to my colleague, Ian Mills, for pointing out the potential problems with this allusion.

nations.[17] After rehearsing the practice of idolatry and Moses's destruction of the Golden Calf in Exodus 32, Ephrem relativizes the chosen status of Israel, leveling religious distinctions: "Glory to you who, by your cross, removed the paganism over which both uncircumcised and circumcised stumbled! Thanksgiving to you, Medicine of Life for all, who plunged down after life for all, and returned it to the Lord of all!"[18] Ephrem alludes to the Canaanite Woman within this discussion of the scope of Jesus' salvific mission, simultaneously vilifying the Jewish people for rejecting him and extolling those once thought "lost" (*'abbidē*)—identifying them with the uncircumcised—who have found blessing in God through accepting him. He closes this passage with a polemically charged reference to the woman's encounter with Jesus: "But those [people] to whom you did not come in your love cry out after you to fill them with the crumbs (*partutē*) which fall from the children's table."[19] Those familiar with the text of Matthew will catch the distinctively Matthean detail as to whom the table belongs. The Syriac New Testament, following the Greek, identifies the table as belonging to the master whereas the bread belongs to the children of the house in Mt 15:27, and the table's owner is not specified in Mk 7:28. By erasing the Lord's position over the table, Ephrem emphasizes the distinction between the children and the dogs. The children, those readily provided for, are identified with the Jews, a link Ephrem accentuates. In light of his accusatory tone when narrating the Golden Calf incident from Exodus, it would appear that the Canaanite woman reinforces Ephrem's condemnation of the Jewish people, a central rhetorical aim.[20] As Amy-Jill Levine notes,

17. The implications of this pericope for Matthew's larger view of Jesus mission and the place of the Gentiles are frequently featured in commentaries. See John Nolland, *The Gospel of Matthew: A Commentary on the Greek Text* (Grand Rapids: William B. Eerdmans Publishing Company, 2005), 628–636.

18. Ephrem, *Sermo de Domino Nostro*, VII.1. The Syriac is edited with a German translation in Edmund Beck, *Des Heiligen Ephraem des Syrers Sermo de Domino Nostro,* CSCO 270 (Louvain: Peeters, 1966); an English translation is available in Edward G. Mathews, Jr., and Joseph P. Amar, *St. Ephrem the Syrian: Selected Prose Works*, FOC 91 (Washington: The Catholic University of America Press, 1994), 273–332.

19. Ephrem, *Sermo de Domino Nostro*, VII.1 (Beck, *Des Heiligen Ephraem des Syrers Sermo de Domino Nostro,* 7; Matthews and Amar, *St. Ephrem the Syrian: Selected Prose Works*, VII.1).

20. Christine Shepardson, *Anti-Judaism and Christian Orthodoxy: Ephrem's Hymns in Fourth Century Syria* (Washington: The Catholic University of America Press, 2008), 51–52. Ephrem returns to the Golden Calf episode frequently to bolster his polemical argument, as Shepardson demonstrates.

readings that interpret Matthew through the lens of the Gentile mission often reify the boundaries between Jews and Gentiles, acquiring a tinge of anti-Judaism in the process.[21]

Within the larger context of Ephrem's *Homily on Our Lord*, this single, passing reference to the Canaanite Woman is distinct from the attention the poet pays to female biblical characters throughout the work. While the narrative of the Sinful Woman receives a thorough treatment, Ephrem punctuates his text with a reference to the Hemorrhaging Woman as another example of an outsider who comes forward to receive from the "Treasury of healing"—an image that both Jacob and Narsai invoke for the Canaanite woman. Combined with the references we have seen in the *Hymns on Paradise,* it becomes clear that the ethnic, cultural, and religious identity of the Canaanite Woman serves Ephrem's polemical ends, but he does not reflect on her speech or details of her specific encounter. Like our earlier example, this passage invokes the Gospel text without portraying the woman herself. Her individuality is lost as she is replaced with the collective who call out; she becomes a cipher for the "peoples" who become enlightened beyond the boundaries of Israel and without the benefit of the Law.

Ephrem's allusions to the Canaanite woman also pay little explicit attention to the gender dynamics of the narrative, extending instead the supplicatory posture to all Christians in light of their utter dependence on God. Not only is her voice largely absent from his portrayal, but her body recedes from view. Throughout his poetic corpus, especially in the *Sermon on our Lord,* Ephrem conjures up the Sinful Woman and the Hemorrhaging Woman through vivid images of their clothing, bodily movements and especially their tears. Indeed, Susan Ashbrook Harvey has shown the central role of the body within Syriac Christian literature, and theology as an "instrument of religious expression" and a reflection of spiritual progress.[22] The lack of attention to the Canaanite Woman's body is therefore striking. In contrast to other female figures from the New Testament, he only limns

21. Amy-Jill Levine, "Matthew's Advice to a Divided Readership," in *The Gospel of Matthew in Current Study: Studies in Memory of William G. Thompson, SJ,* edited by David E. Aune, 22–41 (Grand Rapids: William B. Eerdmans Publishing Company, 2001), 32–35.

22. Susan Ashbrook Harvey, "Embodiment in Time and Eternity: A Syriac Perspective," *St. Vladimir's Theological Quarterly* 43 (1999): 108.

the Canaanite Woman, reducing the narrative to her pre-linguistic cry and gladly accepts the crumbs. The middle of her story, specifically her exchange with Jesus, fades from view. Rather than developing the dramatic tension of her approach and interaction with Jesus through re-narrating her bodily movements, Ephrem uses the images associated with her to expand a larger web of textual allusions to bolster his argument.

The *Commentary on the Diatessaron* Attributed to Ephrem

The role that the narrative of the Canaanite Woman plays in positioning the "peoples" in relationship to Israel is an exegetical direction that carries over from the *Homily on Our Lord* to the *Commentary on the Diatessaron*.[23] The nature of the commentary genre elicits from Ephrem (and his editors) a sustained treatment of the themes and exegetical difficulties of the text itself, reflecting perhaps the *Commentary*'s specialized audience.[24] This larger portrait also provides further material for detecting resonance between Ephrem and later Syriac poets. The moral and spiritual vision of the *Commentary* parallels the views of Narsai and Jacob that the Canaanite woman performs in miniature the struggle each Christian experiences in their own lives.

The Canaanite woman first appears in an excursus on the healing of the paralytic in Matthew 9:2, and here the moral lesson of the text is emphasized. Together these stories from Matthew demonstrate that those steadfast in faith intercede as proxies for those who resemble in Ephrem's words, "buildings that [are] in ruins."[25] Rather than relying on others, however, the *Commentary* exhorts the reader to oversee their own souls with a greater caution. In the conclusion of Jacob's

23. Klancher, *The Taming of the Canaanite Woman*, 65–66. For Klancher, these contrasts form a key part of Ephrem's rhetorical strategy for prescribing "orthodox" identity. For the *Commentary on the Diatessaron* attributed to Ephrem, see Christian Lange, *The Portrayal of Christ in the Syriac Commentary on the Diatessaron*, CSCO 616 (Louvain: Peeters, 2005), 52–55.

24. Harvey, *Song and Memory*, 19.

25. Ephrem, *Commentary on the Diatessaron*, V.19. The Syriac is edited in Louis Leloir, *Saint Éphrem: Commentaire de l'Évangile concordant. Texte syriaque (Manuscript Chester Beatty 709). Folios additionnels* (Louvain: Peeters, 1990), 50–51; an English translation is available in Carmel McCarthy, *St. Ephrem's Commentary on the Diatessaron: An English Translation of Chester Beatty Syriac MS 709* (Oxford: Oxford University Press, 1993). For the authorship of the *Commentary*, see Christian Lange, *The Portrayal of Christ in the Syriac Commentary on the Diatessaron*, CSCO 616 (Louvain: Peeters, 2005), esp. 52–55.

mēmrā we hear an echo of this therapeutic language: "Suffering of the soul is worse than the maiden's demon / Make a request on [i.e. your soul's] behalf, and behold it will be healed as that one [i.e. the maiden] was."[26] Assimilating the mother and daughter into the constituent parts of the self, Ephrem and Jacob counsel assiduous self-care. Narsai achieves a similar end without identifying the daughter with the soul. More heavily laden with martial imagery and often utilizing a more complex theological anthropology, Narsai warns:

> The Hateful One who fights with your lives is not corporeal,
> but rather a spirit who engages in battle with hidden impulses.
> According to his concealment prepare spiritual weapons,
> and wage war, conquer by means of the endurance of your minds.[27]

Without sufficient evidence for textual dependence, these three preachers produce similar applications of the biblical material. This shared approach suggests common literary and interpretative traditions. As Hagit Amirav has demonstrated in the corpus of John Chrysostom's homilies, late antique writers applied exegetical traditions rhetorically, showing the cross-fertilization of literary genres and the embedded nature of these liturgical and performative texts within larger patterns of biblical interpretation.[28] Whereas Ephrem's dexterity as an interpreter leads him to employ the Canaanite Woman in various ways (within his *Commentary* alone), the sustained poems of Narsai and Jacob represent their concerted effort to build this biblical figure into a multi-faceted model for Christian piety.

The remaining two references in the *Commentary* deal more directly with the theme of the relationship between the people and the peoples. Ephrem mentions (like many interpreters) the Canaanite Woman while

26. Paul Bedjan and Sebastian P. Brock, *Homilies of Mar Jacob of Sarug* (Piscataway: Gorgias Press, 2006), 1.441.19–20. Translations from Jacob's "On the Canaanite Woman" are my own.

27. Narsai, *On the Canaanite Woman,* lines 214–215. This *memrā* remains unedited, but I have prepared an edition based on the two available extant manuscripts, along with a translation. In the citations that follow, I reference the homily by the line numbers of the oldest extant manuscript, Diyarbakir 70, f. 204r–212r. This manuscript may be found at the Hill Museum and Manuscript Library under the shelf-mark Chaldean Cathedral (Mardin) 578.

28. Hagit Amirav. *Rhetoric and Tradition: John Chrysostom on Noah and the Flood*, TEG 12 (Louvain: Peeters, 2003), 6–7.

discussing the healing of the Centurion's servant in Mt 8:5–13.[29] He recognizes the tension between these narratives and Jesus' injunction in Matthew 10:5 that the disciples are to enter neither Gentile territory nor Samaritan cities, but Ephrem seems unwilling to impose a resolution upon the text. Instead he notes that "He received the Canaanite Woman with difficulty. Our Lord showed through these [individuals] that his Gospel would spread among the peoples."[30] In light of the scriptural witness to Jesus' amazement, Ephrem affirms the promise of these texts while downplaying the friction they create for interpreters.

Later in the *Commentary*, Ephrem explains Jesus' initial silence as pedagogical, a justification shared by Narsai and Jacob. Reassuring his audiences of Jesus' omniscience, Narsai proclaims: "It was not that he tried her by delaying and not listening to her words, (but) He wanted to reveal the truth of her love to those who did not know."[31] This gradual and intentional revelation is part of God's larger strategy for human redemption that began in Eden and is continually fulfilled in the process of salvation.[32] In the Gospel narrative, Jesus praises the faith of the Canaanite Woman, but these three exegetes additionally stress her love as critical for their audiences to emulate.

The Canaanite Woman Speaks: Narsai and Jacob of Serugh

While Ephrem's poetry and the exegetical traditions attributed to him place the Canaanite woman within a constellation of New Testament figures notable for their religious posture and receptivity to Jesus's healing, later poets such as Narsai and Jacob paint more substantial portraits of her. The *mēmrē* they compose share a special emphasis on the quality of her discernment, affective disposition, and command of argumentation. Love distinguishes her boldness from impudence, a theme Jacob shares in common with Ephrem and Narsai: "Whatever

29. Ephrem, *Commentary on the Diatessaron*, XI.27. Leloir, *Saint Éphrem: Commentaire de l'Évangile concordant. Texte Syriaque (Manuscrit Chester Beatty 709)*, 74–75.

30. Ephrem, *Commentary on the Diatessaron*, XI.27. Leloir, *Saint Éphrem: Commentaire de l'Évangile concordant. Texte Syriaque (Manuscrit Chester Beatty 709)*, 74–75 (translation modified).

31. Narsai, *On the Canaanite Woman*, f. 206r.

32. Van Rompay, "Humanity's Sin in Paradise," 211. As Van Rompay shows, Jacob and Narsai disagree over the significance of Adam and Eve's transgression in paradise, and Narsai's theological program is predicated on a commitment to a gradual process of perfection.

love says will be accepted by its own."[33] The zeal of the Canaanite Woman is evidence of her receptivity and responsiveness to a God whose love for humanity abounds.[34] It is God's loving disposition that provides the context for how Jesus' response is properly understood. Jacob specifies that Jesus specifically accepts her dispute (*drāšāh*). Both Narsai and Jacob characterize the woman as persuading, beseeching, and actively debating with Jesus, an aspect of their re-telling that is muted in Ephrem. For Jacob, Jesus lets himself be "joyously defeated" in this dispute, and according to Narsai "the sound of her words was more pleasing to him than any other sounds."[35] The center of gravity within these later *mēmrē* consists of this woman's speech act, thus emphasizing her agency rather than reducing her to a symbol for the collective of non-Israelites.

Turning back to the *Commentary on the Diatessaron,* it unfolds the inner logic he perceives to be at work within the narrative. The Canaanite Woman exemplifies the bold love found in the peoples (*ḥaṣṣiput reḥmathonā*). The canine imagery flows from this point and recalls the theme of identity: "Compared to dogs, the peoples possess the boldness of dogs and the love of dogs, but Israel, compared to dogs, possesses the fury (or savagery) of dogs."[36] While Jacob and Narsai speak of the woman's love and boldness, they do not embrace the negative valence of the canine image. The root for fury (*pqr*) appears in Narsai as a characteristic of the demons who wage war against humanity, and Jacob also attributes aggression and violence to Satan.

A prominent feature of Narsai and Jacob's re-tellings is their dramatic depiction of Satan and his minions. Narsai frames his poem with a description of the how the "Hater of Mankind" plants snares of iniquity to entrap the unsuspecting. In his hands the Canaanite Woman's confrontation with Jesus is in the context of a larger war in which her true adversary is Satan himself. In contrast, the *Commentary* pays little attention to the demonic forces at play. In a rather obscure passage of the *Commentary,* Ephrem mentions the evil spirit in reference to the history of the Canaanites who battled with Joshua, son

33. Bedjan and Brock, *Homilies of Mar Jacob of Sarug,* 1.439.7.

34. Sebastian P. Brock, *Spirituality in the Syriac Tradition* (Kottayam: St. Ephrem Ecumenical Research Institute, 2005), 85.

35. Bedjan and Brock, *Homilies of Mar Jacob of Sarug,* 1.439.13; Narsai, *On the Canaanite Woman,* f. 206r.

36. Ephrem *Commentary on the Diatessaron,* XII.13. Translation modified.

of Nun, a clear type for Jesus. Ephrem notes that this "impure spirit" (*ruḥā ṭanptā*) alternatively dwelt in the Israelites or in the Canaanites; the times when either of these peoples opposed God and caused war indicate the presence of the impure spirit among them. Accordingly, his contemporaries should recognize the presence of this spirit within Israel, further evidence of how Ephrem harnesses this text to a larger polemical posture towards Jews.[37]

Our three authors read the encounter of Jesus with this woman through the lens of larger biblical narrative and in light of their belief that the Incarnation was a decisive moment in the history of Israel. In his *Commentary,* Ephrem emphasizes the soteriological implications of the passage for the non-Israelites, and Jacob's re-telling of the narrative shares this theme. Jacob builds upon this theme by infusing the woman's persuasive rhetoric with the Pauline language of inheritance:[38]

> Along with the heirs he lets the hired workers and dogs live,
> and he is satisfied.
> The sons eat from the table as heirs;
> And the dogs gather from the crumbs as a flock does.
> The sons and the dogs live from the very same bread of the father;
> He feeds all of them from his table for they are his.[39]

In Jacob's re-telling, the Canaanite Woman describes a domestic scene in which the hierarchy of a household still has a place for her. Her fundamental desire is to belong—she even pledges that her daughter will belong to Jesus if he will only heal her.[40] While Narsai also invokes the binary of Israelite and non-Israelite as a minor premise, he uses this distinction to highlight the remarkable discernment of this woman who "taught the peoples to see the light of faith in the daughter of darkness."[41] Narsai overturns traditional expectations of

37. Klancher, *The Taming of the Canaanite Woman,* 69–70: "The minatory use of Matt 15:21 to restrain an array of sinful behaviors and beliefs, not to mention any felt bonds with Jewish faith, praxis, or people, thus became a critical piece of its usefulness as spiritual paranesis, and as Ephrem's readings demonstrate, rebuke could be directed strategically with a modicum of exegetical effort."

38. Cf. Gal 3:29, 4:1; Rom 8:17.

39. Bedjan and Brock, *Homilies of Mar Jacob of Sarug*, 1.434.8–12.

40. Bedjan and Brock, *Homilies of Mar Jacob of Sarug*, 1.429.9.

41. Narsai, *On the Canaanite Woman*, f. 206r.

who possesses enlightenment, troubling assumptions about religious identity. The woman's speech and actions are a conduit for revelation, and Jesus intentionally involves the woman in the process of teaching and leading others to spiritual transformation.[42]

Narsai presents the Canaanite Woman as seeking Jesus' patronage by pursuing narrative details to link her identity to figures from the Old Testament. Given her lineage as a daughter of Ham and of Eve, the Canaanite Woman uses the language of slavery to describe her own condition as well as that of her daughter. Narsai attends to Mt 15:22 in which the woman addresses Jesus as the "Son of David," casting her own identity as the negative foil.[43] She unfolds the history of her people as bearing upon her current suffering:

> The daughter of the accursed one called out in front of the son of the Just One emotionally:
> "Son of David, have pity and set me free from my enslavement to the Captor.
> Son of Abram, rich in love, have pity upon the daughter of Canaan,
> and save my life from the bondage of slavery to the Evil One.
> The father of your father cursed my fathers through the mouth of the Hidden One,
> and subjected them to the heavy yoke of the Accuser.
> Noah cursed our father who mocked and derided him daringly,
> and he blessed your father who honored and loved wisely.[44]

Narsai elides the servitude to which Noah condemns the descendants of Ham with the enslavement to Satan. This slippage in the identity of the slave-master provides a bridge between the historical particularity of the Canaanite Woman and the universality of the human experience of sin. Like any skilled interpreter, Narsai's "glosses" the Gospel term "Canaanite" for his audience by providing them with the biblical antecedents for the term.

42. Susan Ashbrook Harvey, "Spoken Words, Voiced Silence: Biblical Women in Syriac Tradition," *JECS* 9 (2001): 124.

43. Jacob also frequently includes the epithet "Son of David."

44. Narsai, *On the Canaanite Woman*, f. 205r.

While Narsai contextualizes the Canaanite Woman's ethnic identity within biblical history through the seemingly "fixed" genealogy of Ham, he shares a common rhetorical aim with Ephrem and Jacob. The continuity of Old and New Testaments becomes a central part of these interpretations of the Canaanite Woman whose identity serves as one more way the Gospel reflects and illuminates the history of Israel.[45] To apply the work of Denise Buell, we see that each of these authors argues that the language of peoplehood in reference to the Canaanites (or non-Israelites) is essentially fluid. Presenting faith and love as the means of crossing ethnic boundaries, these poets (to varying degrees) reify the identity of the sons/the people/Israel in a negative light.[46] While Theodore of Mopsuestia stands with Ephrem as an important source of inspiration for Narsai's interpretation, I have found this genealogy neither in the extant fragments of Theodore nor in Ephrem's poetry. Narsai's formulation of the genealogy is reminiscent of a passage from Ephrem's *Hymns on the Nativity*:

> My Son, the free-born woman is also Your handmaiden
> if she serves You, and the enslaved woman
> in You is a freewoman. By You she is consoled that she is a freed woman.
> Invisible emancipation is placed in her bosom if she loves You.[47]

Narsai may or may not have consciously recalled this passage from Ephrem, but like his literary precursor, he reminds his listener that liberation begins with an internal movement of the soul.

The *mēmrē* of both Narsai and Jacob are sustained narrations of the encounter between Jesus and the Canaanite Woman that selectively employ overt intertextual links to build meaning. However, Narsai draws a connection between the Canaanite Woman and Eve that recalls the intricate and finely wrought portions of Ephrem's poetry that relate Mary's role in undoing the work of Eve. As he

45. Shepardson, *Anti-Judaism and Christian Orthodoxy,* 75.

46. Denise Buell, *Why this New Race: Ethnic Reasoning in Early Christianity* (New York: Columbia Press, 2005), 110.

47. Edmund Beck, *Des heiligen Ephraem des Syrers Hymnen de nativitate (Epiphania)*, CSCO 82–83 (Louvain: Peeters, 1959), 17.10 (Syriac); Kathleen E. McVey, *Ephrem the Syrian: Hymns* (New York: Paulist Press, 1989), 155.

recounts the victory of this woman's faith over Satan and his legions who had enslaved her, Narsai celebrates the redemptive qualities of her boldness. Rendering her the locus of this cosmic struggle, Narsai proclaims: "In the Canaanite Woman [the demons] saw their own downfall || how the weak rib prevailed against the might of the demons!"[48] Narsai employs synecdoche to invoke the memory of Eve and the origin of Satan's power over humanity. Whether identified with Eve or with her own daughter, the Canaanite Woman is continually featured in association with other women, and as such she gives voice to the human experience of sin and frailty that is experienced by all humanity regardless of gender.

Not only does the Canaanite Woman bear the burden of her forefather, Ham, but on account of her gender she stands with all women as a daughter of Eve. Here her gender becomes the central identity marker for contextualizing her actions within biblical history. As Narsai explains:

> With the eating of the fruit Satan bound Eve who obeyed his word,
> and the fruit returned from inside [Eve's] limbs and trampled him on the earth.
> With the weapon of fruit the guilty one triumphed and made Adam guilty,
> and in the Son of Adam he was defeated and exposed, for he did not triumph.[49]

The Canaanite Woman engages Jesus in debate, but she is truly sparing with Satan. Jesus and the Canaanite Woman cease to be opponents and become allies in a larger story of redeeming humanity and liberating the earth from Satan's grasp.

Conclusion

Narsai and Jacob imbibed the rich imagery and interpretative strategies of Ephrem's poetry, and both authors frequently reference images

48. Narsai, *On the Canaanite Woman*, f. 208r.

49. Narsai, *On the Canaanite Woman*, f. 207r.

of healing and God's overflowing treasury. By tracing the remnants of this biblical story throughout three Syriac authors, one observes how the re-telling of a single narrative operates as an exegetical strategy for each author.[50] Through their dramatic re-narrations, these authors struggle with the figure of the Canaanite Woman whose story continues to challenge interpreters. As Elisabeth Schüssler Fiorenza laments, "read in a *kyriocentric,* i.e. master-centered, frame the story functions as one more variation of woman's story as outsider in symbolic worlds and social constructions of male discourse."[51] While these authors do not employ the text to overtly challenge socially normative behavior of women in their communities, they all—in particular Narsai and Jacob—forge new exegetical ground for how this text might promote religious zeal and humility, appropriating her as a female exemplar for men and women alike. Especially for Narsai, attention to the woman's ethnic and cultural marginality became a vehicle for deeper reflection on the multiple manifestations of power and the historical legacies of violence and oppression the text expresses. These authors, like modern interpreters, find no easy solutions for containing this woman's words—perhaps Jacob said it best, "Against the Master of the worlds love riposted there in the Canaanite woman, for He said no (and) she said yes."[52]

50. Susan Ashbrook Harvey, "Why the Perfume Mattered: The Sinful Woman in Syriac Exegetical Tradition," in *In Dominico Eloquio, In Lordly Eloquence: Essays on Patristic Exegesis in honor of Robert Louis Wilken,* edited by Paul M. Blowers et al., 69–89 (Grand Rapids: W. B. Eerdmans Publishers, 2002), 89.

51. Elisabeth Schüssler Fiorenza, *But She Said: Feminist Practices of Biblical Interpretation* (Boston: Beacon Press, 1992), 12.

52. Bedjan and Brock, *Homilies of Mar Jacob of Sarug,* 1.439.17.

Translation

5. The Syriac Reception of Plato's *Republic*

❖ Yury Arzhanov

One of the modern apologies of the Christian faith was written by Joseph Ratzinger, who in 2005 became Pope Benedict XVI, the head of the Catholic Church. This book bears an academic title "Introduction to Christianity," and it offers an impressive attempt to make Christianity understandable and attractive to modern readers. One of the central issues dealt with in this book is the relation of Christian theology to non-Christian philosophy, and in that discussion, one name receives special attention. Referring to the central doctrine of Christianity, the sufferings of Jesus, Ratzinger points out that this idea can already be found in the dialogues of Plato:

> According to Plato the truly just man must be misunderstood and persecuted in this world; indeed, Plato goes so far as to write: "They will say that our just man will be scourged, racked, fettered, will have his eyes burned out, and at last, after all manner of suffering, will be crucified." This passage, written four hundred years before Christ, is always bound to move a Christian deeply.[1]

The quotation derives from the second book of Plato's *Republic:*

1. Joseph Cardinal Ratzinger, *Introduction to Christianity*, 2nd ed. (San Francisco: Ignatius Press, 2004), 292 (original German edition: Joseph Ratzinger, *Einführung in das Christentum* [München: E. Beck, 1968], 241).

> They will say that the just man who has such a disposition will be whipped; he'll be racked; he'll be bound; he'll have both his eyes burned out; and, at the end, when he has undergone every sort of evil, he'll be crucified.[2]

Curiously enough, it is not found among the words of Socrates, the usual "alter ego" of Plato. Neither is it related as a plausible view which Socrates would accept. Instead, this passage belongs to the provocative speech of Glaucon who explicitly cites the arguments of the opponents of Socrates (cf. the introductory formula "they will say") that Glaucon himself would be happy to refute.[3] All this, nevertheless, does not prevent Joseph Ratzinger from considering the quotation from the *Republic* as a prophecy "written four hundred years before Christ."

This example, taken from the work of a contemporary Catholic theologian, is a continuation of the long tradition of reception of the figure and philosophy of Plato in the Christian Church.[4] The Syriac Christians form an integrative part of this tradition, which starts with the first Christian apologists. The passage from Plato's *Republic* cited by J. Ratzinger is referred to in a very similar manner by Clement of Alexandria in the *Stromateis* in the late second century / early third century, who introduces the quotation by saying that thus "Plato prophesies the economy of salvation" (ὁ Πλάτων ... προφητεύων τὴν σωτήριον οἰκονομίαν).[5] The "prophecy" of Plato is repeated similarly (and probably directly borrowed from Clement) by Eusebius of Caesarea in the *Praeparatio Evangelica*.[6] Later, in the fifth century, the

2. Allan Bloom, *The Republic of Plato*, 2nd ed. (New York: Basic Books, 1991), 39. Greek: ἐροῦσι δὲ τάδε, ὅτι οὕτω διακείμενος ὁ δίκαιος μαστιγώσεται, στρεβλώσεται, δεδήσεται, ἐκκαυθήσεται τὠφθαλμώ, τελευτῶν πάντα κακὰ παθὼν ἀνασχινδυλευθήσεται (*Republic* 361e–362a).

3. Glaucon himself stresses the provocative character of his speech in *Republic* 358db–d. Cf. Julia Annas, *An Introduction to Plato's Republic* (Oxford: Clarendon Press, 1981), 59–71.

4. See Ernst Benz, *Der gekreuzigte Gerechte bei Plato, im Neuen Testament und in der alten Kirche*, Akademie der Wissenschaften und der Literatur in Mainz; Abhandlungen der geistes- und sozialwissenschaftlichen Klasse, Nr. 12 (Wiesbaden, 1950), 1031–1074; Édouard des Places, "Un thème platonicien dans la tradition patristique: Le juste crucifié (Platon, *République*, 361e4–362a2)," *SP* IX.3, TU 94, ed. by F. L. Cross, 30–40 (Berlin: Akademie-Verlag, 1966).

5. *Stromateis* 5.14.108 (edited in Allain Le Boulluec, *Clément d'Alexandrie. Les Stromates: Stromate* V, t. 1, SC 278 [Paris: Cerf, 1981], 204.5–7). Cf. *Stromateis* 4.7.52 (edited in Annewies Van Den Hoek, *Clément d'Alexandrie. Les Stromates: Stromate* IV, SC 463 [Paris: Cerf, 2001], 144.2–3).

6. *Praeparatio Evangelica* 12.10.4 and 13.13.35 (edited in Karl Mras, *Eusebius Werke*, vol. 8. *Die Praeparatio Evangelica*, pt. 2. *Die Bücher XI bis XV*, GCS 8/2. 2nd ed. [edited by Édouard des Places] [Berlin: Akademie-Verlag, 1983], 99.12–15; 211.12–13).

same passage is treated in the same manner by Theodoret of Cyrrhus in the treatise *De Graecarum affectionum curatione*.[7]

Thus, the tradition of considering the passage in Plato's *Republic* as a prophecy about a just man who has to suffer for his righteousness is as old as Christian theology itself, and the book by Joseph Ratzinger forms the tip of a huge iceberg. The Syriac reception of Plato and his philosophy constitutes an important and, until the present, very little examined part of this iceberg.[8] Moreover, the work of Ratzinger gives witness to the fact that the question of the reception of Plato's philosophy is not directly dependent on the availability or unavailability of the primary sources. Syriac literature (in contrast to the Armenian, for instance)[9] shows no traces of a direct acquaintance with the dialogues of Plato. As in the later Arabic tradition,[10] it has preserved a number of quotations "from Plato," summaries of his ideas and several pseudepigrapha that show that the name of the philosopher was distinguished enough among the Syrian authors.[11] Even though there is no evidence for knowledge of the original Platonic texts in Syriac literature, this does not mean that those texts were not available at that time, especially in the Hellenized centers of Syria.[12] The evidence of the early Christian apologists (and of the apologists of our day, such as Pope Benedict XVI) allows for admitting that even in the case when the Syriac Christian authors could have had access to the original works of Plato, they would prefer to use other sources that formed their own picture of the philosopher, the image of *Plato Christianus*.

7. *Curatio* 7.50 (edited in Clemens Scholten, *Theodoret. De Graecarum affectionum curatione* [Leiden: Brill, 2015], 516.12–14).

8. For an overview of the topic, see Yury Arzhanov, "Plato in Syriac Literature," *Le Muséon* 132 (2019): 1–36. See also Yury Arzhanov, *Syriac Sayings of Greek Philosophers: A Study in Syriac Gnomologia with Edition and Translation,* CSCO 669 (Louvain: Peeters, 2019), 76–81.

9. See Irene Tinti, "On the Chronology and Attribution of the Old Armenian Timaeus: A Status Quaestionis and New Perspectives," *EVO* 35 (2012): 219–282.

10. For which, see Franz Rosenthal, "On the knowledge of Plato's philosophy in the Islamic world," *Islamic Culture* 14/15 (1940): 387–422; Dimitri Gutas, "Platon - Tradition arabe," in *Dictionnaire des philosophes antiques*, edited by R. Goulet, vol. 5/1, 845–863 (Paris: CNRS, 2012).

11. See Henri Hugonnard-Roche, "Platon syriaque," in *Pensée grecque et sagesse d'orient: Hommage à Michel Tardieu*, Bibliothèque de l'École des Hautes Études, Sciences religieuses 142, edited by M. A. Amir-Moezzi, J.-D. Dubois, C. Jullien, and F. Jullien, 307–322 (Turnhout: Brepols, 2009).

12. On Edessa, see Judah B. Segal, *Edessa 'The Blessed City'* (Oxford: Clarendon Press, 1970), 30–35. On the culture of Antioch in the 4th century, see Raffaella Cribiore, *The School of Libanius in Late Antique Antioch* (Princeton: Princeton University Press, 2007).

Several examples of the Syriac image of Plato are contained in one of the Syriac manuscripts preserved in the library of the St. Catherine monastery on Sinai, Sinai Syriac 14, dating from the tenth century. These texts were identified[13] and later published by Sebastian Brock in an article with the expressive title "Some Syriac Pseudo-Platonic Curiosities."[14] The first "curiosity" of the Sinai ms. is a collection of moral sentences ("gnomology") which opens with the two following sayings:

ܦܠܛܘܢ܂ ܠܐ ܓܝܪ ܐܢܫ ܡܫܟܚ ܠܡܕܥ ܠܝܬܗ܂ ܐܠܐ ܐܢ ܒܕܘܒܪܐ ܡܝܬܪܐ܂ ܡܝܬܪܘܬܐ
ܓܝܪ ܪܫܝܬܐ ܕܕܘܒܪܐ ܐܝܬ ܠܗ܂ ܘܕܐܢܫ ܠܐ ܢܚܫܘܒ ܥܠ ܢܦܫܗ ܕܚܟܝܡܐ ܗܘ܀

ܗܘ ܬܘܒ ܐܡܪ܂ ܐܝܢܐ ܕܒܫܪܪܐ܆ ܒܥܐ ܕܢܗܘܐ ܙܕܝܩܐ܂ ܢܬܡܚܐ ܢܬܬܫܝܛ܂
ܢܬܚܣܕ܂ ܢܬܢܓܕ܂ ܢܬܐܣܪ܂ ܢܬܦܣܩܢ ܐܝܕܘܗܝ܂ ܥܡ ܪ̈ܓܠܘܗܝ܂ ܢܬܢܣܚܢ ܥܝ̈ܢܘܗܝ܂
ܢܙܕܩܦ܂ ܘܢܣܒܘܠ ܒܟܠܗܝܢ ܗܠܝܢ ܟܠܗܝܢ ܒ̈ܝܫܬܐ܀

Plato [said]: "A man cannot understand his essence except through a virtuous way of life. For virtue is honorable if it results in one's way of life and if a man does not consider himself as wise."[15]

He also said: "The one who truly seeks to be just, will be struck, scorned, reproached, beaten, fettered, will have his hands cut

13. Sebastian P. Brock, "Stomathalassa, Dandamis and Secundus in a Syriac monastery anthology," in *After Bardaisan: Studies on continuity and change in Syriac Christianity in Honour of Professor Han J. W. Drijvers*, OLA 89, edited by G. Reinink and A. Klugkist, 35–50 (Louvain: Peeters, 1999), 48–50. See also Sebastian P. Brock, "Syriac translations of Greek popular philosophy," in *Von Athen nach Bagdad: Zur Rezeption griechischer Philosophie von der Spätantike bis zum Islam*, edited by P. Bruns, 9–28 (Bonn: Borengässer, 2003).

14. Sebastian P. Brock, "Some Syriac Pseudo-Platonic Curiosities," in *Medieval Arabic Thought: Essays in Honour of F. Zimmermann*, edited by R. Hansberger, M. A. al-Akiti, and C. Burnett, 19–26 (London: Warburg Institute, 2012).

15. This gnomic saying presents certain difficulties in translation. The interpretation of S. Brock: "No one can know himself except by means of a virtuous mode of life. Virtue is the first-fruits of the way of life, and that a person should not think of himself as wise" (Brock, "Curiosities," 22). The Syriac terms translated here as "virtue/virtuous" and "way of life" appear in the title of the collection of moral sentences (that includes sayings ascribed to Isocrates, Menander and Plato) preserved in the ms. Brit. Libr. Add. 14,614: ܡ̈ܠܐ ܡܓܒܝ̈ܬܐ ܕܦܝܠܣܘ̈ܦܐ ܕܥܠ ܕܘܒܪܐ ܕܡܝܬܪܘܬܐ "Select sentences of philosophers concerning virtuous way of life" (Eduard Sachau, *Inedita Syriaca: Eine Sammlung syrischer Übersetzungen von Schriften griechischer Profanliteratur* [Wien: Verlag der Buchhandlung des Waisenhauses in Halle, 1870], 80 [ܦ]). See also the title of the *Book of Ethics* of Bar ʿEbroyo (Barhebraeus) in the list of his works composed by his brother Bar Ṣawmō: ܟܬܒܐ ܕܐܝܬܝܩܘܢ ܒܬܘܩܢܘܬ ܕܘܒܪܐ "The Book of *Ethicon* about moral conduct" (J. S. Assemanus, *Bibliotheca Orientalis Clementino-Vaticana*, vol. 2 [Rome: Typis Sacrae Congregationis de Propaganda Fide, 1721], 270).

> off together with his legs, will have his eyes gouged out, be wounded, and endure all evils of this world."

The first sentence seems to be a summary of the arguments of Socrates in the *Republic.*[16] The second one presents a free translation of the passage cited above about a righteous person who is compelled to endure suffering and death. The Syriac version alters the sentence by adding several categories of suffering (such as the cutting off of the hands and legs) and by omitting the reference to the crucifixion. Both the additions and alterations could be due to the difficulty in understanding the rare verb form ἀνασχινδυλευθήσεται in the Greek text.[17] However, they may also reveal the intention of the Syriac author of the translation (or that of the compilers of the Sinai monastic anthology) to apply the image of the suffering of the righteous not exclusively to Jesus but to all his followers.[18] It is also not unlikely that the idea of suffering and death of a just person adduced by Plato implied, for the Syriac readers, the figure of Socrates,[19] whose execution was often compared with that of Christ.[20] In any case, the two sentences, put together in the Syriac gnomology in the Sinai ms., give evidence of the Syriac reception of the Platonic moral teaching expressed in the *Republic.* Taken as isolated quotations which completely neglect the context, they reveal the tradition which stands behind them, the works of the Christian apologists that stressed particular elements of the dialogues of the philosopher and brought them in line with Christian thought.

This evidence is not exceptional. Syriac readers that were interested in Greek culture could have received information about the

16. Compare the quotations from Plato's *Republic* by Eusebius in *Praeparatio Evangelica* XII.10.4 (Mras, *Eusebius Werke*, vol. 8. *Die Praeparatio Evangelica*, pt. 2. *Die Bücher XI bis XV*, 99.1–12).

17. The Greek word could be understood both as "to be impaled" and "to be crucified."

18. In this way, the words of Plato are already understood by Clement and Eusebius, who cite them in one case as a "prophecy" on Christian martyrs, and this is the only context of using the passage from the *Republic* by Theodoret who cites them in the section "On honoring the martyrs." Compare further examples in Benz, *Der Gekreuzigte*, 1059–1072.

19. Possibly the whole dialogue was intended to serve as an apology of Socrates, see Bloom, *The Republic of Plato*, 307–310.

20. See Benz, *Der Gekreuzigte*, 1059–1072. It is worth noting that this comparison has already been made in one of the earliest Syriac texts, *Letter of Mara bar Serapion*, see William Cureton, *Spicilegium Syriacum: Containing Remains of Bardesan, Meliton, Ambrose and Mara Bar Serapion* (London: Rivingtons, 1855), 43–48, 70–76. Cf. Kathleen E. McVey, "A Fresh Look at the Letter of Mara Bar Serapion to his Son," in *SymSyr* V, 263–270.

ideas of Plato through translations of the anonymous scholia to four homilies of Gregory of Nazianzus ascribed to Nonnus which were intended to explain allusions to Greek mythology found in Gregory.[21] One scholion (cited here according to the Greek version, which was twice translated rather literally into Syriac) presents a summary of the *Republic* as follows:[22]

> Plato the philosopher composed a treatise which he called the *Republic*. In this treatise he describes what a city ought to be like and of what number of men it should be made up and by what customs and laws it should be governed. This city only existed in theory; it never actually existed or was a form of government. Thus, in this treatise he makes this remark, "Let us suppose that the citizens are making the following proposals, so that we can see their minds at work."

It is obvious that the author of the Greek commentaries to the homilies of Gregory (as well as the Syriac translators of his work) is already quite certain that his readers had not ever seen the dialogue of Plato which is summarized here.[23] The same impression is gained from another scholion to the fourth homily of Gregory which was also (in one of the versions) translated into Syriac:[24]

21. Two Syriac translations of these scholia have come down to us: the first dating to the 6th, the second to the 7th century, both edited in Sebastian P. Brock, *The Syriac Version of the Pseudo-Nonnos Mythological Scholia* (Cambridge: University Press, 1971).

22. English translation in Jennifer Nimmo Smith, *The Christian's Guide to Greek Culture: The Pseudo-Nonnus* Commentaries *on* Sermons *4, 5, 39 and 43 by Gregory of Nazianzus*, TTH 37 (Liverpool: Liverpool University Press, 2001), 54. The Greek text reads: Πλάτων ὁ φιλόσοφος συνεγράψατο σύνταγμα ὃ Πολιτείαν ἐπέγραψεν. ἐν τούτῳ τῷ συντάγματι λέγει ὁποίαν δεῖ γενέσθαι πόλιν καὶ ἐκ πόσων ἀνδρῶν συγκειμένην καὶ ποίοις ἤθεσι καὶ νόμοις πολιτευομένην. αὕτη δὲ αὐτῷ ἡ πόλις λόγῳ μόνον συνέστη, ἔργῳ δὲ οὔτε συνέστη οὔτε ἐπολιτεύσατο. ἐν ἐκείνῳ οὖν τῷ συντάγματι λέγει τοῦτο τὸ ῥησίδιον, ὅτι, Ὑποκείσθωσαν ἡμῖν οἱ πολῖται τάδε φθεγγόμενοι, ἵν' ἴδωμεν αὐτῶν κινουμένην τὴν ἐπίνοιαν (Jennifer Nimmo Smith, *Pseudo-Nonniani in IV Orationes Gregorii Nazianzeni Commentarii*, Corpus Christianorum Series Graeca 27, Corpus Nazianzenum 2 [Turnhout: Brepols, 1992], 146). For the two Syriac versions see Brock, *The Syriac Version*, 119 (Engl. transl.); 261 (Syriac text).

23. In fact, it is doubtful that the Greek commentator himself had access to the Platonic dialogues, as the quotation which he puts at the end of his summary is derived not from the *Republic*, but from the *Timaeus*, see Nimmo Smith, *Pseudo-Nonniani in IV Orationes Gregorii Nazianzeni Commentarii*, 146, ad loc.

24. English translation in Nimmo Smith, *The Christian's Guide to Greek Culture*, 39. The Greek text reads: Πλάτων ὁ φιλόσοφος ἐν Πολιτείαις (ἔστι δὲ οὕτως αὐτοῦ λεγομένη πραγματεία) εἰσφέρει τινὰ μῦθον. οὗτος δὲ λέγει ὅτι Γύγης ἦν τις ποιμὴν περὶ τὴν Λυδίαν. οὗτος ποιμαίνων ἐν ὄρει τὰ

> Plato the philosopher introduces a certain myth in the *Republic* (this is a treatise of his with such a title). It says that Gyges was a shepherd in Lydia. He was once grazing his sheep on a mountain, when he came across a certain cave, which he entered and found within it a brazen horse, and he found within the brazen horse a corpse and a ring. The head of this ring was reversible, and it was turned round. The holy Gregory calls this head the bezel. So Gyges took the ring, they say, and went out. When the ring was in the correct position, he was seen by everyone, but when he reversed the bezel of the ring, he became invisible to them all. Plato, therefore, introduces this myth, because, he says, the just man, even if he were to possess the ring of Gyges so as not to be seen by anyone, ought none the less not to do wrong. For good should be practiced for its own sake, and not for any other (reasons).

The myth which is introduced here is found among the words of Glaucon in the *Republic* 359d–360b. Glaucon narrates it just before he expounds upon the suffering of the righteous person in order to make the point which is the contrary to the one made by the author of the scholion: Glaucon postulates that even a righteous person who possesses the ring of Gyges would not be capable of withstanding the temptation to do unrighteous deeds.[25] It will become the aim of Socrates to establish the opposite view, but it will take him all ten books of the dialogue to succeed in that (cf. *Republic* 612b). The fact that the story of Gyges in the scholion cited is interpreted in the way that

---

πρόβατα, περιέτυχε σπηλαίῳ τινι, καὶ εἰσελθὼν ἐν αὐτῷ, εὗρεν ἵππον χαλκοῦν, καὶ εὗρεν ἐν τῷ χαλκῷ ἵππῳ νεκρὸν ἄνθρωπον καὶ δακτύλιον. οὗ δακτυλίου ἡ κεφαλὴ στρεπτὴ ἦν, καὶ ἐστρέφετο. ἣν κεφαλὴν καλεῖ σφενδόνην ὁ θεῖος Γρηγόριος. ἔλαβεν οὖν ὁ Γύγης, φησί, τὸν δακτύλιον, καὶ ἐξῆλθεν. καὶ ἡνίκα μὲν ἦν ἐν τῇ τάξει ὁ δακτύλιος, ἑωρᾶτο ὑπὸ πάντων, ἡνίκα δὲ τὴν σφενδόνην τοῦ δακτυλίου ἔστρεφεν, ἀφανὴς ἐγίνετο πᾶσιν. ὁ οὖν Πλάτων εἰσφέρει τὸν μῦθον τοῦτον, ὅτι, φησίν, ὁ δίκαιος ἀνήρ, κἂν τὸν Γύγου λάβῃ δακτύλιον ἵνα μὴ ὁρᾶται ὑπό τινος, οὐδ' οὕτως ὤφειλεν ἀδικεῖν. δεῖ γὰρ τὸ καλὸν δι' αὐτὸ τὸ ἀγαθὸν ἐπιτηδεύεσθαι, καὶ μὴ δι' ἄλλους τινάς. (Nimmo Smith, *Pseudo-Nonniani in IV Orationes Gregorii Nazianzeni Commentarii*, 122–123). For the Syriac version (*Syr. II*), see Brock, *The Syriac Version*, 108 (Engl. transl.); 244 (Syriac text).

25. Cf. *Republic* 360a: "Now if there were two such rings, and the just man would put one on, and the unjust man the other, no one, as it would seem, would be so adamant as to stick by justice and bring himself to keep away from what belongs to others and not lay hold of it… (…) Men do not take it to be a good for them in private, since wherever each supposes he can do injustice, he does it. Indeed, all men suppose injustice is far more to their private profit than justice" (Bloom, *The Republic of Plato*, 38).

Socrates does after a long discussion demonstrates that the author of the scholion was acquainted with a particular version of it. And it was this particular interpretation that was made known to the Syriac readers of the scholia.

Similar sources of knowledge of Platonic ideas may be identified by two East-Syriac authors who wrote their treatises for school purposes and thus transmitted the school image of Plato of their time. The treatise "On the Cause of the Foundation of the Schools" written at the end of the sixth century by an East-Syriac author Barḥadbšabbā also contains a chapter on the "pagan schools" which starts with that of Plato:[26]

> Although he (i.e., Plato) taught correctly about God and spoke about his only-begotten son as the word begotten from him according to nature and about the holy spirit as the hypostatic power that proceeds from him, nevertheless when he was asked by his fellow citizens whether or not it is right to honour idols, he passed on the tradition to them that it is requisite that they be held in honour, and he said: "It is necessary to sacrifice a white cock to Asclepius." Although he knew God, he did not praise and confess him as God, but he was lacking in his thoughts and darkened in misunderstanding. Also about the soul he passes on the tradition that it migrates from body to body. Sometimes it abides in creeping things, at other times in wild animals, sometimes in domestic animals, at other times in birds, and afterwards in human beings, and then it is raised up to the likeness of angels and it passes through all the orders of angels. Then it is strained and made pure and returns to its place above. Regarding women he commanded that they be (held) in common, as the Manichees say.

26. Adam H. Becker, *Sources for the Study of the School of Nisibis*, TTH 50 (Liverpool: Liverpool University Press 2008), 132–133. Syriac: ܘܟܕ ܠܡ ܐܠܦ ܥܠ ܐܠܗܐ ܬܪܝܨܐܝܬ܆ ܘܐܡܪ ܥܠ ܒܪܗ ܝܚܝܕܝܐ ܕܐܝܟ ܡܠܬܐ ܝܠܝܕ ܡܢܗ ܟܝܢܐܝܬ܆ ܘܥܠ ܪܘܚܐ ܕܩܘܕܫܐ ܕܝܠܗ ܗܘ ܠܗ ܩܢܘܡܝܐ ܕܢܦܩ ܡܢܗ܆ ܐܠܐ ܟܕ ܐܫܬܐܠ ܡܢ ܒܢܝ ܡܕܝܢܬܗ܆ ܕܐܢ ܙܕܩ ܠܡܝܩܪܘ ܠܦܬܟܪܐ ܐܘ ܠܐ܆ ܐܫܠܡ ܠܗܘܢ ܕܡܬܒܥܐ ܕܢܬܝܩܪܘܢ. ܘܐܡܪ܆ ܕܠܐܣܩܠܦܝܘܣ ܠܡ ܬܪܢܓܠܐ ܚܘܪܐ ܡܬܒܥܐ ܠܡܕܒܚܘ. ܘܟܕ ܝܕܥ ܠܐܠܗܐ܆ ܠܐ ܐܝܟ ܕܠܐܠܗܐ ܫܒܚܗ ܘܐܘܕܝ ܠܗ܆ ܐܠܐ ܐܣܬܪܩ ܒܡܚܫܒܬܗ܆ ܘܐܬܚܫܟ ܒܠܐ ܡܣܬܟܠܢܘܬ܀ ܘܐܦ ܥܠ ܢܦܫܐ ܡܫܠܡ ܕܡܢ ܦܓܪܐ ܠܦܓܪܐ ܡܫܢܝܐ. ܘܙܒܢ ܒܪܚܫܐ ܥܡܪܐ܆ ܘܙܒܢ ܒܚܝܘܬܐ܆ ܘܙܒܢ ܒܒܥܝܪܐ܆ ܘܙܒܢ ܒܦܪܚܬܐ܆ ܘܒܬܪܟܢ ܒܒܢܝܢܫܐ܆ ܘܗܝܕܝܢ ܡܬܥܠܝܐ ܠܕܡܘܬܐ ܕܡܠܐܟܐ܆ ܘܥܒܪܐ ܒܟܠܗܘܢ ܛܟܣܐ ܕܡܠܐܟܐ. ܘܗܝܕܝܢ ܡܨܛܠܠܐ ܘܡܬܕܟܝܐ܆ ܘܗܦܟܐ ܠܕܘܟܬܗ ܕܠܥܠ. ܘܥܠ ܢܫܐ ܦܩܕ ܕܢܗܘܝܢ ܓܘܢܝܢ܆ ܐܝܟ ܕܐܡܪܝܢ ܗܘܘ ܡܢܝܚܝܐ܀ (Addai Scher, *Mar Barhadbšabba 'Arbaya, Cause de la fondation des écoles*, PO 4.4 [Turnhout: Brepols, 1981], 363–364).

This summary of the views of Plato can give us an insight into the sources of knowledge of Plato in the East-Syriac schools. If we put aside some definitive Christian elements such as the idea of the Trinity, the allusion to Romans 1:21, and the mentioning of the "orders of angels," we may note that several ideas ascribed to Plato in this passage derive from the *Republic*: e.g., the concept of *metempsychosis* (cf. the tale of Er in *Republic* 613e–621b) and the idea of a common possession of women in the ideal state (cf. *Republic* 449a–450a). Both ideas must have looked quite odd to the Christian audience; however, the first part of this summary is quite sympathetic towards Plato. He is presented as a prophet who understood the mystery of the Trinity, but had to hide his views from his contemporaries.

Both a limited complex of ideas, connected mostly with the *Republic*, and the Christianized view of Plato is expressed by the later East-Syrian author Theodor Bar Koni in his "Book of Scholia" written at the end of the eighth century.[27] Bar Koni stresses especially the philosopher's concept of the four "cardinal virtues" of the soul, an idea which is connected with Plato's theory of the State, expressed in the *Republic* 427d–e. Interestingly enough, both Barḥadbšabbā and Bar Kōnī blame Aristotle for the falsification of the teaching of his master. And for both of them, Christians were those who for the first time interpreted the great Athenian philosopher correctly after centuries of his ideas being misunderstood.

The latter example reveals for us the ways of transmission of the Platonic texts to the Syrians. One of the main channels for this was selected quotations from Plato's works by the Church fathers, who offered their interpretation of his philosophy as a forerunner of Christian theology. And it is quite remarkable that the Syrians took these quotations from Plato and transmitted them separately as part of the collections of sentences, as in the case of the gnomology in ms. Sinai Syriac 14.

Another apophthegm in the Sinai collection could be brought in connection with the Platonic *Republic*:

ܠܦܝܠܘܣܘܦܐ ܚܕ ܒܪ ܐܫܬܐܠ. ܕܡܢ ܝܬܪܬ ܡܢ ܚܟܡܬܐ. ܐܡܪ܆ ܕܗܘܝܬ ܡܟܐ
ܐܢܐ ܒܠܚܘܕܝ ܘܥܒܕ ܐܢܐ ܒܨܒܝܢܐ ܕܡܬܛܦܪܣܝܢ ܒܗܘܢ ܟܠܗ.

27. Syriac text edited in Addai Scher, *Theodorus Bar Kōnī. Liber scholiorum*, Vol. 2, CSCO 69 (Louvain: Peeters), 292–293; French translation in Robert Hespel and René Draguet, *Theodore bar Konai. Livre des scolies. Recension de Séert*, Vol. 2. *Mimrè VI–XI*, CSCO 432 (Louvain: Peeters, 1982), 218.

> When one of the philosophers was asked what is greater than wisdom he said: "That is when I am standing in a harbor and contemplating how the others are beaten by the waves."

This sentence probably goes back to the *Republic* 496d–e.[28] However, Brock pointed out that the Syriac sentence is closer to the Greek apophthegm preserved in the *Gnomologium Vaticanum*:

> Ὁ αὐτὸς [sc. Πλάτων] ἐρωτηθεὶς τί ὠφέληται ἐκ φιλοσοφίας ἔφη· τὸ αὐτὸς ἐν εὐδίᾳ ἑστὼς βλέπειν ἄλλους χειμαζομένους.

> When he (i.e., Plato) was asked what is the advantage received from the philosophy he said: "He (i.e., the philosopher) is standing in peace and looking how the others are suffering from the storm."[29]

The reason for choosing this apophthegm from the others preserved in the Greek *Gnomologium Vaticanum* must be the familiarity of the image it contains.[30] It was often applied by Syriac monastic authors to the soul and its state being affected by the passions and concerns of human life: The Syriac monastic author of the fifth century, John of Apamea, writes in one of his letters that the soul of a solitary ascetic is like a ship standing in the quiet harbor during the storm which other people have to endure.[31] As the ascetic life was seen by Christians as the form of "wisdom" which is higher than that of the pagan philosophers, the answer of the philosopher in the Sinai gnomologium should not surprise us. This example demonstrates quite vividly how the Syrians selected particular maxims from the Greek collections of moral sentences, among which the name and figure of Plato was not any less popular than that of Diogenes the Cynic.[32]

---

28. It was proposed by Leo Sternbach and supported by Sebastian Brock; see Leo Sternbach, *Gnomologium Vaticanum: E Codice Vaticano Graeco 743* (Berlin: De Gruyter, 1963), 161; Brock, "Curiosities," 22 fn. 21.

29. Sternbach, *Gnomologium Vaticanum*, 161 (Nr. 430); see the German translation in Alexander Demandt, *Sokrates antwortet* (Zürich: Artemis und Winkler Verlag, 1992), 32.

30. See Sebastian P. Brock, "The Scribe Reaches Harbour," *BF* 21 (1995): 195–202.

31. Lars G. Rignell, *Briefe von Johannes dem Einsiedler mit kritischem Apparat, Einleitung und Übersetzung* (Lund: H. Ohlsson, 1941), 63–64 (transl.), 49*–51* (Syr. text).

32. On the Greek gnomological tradition connected with Plato, see Karl-Heinz Stanzel, *Dicta*

This tradition of reception of the moral teachings of Plato as represented in the Greek gnomological tradition—but reinterpreted in light of Christian ascetic teachings—can be traced in the collection of aphorisms preserved in ms. Vat. Sir. 135, which shares a large number of maxims with the collection of ms. Sinai Syr. 14.[33] The Syriac Vatican gnomology has both those apophthegms which could be traced back to the philosophy of Plato as it was interpreted by Christians, and some witty aphorisms like the following one:

ܦܠܛܘܢ ܚܙܐ ܐܢܫܐ ܕܩܒܪܝܢ ܘܒܟܝܢ. ܘܐܡܪ ܠܗܘܢ. ܡܢܐ ܒܟܝܢ ܐܢܬܘܢ
ܒܢܝ̈ܐ ܥܠ ܡܢ ܕܒܛܠ ܡܢ ܒܟܝܐ

> Plato saw people who were crying during a funeral and said to them: "People, why are you crying about someone who has ceased crying?"

Nevertheless, in the Vatican collection as well, one may see the main points that the Christians saw in Platonic philosophy. One of the apophthegms stresses the idea of the soul:

ܒܢܝ̈ܐ ܡ̈ܒܙܚܢܐ ܩܪܒܘ ܒܚܕ ܠܘܬ ܦܠܛܘܢ ܘܐܡܪܝܢ ܠܗ. ܡܢܘ ܦܘܪܫܢܐ ܒܝܬ
ܚܟܝܡܐ ܠܣܟܠܐ. ܗܘ ܕܝܢ ܐܡܪ ܠܗܘܢ. ܐܝܟ ܕܐܝܬ ܦܘܪܫܢܐ ܒܝܬ ܢܦܫܐ
ܠܦܓܪܐ. ܗܢܘܢ ܕܝܢ ܐܡܪܝܢ ܠܗ. ܘܐܡܟܢܐ ܢܕܥ ܦܘܪܫܢܐ ܒܝܬ ܢܦܫܐ ܠܦܓܪܐ.
ܕܗܐ ܠܐ ܡܢ ܡܬܘܡ ܚܙܝܢܢ ܠ ܢܦܫܐ. ܐܡܪ ܠܗܘܢ ܗܘ. ܡܕܝܢ ܐܦܠܐ ܚܟܝܡܐ
ܡܟܝܠ ܐܢܬܘܢ ܠܓܫܡܐ ܒܕܚܟܡܬܐ ܗܘ ܐܝܟ ܢܦܫܐ

> Once mockers approached Plato and asked him: "What's the difference between a wise man and a fool?" He answered them: "The same difference which is between the soul and the body."

Platonica: Die unter Platons Namen überlieferten Aussprüche (Darmstadt: s.n., 1987); Alice S. Riginos, *Platonica: The Anecdotes concerning the Life and Writings of Plato* (Leiden: Brill, 1976).

33. The Syriac text of this collection was first published by Ignazio Guidi, "Mosè di Aghel e Simone Abbato," *Rendiconti della Reale Accademia dei Lincei, Classe di scienze morali, storiche e filologiche*, Ser. 4, vol. 2 (1886): 545–556. New edition with Russian translation in Yury Arzhanov, "A Syriac Collection of Sentences of Diogenes, Socrates, Plato and Aristotle," *Simvol* 61: *Syriaca • Arabica • Iranica* (Paris-Moscow, 2012): 238–257. See also Yury Arzhanov, "Das Florilegium in der Hs. *Vat. Sir.* 135 und seine griechisch-arabischen Parallelen," in *Geschichte, Theologie und Kultur des syrischen Christentums: Beiträge zum 7. Deutschen Syrologie-Symposium in Göttingen, Dezember 2011*, edited by M. Tamcke and S. Grebenstein, 35–48 (Wiesbaden: Harrassowitz, 2014).

> They responded to him: "But how shall we know the difference between the soul and the body, as the soul is never visible to us?" He retorted: "That is why you are unable to recognize a wise man, for he remains hidden, like the soul."

The value of the soul and its priority over the body constituted a considerable part of the ascetic philosophy developed in the monasteries of the Egyptian desert. In particular, the treatises and collections of sentences written by Evagrius Ponticus constituted an important channel of transmission of Platonic ideas for Syriac readers.[34] The tendency of Syriac Christians to read Plato through a number of Church authorities made unnecessary the usage of the original dialogues of the philosopher, which were quickly replaced not only by Christian summaries of his works but also by a number of pseudepigrapha. Both the Christian summaries and the pseudepigraphical treatises formed the basis of *Plato Christianus*, whose ideas were concealed until the coming of Christianity but for the first time made open with the coming of Christ. This attitude, as one may see on the basis of the presented sources, constituted to a large extent the Syriac image of Plato. And as the work of Joseph Ratzinger shows, this attitude has been shared by some Christian theologians up to this day.

34. See Yury Arzhanov, "Abba Platon und Abba Evagrius," in *Begegnungen in Vergangenheit und Gegenwart: Beiträge dialogischer Existenz*, edited by C. Rammelt, C. Schlarb, and E. Schlarb, 75–82 (Berlin: LIT, 2015).

6. Did the Dying Jacob Gather His Feet into His Bed (MT) or Stretch Them Out (Peshiṭta)? Describing the Unique Character of the Peshiṭta

❖ Craig E. Morrison

The Peshiṭta translator of Genesis made numerous decisions about how to translate particular Hebrew idioms. These unique Peshiṭta readings are often labeled "clarifications," or "translations into good classical Syriac," though often they interpret the Hebrew text more than they clarify it, exposing how the Peshiṭta retells a particular biblical story. In Gen 49:33 the Hebrew text describes the death of Jacob, noting the patriarch's final gesture: "He gathered his feet to the bed." The meaning of this Hebrew expression is clear and an accurate Aramaic translation was possible, as demonstrated by the literal translation in the Pentateuchal Targums. The Peshiṭta reads, "he stretched out his feet in the bed," the very opposite gesture expressed in the Hebrew text. The Peshiṭta reading could be immediately dismissed as a "clarification" or an example of "good Syriac idiom," but that would be misleading, since the Hebrew is eminently clear and a literal translation would have been good Syriac idiom. This study of the Peshiṭta reading in Gen 49:33 will illustrate how some of the traditional descriptors for the Peshiṭta can obscure the significance of particular readings. What does the translation "he stretched out his feet in the bed" reveal about the nature of the Peshiṭta as a translation of the Hebrew?

Describing the Peshiṭta as a Translation

In the early part of the twentieth century, a spate of Peshiṭta research appeared after the publication of Ceriani's photolithographic edition of the Ambrosian Codex (B 21 inf.; 7a1 in the Leiden edition).[1] Most of these contributions were verse-by-verse text critical studies. There was little focus on the nature of the Peshiṭta as a translation. But in 1922 Joshua Bloch described the Peshiṭta of the Song of Songs as follows: "Occasionally the translator endeavors to amend the text, while at other times he will render it very freely…, though as a whole the Peshitta is faithful to the Hebrew and in some places renders the original slavishly.… Very frequently the Syriac differs entirely from the Hebrew original."[2] One wonders what to make of Bloch's description: The Peshiṭta is sometimes a free translation that is mostly faithful, though very frequently different. However, this oxymoronic description captures the character of the Peshiṭta quite well: The Peshiṭta is faithful to its Hebrew *Vorlage* except where it is not.

In the latter part of the twentieth century, the expression "faithful to the Hebrew" surfaced as the predominant descriptor for the Peshiṭta. M. J. Mulder in his 1985 review of the literature on the Peshiṭta cited various scholars who described it as "faithful" to the Hebrew.[3] In 1992 Piet Dirksen, while reviewing Jerome A. Lund's dissertation, *The Influence of the Septuagint on the Peshitta,*[4] characterized the Peshiṭta "as a work in its own right, testifying to the faithfulness of the translator to the Hebrew Bible and at the same time to his pursuit of idiomatic Syriac and clarity."[5] Dirksen employed the three key descriptors: (1) faithful, (2) clarifying, and (3) idiomatic. This language has been borrowed by other scholars, such as Bas ter Haar Romeny, who described the Peshiṭta of Genesis as "a

1. A. M. Ceriani, *Translatio Syra Pescitto Veteris Testamenti ex Codice Ambrosiano sec. fere 6., photolithographice edita* (Milan: della Croce, 1876).

2. Joshua Bloch, "A Critical Examination of The Text of The Syriac Version of The Song of Songs," *AJSLL* 38 (1922): 137.

3. M. J. Mulder, "The Use of The Peshitta in Textual Criticism," in *La Septuaginta en la investigacion contemporánea (V congreso de la IOSCS)*, Textos y estudios "Cardenal Cisneros" 34; edited by Natalio Fernández Marcos, 37–53 (Madrid: Instituto Arias Montano, 1985).

4. Jerome A. Lund, *The Influence of the Septuagint on the Peshitta: A Re-evaluation of Criteria in Light of Comparative Study of the Versions in Genesis and Psalms* (Ph.D. Diss., Hebrew University, Jerusalem, 1988).

5. P. B. Dirksen, "The Peshitta and Textual Criticism of the Old Testament," *VT* 42 (1992): 390.

translation very close to the supposed Hebrew *Vorlage*,... one that at times uses more idiomatic Syriac.... Difficult sentences have been clarified by slight additions or omissions, or by changes in the order of words."[6] Richard Taylor in his 1994 monograph on the Peshiṭta of Daniel concluded that the Peshiṭta "is a carefully executed and idiomatic translation, faithful to its *Vorlage*."[7] I too employed these same descriptors in my own work on 1 Samuel.[8] Michael Weitzman, in his article, "The Interpretative Character of the Syriac Old Testament," offered a list of fascinating Peshiṭta readings, but at the end of his article he confirmed that the "translators seldom express their own theological concerns. For the most part they felt bound by the plain sense."[9] This conclusion comes after several examples that demonstrate how the theological interests of the translator prevailed over the plain sense of the Hebrew text. Weitzman in his major opus on the Syriac version appealed to this expected language: "P can fairly be described as an idiomatic, though faithful, translation."[10] Lund's 2012 article on the Peshiṭta of Genesis provided a detailed description of some Peshiṭta readings and then concluded: "The Peshitta is an idiomatic translation, concerned about conveying the proper sense of its Hebrew source text without slavish adherence to it. Quantitative literalism (a one-to-one correspondence) and fidelity to the plain sense of the Hebrew text generally characterize the Peshitta of Genesis."[11]

The Peshiṭta translation of Gen 49:33 defies these categories because it does not convey the plain sense of the Hebrew. To label

---

6. B. ter Haar Romeny, "Techniques of Translation and Transmission in the Earliest Text Forms of the Syriac Version of Genesis," in *The Peshitta as a Translation: Papers Read at the II Peshitta Symposium Held at Leiden 19–21 August 1993*, MPI 8, edited by P. B. Dirksen and A. van der Kooij, 177–185 (Leiden: Brill, 1995), 183.

7. Richard A. Taylor, *The Peshitta of Daniel*, MPI 7 (Leiden: Brill, 1994), 319–20.

8. Craig E. Morrison, *The Character of the Syriac Version of the First Book of Samuel*, MPI 11 (Leiden: Brill, 2001), 21.

9. Michael P. Weitzman, "The Interpretative Character of the Syriac Old Testament," in *Hebrew Bible / Old Testament: The History of its Interpretation*, Vol. 1. *From the Beginnings to the Middle Ages (until 1300)*, Part 1. *Antiquity*, edited by M. Sæbø, 587–611 (Göttingen: Vandenhoeck & Ruprecht, 1996), 597.

10. Michael P. Weitzman, *The Syriac Version of the Old Testament: An Introduction*, University of Cambridge Oriental Publications 56 (Cambridge: Cambridge University Press, 1999), 61.

11. Jerome A. Lund, "Genesis in Syriac," in *The Book of Genesis: Composition, Reception, and Interpretation*, Supplements to Vetus Testamentum 152, edited by Craig A. Evans, Joel N. Lohr and David L. Petersen, 537–560 (Leiden: Brill, 2012), 549.

it as "idiomatic" or "good Syriac idiom" would also be misleading because an accurate translation of the Hebrew into Syriac for this phrase would have been equally idiomatic Syriac and certainly more "faithful." The distinction between "reader-oriented" (audience-oriented) or "target translation oriented" and "source text oriented" can be helpful in certain cases, as Brock has illustrated by comparing the Peshiṭta translation of the Letter of James to its Harklean version.[12] But these terms may not be as useful for describing the OT Peshiṭta since it can contain readings that seem to be both text-oriented and reader-oriented translations, such as those readings when the Peshiṭta imitates the formal character of the Hebrew in Syriac and are text-oriented and at the same time offer a lucid, reader-oriented translation.

The recent study of Peshiṭta Kings by Janet W. Dyk and Percy S. F. van Keulen offers a more detailed set of descriptors. They list the Peshiṭta readings as harmonizations, exegetical changes, accommodations, explicitations, clarifications, simplifications, contemporizations, and unexplained variations, namely, perplexing and ambiguous readings in the Peshiṭta that escape explanation.[13] It is precisely the exegetical readings and those that remain obscure that can reveal significant information about the nature of the Peshiṭta version. But a good deal of time is required to isolate them and then to explain, if possible, their genesis.

James Barr, in a 1979 article titled, "The Typology of Literalism in Ancient Biblical Translations," addressed the difficulties in describing the ancient biblical versions: Adjectives such as "free" or "literal" are

12. Sebastian Brock describes the character of text-oriented and reader-oriented translators: "A translator's actual practice will depend very much on how he deals with the tension between *signifiant* and *signifié*. If he is a text-oriented *interpres*, he will lay more stress on the *signifiant*, at the expense (or so it would appear to us today) of the *signifié*; if on the other hand he is a reader-oriented *expositor*, he will lay primary stress on the *signifié*, and show little real interest in the *signifiant*." (Sebastian P. Brock, "The Syriac Background to Ḥunayn's Translation Techniques," *ARAM* 3 [1991]: 146). See also Sebastian P. Brock, "Towards a History of Syriac Translation Technique," in *SymSyr* III, 1–14. Brock lists the distinguishing characteristics of the reader-oriented and text-oriented translators in his "To Revise or Not to Revise: Attitudes to Jewish Biblical Translation," in *Septuagint, Scrolls and Cognate Writings, Papers Presented to the International Symposium on the Septuagint and its Relations to the Dead Sea Scrolls and Other Writings, Manchester, 1990*, Septuagint and Cognate Studies Series 3, edited by G. J. Brooke and B. Lindars, 301–338 (Atlanta: Scholars Press, 1992), 312–313.

13. Janet W. Dyk and Percy S. F. van Keulen, *Language System, Translation Technique, and Textual Tradition in the Peshitta of Kings*, MPI 19 (Leiden: Brill, 2013).

"very rough and impressionistic."[14] Thus, while such generalizations can be helpful guides, they do not account for every divergent reading and can even obscure significant divergences that can reveal the nature of a particular version. Ignacio Carbajosa, in his study of Peshiṭta Psalms 90–150, aptly illustrated this point by noticing the distinct use of *ʿēdtā* to translate various Hebrew terms for "congregation."[15] A careful analysis of this apparently minor reading revealed that *ʿēdtā* is not used in a negative context and is never associated with the term "Israel" or "gods." Carbajosa concludes that *ʿēdtā* means "church" and is distinct from *knuštā*, which can appear in any context. After a review of how the terms are used in Ephrem and Aphrahaṭ, Carbajosa cautiously concludes that the Peshiṭta translation of the Psalms may witness to Christian influence either at the time of translation or during transmission. His observation is based upon a Peshiṭta reading that could easily have been overlooked. The Peshiṭta reading in Gen 49:33 could suffer the same fate since at first glance it appears to be a rather unimportant reading.

The Death of the Translator

Within this conversation regarding the Peshiṭta as a translation, I would suggest that we leave aside the question of the translator's "intentions." A. Aejmelaeus addressed this question for Septuagint studies in 1989, writing: "Officially, we know nothing about what went on in the translators' minds."[16] She concludes:

> The Greek text of the Septuagint—whether good or bad, correct or incorrect, intentional or unintentional—should be interpreted as such according to the meanings and rules of Greek and according to the probable understanding of an original native speaker. It should neither be interpreted according to

14. James Barr, *The Typology of Literalism in Ancient Biblical Translations*, Mitteilungen des Septuaginta-Unternehmens der Akademie der Wissenschaft in Göttingen 15 (Göttingen: Vandenhoeck & Ruprecht in Göttingen, 1979), 280.

15. Ignacio Carbajosa, *The Character of the Syriac Version of Psalms. A Study of Psalms 90–150 in the Peshitta*, MPI 17 (Leiden: Brill, 2008), 156–73.

16. A. Aejmelaeus, "Translation Technique and the Intention of the Translator," in *VII Congress of the International Organization for Septuagint and Cognate Studies*, edited by C. E. Cox, 23–36 (Atlanta, Scholars Press, 1989), 24.

> the Hebrew original nor according to the assumed intention of the translator. If the translator had a particular intention, it comes across through the Greek text. If the intention of the translator does not come across we have little possibility of knowing about it.

As Peshiṭta research moves forward, Aejmelaeus' advice should be given serious consideration. We can describe the Peshiṭta without attributing to the translators our own impressions of what we think that they were thinking or about how we think they arrived at a particular reading. We just cannot know. When, for example, the Peshiṭta imitates the formal character of the Hebrew, borrowing the Hebrew consonants into Syriac but generating an entirely different meaning, did the Peshiṭta translator believe that he had been "faithful" to the original?[17] In the case of doublets (the Peshiṭta offers alternative translations),[18] what can we know about the mind of the translator? What is demonstrable is that sometimes the Peshiṭta translation imitates the formal character of the Hebrew text or offers double translations. The translator's understanding of these translation techniques remains a mystery.

The Peshiṭta of Gen 49:33

The Masoretic text (MT) of Gen 49:33 reads:

וַיֶּאֱסֹף רַגְלָיו אֶל הַמִּטָּה וַיִּגְוַע וַיֵּאָסֶף אֶל עַמָּיו

> [Jacob] gathered his feet to his bed and he breathed his last and then he was gathered to his people.

Three moments describe Jacob's death: (1) he gathers his feet to his bed, (2) he breathes his last, and then (3) he is gathered to his people. The Peshiṭta renders this verse as follows:

---

17. For examples from 1 Samuel see, Morrison, *The Character of the Syriac Version of the First Book of Samuel*, 92–94.

18. See the examples in Weitzman, "The Interpretative Character," 596–597.

ܦܫܛ ܪ̈ܓܠܘܗܝ ܒܥܪܣܐ ܘܐܬܟܪܗ ܘܡܝܬ. ܘܐܬܟܢܫ ܠܘܬ ܥܡܗ.

> [Jacob] stretched out his feet in bed and became sick and died and was gather to his people.

The Hebrew verb √גוע (its precise meaning is obscure) is rendered with Syriac ܘܐܬܟܪܗ ܘܡܝܬ, a harmonization with Gen 25:8, 17 and 35:29 (MT וַיִּגְוַע וַיָּמָת אַבְרָהָם; Syriac ܘܐܬܟܪܗ ܘܡܝܬ ܐܒܪܗܡ). The "gathered" feet in the Hebrew text become the "stretched out" feet.[19] Payne Smith glosses this expression without any particular idiomatic meaning: *extendit pedes in lecto.*[20] Brockelmann glosses this verse with *distendit (membra)* but he includes to the Hebrew text perhaps to signal the reader that the Peshiṭta does not render the Hebrew literally.[21]

The Hebrew Text and the Biblical Versions

The meaning of the Hebrew is plain, though the gesture of gathering one's feet to the bed is unique in the Bible. When Abraham dies, the verbs גוע and אסף appear (Gen 25:8) but there is no mention of "gathering the feet" (see also Gen 25:17 and 35:29). Westermann links the action in Gen 49:33 to Gen 48:2 (וַיֵּשֶׁב עַל־הַמִּטָּה),[22] though it is not obvious how Jacob's action of "gathering his feet" in Gen 49:33 after his discourse parallels his sitting up in bed at the beginning of the scene. Wenham suggests that the verb ויאסף is a play on the name Joseph, which would explain why ויאסף is repeated and why the Hebrew phrase is so odd. The Hebrew text is primarily interested in the alliteration of the two words with the name Joseph, not the meaning of the gesture. Nahum Sarna recognizes that this gesture is strange: "Presumably, he had been sitting with his feet over the side of the bed (cf. 48:2, 12), but this is hardly a likely posture for one about

---

19. The expression "to stretch one's feet" occurs only one other time (Ezek 16:25), where it refers to prostitution.

20. R. Payne Smith, *Thesaurus Syriacus* (Oxford: Clarendon Press, 1868–1897), s.v. ܦܫܛ.

21. Carl Brockelmann, *Lexicon Syriacum*, 2nd ed. (Göttingen: W. Fr. Kaestner, 1928), s.v. ܦܫܛ.

22. "So wird es verständlicher, daß er im zweiten Satz »er zog seine Füße auf das Lager zurück« die Szene abschließt, die mit dem Sich-Aufsetzen Jakobs auf dem Lager 48,2 beginnt" (C. Westermann, *Genesis 37–50*, Biblischer Kommentar Altes Testament I,3 [Neukirchen-Vluyn: Neukirchener, 1982], 224).

to breathe his last."[23] Most biblical scholars do not comment on the gesture in Gen 49:33 since the meaning of the Hebrew words is plain and easily translated into ancient or modern languages.[24]

The Göttingen edition of the Greek OT reads: ἐξάρας τοὺς πόδας ἐπὶ τὴν κλίνην.[25] This is the only instance where the Hebrew verb אסף is rendered with ἐξαίρω.[26] Wevers suggests that ἐξάρας with ἐπὶ means "putting on" but makes no comment on the relationship of this translation to the MT.[27] The phrase "to raise the feet" occurs only one other time in Rahlfs' edition where it means to set out on a journey.[28] Old Latin witnesses follow the LXX (*extollens pedes super lectum*).[29] The Midyat manuscript of the Pentateuch of the Syro-Hexapla[30] reads with the LXX:

ܘܟܕ ܐܪܝܡ ܪ̈ܓܠܘܗܝ ܥܠ ܥܪܣܐ

> And when he raised his feet on his bed...

While the LXX and Peshitta readings are not in agreement, these two versions do agree that the action described in the MT cannot be rendered literally.

The Targums Onkelos, Pseudo-Jonathan, and Neofiti follow the MT, translating ויאסף with כנש, as does the Vulgate (*collegit pedes*).

23. Nahum Sarna, *The JPS Torah Commentary: Genesis* (Philadelphia: Jewish Publication Society, 1989), 347. Jürgen Ebach also notes that the Hebrew expression is rare and follows Westermann's explanation (Jürgen Ebach, *Genesis 37–50*, Herders Theologischer Kommentar zum Alten Testament [Freiburg: Herder, 2007], 636.)

24. Victor P. Hamilton interprets this unexpected idiom to describe Jacob resuming "a sleeping posture, almost fetal-like, on his deathbed" (Victor P. Hamilton, *The Book of Genesis: Chapters 18–50*, The New International Commentary on the Old Testament [Grand Rapids: William B. Eerdmans, 1995], 689])

25. John William Wevers, *Genesis*, Septuaginta: Vetus Testamentum Graecum 1 (Göttingen: Vandenhoeck & Ruprecht, 1974).

26. Edwin Hatch and Henry A. Redpath, *A Concordance to the Septuagint and the Other Greek Versions of the Old Testament*. 2 vols. (Oxford: Clarendon, 1897. Repr., Graz: Akademische Verlagsanstalt, 1975), 485.

27. John William Wevers, *Notes on the Greek Text of Genesis*, Septuagint and Cognate Studies 35 (Atlanta: Scholars Press, 1993), 838.

28. Gen 29:1 וַיִּשָּׂא יַעֲקֹב רַגְלָיו וַיֵּלֶךְ אַרְצָה; καὶ ἐξάρας Ιακωβ τοὺς πόδας ἐπορεύθη εἰς γῆν.

29. Petrus Sabatier, *Vetus Latina. Die Reste der altlateinischen Bibel*, vol. 2. *Genesis* (Freiburg: Herder, 1951), 518.

30. A. Vööbus, *The Pentateuch in the Version of the Syro-Hexapla: A facsimile edition of a Midyat MS. discovered 1964*, CSCO 369 (Louvain: Peeters, 1975), fol. 18.

These readings suggest that the Peshiṭta did not have a different Hebrew *Vorlage* and that its translators could have offered a "more faithful" translation of the Hebrew.

The Expression "To Stretch Out One's Feet" as a Final Gesture Before Death

The Peshiṭta expression "to stretch out the feet" occurs in *Jubilees* 23:1 to describe the death of Abraham:

> He put two of Jacob's fingers on his eyes and blessed the God of gods. He covered his face, stretched out his feet, fell asleep forever, and was gathered to his ancestors.[31]

Van Ruiten argues that in *Jubilees* the description of Jacob's death in Genesis has been transferred to Abraham, but the phrase, "he gathered his feet," has been adjusted to he "stretched out his feet."[32] P. A. Robinson[33] notes that the phrase occurs three times in *The Testaments of the Twelve Patriarchs* to describe the impending death of a Patriarch:[34]

> *T. Levi* 19:4 and *T. Iss.* 7:9
> ἐξέτεινε τοὺς πόδας αὐτοῦ
> He stretched out his feet
>
> *T. Jos.* 20:4
> ἐκτείνας τοὺς πόδας αὐτοῦ
> stretching out his feet[35]

31. J. C. VanderKam, *The Book of Jubilees*, CSCO 510–511 (Louvain: Peeters, 1989), 135 (translation).

32. Jacques T. A. G. M. van Ruiten, *Abraham in the Book of Jubilees: The Rewriting of Genesis 11:26–25:10 in the Book of Jubilees 11:14–23:8* (Leiden: Brill, 2012), 324.

33. P. A. Robinson, "To Stretch out the Feet: A Formula for Death in the Testaments of the Twelve Patriarchs," *JBL* 97 (1978): 369–74. See the critical review of Robinson's study in M. de Jonge, "Again: 'to Stretch out the Feet' in the Testaments of the Twelve Patriarchs," *JBL* 99 (1980): 120–121.

34. The text is taken from M. de Jonge, *The Testaments of the Twelve Patriarchs: A Critical Edition of the Greek Text* (Leiden: Brill, 1978).

35. *T. Gad* 8:4 reads with the LXX: ἐξάρας τοὺς πόδας αὐτοῦ.

This expression also appears in a homily on Blessed Mar Severus, Patriarch Of Antioch, by George, Bishop of The Arabs (born ca. 640 near Antioch) when George describes Mar Severus' death:

ܢܦܠ ܟܘܪܗܢܐ ܥܠ ܩܕܝܫܐ ܘܡܚܝܠܘܬܐ
ܘܦܫܛ ܪ̈ܓܠܘܗܝ ܒܥܪܣܐ ܕܟܐܒ̈ܐ ܕܢܐܙܠ ܢܬܬܢܝܚ
ܘܩܪܒܘ ܬܠܡܝ̈ܕܘܗܝ ܘܡܦܝܣܝܢ ܠܗ ܒܟܝܐܝܬ
ܕܠܐ ܬܫܒܘܩ ܠܢ ܐܒܘܢ ܝܬܡ̈ܐ ܡܢ ܐܠܦܟ

A disease and weakness befell the saint
and he stretched out his feet on his sickbed to go to rest.
His disciples drew near and mournfully urged him:
"Do not leave us behind, our father, orphaned of your aid."[36]

George employs the expression "to stretch out the feet" to signal to the audience and Mar Severus' disciples that the patriarch is about to die. Then, once he is dead, his disciples care for his corpse by stretching him out (ܦܫܛܘܗܝ ܗܘܘ) on a slab. Ephrem does not include this phrase from Gen 49:33 when he describes Jacob's death,[37] but it does appear at the beginning of the commentary in Ephrem's overview of the book of Genesis:[38]

ܒܬܪ ܗܠܝܢ ܐܡܪ ܥܠ ܒܘܪ̈ܟܬܐ ܕܒܪܟ ܝܥܩܘܒ ܠܒ̈ܢܘܗܝ، ܘܟܕ ܫܠܡ ܡ̈ܠܘܗܝ،
ܦܫܛ ܪ̈ܓܠܘܗܝ ܒܥܪܣܐ ܘܐܬܟܢܫ ܠܘܬ ܥܡܗ

After these things he spoke about the blessings with which Jacob blessed his sons and, because he finished his words, he stretched out his feet in the bed and he was gathered to his people.

The fact that Ephrem includes this expression, while at the same time omitting ܘܐܬܟܢܫ ܠܥܡܗ, could suggest that ܦܫܛ ܪ̈ܓܠܘܗܝ ܒܥܪܣܐ was sufficient to signal that Jacob was at the point of death.

36. The text and translation are taken from Kathleen E. McVey, *George, Bishop of the Arabs. A Homily on Blessed Mar Severus, Patriarch of Antioch*, CSCO 531 (Louvain: Peeters, 1993), 28–29.

37. The text reads: ܒܬܪ ܕܝܢ ܕܒܪܟ ܠܒ̈ܢܘܗܝ، ܡܝܬ ܒܪ ܡܐܐ ܘܐܪܒܥܝܢ ܘܫܒܥ ܫ̈ܢܝܢ "After [Jacob] blessed his sons, he died at the age of one hundred and forty-seven."

38. R.-M. Tonneau, *Sancti Ephraem Syri. In Genesim et in Exodum Commentarii*, CSCO 152-153 (Louvain: Peeters, 1955), 8.

Describing the Peshiṭta Reading in Genesis 49:33

How should the Peshiṭta reading in Genesis 49:33 be described? It is not a "clarification" since the Hebrew is clear. Classifying it as a translation into good idiomatic Syriac would be misleading, since a majority of Peshiṭta readings can be so categorized and a literal translation of the Hebrew would also have been good Syriac idiom. It might be categorized as "contemporizing," but this assumes that the Hebrew reading is an ancient expression that has been updated in the Peshiṭta. This reading exposes the limits of traditional language for describing the Peshiṭta.

The Hebrew may be nonsensical, following Wenham's suggestion that it derives from an association between the name "Joseph" (יוֹסֵף) and the Hebrew verb "to gather" (אסף) and is therefore the result of alliteration. The Peshiṭta text highlights the solemnity of Jacob's death by employing an expression that is used in Syriac and Greek literature to solemnize the death of major figures. The Peshiṭta reading cannot be described as faithful or idiomatic. It is divergent, and we can only wonder what the translator was thinking. This sort of Peshiṭta reading requires time to identify and, if possible, to explain. But we should also acknowledge that Peshiṭta studies is, to some extent, still groping around in the dark. The digitization of the OT Peshiṭta has allowed for significant strides in our understanding of the character of this version. The ongoing digitization of all classical Syriac literature will allow Peshiṭta scholars to recognize with ease Syriac idioms in their various contexts and genres and to explain readings that are currently considered obscure or anomalous.

This study of Gen 49:33 in the Peshiṭta also has a significant impact on biblical exegesis beyond traditional textual criticism. Because the Hebrew phrase in Gen 49:33 is clear, most biblical commentators have little to say about it. But the divergent readings in the Peshiṭta and LXX signal that the plain meaning of the Hebrew text was not obvious or acceptable for their audiences in antiquity. These divergent readings support Wenham's intuition that alliteration may be behind this rather unidiomatic expression in Hebrew, and they confirm Nahum Sarna's insight that the Hebrew expression is odd.

The Unique Character of the Peshiṭta

The Peshiṭta reading in Gen 49:33 underscores the Peshiṭta's unique character among the biblical versions that emerged after the turn of the Common Era. The texts discovered in the Judean desert have provided a more complete picture of the transmission of the Hebrew text. Before the turn of the eras, different editions of the same biblical book continued alongside the emerging MT. Tov notes that in the time preceding the Qumran community the scribes "initially approached the text freely." The Qumran evidence illustrates "the exact copying of texts belonging to the Masoretic family", although Tov notes that even biblical manuscripts from Qumran "occasionally reflect the intervention of scribes."[39] The period of textual plurality comes to a close, according to Tov, at the end of the first century and the period of textual uniformity (the emerging MT) is reflected in biblical texts found at Naḥal Ḥever and in Wadi Murabba'at.

The Peshiṭta appeared in this period in which more literal biblical translations accorded greater authority to the Hebrew text.[40] But it does not reflect the same degree of respect for the Hebrew text that appears in biblical translations emerging in Palestine, Asia Minor, and the Babylonian academies.[41] In Gen 49:33, Field reports that Aquila has συνέλεξεν and Symmachus has συναγαγών, both of which are closer to the Hebrew-like Targum Onkelos, the official Targum that is emerging at the same time as the Peshiṭta. Thus, not only were the creators of the Peshiṭta non-rabbinic Jews, as Weitzman argues,[42] but they also had little contact, it seems, with the translation movements during this period.

This lack of contact is further illustrated by interpretative readings in the Peshiṭta that have little to do with commonly shared interpretations of the Hebrew. In Gen 22:2 Mount Moriah, the place

39. Emanuel Tov, *Textual Criticism of the Hebrew Bible* (Minneapolis: Fortress, 2001), 189–191.

40. Barr describes the attitude of Greek-speaking Jews toward the Hebrew Bible: "Among Jews in the Greek world the authority and prestige of the Greek version began in the course of time to be challenged by the deepening conviction that real authority lay in the Hebrew. Under this influence we see the growing use of methods which seek to imitate features of the form of the Hebrew original" (Barr, *Typology*, 325).

41. Klaus Beyer (translated by John F. Healey), *The Aramaic Language: Its Distribution and Subdivisions* (Göttingen: Vandenhoeck & Ruprecht, 1986), 21–23.

42. Weitzman, *The Syriac Version*, 216.

where Abraham should bind Isaac, becomes "a particular mountain" (ܥܠ ܚܕ ܡܢ ܛܘܪ̈ܐ) in "the land of the Amorites" (ܠܐܪܥܐ ܕܐܡܘܪ̈ܝܐ) in the Peshiṭta. As Weitzman notes, this reading is an example of the independence of the Peshiṭta from Targum Onkelos (לארע פלחנא) and Peudo-Jonathan (לארע פולחנא).[43] But there is more. According to the Peshiṭta of 2 Chr 3:1 the Temple was built "on the mountain of the Amorites" (ܒܛܘܪܐ ܕܐܡܘܪ̈ܝܐ) where the Hebrew reads "Mount Moriah" (בהר המוריה).[44] So the Peshiṭta of Gen 22:2 appears to link the Akedah to the future Temple mount if Gen 22:2 is read with 2 Chr 3:1.[45] This link also appears in *Jubilees* 18:13,[46] in Philo,[47] and in rabbinic literature.[48] The Peshiṭta also maintains this link but in an entirely unique way. The land of the Amorites is one of the territories that God promises to bestow on the Israelites (Ex 3:8, 17 and 13:5). Read in light of Exodus, the Peshiṭta's Abraham anticipates this divine gift by taking his son Isaac to Amorite land. Thus, the Peshiṭta links the Temple Mount with the Akedah but in a way unrelated to other traditions.

Conclusion

General observations regarding the nature of a biblical version are necessary, but they may not be helpful guides when considering particular readings. Labels such as "idiomatic Syriac" or "clarification" could bury the Peshiṭta reading in Gen 49:33, since on the surface it appears to be rather insignificant. Then we would lose the opportunity to grasp what it can tell us about the nature of the Peshiṭta, which is

43. Weitzman, *The Syriac Version*, 127.

44. Kilimi suggests that the Peshiṭta reading is the result of the similarity in Hebrew between Moriah (המוריה) and Amorites (אמוריא) and that the association of the Akedah with the Temple was known even in the First Temple period. See Isaac Kalimi, "The Land of Moriah, Mount Moriah, and the Site of Solomon's Temple in Biblical Historiography," *HTR* 83 (1990): 348.

45. See S. Spiegel (translated by J. Goldin), *The Last Trial. On the Legends and Lore of the Command to Abraham to Offer Isaac as a Sacrifice: The Akedah* (Philadelphia: The Jewish Publication Society of America, 1967).

46. "Abraham named that place 'The Lord Saw' so that it is named 'The Lord Saw'. It is Mt. Zion" (Vanderkam, *The Book of Jubilees*, 87–88).

47. Nikolaus Walter, "Jewish-Greek Literature of the Greek Period," in *The Cambridge History of Judaism*, vol. 2. *The Hellenistic Age*, edited by W. D. Davies and L. Finkelstein, 285–408 (Cambridge: Cambridge University Press, 1989), 404–405.

48. According to Genesis Rabbah, פרשה נה, Moriah refers to the place where teaching goes out to the world (מקום שתוראה יוצאה עולם), a reference to the Temple.

faithful to the Hebrew except where it is not. Thus a careful appraisal of every Peshiṭta reading, even those that seem very minor, will continue to be necessary in order to illuminate the nature of this translation. The Peshiṭta reading in Gen 49:33 also impacts biblical exegesis since it (and the LXX reading) suggests that the Hebrew text, though easily translated, is odd. Finally, Peshiṭta research will be greatly assisted by the ever-increasing availability of electronic databases for Syriac literature. Then we may learn more about why the Peshiṭta wanted the dying Jacob to stretch out his feet instead of gathering them in and why Abraham went to the land of the Amorites to bind his son Isaac.

Hagiography

Formation and Transmission

7. The Invention of the *Persian Martyr Acts*

❖ Adam H. Becker

The *Acts of the Persian Martyrs*, or more briefly, the *Persian Martyr Acts* or PMA, are a large corpus of Syriac martyr texts which purport to describe the persecution of Christians during the Sasanian Empire from the third to the seventh century. There are over sixty of these texts, which vary in length in their standard editions from only a few pages, even just one page, to over one hundred.[1] The exact date of composition is uncertain for most, but it is clear that they were written primarily from the fifth through seventh centuries. However, some are from later. About two thirds of the PMA describe events that supposedly took place during the reign of Shapur II (309–379 CE), the period commonly referred to as the "Great Persecution" (beginning ca. 345), although probably all of these texts are from at least a century later.

* I would like to thank the two anonymous readers as well as Aaron Butts, who has encouraged this project since its inception in a paper given in a session co-organized by him and Simcha Gross at the Association of Jewish Studies annual conference in 2014. Patrick Deer and Martha Rust kindly offered bibliographical suggestions.

1. For a guide to the various editions, see Sebastian P. Brock, *History of Mar Ma'in, with a Guide to the Persian Martyr Acts* (Piscataway: Gorgias, 2008) (= Brock, *Guide*). See also Paul Peeters, *Bibliotheca Hagiographica Orientalis* (Brussels: Société des Bollandistes, 1910) and J.-M. Fiey, *Saints syriaques*, ed. Lawrence I. Conrad, Studies in Late Antiquity and Early Islam 6 (Princeton: Darwin Press, 2004). For a good introduction to these texts, see Christelle Jullien, "Martyrs, Christian," *EIr* [accessed August 11, 2015].

FIGURE 1: *Acts of the Persian Martyrs* (purported dates and numbering according to Brock's *Guide*)[2]

Under Vahram II (276–293): 1	Under Yazdgard II (493–457): 52–56
Under Shapur II (309–379): 2–40	Late fifth century: 57–58
Late fourth century: 41–43	Under Khosro I (531–579): 59–61
Under Yazdgard I (399–420): 44–47 (and *Shabur*, ed. Herman)	Under Khosro II (591–628): 62–64
Under Vahram V (421–438): 48–51	Further texts also extant in Greek, Armenian, Georgian, and Arabic.

In this essay, I would like to look at the PMA in some of their early compositional groups and then discuss how originally distinct texts have been compiled and categorized over time. This is important because, in order to understand the complex relationship of these texts and their reception, it is necessary to lay out the different ways they have been configured by their authors, copyists, and the modern scholars who edit and study them. The survey I provide is not strong on argument. Rather, this is an opportunity, first, to describe some of the PMA and their diverse origins; second, to provide a sense of how they are variously gathered in the manuscript tradition; and, third, to discuss how they have been collected since scholars began to print them from the eighteenth century onward.

One important caveat I should make before I begin: Some of these texts require further in-depth manuscript study in order for us to move forward. The manuscript witnesses, many of which I will discuss, vary in date, from the fifth or sixth century to the nineteenth. In them the PMA are combined in various ways and, if we had a stemma for each of the texts, we might be able to discern important patterns. Most of this work still needs to be done, although there has been a greater focus on the corpus in recent years.[3] The PMA are commonly

2. I have used abbreviated references to the titles of these works in the following figures.

3. See the several volumes in the Persian Martyr Acts in Syriac series, published by Gorgias Press, the first of which is Brock, *History of Mar Ma'in*. The CSCO edition of several of the PMA is a welcome addition to the bibliography: Florence Jullien, *Histoire de Mār Abba, catholicos de l'Orient. Martyres de Mār Grigor, général en chef du roi Khusro Ier et de Mār Yazd-panāh, juge et gouverneur*, CSCO 658–659 (Louvain: Peeters, 2015).

employed not only as a source for the spread of Christianity in the Sasanian Empire but also as a resource for understanding Sasanian cultural, religious, political, and linguistic history.[4] For example, Joel Walker's book used the *History of Mar Qardagh* (26), a fictional tale set in the fourth century, to examine Christian conversion, family relations, philosophical culture, and the cult of the saints in the Sasanian Empire in the sixth century (the number that appears after PMA texts in this article is that provided for each in Brock's *Guide*).[5] Richard Payne's book astutely locates the PMA within the context of Sasanian aristocratic anxiety and the development of the cult of the saints.[6] His work also employs this literature as a source for Christian anti-Zoroastrian polemic.[7] Christelle Jullien has published a number of works using the PMA as a historical and geographical source and has addressed the literary construction of these works.[8] Furthermore, scholars working in Rabbinics have demonstrated an emerging interest in the PMA.[9]

---

4. I note in particular the work of Philippe Gignoux, e.g., "À la frontière du syriaque et de l'iranien: Quelques confluences tirées des Actes des martyrs perses," *Semitica et Classica* 3 (2010): 189–193. Other examples include Antonio C. D. Panaino, "References to the Term Yašt and Other Mazdean Elements in the Syriac and Greek Martyrologia, with a Short Excursus on the Semantic Value of the Greek Verb μαγεύω," in *Proceedings of the 5th Conference of the Societas Iranologica Europæa, Held in Ravenna, 6–11 October 2003*, vol. 1. *Ancient & Middle Iranian Studies*, edited by Antonio C. D. Panaino and Andrea Piras, 167–182 (Milan: Mimesis, 2006) and Shaul Shaked, *Dualism in Transformation: Varieties of Religion in Sasanian Iran* (London: SOAS, 1994), 90–91. Claudia Ciancaglini, *Iranian Loanwords in Syriac* (Wiesbaden: Reichert, 2008) also relies on the PMA.

5. Joel T. Walker, *The Legend of Mar Qardagh: Narrative and Christian Heroism in Late Antique Iraq* (Berkeley: University of California Press, 2006).

6. Richard Payne, *A State of Mixture: Christians, Zoroastrians, and Iranian Political Culture in Late Antiquity* (Berkeley: University of California Press, 2015).

7. Richard Payne, "Les polémiques syro-orientales contre le zoroastrisme et leurs contexts politiques," in *Les controversies religieuses en syriaque*, ÉS 13, edited by Flavia Ruani, 239–260 (Paris: Geuthner, 2016).

8. For her more recent work, see Christelle Jullien, "Martyrs en Perse dans l'hagiographie syro-orientale: le tournant du VIe siècle," in *Juifs et Chrétiens en Arabie aux Ve et VIe siècles. Regards croisés sur les sources*, Centre de Recherche d'Histoire et Civilisation de Byzance, Monographies 32; Le massacre de Najrân 2, edited by Joëlle Beaucamp, Françoise Briquel Chatonnet, and Christian Julien Robin, 279–290 (Paris: Association des amis du Centre d'histoire et civilisation de Byzance, 2010); "Les Actes des martyrs perses: Transmettre l'histoire," in *L'hagiographie syriaque*, ÉS 9, edited by André Binggeli, 127–140 (Paris: Paul Geuthner, 2012).

9. See the works of Geoffrey Herman cited below. Jeffrey Rubenstein, "Martyrdom in the Persian Martyr Acts and in the Babylonian Talmud" and Simcha Gross, "A Persian Anti-Martyr Act: The Death of Rabbah Bar Naḥmani," in *The Aggada of the Bavli and its Cultural World*, edited by G. Herman and J. L. Rubenstein, 175–210 and 211–242, respectively (Providence: Brown Judaic Studies, 2018). See also Reuven Kiperwasser and Serge Ruzer, "To Convert a Persian and Teach him the Holy

The PMA are often treated as sources for conversion to Christianity in the Sasanian Empire.[10] I do not discount the possibility of using the corpus in this way—and in fact I praise the scholarship that has done this—but some scholarly work, for example, Kyle Smith's 2016 book, suggests we need to better appreciate the literary constructedness of these texts and perhaps be more hesitant about the kinds of historical claims we can make about the Sasanian Empire based upon them.[11] Furthermore, we have in recent years learned—for example, from Elizabeth Castelli—to appreciate martyrdom in general as a form of meaning making, and not to treat such texts as stories based upon memories of historical violence.[12] And, of course, since 2001 martyrdom and meaningful death have become common scholarly topics in our attempt to grapple with contemporary events, and with the often naïve, even disingenuous, conversations in the public sphere.

Building on the foundational work of Gernot Wiessner, who examined a large selection of the corpus, Smith demonstrates how some of the PMA are in harmony with or at times play a very different tune from the later Roman historians and the ecclesiastical historians of the Roman Empire.[13] He dismantles much of the stage and script upon which the fourth-century history of the Roman-Sasanian frontier were thought to have been acted out. Developing suggestions we find in Wiessner's work, as well as those made by Sebastian Brock, he shows the increasingly Eusebian nature of a certain number of the PMA, that is, that their historiographical frame is Western.[14] By this I mean that the perspective offered in

Scriptures: A Zoroastrian Proselyte in Rabbinic and Syriac Christian Narratives," in *Jews, Christians and Zoroastrians: Religious Dynamics in a Sasanian Context*, edited by Geoffrey Herman, 101–138 (Piscataway: Gorgias, 2014).

10. Muriel Debié, "Devenir chrétien dans l'Iran sassanide: La conversion à la lumière des récits hagiographiques," in *Le problème de la chistianisation du monde antique*, edited by Hervé Inglebert, Sylvain Destephen, and Bruno Dumézil, 329–358 (Paris: Picard, 2010).

11. Kyle Smith, *Constantine and the Captive Christians of Persia: Martyrdom and Religious Identity in Late Antiquity* (Berkeley: University of California Press, 2016). See also Kyle Smith, "Constantine and Judah the Maccabee: History and Memory in the Acts of the Persian Martyrs," *JCSSS* 12 (2012): 16–33.

12. Elizabeth Castelli, *Martyrdom and Memory: Early Christian Culture Making* (New York: Columbia University Press, 2007).

13. Gernot Wiessner, *Untersuchungen zur syrischen Literaturgeschichte: Zur Märtyrerüberlieferung aus der Christenverfolgung Schapurs II* (Göttingen: Vandenhoeck and Ruprecht, 1967).

14. Sebastian P. Brock, Review of G. Wiessner, *Untersuchungen zur syrischen Literaturgeschichte*, *JTS ns* 19 (1968): 300–309, esp. 303–306.

these works is ultimately that of the Christian Roman Empire and the story they tell of Christianity's spread is framed from a Christian Roman perspective. The historical frame of the PMA may be understood as an expansion of the vision of Christian history and empire sketched out in Eusebius's works.

Wiessner's 1967 book moved things forward by taking apart prior scholarly claims about many of these texts deriving from one proto-collection, which since Assemani in the eighteenth century has often been wrongly attributed to Marutha of Maypherqaṭ in the early fifth century.[15]

FIGURE 2: Martyrs of Seleucia-Ctesiphon and Karka d-Ladan in Huzistan (= α)

Simeon A ("Martyrdom") (6) and Simeon B ("History") (7)
Pusai (8)
Martha (9)
Great Slaughter (10)
Tarbo (11)
Azad (12)
Shahdost (13)
111 Men and 9 Women (17)
Barbaʿshmin (18)
Martyrs outside court (38)

Wiessner separated out two broader cycles or families of texts from the PMA: The former, perhaps the most well-known, consists of the two different texts on Simeon Bar Ṣabbaʿe (known as the *Martyrdom* and the *History*, translated by Smith) and a number of closely related texts, several of which concern Simeon's immediate successors or persons close to him.[16] These works describe events in Seleucia-Ctesi-

15. S. E. Assemani, *Acta Sanctorum et Martyrum*, I–II (Rome: Typis J. Collini, 1748); Wiessner, *Untersuchungen zur syrischen Literaturgeschichte*, 11–12. See Sebastian P. Brock, "Marutha of Maypherqaṭ," in *GEDSH*, 273 for discussion and bibliography. Elizabeth Key Fowden, *The Barbarian Plain: Saint Sergius between Rome and Iran* (Berkeley: University of California Press, 1999), 48–59 reviews some of the literature and sets "Martyropolis" within the context of Roman-Persian relations and militarization.

16. Kyle Smith, *The Martyrdom and the History of Blessed Simeon bar Ṣabbaʿe* (Piscataway: Gorgias, 2014).

phon in what is now central Iraq and Karka d-Ladan in Khuzistan in what is now southwestern Iran and seem to have been redacted in Karka d-Ladan. Though describing events in the mid-fourth century, the *Martyrdom of Simeon* is likely from the early to mid-fifth century. The *History* and the various related texts seem to be from the later fifth century, possibly even the sixth. Those persecuted are primarily clergy and devoted laity, and there are formulaic parallels, some of which appear also in other later texts, in how the martyrdoms take place (for example, the martyrs are commonly asked to worship the sun and moon).[17]

One important parallel Greek source we have for the accounts of the fourth century is Sozomen's version of several of these martyrdoms, which must be from before the 440s.[18] It is clear he shares some of these texts' sources. Whereas Wiessner argues for a complex relationship of the two Simeon texts with a prior lost source, Smith suggests the simpler explanation, which is the development of one text from the other. Both Smith and Payne argue that the shifts from the former to the latter are representative of certain changes in the communal self-understanding of Christians in the Sasanian Empire. For example, whereas the *Martyrdom* depicts Simeon as opposed to paying taxes to the Shah, the *History* changes this to a double tax. That is, Simeon—who has become Catholicos of the East in this latter text—had no problems with Christians paying their taxes as long as they were equitable.[19]

Another important shift between these two texts is that as a Eusebian model of history is further taken up, something demonstrated well by Smith, so also the later text self-consciously represents itself as being about the East: In contrast to the *Martyrdom*, the *History* prioritizes that it is about the East and sets this in contrast to the West.[20] The events take place in the "land of the East" and Simeon

17. Wiessner, *Untersuchungen zur syrischen Literaturgeschichte*, 203–205 fn 7.

18. Sozomen, *Ecclesiastica Historia*, edited in *PG*, vol. 67: II.9–14. Sozomen also refers to martyrs from outside this cycle, such as 'Aqebshma (31).

19. Smith, *Constantine and the Captive Christians*, 111–122; *pace* Payne's ultimate acceptance of the historicity of the tax issue (*State of Mixture*, 40–43).

20. "Persia" and "Persians" are mentioned more often in the latter text (Michael Kmosko, *S. Simeon Bar Ṣabba'e: Martyrium et Narratio*, PS I.2 [Paris, 1907]: *Martyrdom*: 727.9 731.15; *History*: 782.15, 790.13, 807.23, 810.18, 887.7, 890.3), while the "East" is fronted in the *History*, where it is also more common (*Martyrdom*: 750.2, 763.3; *History*: 779.4, 5; 782.13; 863.13; 886.4, 11, 12; 890.14, 15 ;

is the "Catholicos of the East."[21] Simeon is even compared to the prophet Daniel in that both were servants to a Persian king.[22]

Furthermore, the *History* makes an explicit connection between the death of Constantine and the persecution under Shapur.[23] Christians, who were associated with Rome, it suggests, were no longer protected. This corresponds with an idea we find traces of in the sources, but which has perhaps been overdeveloped in our own scholarship, that is, that Christians were seen as a "fifth column," or that their position in the Sasanian Empire offers "a case of divided loyalties," to borrow from the subtitle of Sebastian Brock's article which has been so important for this discussion.[24] I am, however, increasingly uncertain about what claims we can make about the status of Christians within the Sasanian Empire based upon the PMA, especially because such claims are then circularly used to explain these same texts. I suspect the political implications we are supposed to draw from these texts are often bound up with their self-location in the East and, therefore, the texts and the images of the East and/or Persia they invoke require closer examination.

The other collection of related texts examined by Wiessner are those linked to Adiabene, the region around modern-day (and ancient) Irbil in northern Iraq.

920.24 ; 950.7; 955.22; 959.1, 11; 955.16 [the latter composition is just under three times longer than the former]).

21. See also, e.g., the *Martyrdom of Pusai* (8), which refers to Shapur's "persecution against the churches of the East" (P. Bedjan, *Acta martyrum et sanctorum* [Paris: Via dicta de Sèvres, 1890–1897], 2.209.3).

22. Kmosko, *Simeon Bar Ṣabba'e*, 887.7.

23. Kmosko, *Simeon Bar Ṣabba'e*, 782–790.

24. Sebastian P. Brock, "Christians in the Sassanian Empire: A Case of Divided Loyalties," in *Religious and National Identity: Papers Read at the Nineteenth Summer Meeting and the Twentieth Winter Meeting of the Ecclesiastical History Society*, Studies in Church History 18, edited by Stuart Mews, 1–19 (Oxford: Basil Blackwell, 1982). Reprinted in his *Syriac Perspectives on Late Antiquity* (London: Variorum, 1984). Note the titles of responding works, Antonio C. D. Panaino, "The 'Persian' Identity in the Religious Controversies: Again on the Case of the 'Divided Loyalty' in Sasanian Iran," in *Iranian Identity in the Course of History: Proceedings of the Conference Held in Rome, 21–24 September 2005*, Serie Orientale Roma 105, Orientalia Romana 9, edited by Carlo G. Cereti, 227–239 (Rome: Istituto italiano per l'Africa e l'Oriente, 2010) and Josef Wiesehöfer, "'Geteilte Loyalitäten'. Religiöse Minderheiten des 3. und 4. Jahrhunderts n.Chr. im Spannungsfeld zwischen Rom und dem sasanidischen Iran," *Klio* 75 (1993): 362–382.

FIGURE 3: Martyrs of Adiabene (= β)

GROUP 1	GROUP 2	GROUP 3
John of Arbela (14) Abraham of Arbela (16) Ḥnanya (19) Jacob and Mary (20) Barḥadbshabba of Arbela (23) Jacob and Azad (29)	Aitallaha and Hophsai (24) Thecla and her companions (25)	ʿAqebshma (31)

Wiessner divides these texts into three groups and only examines closely the first, which consists solely of rather short texts. One of his motivating questions concerns the kinds of original collections (*Ursammlungen*) to which these texts belonged. He theorizes that the Adiabene texts derive from earlier diptych lists and addresses the possible genre of clerical martyr lists, introducing as an example the *Martyrs of Karka d-Beth Slokh* (39, not to be confused with 53).[25] He suggests that these earlier lists were expanded upon and out of this derives such collections as the various Adiabene texts (Another important list in this regard is ms. Brit. Libr. Add. 12,150 from 411/2 CE, mentioned below).[26] Of these Adiabene texts, the *Martyrdom of ʿAqebshma* (31) is perhaps the most interesting for its homiletical introduction, its formulaic use of "Zoroastrian" themes, and its first person account at the end.[27] The manner in which it refers to the "land of the East" suggests it could be a Persian Martyr Act composed not within Persia but in the Roman Empire, perhaps in Edessa (It also refers to the Simeon texts explicitly).[28]

Another series of related PMA are those focused on martyrs purportedly killed under Yazdgard I (399–420) and Vahram V (421–38).

25. Wiessner, *Untersuchungen zur syrischen Literaturgeschichte*, 227.

26. William Wright, *Catalogue of Syriac Manuscripts in the British Museum* (London: British Museum, 1870–1872), 2.631–633 (Ms. 726).

27. Bedjan, *Acta martyrum et sanctorum*, 351–361; 361–362, 369; 394–396. Wiessner, *Untersuchungen zur syrischen Literaturgeschichte*, 27–32 addresses the conclusion of the work.

28. Bedjan, *Acta martyrum et sanctorum*, 371, 394; 379, 395.

FIGURE 4: Martyrs of the Early Fifth Century

Yazdgard I (399–420)	Vahram V (421–438)
ʿAbda (44)	Jacob Intercisus (48)
10 Martyrs (45) (γ)	Jacob the Notary (49) (γ)
Narsai (46) (γ)	Mihrshabur (50)
Tataq (47) (γ)	Peroz (51)
Shabur (ed. G. Herman)	

Devos suggests that several of these were written by a certain monk, Abgar, who is mentioned in the *Ten Martyrs* text (45) (These are marked by the symbol γ).[29] Geoffrey Herman, who has edited the five martyrdoms set during the reign of Yazdgard I, including the previously unpublished, fragmentary *Martyrdom of Shabur,* suggests that several of these texts, for example, in their heavy reliance on Roman terms, seem to be, if not written in, then mediated through the Roman Empire, which would challenge the use scholars have put them to as historical sources.[30] The *Martyrdom of Narsai* (46) seems to describe an actual fire temple, but most of these texts have a feel—although this depends on how they are read and is thus obviously subjective—that they could have been written anywhere: East or West, Edessa or somewhere in Persia. If, for the sake of argument, we require clear evidence that these texts were composed in the Sasanian Empire, it is plausible that some of them were Roman: Take the *Martyrdom of Jacob Intercisus* (48), arguably the most popular of the PMA, judging

29. Paul Devos, "Abgar, hagiographe perse méconnu (début du Ve siècle)," *AB* 83:3–4 (1965): 303–328. See also Lucas Van Rompay, "Abgar," in *GEDSH*, 5. Also, on these texts, see Lucas Van Rompay, "Impetuous Martyrs? The Situation of the Persian Christians in the Last Years of Yazdgard I (419–420)," in *Martyrium in Multidisciplinary Perspective. Memorial Louis Reekmans*, edited by M. Lamboigts and P. van Deun, 363–75 (Louvain: Peeters, 1995); Scott McDonough, "A Second Constantine? The Sasanian King Yazdgard in Christian History and Historiography," *JLA* 1 (2008): 127–140; and Scott J. McDonough, "A Question of Faith? Persecution and Political Centralization in the Sasanian Empire of Yazdgard II (438–457 CE)," in *Violence in Late Antiquity. Perceptions and Practices*, edited by H. A. Drake, 69–81 (Aldershot: Ashgate, 2006).

30. Geoffrey Herman, "The Last Years of Yazdgird I and the Christians," in *Jews, Christians and Zoroastrians*, 88–89. For these texts, see Geoffrey Herman, "The Passion of Shabur, Martyred in the 18th Year of Yazdgird with a Fragment of the Life of Mar Aba Catholicos," *JSS* 58 (2013): 121–130 as well as his *Persian Martyr Acts under King Yazdgird I* (Piscataway: Gorgias, 2016).

from its dissemination in numerous manuscripts and multiple translations. This text treats the slow dismemberment of the martyr's body as a mnemonic lesson in Christian piety. It takes the story of persecution and uses it as an object lesson for catechesis, and the little Sasanian reality depicted, as in others, is, frankly, cartoonish.

Another series of interconnected texts is the rather long Pethion Cycle, which I have addressed in the past as providing a good example of how Syriac Christianity often imagined the devotional life in pedagogical terms.[31] The *Martyrdoms of Adhurhormizd and Anahid* (52), *Pethion* (54), and *Yazdin* (55) describe events that purportedly took place under Yazdgard II (439–457) (They will be marked below by the symbol δ). These works offer the most proximate reflection of actual Zoroastrian learning and have long served as a source for scholars attempting to reconstruct certain Masdean ideas in this period.[32] Richard Payne claims:

> The *Martyrdom of Pethion* articulates a polemic against Zoroastrianism that addresses the Good Religion as a nexus of beliefs, rituals, and landscapes, unlike other East Syrian works, which assail a disembodied, decontextualized body of doctrines that bear little resemblance to actually existing Zoroastrianism. Its hagiographer rightly regarded cosmological doctrines as the cornerstones of the religion. In recognizing that cosmology, and in particular cosmogony, was its most important aspect, the author betrayed an understanding of the religion far deeper than that of his counterparts, who tended to rely on hagiographical models of Greco-Roman paganism.[33]

These texts specifically address cult sites in the highland region of Walashfarr, and in his analysis Payne examines the cycle as negotiating local Christian identity through an Iranian cultural attachment to the land.

31. Adam H. Becker, *Fear of God and the Beginning of Wisdom: The School of Nisibis and the Development of Scholastic Culture in Late Antique Mesopotamia* (Philadelphia: University of Pennsylvania Press, 2006), 31–34.

32. See discussion and earlier bibliography in Peter Bruns, "Antizoroastrische Polemik in den syro-persischen Märtyrerakten," in *Jews, Christians and Zoroastrians*, 47–65.

33. Payne, *State of Mixture*, 78.

The most literarily complex of the PMA are what I would call the "high Sasanian" texts from the reigns of Khosro I and Khosro II (marked below by the symbol ε). These texts include: The *History of Mar Aba* (59), the *Martyrdoms of Gregory* (*Pirangushnasp*) (60), *Yazdpaneh* (61), the fragmentary *Martyrdom of Christina* (*Yazdoy*) (62), and the *Histories of George* (*Mihramgushnasp*) (63), *Isho'sabran* (*Mahanosh*) (64), and *Qardagh* (26). These are often long, and several contain an abundance of what look like authentic details of Sasanian political, military, and social life. The *History of Mar Qardagh* belongs to this group, although its story is a projection back onto the fourth century. Two of the authors of these texts, Babai the Great (d. 628) and Isho'yahb III (d. 659), are well-known church figures of the seventh century, whereas Aba (d. 552), technically a confessor, is a relatively well-known Catholicos of the church from the mid sixth century (the *History of Sabrisho'* is comparable but not always listed with the texts by these authors).[34] It is important to note that we have manuscripts of some of the other PMA that antedate the composition of these high Sasanian texts. The significance of this will become apparent below as I address the compilations contained in these early manuscripts. For now, I point out that almost all of these later texts are attested only in East Syrian manuscripts (in what is generally a weaker manuscript tradition than that of the earlier martyrdoms). This may be because their content is more explicitly East Syrian and they sometimes provide accounts of well-known "Nestorians," such as Mar Aba (as opposed to the more obscure figures of the Christologically less charged and thus less politically fraught fourth century).

Another category of the PMA we may refer to as "late mythical" or "legendary," although such labels are problematic because applying them could imply that texts in other categories can be read as transparently historical (Such a distinction appears in Paul Devos's division of the PMA into *historiques*, *épiques,* and *romantiques*, or *romanesque*, which overtly employs European literary categories for these texts).[35] These martyrdoms (which I mark below by the symbol

34. Paul Bedjan, *Histoire de Mar-Jabalaha et trois autres Patriarches, d'un prêtre et deux laïques nestoriens* (Paris-Leipzig: Harrassowitz, 1895), 288–331.

35. Paul Devos, "Les martyrs persans à travers leurs actes syriaques," in *Atti del Convegno sul tema: La Persia e il mondo greco-romano (Roma 11–14 aprile 1965)*, Accademia Nazionale dei Lincei 363, Problemi attuali di scienza e di cultura 76, 213–225 (Rome: Accademia Nazionale dei Lincei, 1966); see summary at Jullien, "Martyrs en Perse dans l'hagiographie syro-orientale," 280–281.

ζ) include the *Martyrs of Mount Ber'ain* (2), the *Martyrdoms of Behnam and Sarah* (22), and *Gubralaha and Qazo* (4), *History of ʿAbda da-Mshiḥa* (43), the *Memra on Bassus and Susanna* (42), and the *History of Pinḥas* (41).[36] They often describe the miraculous conversion to Christianity of young people of royal or elite descent, and their subsequent punishment by their families.[37] Several are related to specific cult sites, even if the texts themselves had wide distribution later. They are all very late or post-Sasanian, and they seem to be, if not playing with the genre, to have inherited certain set figures, motifs, and terms that they use to mark events as belonging to Sasanian times. There are *mobeds* (Zoroastrian priests) who persecute, and the heroes often reject their upbringing in magianism (*māgošutā*), but the evidence for actual Sasanian culture and society is thin. Both the *Martyrs of Mount Ber'ain* (2), which was written in the seventh century, and the *History of Behnam and Sarah* (22) are exemplars of this type of act.

The latter of these two texts, which is Medieval, is associated with the local martyr cult in a monastic center near Mosul, a site destroyed by the so-called Islamic State in 2015.[38] It is set in a fantastical past: Behnam and Sarah, the children of the ancient Assyrian king Sennacherib (d. 681 BCE), are persecuted by their father because they reject their Zoroastrian heritage. The *Martyrdom of Gubralaha and Qazo* (4) raises, among other things, the problem of the first person voice employed in some of these texts: The story is clearly not true, and yet the narrator describes himself as a witness to some of the events.[39] The *History of ʿAbda da-Mshiḥa* (43), in fact, even begins

36. *Tahmazgard* (56) could be included among these texts, but it is an anomaly in the larger collection: The only narrative about him is a thirteenth-century poem by Gewargis Warda, who also wrote on Jacob Intercisus, Heinrich Hilgenfeld, *Ausgewählte Gesänge des Giwargis Wards von Arbel* (Leipzig: Harrassowitz, 1904), poems 8 and 9 (pp. 37–40 and 40–44; translation: 74–79 and 80–86).

37. See also the distinction of "Acta Legendaria" after the section on "Martyres Persiae" in Ortiz de Urbina, *Patrologia Syriaca*, 2nd ed. (Rome: Pont. Institutum Orientalium Studiorum, 1965), 194–198. On child martyrs in Syriac tradition, see Cornelia B. Horn, "Children as Pilgrims and the Cult of Holy Children in the Early Syriac Tradition: The Cases of Theodoret of Cyrrhus and the Child-Martyrs Behnām, Sarah, and Cyriacus," *ARAM* 19 (2007): 439–462.

38. Jeanne-Nicole Mellon Saint-Laurent and Kyle Smith, *The History of Mar Behnam and Sarah* (Piscataway: Gorgias, 2017).

39. E.g., "Now God bears witness as do his Christ and the Holy Spirit that anything our eyes have seen and our ears have heard we have written down, while we were in severe oppression from the religion (*lit.* fear) of the Magi and in constant vigil, fasting, and daily prayer, ... We have informed Christ that our eyes have seen ..." (Bedjan, *Acta martyrum et sanctorum*, 4.162).

with a reference to the time when "magianism" was dominant, and thus provides more explicit acknowledgement of its post-conquest date of composition.[40] In the introduction to their new critical edition of the two recensions of the text, Butts and Gross demonstrate how an anti-Jewish legend attested in Latin and Greek sources was grafted onto a cult site in the Sinjar region and then reframed as a Persian Martyr Act.[41]

The metrical homily (*mēmrā*) on *Bassus and Susanna* (42), which is a very late poetical text, is linked to a monastery near Apamea which was in epistolary correspondence with Jacob of Serugh.[42] This work seems to be a *West Syrian* Persian Martyr Act written after Sasanian times and outside of any post-Sasanian context. The *History of Pinḥas* (41) is late and associated with Mar Awgen and his disciples.[43] Pinḥas was a saint shared between West and East Syrians, and yet the text is only extant in a West Syrian manuscript from 1199 CE and in an Arabic translation in a manuscript that was originally East Syrian but was brought to Jerusalem in the early 17th century. It now belongs to the Greek Patriarchate in Jerusalem.[44]

Some of the PMA were apparently produced in a Roman imperial context. The *History of Mar Ma'in* (37), which has links to the Sinjar region, seems to be from the western side of the border, whereas the related *Heroic Deeds of Zebina and His Companions* (3) and the *Martyrdom of Shabur of Niqator, Isaac of Karka d-Beth Slokh, and their Companions* (5), though about Beth Slokh (Kirkuk), seem to be from Edessa. The *Martyrdom of Shabur* was in turn a source for the *History of Karka d-Beth Slokh* (53), a text from the Sasanian Empire.[45]

40. Bedjan, *Acta martyrum et sanctorum*, 1.173. Aaron Michael Butts and Simcha Gross, *The History of the "Slave of Christ": From Jewish Child to Christian Martyr* (Piscataway: Gorgias, 2016).

41. Butts and Gross, *The History of the "Slave of Christ"*, 1–79. See also the next essay by Simcha Gross (pp. 149–173).

42. E.g., Volker L. Menze, *Justinian and the Making of the Syrian Orthodox Church* (Oxford: Oxford University Press, 2008), 127–128.

43. Adam Carter McCollum, *The Story of Mar Pinḥas* (Piscataway: Gorgias, 2013).

44. Brit. Libr. Add. 14733, Wright, *Catalogue*, 3. 1139–1140 (Ms. 961); Greek Patriarchate, Jerusalem, ms. 17, J.-B. Chabot, "Notice sur les manuscrits syriaques conservés dans la bibliothèque du patriarcat grec orthodoxe de Jérusalem," *JA* 9.3 (1894): 110–111.

45. Muriel Debié, "Writing History as 'Histoires': The Biographical Dimension of East-Syriac Historiography," in *Writing 'True Stories': Historians and Hagiographers in the Late Antique and Medieval Near East*, edited by A. Papaconstantinou in collaboration with M. Debié and H. Kennedy, 43–75 (Leiden: Brill, 2010), 68–69.

(The possibly Edessene, or at least Western, produced works from the pre-Islamic period are marked below by the symbol η).

Space does not permit me to address a number of texts with certain striking or idiosyncratic features.[46] Some are useful local sources, such as the two Karka d-Beth Slokh works (39, 53), whereas others raise questions about the history of the patriarchs of the Church of the East, or at least how that history was imagined, such as the *Martyrdom of Miles* (40).[47] The two works on Saba (28 and 58) are interesting because the former depends partly upon the latter, but they differ so much: The former is a martyr tale set in the Sasanian Empire; the latter is much longer and the similar hero leads a long life as a holy man. The latter seems to be post-Sasanian and its hero even comes up against fictional Sadducees—very odd—who are harassing local Kurds—even more odd![48]

As I mentioned, Kyle Smith has demonstrated the fundamentally western ecclesiastical historical basis for the development of the Simeon bar Ṣabba'e texts. Geoffrey Herman has even argued that certain PMA from the West tend to be less conciliatory to the Shah.[49] He contrasts these texts with contemporary church canons which are supportive of him. The interest in exiles in some of this literature has primarily been used to extract some history of the Christian communities of the Sasanian Empire. However, it is possible that this focus on captivity reflects something else, especially if some texts are from the West: Narratives of captivity are a common romantic theme, and so for example the *Martyrdom of Candida* (1), the story of the Christian martyr queen of the third century, may just be an invention.[50] Anomalies exist in a number of the texts; for example, Zoroastrians are

46. These texts include: Captives (27); Miles (40) and Daniel and Warda (36); Barshebya (34); Candida (1); History of Beth Slokh (53); Saba (28) and Saba (58).

47. Philip Wood, *The* Chronicle of Seert: *Christian Historical Imagination in Late Antique Iraq* (Oxford: Oxford University Press, 2013), 82–87.

48. Bedjan, *Acta martyrum et sanctorum*, 2.673–675.

49. Geoffrey Herman, "'In Honor of the House of Caesar': Attitudes to the Kingdom in the Aggada of the Babylonian Talmud and Other Sasanian Sources," in Herman and Rubenstein, eds., *The Aggada of the Bavli and its Cultural World*, 103–124.

50. *Pace* Brock, who sets it apart from other fifth-century martyrdoms but suggests there may be a historical kernel in it, Sebastian P. Brock, "A Martyr at the Sasanid Court under Vahran II: Candida," *AB* 96 (1978): 167–181 (reprinted in his *Syriac Perspectives on Late Antiquity*, ch. 9).

depicted as burning the bodies of the dead in *Gubralaha and Qazo*.[51] Furthermore, I would note how uninterested in the Persian Martyrs most East Syrian texts from late antiquity and the early Islamic period are. Martyrs in the abstract appear in the school tradition, but we would not be able to infer the content of the PMA from East Syrian sources until later Medieval syntheses, such as the *Chronicle of Seert*.[52]

The appearance of some of the Persian martyrs in Western texts of the fifth century, in particular Sozomen's *Ecclesiastical History*, typically serves as a reference point for the general dating of the stories in some of the PMA. However, Sozomen's text is also an important example of the movement of these texts into the Roman Empire. He notes that, with regard to the reckoning of all the martyrs' names, the "inhabitants of Edessa ... have devoted much care to this matter."[53] One instance of this Edessene "care" for the martyrs' names may be the list of martyrs from ms. Brit. Libr. Add. 12,150, dated to 411/412 CE, which is famous for being the oldest extant dated Syriac manuscript.[54] It is often speculated that this list was brought to the Roman Empire by Marutha of Maypherqaṭ in the early fifth century. This is possible. Two things, however, are significant here. First, this

51. Bedjan, *Acta martyrum et sanctorum*, 4.143. See Herman's discussion of Roman terms in supposedly Sasanian texts in "The Last Years of Yazdgird I and the Christians," esp. 87 and 89; and also Hector Ricardo Francisco, "Corpse Exposure in the Acts of the Persian Martyrs and its Literary Models," *Hugoye* 19 (2016): 193–235, where the author argues that the theme of corpse exposure derives from Western models. Herman's earlier article relies more heavily than his later works on the PMA as a transparent historical source: Geoffrey Herman, "'Bury My Coffin Deep!' Zoroastrian Exhumation in Jewish and Christian Sources," in *Tiferet Leyisrael: Jubilee Volume in Honor of Israel Francus*, edited by Joel Roth, Menahem Schmelzer, and Yaacov Francus, 31–59 (New York: The Jewish Theological Seminary of America, 2010).

52. Barḥadbshabba's *Ecclesiastical History* is, like John of Ephesus's work for West Syrians, a history of suffering, but it ends with flight *into* the Sasanian Empire (F. Nau, *La second partie de l'histoire de Barhadbešabba 'Arbaïa*, PO 9.5 [Paris: Firmin-Didot, 1913]). Among Narsai's numerous *mēmrē*, martyrs are generally treated in the abstract, e.g., Alphonse Mingana, *Narsai doctoris syri homiliae et carmina*, I–II (Mosul, 1905), 2.46–55, but there are a few possible traces of the contents of the PMA tradition (the "mumbling of the magianism" [2.49], the command to worship the sun and the moon [2.52], and the martyrs' yielding "their necks over to the slaughter of the sword [2.53]). John of Phenek only briefly touches upon the Persian martyrs but emphasizes that persecution took place in both the West and the East and shows much more interest in Julian the Apostate (Alphonse Mingana, *Sources syriaques*, vol. 1 [Leipzig: Harrassowitz, 1908], 121 and 124 respectively).

53. Translation from *NPNF* II.14 (p. 268).

54. François Nau, *Un martyrologe et douze ménologes syriaques*, PO 10.1 (Paris: Firmin-Didot, 1915), 7–26. For an English translation, which includes the material from Dayr al-Suryān, see Brock, *History of Mar Ma'in*, 123–4. See also Sebastian P. Brock and Lucas Van Rompay, *Catalogue of the Syriac Manuscripts and Fragments in the Library of Deir al-Surian, Wadi al-Natrun (Egypt)*, OLA 227 (Louvain: Peeters, 2014), 389–392 (Fragment 27).

manuscript confirms Sozomen's claim about the interest in the Persian Martyrs in Edessa, which is further bolstered by the reference to Jacob Intercisus in the sixth-century *Chronicle of Edessa.*[55] Second, the martyrs are categorized in this manuscript by whether they were from the East or the West, which was therefore apparently a meaningful distinction. After providing a menologion (a list of saints organized according to the festal calendar) translated from Greek, the text provides the names of the saint "confessors [i.e., martyrs] who were killed in the East."[56]

Ms. Brit. Libr. Add. 12,150 was produced not long before the so-called Edessene martyr acts, and both possibly derive from the broader context in which Eusebius's influential *Martyrs of Palestine* was translated.[57] The Edessene martyr acts consist of the *Martyrdom of Habib* and the *Acts of Shmona and Gurya*, which are based on some historical events from the early fourth century, and the *Acts of Sharbel* and the *Martyrdom of Barsamya*, which purport to take place under the emperor Trajan in the early second century CE but were probably composed in the fifth century and are related to the well-known *Teaching of Addai*. These texts were part of an emerging narrative about the conversion of Edessa and contributed to the projection of orthodoxy into the city's past. Details about local non-Christian practice (both pagan and Jewish), stories of the clout of local elites, a Eusebian tale about the city (an earlier version of which may have been in circulation in Edessa before Eusebius), and the developing tradition around Julian the Apostate (d. 363) were all synthesized to Christianize the history of Edessa.[58] Sebastian Brock already pointed out a possible connection between the Edessene Martyr Acts and the PMA in his review of Wiessner's book.[59] Certain vocabulary suggests there may be an awareness of some of these Edessene texts in some of the PMA.

55. I. Guidi, *Chronica Minora I*, CSCO 1–2 (Louvain: Peeters, 1903): 6.29–30 (trans. 7.9–10) (liv).

56. The Western section ends with Nau's speculative correction: "Here ends the confessors of the West" (*šlem[w] mawdyānē d-ma'rbā*) (Nau, *Un martyrologe*, 23).

57. William Cureton, *History of the Martyrs in Palestine* (London: Williams and Norgate, 1861).

58. For work on these martyr acts, see Lutz Greisiger, "Saints populaires d'Édesse," in *L'hagiographie syriaque*, 171–200; Josef Rist, "Geschichte und Geschichten: Die Christenverfolgungen in Edessa und ihr populäres Echo in den syrischen Märtyrerakten," in *Volksglaube im antiken Christentum*, edited by Heike Grieser and Andreas Merkt, 157–75 (Darmstadt: Wissenschaftliche Buchgesellschaft, 2009).

59. Brock, "Review of G. Wiessner," 303–6.

When scholars look at the PMA, they tend to think about the Sasanian East, even while acknowledging the influence from the West. However, if it turns out that some of the PMA were composed in Edessa and that this literature has links to Edessa—and we certainly know some of it was preserved there—then the PMA, on the one hand, and the Edessene martyrdoms and those texts related to the latter, on the other, may have existed side by side with one another as different imaginative, even generic landscapes. This has significant implications for how we do history. Instead of treating our sources as direct reflections of their historical environments, we should take deeper interest in the kind of textual, imaginative landscapes they establish and how those landscapes correspond in certain ways. An increasingly Christian Edessa and an anti-Christian, Zoroastrian Persia may be two textual worlds that, as we will see when we look at the manuscripts, often share manuscripts and therefore may have helped constitute one another for their audience.[60]

Turning to the reception of the PMA, we should observe where these texts are attested in the early manuscripts, and in what kinds of compilations we find them. I would suggest that we think about our manuscript witnesses as "assemblages," that is, that we treat the PMA "codicologically." What I mean by this is something similar to what Arthur Bahr suggests when, in examining late Medieval manuscripts from London, he argues that "compilation" should be understood "not as an objective quality of either texts or objects, but rather as a mode of perceiving such forms so as to disclose an interpretably meaningful arrangement, thereby bringing into being a text/work that is more than the sum of its parts."[61] We might even "read compilationally" "disparate texts whose assemblage into a larger structure is meaningfully interpretable." This is to interpret compilations as compositions in themselves, thus understanding compilation itself as providing an interpretative approach. In such an approach compilations resemble constellations of stars: Although our ancestors constructed Orion or Ursa Major from stars that had no inherent connection

60. This is in a way comparable to how Ḥarran and Edessa are set against one another in the *Julian Romance*. See Daniel L. Schwartz, "Religious Violence and Eschatology in the *Syriac Julian Romance*," *JECS* 19 (2011): 580–581.

61. Arthur Bahr, *Fragments and Assemblages: Forming Compilations of Medieval London* (Chicago: University of Chicago Press, 2013), 3.

to one another, the constellated constructions they formed had no less meaning for them or their posterity despite their constructedness. Many of the PMA were written in different contexts from one another, and so the compilations are not instances of collective biography—a genre that includes the lives of the fathers, the stories of holy women, or John of Ephesus's *Lives of the Eastern Saints*.[62] However, the PMA were sometimes deliberately gathered together and in their reception were read collectively. To be sure, practical and material strictures also led to the production of certain compilations, but from the perspective of reader reception we can treat these compilations as coherent and meaningful.[63]

The earliest manuscripts of the PMA are from the fifth and sixth centuries, some most likely from Edessa.

FIGURE 5: Edessene and Late Antique Manuscripts

5th Century	Brit. Libr. Add. 17,204, includes *Martyrdom of Miles* (40)
5/6th Century	Brit. Libr. Add. 14,644, includes *Martyrdom of Jacob Intercisus* (48)
6th Century	Brit. Libr. Add. 12,142, includes *Martyrdom of Candida* (1)[64]
6th Century	Brit. Libr. Add. 14,654, Collection of PMA
6th or 10th Century	Vatican Syr. 160, Collection of PMA

Thus, some are from Edessa when it was becoming predominantly Syrian Orthodox and certainly less Dyophysite. (The School of the Persians, apparently a bastion of Dyophysite theology, was expelled in the late fifth century.) All of these manuscripts were eventually

62. E.g., Agnes Smith Lewis, *Select Narratives of Holy Women: From the Syro-Antiochene or Sinai Palimpsest* (London: Cambridge University Press, 1900).

63. For discussion of the difficulties of studying monastic miscellanies, see Grigory M. Kessel, "Syriac Monastic Miscellanies," in *Comparative Oriental Manuscript Studies: An Introduction*, ed. Alessandro Bausi et al., 411–414 (Hamburg: COMSt, 2015). On different hagiographical collections, including the PMA, and their function, see André Binggeli, "Les collections de vies de saints dans les manuscrits syriaques," in Binggeli, ed., *L'hagiographie syriaque*, 49–75, esp. 62–65.

64. Wright, *Catalogue*, 3.1092–109 (Ms. 944).

preserved in Egypt. Some were possibly from further east and were only brought to Egypt centuries later, for example, from Takrit, the growing Metropolitan center of the Syrian Orthodox Church.[65]

Of the PMA, ms. Brit. Libr. Add. 17,204 contains only the *Martyrdom of Miles* (40).[66] Preceding it are translations of the *Martyrdom of Paphnutius* and the *Martyrdom of Apollonius and Philemon*, both Diocletianic martyrdoms set in Egypt.[67] It is followed by translations of the *History of Mary the Egyptian* and the allegorical *Martyrdom of Sophia and Her Daughters, Sophia, Pistis, Elpis, and Agape*, which takes place in Rome.[68]

Brit. Libr. Add. 14,644 also has only one Persian Martyr Act, the *Martyrdom of Jacob Intercisus* (48), which as I mentioned, may not actually be from the East.[69]

FIGURE 6: Brit. Libr. Add. 14,644

Teaching of Addai	Julian Saba
Teaching of the Apostles	Sophia and her Daughters
Teaching of Peter	Sharbel
Discovery of Cross	Cosmas and Damianus
Judas the Jewish Convert	Man of God of Edessa
Abraham Qidunaya	
Jacob Intercisus (48)	

Many of the texts in this manuscript are connected in some way to Edessa, whereas the *Martyrdom of Jacob Intercisus* (48) explicitly claims its hero was persecuted before the "Persian king."[70] It is noteworthy that this manuscript seems to preserve two copies of the

65. Lucas Van Rompay and Andrea B. Schmidt, "Takritans in the Egyptian Desert: The Monastery of the Syrians in the Ninth Century," *JCSSS* 1 (2001): 41–60. On Takrit, see Amir Harrak, "Tagrit," in *GEDSH*, 395–396.

66. Wright, *Catalogue*, 3.1081 (Ms. 934).

67. BHO 80 (for Armenian of the former) and BHO 839.

68. BHO 684 and 1084.

69. Wright, *Catalogue*, 3.1083–1086 (Ms. 936).

70. Bedjan, *Acta martyrum et sanctorum*, 2.539, 557.

Jacob text, for it has lost some pages, and they have been replaced (or perhaps the ones that fell out were recopied because of damage). I wonder how these individual PMA were read next to these other texts within Brit. Libr. Add. 17,204 and Brit. Libr. Add. 14,644: As stories of comparable martyrdom? As evidence of Christianity's ecumenical dissemination?

Brit. Libr. Add. 14,654, which is apparently from the sixth century, is the first of our large collections of PMA.[71]

FIGURE 7: Brit. Libr. Add. 14654

ʿAqebshma (31) (β)	Eleutherius and others at Rome
Miles (40)	Lucius and others
Zebina (3) (η)	Crescens
Shabur of Niqator (5) (η)	Alexander and Theodulus at Rome
Badma (33)	Fragment of the Protonike Legend
Shahdost (13) (α)	Fragment of *Teaching of Addai*
Barḥadbshabba (23) (β)	Selections of Ephrem, including *mēmrē* on the Fear of God
Tarbo (11) (α)	
111 Men (17) (α)	

It begins with several PMA from different backgrounds, including the possibly Edessene *Martyrdom of Shabur of Niqator* (5). Then there follows translations of several martyrdoms from the Roman Empire, both Diocletianic and Hadrianic. These are implicitly from the West in their grouping. The manuscript then contains several texts that also suggest an Edessene context, such as the *Teaching of Addai*. A sixth-century reader could derive from such a manuscript a sense that Rome and Edessa have changed after Constantine but that Persia has not.

Vatican Syr. 160 offers a more explicit spatial distinction in how the texts are organized.[72]

71. Wright, *Catalogue*, 3.1081–1083 (Ms. 935).

72. J. S. Assemani and S. E. Assemani, *Biblioteca apostolica vaticana* (Reprint, Paris: Maisonneuve frères, 1926), 3.319–324.

FIGURE 8: Vatican Syr. 160

Life and Letters of Simeon the Stylite	Daniel (36)
[ACTS OF THE PERSIAN MARTYRS]	Narsai (46) (γ)
Simeon (6) (α)	Badma (33)
Tarbo (11) (α)	Jacob and Mary (20) (β)
111 Men and 9 Women (17) (α)	Thecla (25)
Barba'shmin (18) (α)	Barḥadbshabba (23) (β)
Miles (40)	'Aqebshma (31) (β)
Barshebya (34)	[LIVES OF THE WESTERN MARTYRS]

The earlier part of this manuscript, which consists of documents pertaining to Simeon the Stylite, is from the sixth century, but the portion with the PMA may be much later, perhaps the 10th century.[73] The PMA are clustered together in this manuscript, marked off as being about the "martyrs of the East," and they all relate events under Shapur II. "The History of the Martyrs in the Land of the East" (*Taš'ītā d-sāhdē d-b-ar'ā d-madnḥā*) is the title for this cluster in the manuscript.[74] After this there is a long series of martyrdoms most of which are from the Syriac translation of Eusebius's *Martyrs of Palestine*, who in this case become the "Martyrs of the West."

The manuscripts that were produced in the West, most likely in Edessa, possibly in West Syrian circles, may reflect the development of a distinctly Syrian Orthodox position and politics.[75] Furthermore, it must be remembered: These manuscripts were compiled often *before* the composition of some of the other PMA, such as those I labeled the "high Sasanian" and "legendary" (or "mythical") above.

In the Islamic period, the Persian martyrs became part of the age of the martyrs of the past, a past that is reimagined with the

73. On this manuscript, see Dina Boero, "The Context of Production of the Vatican Manuscript of the Syriac Life of Symeon the Stylite," *Hugoye* 18 (2015): 319–359.

74. Vatican Syr. 160, 80v, but see Assemani and Assemani, *Biblioteca apostolica vaticana*, 319–20 for fuller reading.

75. See, for example, the relevant discussion of the *Teaching of Addai* and the *Julian Romance* in Philip Wood, *'We have no king but Christ': Christian Political Thought in Greater Syria on the Eve of the Arab Conquest (c. 400–585)* (Oxford: Oxford University Press, 2010).

production of new collections of the PMA and the composition of a few new ones, such as *History of ʿAbda da-Mshiḥa* (43).

FIGURE 9: PMA in Egypt

9th Century	Vatican Syr. 161, Collection
936 CE	Brit. Libr. Add. 14,645, Collection
10th Century	Brit. Libr. Add. 14,665 (Palimpsest with Simeon A)[76]
1199 CE	Brit. Libr. Add. 14,733 (Behnam and Sarah [22])

This age of the martyrs, for both the East and West Syrians, is the eastern equivalent of the pre-Constantinian age of martyrs in the West. Perhaps there was a shift from the spatial horizontal understanding of martyrdom in the post-Constantinian period as something that happens still over there in Persia (or over here depending on where the author, scribe, or audience is) to a vertical temporal relation where pagan Rome and Zoroastrian Persia are both persecuting empires of the past. In general, in the post-conquest period Christians no longer composed martyr texts. There are a number of exceptions, such as the Neo-Martyrs of Cordova, or in Syriac the *Martyrdom of Cyrus of Ḥarran*, or the late *Martyrdom of John of Phanijoit* in Coptic, but most new martyr texts seem to come from the Chalcedonian community, not because they necessarily suffered particular violence but perhaps because they lost the most in status after the conquest.[77] However, these issues require further examination.

The various fifth- and sixth-century manuscripts of the PMA were eventually brought to Egypt to the community centered around Dayr

76. Wright, *Catalogue*, 3.1151 (Ms. 981).

77. Jessica A. Coope, *The Martyrs of Cordoba: Community and Family Conflict in an Age of Mass Conversion* (Lincoln: University of Nebraska, 1995); Amir Harrak, "Piecing Together the Fragmentary Account of the Martyrdom of Cyrus of Ḥarrān," *AB* 121:2 (2003): 297–328; Jason R. Zaborowski, *The Coptic Martyrdom of John of Phanijōit: Assimilation and Conversion to Islam in Thirteenth-Century Egypt* (Leiden: Brill, 2005); Jack Tannous, "L'hagiographie syro-occidentale à la période islamique," in Binggeli, ed., *L'hagiographie syriaque*, 225–245. For a treatment of the Neo-Martyrs as a broader phenomenon, see Christian Sahner, "Old Martyrs, New Martyrs, and the Coming of Islam: Writing Hagiography after the Conquests," in *Cultures in Motion: Studies in the Medieval and Early Modern Periods*, edited by Adam Izdebski and Damian Jasiński, 89–112 (Krakow: Jagiellonian University Press, 2014).

al-Suryān, the "Monastery of the Syrians," which depended on the lay Syrian Orthodox community in Fustat (Old Cairo).[78] The Egyptian preservation of these manuscripts raises a standard problem in the scholarly inquiry into the transmission of early Syriac material: The West Syrian transmission consists of much older manuscripts, and many of them passed through Egypt. Furthermore, the West Syrian transmission of the PMA reflects another instance of the frequent reception of East Syrian texts by West Syrians.[79] A similar reception of East Syrian monastic authors occurred.[80] Furthermore, we find the reworking of East Syrian texts by West Syrians, for example, in Moses bar Kepha's creation of his own *cause* literature after the East Syrian school texts of the sixth and seventh century.[81] It is noteworthy that here again we find Takrit as an important locus in this transmission, for Moses was from nearby.

Now that we have an excellent catalog of the library at the Syrian monastery, and as work on post-conquest Coptic Christianity progresses, we may begin to think more deeply about the relationship between West Syrians and Copts in Egypt.[82] Within this context the Persian Martyr Acts described a doubly distant world: events that took place centuries ago and in the East, that is, Persia.

---

78. Sebastian P. Brock, "Abbot Mushe of Nisibis, Collector of Syriac Manuscripts," in *Gli studi orientalistici in Ambrosiana nella cornice del IV centenario, 1609–2009: primo dies academicus, 8–10 novembre 2010*, Orientalia Ambrosiana 1, edited by Carmela Baffioni, Rosa Bianca Finazzi, Anna Passoni Dell'Acqua, and Emidio Vergani, 15–32 (Rome: Bulzoni / Milan: Biblioteca Ambrosiana, 2012).

79. Note the list of "Eastern saints" cited as from a "Nestorian" source in ms. Vatican 37 (201r), a late West Syrian manuscript brought from Mesopotamia to Rome by Andrea Scandar (d.1748). Assemani and Assemani, *Biblioteca apostolica vaticana*, 2.273–274 (244–274 for the manuscript as a whole).

80. Grigory M. Kessel, "A Manuscript Tradition of Dadīšōʿ Qaṭrāyā's Work 'On Stillness' (*'al šelyā*) in the Syrian Orthodox Milieu," in *Geschichte, Theologie und Kultur des syrischen Christentums: Beiträge zum 7. Deutschen Syrologie-Symposium in Göttingen, Dezember 2011*, Göttinger Orientforschungen: Reihe 1, Syriaca 46, edited by Martin Tamcke and Sven Grebenstein, 103–122 (Wiesbaden: Harrassowitz, 2014).

81. James F. Coakley, "The Explanations of the Feasts of Moše bar Kepha," in *SymSyr* IV, 403–410. On the intellectual rapprochement in the later period, see Lucas Van Rompay, "La littérature exégétique syriaque et le rapprochement des traditions syrienne-occidentale et syrienne-orientale," *PdO* 20 (1995): 221–235. For an example of later reception of East-Syrian exegesis into the Miaphysite churches, see Aaron Michael Butts, "Embellished with Gold: The Ethiopic Reception of Syriac Biblical Exegesis," *OC* 97 (2013/2014): 147–149.

82. Brock and Van Rompay, *Catalogue of the Syriac Manuscripts and Fragments in the Library of Deir al-Surian*. For martyrdom in Coptic Christianity, see, e.g., Arietta Papaconstantinou, "Historiography, Hagiography, and the Making of the Coptic 'Church of the Martyrs' in Early Islamic Egypt," *DOP* 60 (2006): 65–86.

Vatican Syr. 161 is quite like Vatican Syr. 160 as a collection with two clearly demarcated portions of Eastern and Western martyrs.[83]

FIGURE 10: Vatican Syr. 161

Panegyric on the Martyrs	Daniel and Warda (36)
Prologue of Simeon A (6) (α)	Forty Martyrs (30)
Simeon B (7) (α)	Badma (33)
Sergius and Bacchus	Captives (27)
Shahdost (13) (α)	ʿAqebshma (31) (β)
Tarbo (11) (α)	Zebina (3) (η)
111 Men (17) (α)	Shabur (5) (η)
Barbaʿshmin (18) (α)	Mihrshabur (50)
Martyrs outside court (38) (α)	VARIOUS WESTERN MARTYRS
Miles (40)	Ishoʿsabran (64) (ε)
Barshebya (34)	

Note that the late "high Sasanian" *History of Ishoʿsabran* (64) has been tacked onto the end. The manuscript begins with a long text, often referred to as a panegyric in the secondary literature. This homily "on the glory of all the martyrs in the land of the East" (*ʿal tešboḥtā w-neṣḥānā d-sāhdē kollhon d-b-arʿā d-madnḥā*) was attributed by the Assemanis to the West Syrian Marutha of Takrit (an attribution that may not be correct but makes sense).[84] It discusses the martyrs' bones and their power, but it also has a broader exhortation on sin and redemption and provides consolation for suffering. It specifically refers to the "Church of the East" and prays that the "crown of the East" be kind.[85] It even quotes God's statement at Zachariah 8:7: "I will save my people from (*men*) the East," but changes the text to "in (*b*) the East."[86]

Another large medieval collection is ms. Brit. Libr. Add. 14,645, a manuscript dated to 936 CE.[87]

83. Assemani and Assemani, *Biblioteca apostolica vaticana*, 3.324–8.

84. Vatican Syr. 161, 18v; Assemani and Assemani, *Biblioteca apostolica vaticana*, 3.324.

85. Bedjan, *Acta martyrum et sanctorum*, 2.104, 91.

86. Bedjan, *Acta martyrum et sanctorum*, 2.117.

87. Wright, *Catalogue*, 3.1111–1116 (Ms. 952).

FIGURE 11: Brit. Libr. Add. 14,645

Acts of Thomas
Acts of Matthew and Andrew
Narrative of Dionysius the Areopagite
Image of the Messiah made by the chief priests of the Jews at Tiberias
Simeon the Holy Fool by Leontios
Miracles of Nicolaus
Massacre of Monks of Mt Sinai by Ammonius
Julian Saba
John, bishop of Alexandria
Story of a monk and his sister
Story of a man who robbed a grave
Domitius the physician
Mar Saba of the mountain
Mar Ḥannina by Jacob of Serugh
Martinianus
Life of Marutha of Takrit
History of Aḥudemmeh
Sharbel
Barsamya
Ḥabib
Simeon A (6) (α)
Tarbo (11) (α)
Paphnutius and his disciples
Theopompus and others
Procopius at Caesarea
Sophia and her Daughters
Tarachus, Probus, and Andronicus
Lucian and Marcian
Ammonius and others
Charisius and others
Acacius at Byzantium
Barshebya (34)
Shahdost (13) (α)
Barbaʿshmin (18) (α)
Ḥnanya of Arbela (19) (β)
Forty Martyrs (30)
Stratonice and Seleucus at Cyzicus
Mamas
Babylas
Eugenia, Claudia, and others in Egypt
John the Little of Scetis

This West-Syrian collection was produced at Dayr al-Suryān in Egypt. The fragmentary table of contents demonstrates that the manuscript once contained even more texts than it now does. The PMA are clustered in this carefully produced volume, but they are not completely set off as they are in others.

There are other medieval manuscripts from Egypt containing individual martyrdoms (Brit. Libr. Add. 14,735 of the 12/13th century, which contains the *History of Behnam and Sarah* [22] and Brit. Libr.

Add. 17,267 of the 13th century, which contains this same work as well as fragments of a second recension of the *Martyrdom of ʿAbda da-Mshiḥa* [43]).[88] One massive collection is Brit. Libr. Add. 12,174, which is dated to October 1196.[89]

FIGURE 12: Brit. Libr. Add. 12,174

1–50 Saints Lives and Egyptian Monastic Lives
Mamas and others
Christopher and others
Placidus and family
ʿAbda da-Mshiḥa (43) (ζ)
Theodore
Stratonice and Seleucus at Cyznicus
Babylas and others
Onesimus
Tur Berʾain (2) (ζ)
Simeon B (7) (α)
Pusai (8) (α)
Martha (9) (α)
Shahdost (13) (α)
Tarbo (11) (α)
111 men (65) (α)
Pethion (54) (δ)
Maʾin (37) (η)
Praepositus Romulus and others
Cosmas and Damianus
Behnam (22) (ζ)
Jacob the Egyptian
Leontius
Ṭalya
Probus, Tarachus, and Andronicus
4 Macc
Thecla
Virgin of Caesarea
History of the Death of the Blessed Mother of God

This manuscript was written at the Monastery of Mar Barṣawma outside of Melitene (Malatya), a center of learning associated with Michael the Great and the so-called Syriac Renaissance.[90] Michael the Great subscribes (via the scribe) to the manuscript in its colophon. The first life in it is, in fact, that of Mar Barṣawma, the great fifth-century monastic founder and advocate of the Miaphysite cause. The PMA are scattered

88. Wright, *Catalogue*, 3. 1148 (Ms. 969) and 3.1146 (Ms. 964). The second recension was edited and translated by Butts and Gross (*The History of the "Slave of Christ"*).

89. Wright, *Catalogue*, 3.1123–1139 (Ms. 960). This is the manuscript used in the *Martyrs of Mount Berʾain* edition of Sebastian Brock and Paul Dilley.

90. Ernest Honigmann, *Le couvent de Barsaumā et le patriarcat Jacobite d'Antioche et de Syrie* (Louvain: L. Durbecq, 1954). The scribe was in fact from the nearby Monastery of Abu Galib (p. 80).

in the latter part of this beautifully produced volume with the various Simeon-related texts (α) clustered together. Another compendious collection of lives similar to Brit. Libr. Add. 12,174 is in mss. Damascus, Syriac Orthodox Patriarchate 12/17 and 12/18, which were originally one manuscript compiled in the late twelfth century, also in connection with Michael the Great's project of collecting.[91]

Another important compilation, one that is our only source in some cases of certain PMA, is Brit. Libr. 7,200.[92]

FIGURE 13: Brit. Libr. 7,200

Febronia	Narsai (46) (γ)
Trypho	Jacob the Notary (49) (γ)
George (63) (ε)	Behnam (22) (ζ)
Saba (58)	Cyprian and Justina
Saba (28)	Ignatius of Antioch
Dadu (35)	Shabur (ed. Herman)
Miles (40)	Peroz (51)
Yazdpaneh (61) (ε)	ʿAbda (44)
Gregory (60) (ε)	Material from the History of Mar Aba (59)
History of Beth Slokh (53)	

This manuscript was brought to London by Claudius James Rich in the early nineteenth century. He acquired it in Ottoman Iraq, most likely from Chaldeans. It has been dated to the twelfth or thirteenth century.[93] It is possible this manuscript was an intentional collection of PMA. Judging from the numeration of its folios, it was originally much longer. There are notes from a certain Sulayman in it. On the margin of one page it reads: "Go and read the story of Mar Gregory the Martyr. Behold, it was written after this one. And pray for Sulayman who gathered them."[94] That Sulayman "gathered" (*kanneš*) the texts may refer to his putting together of the quires,

91. Most recently, see Butts and Gross, *The History of the "Slave of Christ,"* 12–15.

92. F. Rosen and J. Forshall, *Catalogus codicum manuscriptorum orientalium qui in Museo Britannico asservantur* (London: British Museum, 1838), 92–93 (Ms. 59); Jullien, *Histoire* (édition), xxii–xxxi.

93. Wright, *Catalogue*, 3.1207.

94. Jullien, *Histoire* (édition), xxii.

but it could also mean that he is the one who put these various martyrdoms together in one collection.

Another manuscript which is of clearly East Syrian provenance and contains, or rather contained, PMA that never crossed over into the West Syrian tradition is Diyarbakir 96, which was originally held in the Mar Pethion Church in Diyarbakir.[95]

FIGURE 14: Diyarbakir 96

Panegyric on the Martyrs
Prologue to Simeon A (6) (α)
Simeon B (7) (α)
Pusai (8) (α)
Martha (9) (α)
Tarbo (11) (α)
Shahdost (13) (α)
Barbaʿshmin (18) (α)
Great Slaughter (10) (α)
111 Men (17) (α)
40 Martyrs (30)
Badma (33)
Captives (27)
Narsai (15)
John of Arbela (14) (β)
Abraham (16) (β)
Ḥnanya (19) (β)
Jacob and Mary (20) (β)
Thecla (25)
Martyrs of Beth Slokh (39)
Barḥadbshabba (23) (β)
Aitallaha and Hophsai (24) (β)
Jacob and Azad (29) (β)
Gubarlaha and Qazo (4) (ζ)
Baday (32)
ʿAqebshma (31) (β)
Zebina (3) (η)
Shabur (5) (η)
Martyrs of Gilan (21)
Qardagh (26) (ε)
Miles (40)
Barshebya (34)
Daniel and Warda (36)
"The end of the acts of the holy martyrs martyred under Shapur King of the Persians."
Gregory (60) (ε)
Yazdpaneh (61) (ε)
History of Beth Slokh (53)
Narsai (46) (γ)
Tataq (47) (γ)
10 Martyrs (45) (γ)
Jacob the Notary (49) (γ)
Jacob Intercisus (48)
Pethion, Adurhormizd and Anahid (δ)
On Himyarite Martyrs from Bar Sahde Baboi (57)
Mar Aba (59) (ε)
Letter of Mar Aba
History of Sabrishoʿ
George (63) (ε)
Christina (62) (ε)

95. Jullien, *Histoire* (édition), xv–xvi.

I use the word "contained" because this manuscript was lost in 1915 at the time of the execution of Addai Scher, whose catalog entry remains for it.[96] Scher dates the manuscript to the eleventh or twelfth century (whereas elsewhere it has been dated to the seventh or eighth).[97] Note the clustering we find in this manuscript, which begins with the introductory so-called panegyric and contains almost only PMA. Some of its texts may have been faux eastern, such as the *Heroic Deeds of Zebina and His Companions* (3) and *Martyrdom of Shabur of Niqator* (5). Scher notes that between the *Martyrdom of Daniel and Warda* (36) and the *Martyrdom of Gregory* (60) the manuscript states: "The end of the acts of the holy martyrs martyred under Shapur King of the Persians."[98] The compilation therefore had a chronological structure. Fortunately, a copy of this lost manuscript was made in 1882 for J. B. Abbeloos. This is now in Berlin (after its removal from Marburg).[99]

Aside from the Medieval Egyptian reception of the PMA and the large later collections, we also have from late antiquity and the Islamic period translations of the PMA into several languages. There are several Greek versions, in some cases with a number of recensions. The main edited collection from 1905 has not been sufficiently incorporated into how we read the PMA, nor has there been any work on the reception of these texts into Greek hagiography.[100] It seems that the idea of Persia as an exotic land where Christians were persecuted took on a life of its own in the Byzantine tradition.[101]

96. Addai Scher, "Notice sur les manuscrits syriaques et arabes conserves à l'archevêché chaldéen de Diarbékir," *JA* 10.10 (1907): 398–401. On Scher, see Adam H. Becker, "Mar Addai Scher and the Recovery of East Syrian Scholastic Culture," in *Griechische Wissenschaft und Philosophie bei den Ostsyrern: Zum Gedenken an Mār Addai Scher (1867–1915)* edited by Matthias Perkams and Alexander Schilling, 13–28 (Berlin: De Gruyter, 2020).

97. Jullien, *Histoire* (édition), xv.

98. Scher, "Notice sur les manuscrits syriaques," 400: "Fin des actes des saints martyrs martyrisés sous Sapour, roi des Perses."

99. Ms. Berlin or. Oct. 1256–7 (Julius Assfalg, *Syrische Handschriften*, Verzeichnis der Orientalischen Handschriften in Deutschland 5 [Wiesbaden: Franz Steiner, 1963], 53–59); Jullien, *Histoire* (édition), xvii–xxii.

100. H. Delehaye, *Les versions grecques des martyrs persans sous Sapor II*, PO 2.4 (Paris: Firmin-Didot, 1907). On Persian martyrs in Greek hagiography, see Marina Detoraki, "Greek *Passions* of the Martyrs in Byzantium," in *The Ashgate Research Companion to Byzantine Hagiography*, vol. II. *Genres and Contexts*, edited by Stephanos Efthymiadis, 61–101 (Farnham: Ashgate, 2014), 73–74.

101. Xavier Lequeux, "La Passion grecque (BHG 2245) inédite de Mamelchta, mystérieuse martyre en Perse," *AB* 131 (2013): 268–275.

Some of the PMA that were translated are no longer extant in Syriac. For example, the Greek *Life of Golindouch* is a reworking by Eustratius of Constantinople in the late sixth century of a lost work by Stephen of Hierapolis (Mabbug).[102] The Syriac is lost, but there is also a version of this text in Georgian. That someone from Mabbug was composing PMA is itself striking: This is not in Persia. Moreover, the author seems to be Miaphysite.

There are several translations of PMA extant in Armenian and Georgian, and these are not always close translations.[103] We even have what seem to be imitations of the PMA, such as the *Martyrdom of Makhoz-Yazdbozhid*, which resembles one of the PMA but was probably not written in Syriac.[104] From further afield there are also the Soghdian translations: What did these stories mean in Central Asia in such a different context and how do they fit into the broader Soghdian archive?[105] Furthermore, some PMA had an active reception into Arabic, such as the *Martyrdom of Behnam and Sarah* (22) and the *Martyrdom of Jacob Intercisus* (48). Finally, with regard to the reception of the PMA there are also later works that employ material from them. Philip Wood's book on the *Chronicle of Seert* begins to address the incorporation of some of the PMA into this medieval Arabic work.[106] Some of the heroes of the PMA were celebrated at a number of regional cult sites and continued to receive literary attention: Behnam and Sarah are associated with several sites in the Mosul region, and there are metrical homilies about them falsely attributed to Jacob of Serugh and Ephrem (The former, rather long compositions are also attributed to

102. Paul Peeters, "Sainte *Golindouch*, martyre perse († 13 juillet 591)," *AB* 62 (1944): 74–125; G. *Garitte*, "La passion géorgienne de sainte *Golindouch*," *AB* 74 (1956): 405–440.

103. M. van Esbroeck, "Abraham le confesseur (Ve s.), traducteur des passions des martyrs perses: À propos d'un livre recent," *AB* 95 (1977): 169–179; Louis Gray, "Two Armenian Passions from the Sasanian Period," *AB* 67 (1949): 361–376; Paul Peeters, "Une passion arménienne des ss. Abdas, Hormisdas, Šâhîn (suenes) et Benjamin," *AB* 28 (1909): 399–415. The so-called panegyric, mentioned above, was translated into Armenian (BHO 707). Several Armenian versions of the PMA were published in Վարք եւ վկայաբանութիւնք սրբոց. Հատընտիր քաղեալք ի ճառընտրաց [Lives and Martydoms of the Saints: Collected Selections from Collections of Sermons] (Venice, 1874).

104. BHO 433. See the translation of the "Acts of S. Hiztibouzit" in F. C. Conybeare, *The Apology and Acts of Apollonius and Other Monuments of Early Christianity* (New York: Macmillan, 1894), 257–271.

105. For the Pethion (43) text, see Nicholas Sims-Williams, *The Christian Soghdian Manuscript C2* (Berlin: Akademie, 1985), 31–68.

106. Wood, *The* Chronicle of Seert.

West Syrian Patriarch Behnam Ḥedlaya [d. 1454]).[107]

One other possible manuscript of interest is Berlin Syriac 75/ Sachau 222, which contains a number of the PMA but may be of little use because it was perhaps copied from manuscripts we already have.

FIGURE 15: Berlin Syriac 75/Sachau 222

Acts of Thomas	Sergius and Bacchus
Mar Mari	Simeon (7) (α)
Image of Christ	Tarbo (11) (α)
Matthew and Andrew	40 Martyrs (30)
First Inventio Crucis	Rabban Hormizd
Stephen	Shahdost (13) (α)
Ignatius	Mar Awgen
Second Inventio Crucis	Abba Yawnan
John bar Malke	Mar Mika
Behnam (22) (ζ)	Mar Saba (58)
Qardagh (26) (ε)	Mar Daniel
History of Beth Slokh (53)	Isaiah of Aleppo
Tur Ber'ain (2) (ζ)	Himyarite Martyrs
Jacob Intercisus (48)	Mimes
Gordianus, Father of George	Placidus and others
St. George	Cyprian and Justina
Cyriacus and Julitta	Thecla (25)
Pantaleon	Juliane
Seven Sleepers	Thecla
Christopher	

This manuscript, produced at Alqosh, is dated Aug. 10, 1881. The scribe was asked to produce it by Shmuel Jamil, who was one of those scholarly-inclined Chaldeans who studied in Rome in the nineteenth century.[108] We know, for example, from a manuscript dated July 23,

107. E.g., Vatican Borgia Syriac 128; Kristian S. Heal, "Vatican Borgia Syriac 128: A New Description," cpart.byu.edu: The Center for the Preservation of Ancient Religious Texts, Brigham Young University [accessed 12/19/2016]. For the Pseudo-Ephrem text, see Mingana 409 (Alphonse Mingana, *Catalogue of the Mingana Collection of Manuscripts* [Cambridge: Heffer and Sons, 1933], 1.731).

108. On Jamil, see Rudolf Macuch, *Geschichte der spät- und neusyrischen Literatur* (Berlin: De Gruyter, 1976), 405–7. See also Becker, "Mar Addai Scher and the Recovery of East Syrian Scholastic Culture."

1882 that, not long after, Jamil had a scribe reproduce a copy—this was obviously before photocopying—of the printed edition of Assemani's *Acta Martyrum* from the patriarchal library in Mosul.[109] The colophon of Sachau 222 states that it was gathered from several places and put in chronological order.[110] So it is not clear yet what this compilation is exactly.[111] It may include hand copies of the printed texts, which began to circulate within the region in the nineteenth century.

As Wiessner notes, Stephen Assemani (1711–82), in his *Acta Sanctorum Martyrum Orientalium et Occidentalium* (1748), treats many of the PMA as "a literary unity" ("eine literarische Einheit").[112] Assemani began to order the texts chronologically, and in his editing makes an important emendation to how they are titled. He calls them: "The Martyrdoms the Holy Martyrs of the East suffered in the land of Persia" (*sahdwātā d-sāhdē qaddišē d-madnḥā b-arʿā d-Pāres ḥaš[w])* or in the Latin, "The Acts of the Eastern Martyrs who suffered in Persia" (*Acta martyrum orientalium qui in Perside passi sunt*).[113] With this, martyrdoms which had previously been located in "the East" were now more explicitly set in "Persia."

Translations of Assemani's texts appeared in the following century, one in French, another in German.[114] Later Georg Hoffmann's 1880 volume, *Auszüge aus syrischen Akten persischer Märtyrer*, demonstrates a new scholarly interest in the PMA and refers to them as "Syrisch" and now the martyrs are not from the vague "East" (*Morgenland*) of Pius Zingerle's 1836 translation, but are "Persian." More significantly, the Chaldean missionary and Orientalist, Paul Bedjan, published most of the PMA in volumes 2 and 4 of his *Acta Martyrum*

109. J.-M. Vosté, *Catalogue de la Bibliothèque Syro-Chaldéenne du Couvent de Notre-Dame des Sémences près d'Alqoš (Iraq)* (Rome: Angelicum, 1929), 86 (Codex 218).

110. E. Sachau, *Verzeichnis der syrischen Handschriften der Königlichen Bibliothek zu Berlin* (Berlin: A. Asher, 1899), 289–91 (number 75). See Brock's comments on this manuscript at Brock and Dilley, *Martyrs of Mount Ber'ain*, xxxi.

111. It also bears some resemblance in its contents to Vatican Syr. 597. See Jullien, *Histoire (édition)*, xxxii–xxxiii.

112. Wiessner, *Untersuchungen zur syrischen Literaturgeschichte*, 11.

113. Assemani, *Acta Sanctorum Martyrum*, 1.1.

114. F. Lagrange, *Les Actes des martyrs d'Orient* (Paris: Eugène Belin, 1852); Pius Zingerle, *Echte Akten heiliger Märtyrer des Morgenlandes* ["Authentic Acts of the Holy Martyrs of the East"] (2 vols.; Innsbruck: Wagner, 1836).

et Sanctorum Syriace (1891 and 1894 respectively).[115] Several other later PMA appeared in a separate volume in 1895. He also published a Neo-Aramaic translation of some of the PMA in his *Ḥayyē d-Qaddišē* (*Vies des saints*) in 1912.[116] Bedjan relied on manuscripts in European collections and published some texts that East Syrians had possibly not seen for centuries. Addai Scher published his two volume hagiographical collection in Arabic, *Šuhadāʾ al-mašriq* ("The Lives of the Saints of the East") in 1900 and 1906, further disseminating the PMA published by Bedjan.[117] Scher's work puts the texts in chronological order, as opposed to ordering them in a more traditional manner according to the calendar. For him these were also historical documents, and their chronological order mattered. To be sure, there was no East Syrian synaxarion (a collection of hagiographies arranged by the calendar), but as a Chaldean, Scher would have been aware of the Catholic calendrical system of holy days and decided not to use it.[118]

Scher had in fact read Jérôme Labourt's 1904 *Le christianisme dans l'empire perse* and therefore was aware of Labourt's historico-critical approach to these texts.[119] Both Bedjan and especially Scher were part of circles interested in developing and promulgating a national literary culture, one that could offer a vision of a reformed Christian life for lay readers. They both thus contributed to an emerging national and ethnic identity among Syriac Christians.[120] However, at the same time, within the new emphasis on literary culture at the turn of the century, texts like the PMA were generally ignored, most likely because of the bias against hagiography and authorless works in general. It is noteworthy that the anthologies at the time, both Eugène Manna's and that of the Archbishop of Canterbury's Mission, are chronological and

115. On Bedjan's life, see J.-M. Vosté, "Paul Bedjan, le lazarist persan (27. nov. 1838 – 9. juin 1920). Notes bio-bibliographiques," *OCP* 11 (1945): 45–102; Heleen L. Murre-van den Berg, "Paul Bedjan, Missionary for Life (1838–1920)," *apud* Paul Bedjan and Sebastian P. Brock, *Homilies of Mar Jacob of Sarug* (Piscataway: Gorgias, 2006), 6.339–69.

116. Jean-Maurice Fiey, "L'apport de Mgr Addaï Scher (†1915) à l'hagiographie orientale," *AB* 83 (1965): 130–131.

117. Ibid., 129–133.

118. Fiey, "L'apport de Mgr Addaï Scher," 130, 135 on Scher's treatment of historicity.

119. Jérôme Labourt, *Le christianisme dans l'empire perse, sous la dynastie sassanide (224–632)* (Paris: V. Lecoffre, 1904), 43–82.

120. Adam H. Becker, *Revival and Awakening: American Evangelical Missionaries and the Origins of Assyrian Nationalism* (Chicago: University of Chicago Press, 2015).

provide timetables.[121] Manna's inclusion of selections from the PMA in his 1901–2 anthology is the exception that confirms this authorial rule: He attributes the material to Marutha of Maypherqaṭ.[122]

We witness the new understanding of the PMA as "Persian" chronological sources for ecclesiastical and late ancient history in Oscar Braun's *Ausgewählte Akten persischer Märtyrer* (1915), which provides a translation of these "patrischer Werke."[123] I myself have commonly called these texts "The Persian Martyr Acts." They are not actually called "acts" in Syriac but variously *sahdwātā* ("martyrdoms"), *neṣḥānē* ("heroic deeds"), or *tašʿyātā* ("histories"). The series of translations with commentary of these texts that I edit for Gorgias Press is called "Persian Martyr Acts in Syriac: Text and Translation." "In Syriac" was added because George Kiraz, who as the publisher has to worry about the audience knowing what something is, was concerned that "Syriac" be in the title. The earliest attestation for the usage "Persian Martyr Acts" in English may be from Sebastian Brock (Wiessner already refers to "die sog. Syro-persischen Märtyrerakten").[124] His well-known teaching handouts, many of which have now been put online, go back into at least the 1990s, and the one on the PMA is the source for the guide he published in 2008.[125] Brock orders them according to the purported date of martyrdom and includes references to where they are published and translated (the system is borrowed from Ignatius Ortiz de Urbina's 1958 *Patrologia Syriaca*).

The PMA have also become a tool used by some Syriac Christians for reflecting upon modern events: The age of martyrs of the Church of the East, the "Great Persecution," has been used to understand the suffering of Syriac Christians in the twentieth century, and as is common to many nationalisms, past suffering has been used to lay a foundation for certain kinds of political identification. In his 1910 *History of the Syrian Nation and the Old Evangelical-Apostolic Church*

121. *Book of Crumbs* [*ktābonā d-partutē*] (Urmia: Archbishop of Canterbury's Mission, 1898); Jacques Eugène Manna, *Morceaux choisis de littérature araméenne* (Mosul: Dominican Press, 1901–1902).

122. Manna, *Morceaux choisis*, 1.120–149.

123. Kempten and Munich: Verlag der Jos Köselschen.

124. Wiessner, *Untersuchungen zur syrischen Literaturgeschichte*, 7.

125. http://www.doaks.org/research/byzantine/resources/syriac/brock [accessed 8/17/2015]. Richard W. Burgess and Raymond Mercier, "The Dates of the Martyrdom of Simeon bar Sabbaʿe and the 'Great Massacre,'" *AB* 117 (1999): 9–66 uses the expression "Persian Martyr Acts," but they thank Brock.

of the East, a book suggesting that Arameans, Chaldeans, Assyrians, and Syrians are a single nation with a shared basic language, George David Malech uses the PMA to describe the history of the Church of the East.[126] In his day, many of these texts had only newly been uncovered. His son, David George Malik (a variant spelling of "Malech"), writing in Neo-Aramaic in Chicago in 1916, connected the current events of the genocide of Christians in the Middle East to this martyrological past when he wrote:

> Our patriarch, the successor of Peter,
> The Simeon of our time, the bishop,
> From the wicked and the plunderer
> Save him as from the persecutor.
>
> The throne of Saliq, pillar of truth,
> Giver of light to the sons of the East,
> By the blood of its martyrs from generation to generation
> It was a source of glory for the church of Christ.[127]

In this poem about exile and the suffering of his people, Malik describes the East Syrians, now Assyrians, as participating in a long tradition of suffering going back to the time of the Great Persecution.

My title, "*The Invention of the* Persian Martyr Acts," was intentionally vague. These texts have been invented in both senses of the word: They have been uncovered, discovered anew in different places, but also the corpus itself has been cultivated, created, and invented as a corpus over time and that invention and its function have changed. The various PMA have been local documents. They have been compiled with other texts, clustered together as "Eastern," and this East was at first imagined as contemporaneous with the Roman West, which was understood to be fostering the church in post-Constantinian times. Then later in the Middle Ages this East became temporally equivalent to the Roman past. The division between East and West that appears in these texts and in how these texts were organized functioned as

126. George David Malech, *History of the Syrian Nation and the Old Evangelical-Apostolic Church of the East: From Remote Antiquity to the Present Time* (Minneapolis: s.n., 1910). On Malech and his son David George Malik, see Becker, *Revival and Awakening*, 339–353.

127. "Lamentation and Entreaty," stanzas 46–47, translation from Becker, *Revival and Awakening*, 346.

a horizontal political boundary in space but then also as a vertical boundary in the post-conquest period. More recently the textual East has served as a tool of ethno-national difference: As the PMA have come to be used as historical documents, they have increasingly been labeled and thought of as Persian in a way that reflects Sasanian history, a kind of history that could only be done after the development of nationalism in the nineteenth century. Simultaneously, this diverse collection of texts has served as a tool for the contemporary East Syrian making of meaning. Unfortunately, the history of the Church of the East and the Syriac churches in general is one in which tales about enduring persecution remain useful.

8. The Sources of the *History of ʿAbdā damšiḥā*

The Creation of a Persian Martyr Act

❖ Simcha Gross

Introduction

The collection of texts known as the "Acts of the Persian Martyrs" or the "Persian Martyr Acts" has received increased scholarly attention in the past decade.[1] The texts in this corpus usually describe the martyrdom of Christians—often converts from Zoroastrianism—at the hands of Sasanian kings, clerics, or other officials.[2] Whereas prior scholars—such as the Bollandists—tended either to trust the historicity of these texts or to mine them for reliable historical data, recent scholarship, following the approach of scholars of Christian

* I owe special thanks, first and foremost, to Aaron M. Butts (The Catholic University of America), for his indispensable help with this paper as well as for his partnership in the larger project from which this study emerged; to Adam Becker (New York University) for reading and providing helpful feedback on an earlier draft of this paper; to Sergey Minov (Oxford University), for helpful comments and bibliography; and to Yakir Paz (Hebrew University), for his constant feedback throughout the conceptualization and writing of this paper.

1 The closest to a standard list is found in Sebastian Brock, *Acts of Mar Ma'in* (Piscataway: Gorgias Press, 2009), 77–86. There are other texts that might be included, and some that might be excluded, from this list. For the former, see Geoffrey Herman, "The Passion of Shabur, Martyred in the 18th Year of Yazdgird with a Fragment of the Life of Mar Aba Catholicos," *JSS* 58 (2013): 121–30. To be sure, the question of what to include or not to include is not an objective one. For instance, there is significant variety in the way these texts were collected in antiquity (and the present). See the contribution by Adam Becker in this volume (pp. 113–148).

2. See the helpful schema in Adam Becker, "Martyrdom, Religious Difference, and 'Fear' as a Category of Piety in the Sasanian Empire: The Case of the *Martyrdom of Gregory* and the *Martyrdom of Yazdpaneh*," *JLA* 2 (2009): 300–336.

and Jewish martyrdoms composed in the Roman Empire,[3] assumes that many of these martyrdom accounts are largely works of literature rather than of history.[4] This perspective is strengthened by the related conclusion that many—if not most—of the Persian Martyr Acts were written centuries after the purported events described in them and at times were even composed in the Roman Near East rather than in the Sasanian Empire.[5] Instead of relaying historical information, these

---

3. Tessa Rajak, "Dying for the Law: The Martyrs Portrait in Jewish-Greek Literature," in *Portraits: Biographical Representation in the Greek and Latin Literature of the Roman Empire*, edited by M. J. Edwards and Simon Swain, 39–67 (Oxford: Clarendon Press, 1997); Daniel Boyarin, *Dying for God: Martyrdom and the Making of Christianity and Judaism* (Stanford: Stanford University Press, 1999), and esp. 116 there for his oft quoted remark: "Being killed is an event. Martyrdom is a literary form, a genre." Elizabeth Castelli, *Martyrdom and Memory: Early Christian Culture Making* (New York: Columbia University Press, 2004). See also Candida Moss, *The Other Christs: Imitating Jesus in Ancient Christian Ideologies of Martyrdom* (Oxford: Oxford University Press, 2010), and the edited collection Johan Leemans, eds., *More than a Memory: The Discourse of Martyrdom and the Construction of Christian Identity in the History of Christianity* (Louvain: Peeters, 2005).

4. Sebastian Brock ("Christians in the Sasanian Empire: A Case of Divided Loyalties," in *Religion and National Identity*, edited by S. Mews, 1–19 [Oxford: Basil Blackwell, 1982]) famously argues, echoing a sentiment found in a number of martyrdoms, in particular the *History of Simeon bar Sabba'e,* that Christians in Persia were persecuted because they were viewed by the Persians as a fifth column. Cf. T. D. Barnes, "Constantine and the Christians of Persia," *JRS* 75 (1985): 126–36. Kyle Smith has critiqued this approach. See his "Constantine and Judah the Maccabee: History and Memory in the Acts of the Persian Martyrs," *JCSSS* 12 (2012): 16–33, and idem, *Constantine and the Captive Christians of Persia: Martyrdom, Politics, and Religious Identity in Late Antiquity* (Berkeley: University of California Press, 2016). For the persecution under Yazdgird I, Lucas Van Rompay ("Impetuous Martyrs? The Situation of the Persian Christians in the Last Years of Yazdgard I [419–420]," in *Martyrium in multidisciplinary Perspective. Memorial Louis Reekmans*, ed. M. Lamboigts and P. van Deun, 363–375 [Louvain: Peeters, 1995]) challenges the idea, derived from a few Persian Martyr Acts and their Western parallels, that Christians were killed because of violent attacks on magi and fire temples. More recently, Geoffrey Herman ("The Last Years of Yazdgird I and the Christians," in idem, ed., *Jews, Christians and Zoroastrians: Religious Dynamics in a Sasanian Context*, 67–90 [Piscataway: Gorgias Press, 2014]) has argued that there may never even have been a persecution under Yazdgird I. An early attempt at classifying "historical" versus "romantic" martyrdom accounts can be found in Paul Devos, "Les martyrs persans à travers leurs actes syriaques," in *Atti del Convegno sul tema: La Persia e il mondo greco-romano (Roma 11–14 aprile 1965)*, Accademia Nazionale dei Lincei 363, Problemi attuali di scienza e di cultura 76, 213–225 (Roma: Accademia Nazionale dei Lincei, 1966).

5. In terms of dating, see Brock, *Mar Ma'in*, 4–5. Smith (*The Martyrdom and History*, xx–xxiv) argues that the dates we find in the *Martyrdom* and *History* are typological and are not historically accurate. Many earlier articles sought precisely to date Simeon's martyrdom, but Smith's approach is persuasive. For the latest attempt to date the martyrdom of Simeon, see Sacha Stern, "Near Eastern Lunar Calendars in the Syriac Martyr Acts," *Le Muséon* 117 (2004): 447–72, and references there. In terms of Persian Martyr Acts composed in the Roman Near East, see Geoffrey Herman, "The Last Years of Yazdgird I and the Christians," who argues that a number of martyrdoms said to take place under the reign of Yazdgird I seem to have been composed in the Roman Near East. Brock (*Mar Ma'in*, 4–5) makes a similar argument.

works, according to these scholars, addressed issues related to identity construction, boundary maintenance, attitudes towards ruling powers, and more.[6]

The fictional nature of these texts is often proven by appealing to evidence in the martyrdoms themselves, such as anachronisms or hagiographic tropes, which underscore that the account in part or as a whole is ahistorical.[7] In the first part of this paper, I will similarly argue that the *History of ʿAbdā damšiḥā*, usually included among the Persian Martyr Acts, has no historical kernel. However, I will do this in a different way, by showing that the *History of ʿAbdā damšiḥā* is a reworking of an earlier Western source, which guarantees that the text—in its new Syriac form—is not reporting an actual historical event.

After studying the sources behind the text, in a sense taking it apart, I will piece the text back together by studying how it took its current form. Given that it is a reworking of an earlier Western source, the *History of ʿAbdā damšiḥā* allows us to see the nuts and bolts process by which the composer altered his source material to craft a "Persian Martyr Act." Through this we can better understand how the various martyrdom accounts in the Persian Martyr Acts, despite emerging in different times and places and under different conditions, nevertheless came to resemble each other. Thus, whereas elsewhere in this volume Adam Becker gives a macro-level analysis of the different ways the Persian Martyr Acts were collected in antiquity, I will make a point similar to Becker's through a micro-level analysis, focusing on how one specific Persian Martyr Act was created and crafted to resemble other Persian Martyr Acts.

The *History of ʿAbdā damšiḥā*

The *History of ʿAbdā damšiḥā*, also known as the *History of ʿAbd al-masīḥ*, is typically included as part of the Persian Martyr

6. See Joel Walker, *Narrative and Christian Heroism in Late Antique Iraq: The Legend of Mar Qardagh the Assyrian* (Berkeley: University of California Press, 2006); Adam Becker, "Martyrdom, Religious Difference, and 'Fear' as a Category of Piety in the Sasanian Empire"; Richard E. Payne, *A State of Mixture: Christians, Zoroastrians, and Iranian Political Culture in Late Antiquity* (Berkeley: University of California Press, 2015); Philip Wood, *Chronicle of Seert: Christian Historical Imagination in Late Antique Iraq* (Oxford: Oxford University Press, 2013).

7. See, for instance, Joel Walker, *Mar Qardagh*, 117–20 and Geoffrey Herman, "The Last Years of Yazdgird I."

Acts.[8] The story appears in Sebastian Brock's list of Persian Martyr Acts[9] and indeed is grouped with other Persian martyrdom accounts in the surviving Syriac manuscripts (mss. Damascus, Syriac Orthodox Patriarchate 12/18, ff. 128r–132r; Brit. Libr. Add. 12174; and Brit. Libr. Add. 17267).[10] And yet, in its content, plotline, and more, the *History of ʿAbdā damšiḥā* does not quite conform to the other texts in the corpus. As opposed to other Persian Martyr Acts, which typically involve an elite Persian or Zoroastrian who converts to Christianity and is martyred at the hands of Sasanian or high ranking Zoroastrian officials, the *History of ʿAbdā damšiḥā* features a young Jewish boy who converts to Christianity and is ultimately martyred by his own father, in private, without any of the spectacle we might expect in a martyrdom account. Persians or Zoroastrians (*bnay mgošē*), usually the main persecuting forces in the Persian Martyr Acts, appear in the narrative but only as background to the story itself. Thus, unlike most Persian Martyr Act accounts, where the chief concern is Zoroastrianism or imperial Persian rule, the chief concern in the *History of ʿAbdā damšiḥā* is Jews and Judaism. Once the Sasanian Empire and Zoroastrianism are no longer central to the narrative, the central scene of debate and public martyrdom is no longer fitting. It is replaced instead with what is, essentially, a private event: the murder of a son by his father.

As with many other martyr acts, there are clear indications that the *History of ʿAbdā damšiḥā* was composed centuries after the events

8. The Syriac text and English translation of the *History of ʿAbdā damšiḥā* in this paper are taken from Aaron Michael Butts and Simcha Gross, *The History of 'The Slave of Christ': From Jewish Child to Christian Martyr* (Piscataway: Gorgias Press, 2016), cited as "*HAdM*, page number." See there for discussion of manuscripts and recensions.

9. Brock, *Mar Maʾin*, 82 and 89–90.

10. In ms. Damascus, the *History of ʿAbdā damšiḥā* is followed by the martyrdom of Pethion, and there are Persian and Edessene martyr acts elsewhere in this manuscript. In the case of ms. Brit. Libr. Add. 17,267, a very fragmentary manuscript, the *History of ʿAbdā damšiḥā* is followed by the martyrdom of Behnam, a late Persian Martyr Act, but preceded by the martyrdoms of Leontius and Publius, who were not martyred by the Sasanians or in Persia but rather in the Roman Near East, in Syria. It seems this may be a collection of "Eastern martyrs" more generally, and not just of Persian Martyr Acts in particular. For more on ms. Brit. Libr. Add. 17,267, see William Wright, *Catalogue of Syriac Manuscripts in the British Museum* (London: British Museum, 1870–1872), 3.1146. For the ordering of Persian Martyr Acts in manuscripts, see Adam Becker's contribution to this volume (pp. 129–144). It is also worth noting that Georg Hoffman, *Auszüge aus syrischen Akten persischer Märtyrer* (Leipzig: Brockhaus, 1880) and Oskar Braun, *Ausgewählte Akten persischer Märtyrer* (Kempten and Munich: Kösel-Verlag, 1915) did not include the *History of ʿAbdā damšiḥā* among their excerpts and translations of the Persian Martyr Acts.

it describes. The martyrdom itself is said to have taken place in "the year 701 according to the reckoning of the Greeks (= 390 CE)" (*HAdM*, 88–89). However, the text begins by noting that the events described took place when "Magianism was still widespread," suggesting that it was composed after Magianism, or Zoroastrianism, was no longer as prominent, which would probably date it sometime after the Arab conquests (see below for further support of this dating).[11] There is a firm *terminus ante quem*, as several of the manuscripts of the Armenian version contain a note indicating that the Armenian was translated from Syriac in year 322 of the Armenian era (= 873 CE) at the order of Gourgēn Arcruni.[12] There is therefore a window of about two hundred years in which the *History of ʿAbdā damšiḥā* was likely composed, which postdates the purported events of the story by a number of centuries.

The Storyline

The story of the *History of ʿAbdā damšiḥā* begins with a Jewish boy, named Asher, who is a shepherd near Shigar (modern Sinjar), tending to the flocks of his father, Levi. Upon arriving at the watering station where all the shepherds in the area gather to eat, Asher feels left out because he must eat alone, as there are no other Jewish children in the area. Asher enviously watches a large group of Christian children breaking bread together and beseeches them to allow him to join them. They refuse, explaining that it is prohibited for Christians to eat with a Jew; he can only join them if he is baptized. Asher insists that they baptize him immediately rather than wait for a bishop. The Christian children agree, baptize Asher, and change his name to ʿAbdā damšiḥā, meaning "slave of Christ." Soon after this, the Christian children regale Asher with tales of the martyrdom of Babylas of Antioch and his three child companions, and Asher prays that he might also be granted the crown of martyrdom.[13] When Asher

11. On the term "Magianism," see *HAdM,* 89 fn. 6.

12. Gérard Garitte, "La passion géorgienne de saint ʿAbd al-Masīh," *Le Muséon* 79 (1966): 188 and fn. 6 there.

13. For a recent discussion of Babylas, see Christine Shephardson, *Controlling Contested Places: Late Antique Antioch and the Spatial Politics of Religious Controversy* (Berkeley: University of California Press, 2014), 58–91. He is perhaps best known from John Chrysostom's *De sancto Babyla.* For discussion and translation, see Margaret Schatkin and Paul Harkins, *Saint John Chrysostom: Apologist* (Washington: The Catholic University of America Press, 1985).

returns home, his mother learns of his baptism and tries to conceal it from Asher's zealous father, Levi. But one Friday night, when Asher's father and his guests are gathered around for Shabbat dinner, his father demands that Asher join them. Asher arrives but refuses to eat, declaring that Christians are prohibited from eating with Jews, mimicking the response the Christian children gave him at their first encounter. Asher boldly defends Christianity and is thereupon chased by his father and martyred near the very stream at which he was baptized. Eventually, his relics are translated to two martyria, one in the West and one at the site of his martyrdom near Shigar, at which miracles are performed.

The Source(s) of the *History of ʿAbdā damšiḥā*

There are several roughly contemporaneous Greek and Latin sources from the mid- to late sixth century CE that share striking similarities with the *History of ʿAbdā damšiḥā*, and the relationship between them is therefore worth considering.

Three of these texts narrate a story of a Jewish (Greek Ἑβραῖος or Ἰουδαῖος, Latin *Iudaeus*) boy, the son of a Jewish glassblower, who partakes of the Eucharist with Christian children. As a result, the boy's father attempts, unsuccessfully, to kill him in his glassblowing furnace, leading to the father's death instead. The sources are a) Gregory of Tours (d. 594), *Glory of the Martyrs* 9;[14] b) Evagrius Scholasticus (d. 590), *Ecclesiastical history* IV.36;[15] and c) a text attributed to John Moschos by Elpidio Mioni (hereafter Mioni 12, date unknown).[16] The theme of youths thrown into a furnace and surviving through divine

14. *Glory of the Martyrs*, or *Liber in gloria martyrum*, is the first book in *Gregory's Eight books of Miracles*, or *libri octo miraculorum*. The standard edition is B. Krusch and W. Levison, *Gregorii Turonesis opera*, Part 2. *Miracula et opera minora*, Scriptores Rerum Merovingicarum 1 (Hannover: Impensis Bibliopolii Hahniani, 1885; repr. 1969 with new pagination and revised index, 1988), 44. Krusch added additional manuscript data on the *Libri octo miraculorum* in an appendix in *Passiones vitaeque sanctorum aevi merovingici* (Hannover: Impensis Bibliopolii Hahniani, 1910), 707–756. English translation in Raymond Van Dam, *Glory of the Martyrs*, 2nd ed. (Liverpool: Liverpool University Press, 2004), 11–12. Gregory seems to have composed *Glory of the Martyrs* sometime around the late 580s or early 590s. See Van Dam, *Glory of the Martyrs*, xii.

15. Standard edition by J. Bidez and L. Parmentier, *Evagrius, Ecclesiastical History* (London: Methuen & Co., 1898), 185–186. English translation by Michael Whitby, *Evagrius Scholasticus, The Ecclesiastical History* (Liverpool: Liverpool University Press, 2000), 241–242.

16. E. Mioni, "Il Pratum Spirituale di Giovanni Mosco: Gli episodi inediti del cod. Marciano greco II.21," *OCP* 17 (1951): 61–94.

intervention of course comes from Daniel 3, and this comparison is made explicitly in one of the sources (Gregory).[17] While in Evagrius and Mioni 12 the story is set in Constantinople, Gregory refers only to "the East/*in Oriente*."[18] These sources are clearly products of the broad exchange of hagiography in late antiquity.[19]

These stories therefore share a number of plot components:

- a Jewish boy;
- son of a glassblower
- converting to Christianity;
- the presence of Christian children;
- the near martyrdom of the boy,
- at the hands of the boy's father,
- in the father's glassblowing oven;

17. *Sed non defuit illa misericordia, quae tres quondam Hebraeos pueros Chaldaico in camino proiectos nube rorolenta resperserat.* Of course, Daniel 3 was also utilized as a precedent in other martyrdoms. See the *Passion of Montanus and Lucius* 3.4, in Herbert Musurillo, *Acts of the Christian Martyrs* (Oxford: Clarendon Press, 1972), 214. Daniel 3 appears in some Persian Martyr Acts as well; see Van Rompay, "Impetuous Martyrs?" See also Amir Harrak, *The Acts of Mar Mari the Apostle* (Leiden: Brill, 2005), xxi—xxii. Daniel and his companions were also a prominent subject in Syriac poetry, such as in Jacob of Serugh and Narsai. Jacob, in his *Homily on Habib the Martyr*, actually points out the difficulty in using Daniel 3 as a precedent for martyrdom, precisely because the three companions survive. See William Cureton, *Ancient Syriac Documents* (London: Williams and Norgate, 1864), 86–87. Interestingly, the three companions of Daniel *do* die in some later traditions, such as in Armenian; see Michael Stone, *Armenian Apocrypha Relating to Adam and Eve* (Leiden: Brill, 1996), 155 as well as idem, "An Armenian Tradition Relating to the Death of the Three Companions of Daniel," *Le Muséon* 86 (1973): 111–23. In *The History of Cyriacus and Julitta*, the house of Ḥananiah is invoked, as is Daniel and the lion pit. See Paul Bedjan, *Acta Martyrum et Sanctorum* (Paris-Leipzig: Harrassowitz, 1892), 3.273–274. On the potential Ancient Near Eastern background to Daniel 3, see Tawny L. Holm, "The Fiery Furnace in the Book of Daniel and the Ancient Near East," *JAOS* 128 (2008): 85–104. Miraculously surviving ovens is found in many other texts, such as Cyril of Scythopolis, *Life of Sabas* 5 (edited in E. Schwartz, *Kyrillos von Skythopolis* [Leipzig: J. C. Hinrichs, 1939], with an English translation in R. M. Price, *Cyril of Scythopolis. Lives of the Monks of Palestine* [Kalamazoo: Cistercian Publications, 1991]. Similarly, John Rufus, *Plerophories* 14, has a vision in which Christ is placed in an oven for three days before being retrieved (F. Nau, *Jean Rufus, évêque de Maïouma. Plérophories*, PO 8.1 [Paris: Firmin-Didot, 1912]).

18. Though it is worth noting that Constantinople was indeed to the east of Gregory's home in Gaul.

19. For Gregory's sources and informants from around the Mediterranean, see G. Kurth, *Études franques* (Paris: H. Champion; Brussels: A. Dewit, 1919), 2.131–145 and Van Dam, *Glory of the Martyrs*, xv–xvi. Indeed, as Lucas Van Rompay pointed out to me, after the oral presentation of this paper, Gregory mentions Syrian merchants a number of times in his *History*. It is interesting to note that a Jewish glassblower converts to Christianity at the instigation of Symeon the Holy Fool. See Derek Krueger, *Symeon the Holy Fool: Leontius's Life and the Late Antique City* (Berkeley: University of California Press, 1996), 122.

- the father's death;[20]
- a reference or allusion to Daniel 3; and
- a setting in (or near) Constantinople.[21]

While these three stories share many features with the *History of ʿAbdā damšiḥā*, the most striking parallel to the *History of ʿAbdā damšiḥā* can be found in a fourth text which appears in several manuscripts that contain the *Spiritual Meadow* by John Moschos (d. 619).[22] In 1938, Theodor Nissen published fourteen short Greek stories as a supplement to Migne's edition of Moschos' *Spiritual Meadow*.[23] The eighth story in this collection, which I will hereafter refer to as "Nissen 8," contains several striking parallels to the *History of ʿAbdā damšiḥā*.[24]

20. The father is thrown in the furnace in Gregory but is executed in a different manner in the Greek versions of the story. From this John Duffy ("Passing remarks on three Byzantine texts," *Palaeoslavica* 10 [2002]: 54–64) originally concluded that the father's death in the furnace was a "Western" reworking of an original Greek tradition. However, he has since changed his mind. See John Duffy, "The Jewish Boy Legend and the 'Western Twist,'" in *Byzantine Religious Culture: Studies in Honor of Alice-Mary Talbot*, edited by D. Sullivan, E. Fisher, and S. Papaioannou, 313–322 (Leiden: Brill, 2012).

21. Parallels between these Greek and Latin texts have been noted before. Theodor Nissen drew connections between many of these sources already in his "Zu den ältesten Fassungen der Legende vom Judenknaben," *Zeitschrift für französische Sprache und Literatur* 62 (1939): 393–403. Krusch in his edition of Gregory notes the parallel to Evagrius, and he was followed by Van Dam, *Glory of the Martyrs*, 11 fn. 16, Whitby, *Evagrius Scholasticus*, 242 fn. 17, and Miri Rubin, *Gentile Tales: The Narrative Assault on Late Medieval Jews* (Philadelphia: University of Pennsylvania Press, 1999), 8–9. H. Chadwick ("John Moschos and his friend Sophronios the Sophist," *JTS* 25 [1974]: 47–49) notes general parallels between Evagrius and Mioni 12. Finally, Robert Hoyland (*Seeing Islam as Others Saw it: A Survey and Evaluation of Jewish, Christian, and Zoroastrian Writings on Early Islam* [Princeton: Darwin Press, 1997], 65–67 and notes 37–38 there) and Chadwick ("John Moschos and his friend Sophronios the Sophist," 47–49) note the parallel between Nissen 8 and Evagrius.

22. On John Moschos, see Chadwick, "John Moschos and his friend Sophronios the Sophist"; Elpidio Mioni, "Jean Moschus Moine," *Dictionnaire de Spiritualité* 7 (1973), cols. 632–640; Brenda Llewellyn Ihssen, *John Moschos'* Spiritual Meadow: *Authority and Autonomy at the End of the Antique World* (Farnham: Ashgate, 2014). There continues to be no reliable edition of the Greek text of the *Spiritual Meadow*; thus, recourse must still be made to *PG* lxxxvii (1863). A French translation is available in M.-J. Rouët de Journel, *Le pré spirituel*, SC 12 (Paris: Cerf, 1946), and an English translation is available in John Wortley, *The Spiritual Meadow* (Kalamazoo: Cistercian Publications, 1992). On its textual history, see in addition to the literature already cited Philip Pattenden, "The Text of the Pratum Spirituale," *JTS* 26 (1975): 38–54.

23. Nissen based his edition on two manuscripts, which contain other material from John Moschos: ms. Berlin Gr. 221 (= Phillipp. 1624) and ms. Vienna Hist. Gr. 42. In 1951, E. Mioni argued that both of these manuscripts are dependent on ms. Venice Marcianus Gr. II.21, though Nissen 8 does not appear in ms. Venice. For further information on this manuscript, see Pattenden, "The Text of the Pratum Spirituale," 40 and fn. 4 there.

24. Nissen, "Unbekannte Erzählungen aus dem Pratum Spirituale." The story is translated in Wortley, *The Spiritual Meadow*, 205–210.

The tale in Nissen 8 cannot, at least in its present form, be a faithful reproduction of John Moschos's original text, though it is attributed to Abba Basil, who was a monk at the New Laura where John Moschos once lived. This later date is most clearly demonstrated by the use of terms such as 'emir' (ἀμηρᾶς), which establish a *terminus post quem* for the text a few years after 638 CE, when Jerusalem was captured in the Arab conquests, and thus two decades after John Moschos' death (d. 619).[25] Indeed, it is far more likely that Nissen 8 was attached to the *Spiritual Meadow* in the manuscript tradition, which was quite a common occurrence.[26]

Nissen 8 is set not in Constantinople but in Palestine, in a town in which both Jewish and Christian children are shepherds. One day, as the Christian children sit to eat, they decide to playact the Eucharist. A Jewish youth who is shepherding the flock of his father, identified as the "chief rabbi" (ἀρχιρεμβής),[27] wishes to join them but is rebuffed because he is a Jew; a Jewish boy cannot, of course, partake in the Eucharist. But the Jewish boy agrees to convert, and what began as a playful Eucharist turns real as the Jewish boy is baptized at the hands of the Christian children. Upon returning home, the Jewish boy refuses to eat with his father and confesses that he has become a Christian. The father tries to kill the boy in a furnace in the local bathhouse, but, like the youths in Daniel 3, to whom he is explicitly

25. So already Nissen, "Unbekannte Erzählungen aus dem Pratum Spirituale," 353; Chadwick, "John Moschos and his friend Sophronios the Sophist," 43. Phil Booth, *Crisis of Empire: Doctrine and Dissent at the End of Late Antiquity* (Berkeley: University of California Press, 2013), 93 fn. 12 argues on stylistic grounds that Nissen 8 was not composed by John Moschos.

26. Booth, *Crisis of Empire*, 91 provides an explanation for the proliferation of Pseudo-Moschos texts.

27. The word ρεμβής results from the dissimilation of Hebrew or Aramaic **bb* > *mb*. See Paul Wexler, *Explorations in Judeo-Slavic Linguistics* (Leiden: Brill, 1987), 26 and fn. 93 there, as well as idem, *Three Heirs to a Judeo-Latin Legacy: Judeo-Iberio-Romance, Yiddish, and Rotwelsch* (Wiesbaden: Harrassowitz, 1988), 17–18 and fn. 18 there; Victor A. Tcherikover, Alexander Fuchs, and Menahem Stern, *Corpus Papyrorum Judaicarum*, vol. 3 (Cambridge: Harvard University Press, 1964), sec. XIII, 44. A Christian baptismal formula dated to 1027 includes the equivalent of rabbi with and without ἀρχι, each with two forms due to a vowel change: ρέμβι, ράμβι, ἀρχιρεμβίται, and ἀρχιραμβίται (J. Starr, *The Jews in the Byzantine Empire, 641–1204* [New York: B. Franklin, 1970], 175–178). These seem to represent accurately Jewish titles, as they are paired with ἀρχιφερέχεται, which may be a calque on the title *resh pirqa*, or head of assembly or session (on which, see D. Goodblatt, *Rabbinic Instruction in Sasanian Babylonia* [Leiden: Brill, 1975], 171–196). Moreover, the baptismal formula has a *scholion* explaining the titles ραβίς and ἀρχιραμβός, suggesting that they were real words with which the Christian audience might not have been familiar. This is corroborated by a twelfth-century list where these titles appear with other real ones (see A. Sharf, *Byzantine Jewry from Justinian to the Fourth Crusade* [London: Routledge, 1971], 178–179).

compared, the Jewish boy miraculously survives, and his father is, in turn, beheaded.

All of the aforementioned Greek and Latin stories share a number of elements:

- a Jewish boy;
- encounters Christian children
- converts to Christianity;
- the near martyrdom of the boy;
- at the hands of the boy's father;
- the father's death;
- A reference or allusion to Daniel 3.

However, the account in Nissen 8 is different in a number of ways from these other stories, and each of the features distinctive to Nissen 8 is also found in the *History of ʿAbdā damšiḥā*:

- The stories in Nissen 8 and the *History of ʿAbdā damšiḥā* do not take place in Constantinople but in Palestine and Shigar, respectively.
- In both Nissen 8 and the *History of ʿAbdā damšiḥā*, the Jewish and Christian youths are now shepherds tending to their fathers' flocks and meet while taking a break to eat.
- In both Nissen 8 and the *History of ʿAbdā damšiḥā*, the Jewish boy is not only in the presence of Christian youths when he becomes a Christian, but he is baptized *by* their very hands, in a kind of makeshift ritual only later confirmed to have been successful (either by a divine sign in Nissen 8, or by a divinely-guided itinerant bishop in the *History of ʿAbdā damšiḥā*).
- Only in Nissen 8 and the *History of ʿAbdā damšiḥā* does the Jewish youth refuse to eat with his father, at which point the father learns that he has become a Christian.
- Finally, in Nissen 8 the Jewish boy's father is said to be the "chief rabbi" (ἀρχιρεμβής), and similarly in the *History of ʿAbdā damšiḥā* he is said to be the "chief of the Jews" (ܪܝܫܐ ܗܘܐ ܕܝܗܘܕܝܐ). By contrast, the three Greek and Latin stories do not ascribe any significant leadership role to the boy's father.

Of course, Nissen 8 shares some elements with the Greek and Latin stories that are missing from the *History of ʿAbdā damšiḥā*, namely the father throwing his son in a furnace and the boy miraculously surviving. In the *History of ʿAbdā damšiḥā*, unlike in all of these other texts, the boy is actually martyred.

How should we treat these parallel texts? It seems fair to speculate that the first three sources—Gregory, Evagrius and Mioni 12—are working with a shared original kernel, in which the father's occupation as a glassblower perfectly explains why he later uses a furnace to try and kill his son. Nissen 8 seems to revise this earlier kernel, leading to a less symmetrical story. Nissen 8 moves the story to Palestine and changes the occupation of the father from glassblower to shepherd. Once the father's occupation is changed, Nissen 8 must find a different way to account for the furnace, which it does by adding a lengthy portion explaining the existence and relevance of a bathhouse. Finally, while in the first three stories the Christian youths and the Jewish boy partake of a Eucharist officiated by a bishop, Nissen 8 has the Christian youths perform the Eucharist themselves. The youth-led Eucharist is in line with a preoccupation found predominately in sources from the seventh century in the Eastern Mediterranean of makeshift Eucharists, oftentimes at the hands of children.[28] The appearance of this motif in Nissen 8 would therefore represent an insertion of a contemporary and local concern into an earlier story that did not share this preoccupation.

What then is the relationship between these stories and the *History of ʿAbdā damšiḥā*? Plainly, the strongest relationship is between the *History of ʿAbdā damšiḥā* and Nissen 8.[29] The stronger relationship between these texts jibes well with the chronological data, as both are clearly written post-conquest, whereas the other stories all come from the end of the sixth century.

28. Derek Krueger, "The Unbounded Body in the Age of Liturgical Reproduction," *JECS* 17 (2009): 267–279. This was already noted by George Graf, *Geschichte der christlichen arabischen Literatur* (Vatican City: Biblioteca apostolica vaticana, 1944-1952), 1.523. See Robert Hoyland, *Seeing Islam as Others Saw It*, 65–67 and fn. 37–38 where he notes the parallel between Nissen 8 and John Moschos, *Pratum Spirituale*, 96 (Wortley, *The Spiritual Meadow*, 172–174).

29. The similarity between these two texts was noted briefly by Christian Sahner, "Old Martyrs, New Martyrs, and the Coming of Islam: Writing Hagiography after the Conquests," in *Cultures in Motion: Studies in the Medieval and Early Modern Periods*, edited by Adam Izdebski and Damian Jasiński (Krakow: Jagiellonian University Press, 2014), 111 fn. 101.

Moreover, whereas Nissen 8 helps explain many of the differences we find between the *History of Abdā damšiḥā* and the three earlier stories, the reverse is not the case. In other words, whereas Nissen 8 is directly dependent on these earlier sources, the existence of Nissen 8 is crucial for understanding how the *History of ʿAbdā damšiḥā* received its current form in relation to the earlier kernel, the "missing link" in the text's evolution. To be clear, I do not mean to suggest a direct line of influence between Nissen 8 and the *History of ʿAbdā damšiḥā.* The story could have traveled Eastward in many different ways, and Nissen 8 and *History of ʿAbdā damšiḥā* may each be dependent on a common source.

Thus, the full genealogy of these sources would seem to be as follows: A basic kernel shared by Gregory, Evagrius, and Mioni 12 is reshaped in Nissen 8 and is then reshaped once more in the *History of ʿAbdā damšiḥā.*[30]

The Creation of the *History of ʿAbdā damšiḥā*

With this proposed genealogy, we can better appreciate the kinds of revision and reworking performed by the composer of the *History of ʿAbdā damšiḥā* on the source(s) he had before him. As we will see, the composer adapted his Western hagiographical source in order for it to better resemble other Persian Martyr Acts.

First, the miraculous survival of the youth in Nissen 8 and the other sources is changed in the *History of ʿAbdā damšiḥā* to martyrdom, as the Jewish boy is now indeed killed (*HAdM,* 122–125; 130–131):

> Then, Levi, his father, got up angrily and with a hard heart, took a knife in his hand from the table that was before them, and ran after him in great anger...
>
> He lowered his head onto the stone on which he was reclining, and he slew him like a lamb with the knife in his hand. He poured out his blood on that stone. While he was

30. The story of the Jewish boy was to have a very long legacy in the Medieval West, as described by Rubin, *Gentile Tales,* 7–39. On the *Judenknaben,* see the classic work by Eugen Wolter, *Der Judenknabe. 5 griechische, 14 lateinische und 8 französische texte* (Halle: M. Niemeyer, 1879) and more specifically for my purposes see Nissen, "Zu den ältesten Fassungen der Legende vom Judenknaben."

> being sprinkled with his own blood, he shouted with the flow of his own blood and said, "Christ, my Lord, I entrust my spirit into your hands" (Lk 23:46).

This point is stressed as well by the change from Daniel 3 as the precedent for divine saving in the Greek and Latin sources, to Babylas and the three youths as precedent for divinely sanctioned martyrdom (*HAdM*, 102–105).

> When some of the parents of the Christian children gathered at one of the monasteries of the holy solitary ones on the mountain for the feast of the martyr Babylas and of the three children (ܒܥܐܕܐ ܕܣܗܕܐ ܒܒܘܠܐ ܘܕܬܠܬܐ ܛܠܝ̈ܐ) who were martyred with him, they heard there the story (ܬܫܥܝܬܐ) of their heroic deeds. They went and told them in their homes, as praise to God and a panegyric of the holy martyrs. These children were telling one another the things that they had heard from their parents at that place where they would gather at the time of watering (the flock) so that, when this holy one learned these things at this place, he was even more ablaze in faith. The fire of Christ shown upon him, and he was also smoldering with love for the victories of the holy ones. He was praying that he also might be worthy of the crown of confession like this.[31]

As in many other Persian Martyr Acts, the story does not end with the martyrdom of the protagonist but instead is followed by relic hunting scenes and the establishment of martyria (*HAdM*, 136–139):[32]

> After a few days, a caravan of merchants came from the east, and it passed to the west at night on the road near the grave of the holy one. The merchants looked and saw at that place a fire burning and blazing on the grave. It was lighting up the entire

31. Perhaps the references to fire near the end of this passage is another way of alluding to the Daniel 3 story or to the previous story about the furnace. "...he was even more ablaze in faith. The fire of Christ shown upon him, and he was also smoldering with love for the victories of the holy ones."

32. See, for example, the similar scenes in Mar Pinḥas and Narsai the Ascetic. For Mar Pinhas, see now Adam McCollum, *The Story of Mar Pinhas* (Piscataway: Gorgias Press, 2013), 14–17. For Narsai, see Bedjan, *Acta martyrum et sanctorum*, 4.179–80.

> valley, so to speak, with its rays. Some of the merchants came to see that great marvel. When they arrived at the grave, they saw the stone from under which rays were coming forth like the sun. They were smelling from those rays a pleasing and sweet smell that was more agreeable than every spice. Since they were Christians from the Arab peoples in the West, they understood in their thoughts and were saying to one another, "This is a great tomb of one of the holy ones, which has not been disclosed to anyone from this land. Come, let us pillage it and take it to our land. Let us acquire from it spiritual wealth.

These basic changes—martyrdom instead of divine saving, Babylas instead of Daniel—and the addition of the establishment of martyria, effectively alter the original kernel from a story about the miraculous survival of the boy into a martyrdom.

Persian Martyr Act "Window Dressing"

The composer of the *History of ʿAbdā damšiḥā* also added a number of literary features and motifs common to other Persian Martyr Acts, as a sort of "window dressing." The story begins with a common Persian Martyr Act dating formula (*HAdM*, 88–89), in which the date, usually according to the Seleucid calendar, is given:

> In the year 701 according to the reckoning of the Greeks (= 390 CE), while Magianism (ܡܓܘܫܘܬܐ) was still triumphant (ܢܨܝܚܐ) in the land of the Persians, and Judaism was also bold in the land of the inhabitants of Shigar...

The *History of ʿAbdā damšiḥā* does not, however, date the event according to the reign of the king, since, as we have seen, the king plays no role in the story at all. What's more, the date of the martyrdom—390 CE—falls in between rather than during the reigns of Shapur II and of Yazdgird I, under whom a number of martyrdoms are said to have occurred. In fact, the *History of ʿAbdā damšiḥā* is the *only* martyrdom said to take place during the period between these kings.[33] This reinforces the point that the *History of ʿAbdā damšiḥā*

33. Brock, *Mar Maʾin*, 78–84.

is made to resemble the Persian Martyr Acts, despite not actually conforming to their underlying premise(s).

Similarly, as in other Persian Martyr Acts, magi or Zoroastrians appear in a few places in the text, but they serve no function in the larger narrative (*HAdM,* 90–91):

> A large number of children of his age would congregate there, some of whom were Christians and others of whom were magi (ܒ̈ܢܝ ܡ̈ܓܘܫܐ). Congregating there often, they would gather with each other and eat bread together, the magi and the Christians (ܒ̈ܢܝ ܡܓܘ̈ܫܐ ܘܒ̈ܢܝ ܟܪ̈ܣܛܝܢܐ), so that Asher would remain alone, because he did not have a Jewish friend to eat with him.

Later in the narrative, the story notes in passing that the magi marvel at Asher's baptism and the subsequent celebration of the Christian children (*HAdM,* 96– 97). The magi serve as set pieces but do not contribute directly to the events in the story.

The Old Testament and Judaism

Beyond the incorporation of Persian Martyr Act "window dressing," perhaps the most consistent and noticeable feature of the composition of the *History of ʿAbdā damšiḥā* is its extensive reliance upon Old Testament themes.[34] For example, the Jewish characters are given Biblical names, such as Levi and Asher, two of the sons of Jacob, who, it should be noted, were also shepherds tending their father's flock (*HAdM*, 88–91).[35]

> ...there was a Jewish man from the city of Shigar. He had possessions and a great household, and he was increasing in great wealth. His name was Levi (ܠܘܝ), and he was the chief of the Jews. He had sons, and he entrusted to each of them a flock from his possession. The youngest of them was about eleven years old more or less, and his name was Asher (ܐܫܝܪ).

34. This was a choice, as the author could have alternatively constructed the Jew from the New Testament, as Ephrem often seems to do. See Christine Shepardson, "'Exchanging Reed for Reed': Mapping Contemporary Heretics onto Biblical Jews in Ephrem's Hymns on Faith," *Hugoye* 5 (2002): 15–33.

35. See, for instance, Genesis 37:12.

The setting—a shepherd's watering station in a desert—is, of course, a familiar motif from both Genesis and Exodus.[36]

The *History of ʿAbdā damšiḥā* employs the *aqedah* in Genesis 22 as precedent for the attempted murder by another father, Abraham, of his son Isaac, a text which also served as precedent for Christ and many other martyrs (*HAdM,* 122–125; 130–131):[37]

> Then, Levi, his father, got up angrily and with a hard heart, took a knife in his hand (ܘܢܣܒ ܒܐܝܕܗ ܣܟܝܢܐ) from the table that was before them, and ran after him in great anger...
>
> He lowered his head onto the stone on which he was reclining, and he slew him (ܘܢܟܣܗ) like a lamb with the knife in his hand. He poured out his blood on that stone. While he was being sprinkled with his own blood, he shouted with the flow of his own blood (in his mouth) and said, "Christ, my Lord, I entrust my spirit into your hands." (Lk 23:46).

The composer here incorporated the language that is undeniably from the Peshiṭta to Genesis 22:10:

ܘܐܘܫܛ ܐܝܕܗ ܐܒܪܗܡ. ܘܢܣܒ ܣܟܝܢܐ ܠܡܟܣܗ (ܠܡܢܟܣܗ) ܠܒܪܗ

> And Abraham stretched forth his hand, and took the knife to slay his son.

36. For the type-scene of the encounter at the watering station in the Bible, see Robert Alter, "Biblical Type-Scenes and the Uses of Convention," *Critical Inquiry* 5 (1978): 355–68 and idem, *The Art of Biblical Narrative* (New York: Basic Books, 1981), chapter 3.

37. The *aqedah* is already invoked in 4 Macc 16:20–22 (which also invokes Daniel and his three companions). See Jan Willem van Henten and Friedrich Avemarie, *Martyrdom and Noble Death: Selected Texts from Graeco-Roman, Jewish and Christian Antiquity* (London: Routledge, 2002), 21, and Leroy Andrew Huizenga, "The Aqedah at the End of the First Century of the Common Era: *Liber Antiquitatum Biblicarum, 4 Maccabees,* Josephus' *Antiquities, 1 Clement,*" *JSP* 20 (2010): 105–133. The list of publications on the Binding of Isaac and its relationship to martyrdom is vast. For the importance of the *aqedah* in Syriac texts, see Sebastian Brock, "Genesis 22 in Syriac Tradition," in *Mélanges Dominique Barthélemy: Études bibliques offertes à l'occasion de son 60e anniversaire*, edited by Pierre Casetti, Keel Othman, and Adrian Schenker, 1-30 (Göttingen: Vandenhoeck & Ruprecht, 1981); idem, "Two Syriac Verse Homilies on the Binding of Isaac," *Le Muséon* 99 (1986): 61–129. For a brief look at a number of rabbinic and Jewish approaches to the story, see Wout van Bekkum, "The Aqedah and its Interpretation in Midrash and Piyyut," in *The Sacrifice of Isaac: The Aqedah (Genesis 22) and its Interpretations*, edited by E. Noort and E. J. Tigchelaar, 86–95 (Leiden: Brill, 2002).

Levi, like Abraham, takes (ܢܣܒ) a knife (ܣܟܝܢܐ) in order to slay (ܢܟܣ) his son.[38] The verb used for "slay" (*nks*) is noteworthy because it is usually used to refer to the slaughter of sacrifices. This word fits well in the Binding of Isaac, where Abraham is told to offer Isaac as a sacrifice (Gen. 22:2); however, it is far less commonly used to refer to killing a human, even in a martyrological context, in which the roots *qtl, kll,* and *ʾbd* are far more common. The fact that these words are unexpected in this context would have made it clear to a reader or listener that the Binding of Isaac was being invoked.

In short, unlike the Greek and Latin sources discussed above, Old Testament motifs appear extensively throughout the *History of ʿAbdā damšiḥā*. This use of the Old Testament relates to the larger invocation of Jewish practices throughout the *History of ʿAbdā damšiḥā*. I suggest that this thematization of Judaism is also modeled on a certain subset of the Persian Martyr Acts in which the gods and practices of the persecutor are repeatedly invoked and contested. Examples of the polemic against Zoroastrianism in the Persian Martyr Acts include the Pethion, Adurhormizd, and Anahid cycle, as well as the martyrdoms of Gregory, Yazdepaneh, Ishoʿsabran, and George.[39] While mockery of the persecutor's gods and practices may figure in many martyrdoms in many traditions, it is the specific way they are invoked and contested that is shared with the *History of ʿAbdā damšiḥā*, as we will now see.

In many of these martyr acts, the protagonist changes their name from a Persian to a good Christian name. Thus, both Gregory and Mar

38. The Peshiṭta here is nearly identical to the rendering (not including the expansions) of the Hebrew verse in the Targumim of Onqelos, Neofiti, Pseudo-Jonathan, and the Fragmentary Targum, all of which have the verbal root *nks* and *sakinā*.

39. Becker, "Martyrdom, Religious Difference," discusses these various martyrs. For the Pethion cycle, see Richard E. Payne, *A State of Mixture: Christians, Zoroastrians, and Iranian Political Culture in Late Antiquity* (Berkeley: University of California Press, 2015) and Adam Becker, *Fear of God and the Beginning of Wisdom: The School of Nisibis and the Development of Scholastic Culture in Late Antique Mesopotamia* (Philadelphia: University of Pennsylvania Press, 2006), 31–35. For Ishoʿsabran, see Reuven Kiperwasser, "Zoroastrian Proselytes in Rabbinic and Syriac Christian Narratives: Orality-related markers of cultural identity," *History of Religions* 51 (2012): 203–35, and more recently Reuven Kiperwasser and Serge Ruzer, "To Convert a Persian and Teach him the Holy Scriptures: A Zoroastrian Proselyte in Rabbinic and Syriac Christian Narratives," in *Jews, Christians and Zoroastrians: Religious Dynamics in a Sasanian Context*, edited by Geoffrey Herman, 101–138 (Piscataway: Gorgias, 2014). For George, see G. J. Reinink, "Babai the Great's Life of George and the Propagation of Doctrine in the Late Sassanian Empire," in *Portraits of Spiritual Authority: Religious Power in Early Christianity, Byzantium & the Christian Orient*, edited by J. W. Drijvers and J. W. Watt, 171–193 (Leiden: Brill, 1999).

Saba are formerly known as Pīr-Gušnasp (ܦܝܪ ܓܘܫܢܣܦ);[40] Yeshuʿsabran is formerly known as Mahānūš (ܡܗܐܢܘܫ);[41] Giwargis (George) is formerly known as Mīhr-Mah-Gušnasp (ܡܗܪܡܗܓܘܫܢܣܦ);[42] and Christina is formerly known as Yazdoi (ܝܙܕܘܝ).[43] In the *History of ʿAbdā damšiḥā*, ʿAbdā damšiḥā is originally known by the Biblical name Asher (ܐܫܝܪ), but upon baptism he is renamed "slave of Christ." By contrast, in the Greek and Latin sources, the Jewish boy does not undergo a name-change.[44]

Another common feature these Persian Martyr Acts share with the *History of ʿAbdā damšiḥā* but not found in the Greek and Latin parallels is the debate or dialogue scene in which the future Christian martyr extols the virtues of Christianity while mocking the king, or his messengers, and a caricature of their gods and practices. However,

40. For Gregory, see Florence Jullien, *Histoire de Mār Abba, catholicos de l'Orient. Martyres de Mār Grigor, général en chef du roi Khusro Ier et de Mār Yazd-panāh, juge et gouverneur*, CSCO 658–659 (Louvain: Peeters, 2015), 1.49–50 (Syriac), 2.50 (French). Though see the variant Pirāngušnasp (ܦܝܪܢܓܘܫܢܣܦ) in P. Gignoux, F. Julien, and C. Julien, *Noms propres syriaques d'origine iranienne* (Vienna: Verlag der Österreichischen Akademie der Wissenschaften, 2009), 115 (#344). For Mar Saba, see Bedjan, *Acta martyrum et sanctorum*, 4.228–229, and Gignoux et al., *Noms propres syriaques d'origne iranienne*, 116 (#346).

41. J. B. Chabot, "Histoire de Jésus-Sabran écrite par Jésus-Yab d'Adiabène," *Nouvelles archives des missions scientifiqueset littéraires* 7 (1897): 509, and Gignoux et al., *Noms propres syriaques d'origne iranienne*, 94 (#265).

42. Paul Bedjan, *Histoire de Mar-Jabalaha et trois autres Patriarches, d'un prêtre et deux laïques nestoriens* (Paris-Leipzig: Harrassowitz, 1895), 436, and Gignoux et al., *Noms propres syriaques d'origne iranienne*, 101 (#298).

43. Bedjan, *Acta martyrum et sanctorum*, 4. 201, and Gignoux et al., *Noms propres syriaques d'origne iranienne*, 145 (#454b). See also the case of Anastasius, a Persian soldier originally named Magundat, discussed below.

44. There are other similar texts that should be noted here as well. In the Georgian *Martyrdom and Passion of St. Eustace of Mtskheta*, the protagonist is a Magian who is baptized before being martyred and undergoes a change of name from Gvirobandak to Eustace. For an English translation of this text, see David Marshall Lang, *Lives and Legends of the Georgian Saints* (Crestwood: St. Vladimir's Seminary Press, 1976), 95–99, and discussion in Dan Shapira, "Gleanings on Jews of Greater Iran under the Sasanians (According to the Oldest Armenian and Georgian Texts)," *Iran and the Caucasus* 12 (2008): 202–209. See Sebastian Brock, "An Early Syriac Life of Maximus the Confessor," *AB* 91 (1973): 299–346, reprinted in *Syriac Perspectives on Late Antiquity* (London: Variorum Reprints, 1984), ch. 12, pages 303 and 314, where the name of the Persian slave-girl *šndh* (ܫܢܕܗ) is changed to Mary. In contrast, there are other Persian Martyr Acts that thematize the teaching of the magi and the conversion of Zoroastrians without changing the Persian names of the protaganists. See, for instance, the Martyrs of Mount Berʾain, named Adarparwa (ܐܕܪܦܪܘܐ), Mihrnarse (ܡܗܪܢܪܣܐ), and Mahdukht(y) (ܡܗܕܘܟܬܝ). Interestingly, however, the Greek and Latin versions of the Martyrdom of Theonilla, who was killed during the Diocletian persecutions, does not mention a name change, whereas in the Syriac version she responds to a request for her name by saying: "My real name? I am Christiana. My common, regular name? I am called Theonilla." See Adam McCollum, "The Martyrdom of Theonilla in Syriac," *AB* 128 (2010): 319 (Syr.) and 323 (Eng.).

given that the story was about Jews and Judaism, rather than about Zoroastrianism, the composer of the *History of ʿAbdā damšiḥā* added a long dialogue scene that pitted the Jewish boy against his father and guests. In some Persian Martyr Acts, the stakes of the debate are raised by the fact that they take place on the persecutor's festival. For instance, Gregory, here still called by his former name Pirangušnasp, confronts his former colleagues on the Zoroastrian festival of Frawardīgān.

> When the festival (ܥܐܕܐ) that the magi perform for Satan arrived, which they call Frawardīgān (ܦܪܘܪܕܝܓܢܐ), before the day itself arrived for Pirangušnasp to perform that festival for Satan...[45]

Similarly, in the *History of ʿAbdā damšiḥā,* the debate occurs on the Sabbath, which is called a "great festival" (*HAdM,* 116–117):

> That day was Friday (ܥܪܘܒܬܐ), and when Saturday (ܫܒܬܐ)[46] was approaching, the Jews had a great festival (ܥܐܕܐ ܪܒܐ), during which his father prepared a great banquet. He invited and called his friends to supper, and he sent his servants after all of his sons. He commanded that before Saturday (ܫܒܬܐ) come they should gather apart from their flocks.

Thus, in both accounts, those participating in the festival attempt to convince their former coreligionist(s) to join them in feasting, but to no avail.[47]

---

45. Syriac from Bedjan, *Histoire de Mar-Jabalaha*, 351. English translation from Becker, "Martyrdom, Religious Difference," 327.

46. The word here is *šabbtā*, which could also be translated 'Sabbath'.

47. *HAdM*, 118–119; Bedjan, *Histoire de Mar-Jabalaha*, 355. *HAdM*, in turn, seems to have influenced the "festival scene" in the much later *Mēmrā on Basus and Susanna* (Bedjan, *Acta martyrum et sanctorum*, 4.484.13–485.15). Here too, Basus confronts his father, a Zoroastrian priest and Sasanian official, on a festival day (ܥܐܕܐ ܗܘ ܪܒܐ, found in Bedjan, *Acta martyrum et sanctorum*, 4.485.1), at which time Basus makes clear, in words strikingly similar to those in the *History of ʿAbdā damšiḥā,* that he has indeed become a Christian. There is in fact much in common between the *Mēmrā on Basus and Susanna* and the *History of ʿAbdā damšiḥā.* Both involve children who are killed by their father for converting to Christianity (from Judaism or from Zoroastrianism), and similar miracles are performed following the death of the martyrs. These similarities were already noted in J.-M. Fiey (ed. L. Conrad), *Saints syriaques*, Studies in Late Antiquity and Early Islam 6 (Princeton: Darwin Press,

These are just some of the additions made by the composer of the *History of ʿAbdā damšiḥā* that would have resonated with a specific subset of Persian Martyr Acts that target the persecutor's religion.[48]

The Case of the Golden Earring

Another motif of the *History of ʿAbdā damšiḥā* that may similarly mimic the Persian Martyr Acts that target Zoroastrianism is the most central element in the text: the prohibition against free Jewish males wearing earrings. This is the central narrative device in the larger narrative of ʿAbdā damšiḥā becoming a slave of Christ. As we have just seen, following his conversion to Christianity and baptism, Asher receives the new name ʿAbda damšiḥā, "slave of Christ." The imagery of slavery does not, however, end with this new name. Immediately following this episode, the text narrates the story of the newly baptized ʿAbdā damšiḥā receiving a golden earring. This earring serves as a further marker of his newfound identity as a slave of Christ. As ʿAbdā damšiḥā's mother explains, only slaves wear earrings (*HAdM,* 98):

> Have you not heard in the law of Moses that he commands thus, "The ear of a male in Israel shall not be pierced, aside from a slave who wishes to stay with his master forever"?

All of the characters in the story—Jews and non-Jews—are apparently aware of this law: The Christian children convince ʿAbdā damšiḥā to pierce his ear in order to mark him as a Christian and thus prevent him from returning to Judaism; ʿAbdā damšiḥā's mother hides him

2004), 52. The opening formula in both stories are also nearly identical. The opening formula of Basus reads: "In the year 699 (= 387–388 CE) of the Macedonians (= Greeks), and the 76th year of the reign of Shapur, the great king of Persia, when Magianism (ܡܓܘܫܘܬܐ) and idolatry were still greatly flourishing (ܢܨܝܚܐ)..." (Bedjan, *Acta martyrum et sanctorum*, 4.474). As in the *History of ʿAbdā damšiḥā,* this introduction mentions the time when Magianism (ܡܓܘܫܘܬܐ) was still flourishing (ܢܨܝܚܐ).

48. To be sure, some features of the Greek and Latin sources already resonated with features of this subset of the Persian Martyr Acts, for example, the refusal to eat with one's parents after joining a different group, for which see Adam Becker, "Beyond the Spatial and Temporal *Limes*: Questioning the 'Parting of the Ways' Outside the Roman Empire," in *The Ways That Never Parted*, edited by A. H. Becker and A. Y. Reed, 373–392 (Tübingen: Mohr Siebeck, 2003), 380 and fn. 31. In this paper, however, I am interested in features unique to the *History of ʿAbdā damšiḥā* that parallel this subset of Persian Martyr Acts.

from his father because of the earring; and it is the earring that ultimately signals to his father and the Jewish guests at the Shabbat feast that something has happened to the boy. The *History of ʿAbdā damšiḥā* thus presents this prohibition against piercing the ear of a male Jew as an established and widely-known Jewish law.

A prohibition against piercing the ear of a male from Israel is not found in the Bible. Despite this, the statement by ʿAbdā damšiḥā's mother—along with the ensuing narrative—appears to be based on the slavery law found in Ex 21:5–6, which reads as follows:

> ܘܐܢ ܢܐܡܪ ܥܒܕܐ ܕܪܚܡ ܐܢܐ ܠܡܪܝ. ܘܠܐܢܬܬܝ ܘܠܒܢܝ. ܠܐ ܢܦܩ ܐܢܐ
> ܒܪ ܚܐܪܐ. ܢܩܪܒܝܘܗܝ ܡܪܗ ܠܘܬ ܕܝܢܐ. ܘܢܩܪܒܝܘܗܝ ܠܘܬ ܬܪܥܐ ܐܘ ܠܘܬ
> ܐܣܟܘܦܬܐ. ܘܢܢܩܘܒ ܡܪܗ ܐܕܢܗ ܒܡܪܨܥܐ. ܘܢܗܘܐ ܠܗ ܥܒܕ ܦܠܚ ܠܥܠܡ.

> If a slave says, "I love my master, my wife, and my sons; I will not go out as a free person," then his master should bring him to the judges and bring him to the door or the threshold, and his master should pierce his ear with an awl, and then he will be to him a slave forever.[49]

ʿAbdā damšiḥā invokes language very similar to this verse when explaining to his mother that he has become a Christian (*HAdM,* 100):

> I am a Christian from this moment and ʿAbdā damšiḥā (i.e., a slave of Christ) forever (ܠܥܠܡ). I am his slave (ܥܒܕ ܦܠܚ), because I have come to love him (ܪܚܡܬܗ), and he is my Lord (ܡܪܝ) and my God. The law of Moses does not reproach slaves who love their masters (ܪ̈ܚܡܝ ܡܪ̈ܘܗܘܢ), but rather commands that the ear of such a slave be pierced at the door of the house of his master's household (ܕܬܬܢܩܒ ܐܕܢܗ ܕܥܒܕܐ ܗܘ ܒܬܪܥܐ ܕܕܪܬܐ ܕܒܝܬ ܡܪܗ), and then he will become a slave forever (ܘܢܗܘܐ ܥܒܕ ܦܠܚ ܠܥܠܡ). This is what happened to me today, for at the door (ܬܪܥܐ) of baptism I pierced my own ear (ܢܩܒܬ ܠܐܕܢܐ ܕܝܠܝ) and confirmed the covenant with my Lord (ܡܪܝ) forever (ܠܥܠܡ).

49. A similar law is found in Dt 15:16–17: 'If he (i.e., a slave) says to you, "I will not go out from you, because I have loved you and your household, and it is better for me (to be) with you," then take an awl and pierce his ear at (or: to) the door, and he will be for you a slave forever'.

The *History of ʿAbdā damšiḥā* thus bases this supposedly Jewish prohibition against piercing the ear of a male on Ex 21:5–6.

Elsewhere, Butts and I have argued at length that there is no evidence for a prohibition against free Jewish males wearing earrings in the Jewish literary sources available to us and that the *History of ʿAbdā damšiḥā* has constructed this prohibition based on the Bible.[50] In fact, all of the Jewish laws and practices mentioned in the *History of ʿAbdā damšiḥā* are derived directly from the Bible. The prohibition against piercing the ear of a male is no exception: The *History of ʿAbdā damšiḥā* has constructed this prohibition based on the Bible; it does not depict real Jewish practice.[51]

This would fit quite well with the composer's aim to structure the *History of ʿAbdā damšiḥā* around the Persian Martyr Acts that thematize Zoroastrianism. While some of these texts do have direct knowledge of Zoroastrian practice and belief, others veer quite far from actual Zoroastrianism. Indeed, one of the problems of earlier scholarship was its mistaken reliance on the Persian Martyr Acts as evidence for actual Zoroastrian belief, much as earlier scholars mistakenly relied on heresiologists for accurate depictions of real communities and their beliefs.[52] Here too, the composer seems to have invented a Jewish practice for the sake of polemicizing and creating a strong contrast between Christians who commit themselves to servitude of Christ, and Jews who refuse the markings of servitude.[53]

50. *HAdM*, 53–62.

51. This fits quite well within larger trends in Syriac literature. A. P. Hayman ("The Image of the Jew in the Syriac Anti-Jewish Polemical Literature," in "*To See Ourselves as Others See Us*": *Christians, Jews, and "Others" in Late Antiquity*, edited by J. Neusner and S. Frerichs, 423-441 [Chico: Scholars Press, 1985], 440–441), argues that this is true of all Syriac Christian writers; they show no awareness of post-biblical Jewish practice and instead conceive of and discuss the Jew as if they were still adhering exclusively to the Old Testament and the religion of that period. This position has been challenged many times. For a theoretical reflection on this issue, as well as how it relates to scholarship of Jews in Christian texts from the Roman Empire, see Adam Becker, "Anti-Judaism and Care of the Poor in Aphrahat's *Demonstration* 20," *JECS* 10 (2002): 305–327.

52. See, for example, A. V. Williams, "Zoroastrians and Christians in Sasanian Iran," *Bulletin of the John Rylands University Library of Manchester* 78 (1996): 37–54.

53. Based, undoubtedly, in part on John 8:33.

Conclusions

There are three conclusions that can be drawn from the arguments offered above, from the specific to the more general. It must be kept in mind, however, that all of these conclusions are drawn from a single case study. While the conclusions do follow from the study, the scope of these conclusions beyond this one text are in need of further corroboration and support.

First, this study shows that the *History of 'Abdā damšiḥā* is a creative revision (of a creative revision) of a tradition circulating in the West in late antiquity. The *History of 'Abdā damšiḥā* is a very clear example of how martyrdom accounts can be constructed out of whole cloth, or in this case, out of earlier sources.

As a result, the *History of 'Abdā damšiḥā* can be added to the growing list of clearly late and fictional Persian Martyr Acts, though it is arguably the most obviously fictional and constructed account.[54] This conclusion is supported by the lack of awareness of any recognizable Jewish law, practice, ritual or behavior that is not already found in the Hebrew Bible—in other words, by the "imaginary Jew" constructed in the text. Moreover, the story reveals no in-depth knowledge of the area around Shigar, where the story is supposed to have taken place. Therefore, like other Persian Martyr Acts that have proven to be unreliable sources for information about Zoroastrianism, the *History of 'Abdā damšiḥā* should not be viewed as a source of reliable information about Jews, Christians and Zoroastrians at Shigar, or about the local Jewish practices.[55]

Second, this study shows that the composer of the *History of 'Abdā damšiḥā* was already aware of a genre of what we now might call the Persian Martyr Acts. This is clear from the 'window dressing' and other motifs that the composer added to his earlier source(s).

54. Indeed, 'Abdā damšiḥā's name does not appear in the list of Persian martyrs found in Brit. Libr. Add. 12,150, dated 411 CE. For the text, see F. Nau, *Martyrologes et ménologes orientaux, I–XIII. Un martyrologie et douze ménologes syriaques édités et traduits*, PO 10.1 (Paris: Firmin-Didot, 1912), 7–26; and English translation, with additions from Deir al-Surian Fragment 27, is available in Brock, *History of the Holy Mar Ma'in*, 123–25.

55. Contra those scholars who have treated it historically. See J.-M. Fiey, "Encore 'Abdulmasīḥ de Singār," *Le Muséon* 77 (1964): 215–23; Michael Morony, *Iraq After the Muslim Conquest* (Princeton: Princeton University Press, 1984), 182, 307, 314; Sacha Stern, "Near Eastern Lunar Calendars in the Syriac Martyr Acts," 468. Fiey is especially interesting because he believes the date for these events in the text (390 CE) is wrong but then proffers an alternative date for when they did in fact occur.

The use of Persian Martyr Act window dressing is, in fact, not limited to the *History of ʿAbdā damšiḥā*. For instance, the story of Anastasius, a Persian soldier formerly named Magundat, whose account is clearly composed in Greek and outside of the Sasanian Empire, incorporates many of the same stock features of the Persian Martyr Acts as the *History of ʿAbdā damšiḥā*, such as a Persian convert who changes his name. The story goes so far as to have Anastasius killed by the *shah*.[56] Another example is a story that appears in the Babylonian Talmud which, I argue elsewhere, invokes certain features and *topoi* from the Persian Martyr Acts but ultimately subverts them.[57] This genre was not only known but also popular and presented an important model that, for various reasons, was appealing to imitate and adapt in the creation of new works.

Lastly, this study has implications for the transmission of information and knowledge in late antiquity. There is plenty of evidence for the transmission of material from West to East, and between Greek and Syriac, in late antiquity, as well as a wealth of secondary literature on the subject. This literature mainly focuses on translations of patristic, philosophical, and scientific texts.[58] In part, this may be due to the growing wealth of studies about the importance of Syriac Christians and Syriac as an intermediary language in the translation of major scientific, philosophical, and other works into Arabic.[59] To a lesser

56. Text and commentary in B. Flusin, *Saint Anastase le Perse et l'histoire de la Palestine au début du VIIe siècle* (Paris: Centre national de la recherche scientifique, 1992).

57. Simcha Gross, "A Persian Anti-Martyr Act: The Death of Rabbah Bar Naḥmani," *The Aggada of the Bavli and its Cultural World*, edited by G. Herman and J. L. Rubenstein, 211-242 (Providence: Brown University Press, 2018).

58. The bibliography is vast. For a helpful overview, see Sebastian Brock, "Charting the Hellenization of a Literary Culture: The Case of Syriac," in *New Horizons in Graeco-Arabic Studies*, edited by D. Gutas, S. Schmidtke, and A. Treiger, 98–124 (Leiden: Brill, 2015), as well as Adam McCollum's contribution to the same volume, "Greek Literature in the Christian East: Translations into Syriac, Georgian and Armenian," 15–66, both of which include an extensive bibliography. For the migration of historiography and historical details between Arabic, Syriac, and Greek during the early Abbasid period, see Robert Hoyland, "Arabic, Syriac and Greek Historiography in the First Abbasid Century: An Inquiry into Inter-Cultural Traffic," *ARAM* 3 (1991): 211–33, as well as idem, *Theophilus of Edessa's Chronicle and the Circulation of Historical Knowledge in Late Antiquity and Early Islam* (Liverpool: Liverpool University Press, 2011).

59. See Dimitri Gutas, *Greek Thought, Arabic Culture: The Graeco-Arabic Translation Movement in Baghdad and Early ʿAbbāsid Society (2nd–4th/8th–10th C.)* (London: Routledge, 1998), and idem, "Graeco-Arabic Studies from Amable Jourdain through Franz Rosenthal to the Future," in Gutas et al., eds., *New Horizons in Graeco-Arabic Studies*, 1–14 and the other contributions in that volume.

extent, this work has extended to the translation of hagiography.[60] These texts are often studied for translation style and technique.[61] However, the *History of ʿAbdā damšiḥā* shows that it would be productive to expand our focus beyond explicit translations of texts in order to see how information not only traveled eastward but was also reworked and reshaped in the process, without explicitly identifying—indeed, in this case erasing—its original source and context.[62]

60. The Persian Martyr Acts are themselves a useful example of texts traveling from East to West. See Kyle Smith, *The Martyrdom and History of Blessed Simeon Bar Ṣabbaʿe* (Piscataway: Gorgias Press, 2014). Sebastian Brock, "Saints in Syriac: A Little-Tapped Resource," *JECS* 16 (2008): 181–196, is the best article to date on the way hagiography traveled between West and East and how that relates in particular to hagiography in Syriac. The example of the "Sleepers of Ephesus" is a useful parallel to the *History of ʿAbdā damšiḥā*, as it also appears in Gregory of Tours (indeed, in his *Glory of the Martyrs*!), Jacob of Serugh, and the Qurʾān. See Brock, "Saints in Syriac," 183–184. Indeed, Gregory in this case even says he heard this story from "a certain Syrian." Brock also makes the important point that hagiography traveled in both directions.

61. See, for instance, Sebastian Brock "Aspects of Translation Technique in Antiquity," *GRBS* 20 (1979): 69–87 and his "Towards a History of Syriac Translation Technique," *SymSyr* III, 1-14, but also the nuanced comments in McCollum, "Greek Literature in the Christian East," 29–31.

62. The changes made to the Syriac translation of the *Life of Antony* in order to 'nativize' it to the Syriac tradition is somewhat analogous to the case of the *History of ʿAbdā damšiḥā,* with the major difference being that the *Life of Antony* is still marked as a Western source, whereas the *History of ʿAbdā damšiḥā* nativizes the tradition entirely. See Fumihiko Takeda, "The Syriac Version of the Life of Antony: A Meeting Point of Egyptian Monasticism with Native Syriac Asceticism," in *SymSyr* VII, 185–94; idem, "Monastic Theology of the Syriac Version of the Life of Antony," *SP* 35 (2001): 148–157. In the first piece, Takeda insists on calling the Syriac *Life of Antony* a "separate creation" from the original, but this may be an overstatement. A similar effort to "Christianize" Greek literature in Syriac translation is studied by Alberto Rigolio, "From 'Sacrifice to the Gods' to the 'Fear of God': Omissions, Additions and Changes in the Syriac Translations of Plutarch, Lucian and Themistius," *SP* 64 (2013): 133–143. See also the recent work by Richard Kalmin, *Migrating Tales: The Talmud's Narratives and Their Historical Context* (Berkeley: University of California Press, 2014), on the transmission and integration of Western sources—Jewish and not Jewish—by the Babylonian rabbis.

9. Stories, Saints, and Sanctity between Christianity and Islam

The Conversion of Najrān to Christianity in the Sīra *of Muhammad*

❖ Reyhan Durmaz

At the beginning of Ibn Isḥāq's (d. 768) *al-Sīra al-Nabawiyya* (*the Life of Muhammad*) there is a story of an ascetic man, Fīmyūn, who converted a community of tree-worshipping pagans of south Arabia to Christianity.[1] Yet, Ibn Isḥāq also claims that Fīmyūn was a Muslim, and that one of his young followers became the *imām* of the community. This conversion narrative appears to be a shortened version of a late-fifth-century Syriac hagiographical text, *The History of the Great Deeds of Bishop Paul of Qenṭos and Priest John of Edessa,* transformed to serve Ibn Isḥāq's larger narrative of a world history from Adam to Muhammad.[2] How are we to understand the transformation of the holy narrative that Ibn Isḥāq here presents? What

* I am deeply grateful to Susan Ashbrook Harvey, Nancy Khalek, Volker Menze, and Suleiman Mourad for their extensive comments and guidance.

1. Alfred Guillaume, *The Life of Muhammad: Translation of Isḥāq's Sīrat Rasūl Allāh* (Oxford: Oxford University Press, 1955); *al-Sīra al-Nabawiyya* (al-Qāhira: s.n., 1996). The *Sīra* has been preserved in an edition of it by Ibn Hishām (d. 833). All citations in the present article are from this translation. However, I have occasionally emended for clarification.

2. The Syriac text is edited with an English translation in Hans Arneson, Emanuel Fiano, Christine Luckritz Marquis, and Kyle Smith, *The History of the Great Deeds of Bishop Paul of Qenṭos and Priest John of Edessa* (Piscataway: Gorgias Press, 2010); for a summary, see François Nau, "Hagiographie syriaque," *ROC* 15 (1910): 56–60. Guillaume transliterates the saint's name as Faymiyūn, although Fīmyūn is most probably a better transliteration, as I will demonstrate below.

were the contexts and agents enabling the transmission of a Christian story to Islam? What do the changes in the text during this transmission signify? And how does this textual phenomenon contribute to our understanding of sanctity in Islam, particularly with regard to Christian holy men? The current paper seeks answers to these questions through a close analysis of this particular story and its transmission.

Multiple overlapping genres in late antique and medieval writing fall under the two modern categories that I frequently refer to in this study, hagiography and historiography.[3] In the Syriac Christian tradition a text narrating the life, deeds, and sayings of a holy person is usually called a *taš'ītā* (story), the equivalent of *diegesis* in Greek hagiography.[4] A writing that has the primary concern of chronologically documenting past events is called *maktbānut zabnē* (chronography, lit. "writing of times"). While the latter term roughly corresponds to *ta'rīkh* in the Islamic tradition, the former is difficult to find a counterpart for. The closest terms would be *qiṣaṣ* (tales), *sīra* (life-story), *tarjama* (biographical note), or simply a *khabar* (report, pl. *akhbār*). Yet, *maghāzī* (exploitations), *ḥikāyāt* (stories), *tadhkīra* (remembrance), *manāqib* (marvelous accomplishments), and *faḍā'il* (excellences) are also among the prominent genres in the Islamic tradition in which writings about sayings and deeds of holy men and women appear.[5] As for stories transmitted particularly from Christian and Jewish traditions, they are mostly found in the *qiṣaṣ al-anbiyā* (stories of prophets) and *isrā'īliyyāt* literature (narratives from Jewish and Christian traditions), although hagiographical narratives are by no means restricted to these two.[6]

In this complex matrix of nomenclature, genres, forms, and contents, it is difficult to identify and trace texts across different religious

3. Stephanos Efthymiadis, "Introduction," in *The Ashgate Research Companion to Byzantine Hagiography*, vol. 1. *Periods and Places*, edited by Stephanos Efthymiadis, 1–14 (Surray and Burlington: Ashgate, 2011), 2; Chase Robinson, *Islamic Historiography* (Cambridge: Cambridge University Press, 2003), 5; Martin Hinterberger, "Byzantine Hagiography and its Literary Genres. Some Critical Observations," in *The Ashgate Research Companion to Byzantine Hagiography*, vol. 2. *Genres and Contexts*, edited by Stephanos Efthymiadis, 25–60 (Surray and Burlington: Ashgate, 2014), 29.

4. Claudia Rapp, "Storytelling as Spiritual Communication in early Greek Hagiography: The Use of *diegesis*," *JECS* 6 (1998): 431–448, especially 436–439.

5. John Renard, *Friends of God: Islamic Images of Piety, Commitment and Servanthood* (Berkeley: University of California Press, 2008), 243.

6. Tarif Khalidi, *The Muslim Jesus: Sayings and Stories in Islamic Literature* (Cambridge: Harvard University Press, 2001), 27–29; Renard, *Friends of God*, 7ff, 239–40.

traditions. The vast world of Christian hagiography, coupled with the multitude of genres in Islam, constitutes a limitless field to trace especially the transmission of extra-biblical stories. Moreover, the predominance of oral tradition and storytelling in late antiquity and beyond adds another layer of complexity to these processes. Yet, when possible, it is a rewarding scholarly endeavor, shedding light not only on the complete dossier of saints expanding across languages and religions but also on the development of the notion of sanctity in Islam vis-à-vis Christianity. The story of Fīmyūn and Ṣāliḥ's ventures in south Arabia is a short yet helpful example in this regard.

Substantial modern and ancient historiography has been dedicated to the history of Christianity in south Arabia. The accounts mostly focus on the region's role in religious, economic, and military encounters between Byzantium, Persia and the Kingdom of Axum, and on the oppression and persecution of Christians under Jewish kings in the sixth century.[7] The Syriac story I analyze here does not dwell on either of these topics. It is one of the many traditions that narrate the introduction of Christianity to the region.

Texts in their Contexts

The History of the Great Deeds of Bishop Paul of Qenṭos and Priest John of Edessa is a hagiographical composition narrating the adventures and pilgrimages of two ascetic men in the setting of the fifth-century eastern Mediterranean (though at points extending to Italy and south

7. Paul Maier, *Eusebius. The Church History: A New Translation with Commentary* (Grand Rapids: Kregel Publications, 1999), V.10; Henry Bronson Dewing, *Procopius. History of the Wars* (London: W. Heinemann; New York: Macmillan, 1914–1940), I, xvii 43–48, xix 1–7; Edward Walford, *Epitome of the Ecclesiastical History of Philostorgus* (London: Henry G. Bohn, 1855), III.4; Witold Witakowski, *Chronicle of Pseudo-Dionysius of Tel-Mahre* (Liverpool: Liverpool University Press, 1996), 51ff; R. H. Charles, *The Chronicle of John of Nikiu* (London: Williams & Norgate, 1916), 69; E. W. Brooks, *James of Edessa. The Hymns of Severus of Antioch and Others*, PO 7.5 (Paris: Firmin-Didot, 1911), 613–614; E. Carpentier, "Martyrium Sancti Arethae et Sociorum in Civitate Negran," *Acta Sanctorum* October X (1869): 721–759; Axel Moberg, *The Book of the Ḥimyarites: Fragments of a Hitherto Unknown Syriac Work* (Oxford: Oxford University Press, 1924); Irfan Shahīd, *Byzantium and the Arabs in the Fourth Century* (Washington: Dumbarton Oaks Trustees for Harvard University, 1984); J. Spencer Trimingham, *Christianity Among the Arabs in Pre-Islamic Times* (Beirut: Librarie du Liban, 1990); René Tardy, *Najrān: Chrétiens d'Arabie avant l'islam* (Beirut: Dar el-Machreq Éditeurs, 1999); Irfan Shahīd, *Martyrs of Najrān: New Documents* (Brussels: Société des Bollandistes, 1971); Marina Detoraki, *Le Martyre de Saint Aréthas et de ses compagnons*, Bibliotheca Hagiographica Graeca 166 (Paris: Association des amis du Centre d'histoire et civilization de Byzance, 2007); Sidney Griffith, *The Bible in Arabic* (Princeton: Princeton University Press, 2013), 9ff.

Arabia). The earliest manuscripts that include the story are from the sixth century, although the story itself probably was written in the fifth century.[8] Whether it was originally written in Greek or Syriac is uncertain; yet, it is likely that it circulated in both languages.[9] The text can thematically be divided into four sections: 1) Paul, a bishop in Italy, leaves his city and arrives in Edessa during the episcopacy of Rabbula (r. 411–435). While he works in this city as a day-laborer he meets Priest John, who becomes his admirer, companion, and disciple. 2) Paul and John go on a pilgrimage, during which they are kidnapped by Arabs and taken to the "land of the Himyarites," south Arabia.[10] With the help of miracles they convert the tree-worshipping Himyarites to Christianity. 3) During their return to Syria they encounter a dendrite on the way who claims to have been waiting for them. Following the demise of the dendrite, Paul and John go to Jerusalem and then arrive back at Edessa. 4) Paul goes on another journey alone; John seeks for him until he hears in one of his dreams that Paul passed away in Nisibis.

The story of Paul and John closely resembles another fifth-century hagiographical composition that is associated with the episcopacy of Rabbula, *The Man of God*.[11] Although anonymous, the Man of God was a holy man in Italy who left his hometown and came to Edessa. Also, his relationship to his servant closely resembles the one between Paul and John.[12] Within the Syriac manuscript tradition, in all of the surviving seven manuscripts dating between the sixth and thirteenth centuries, the story of the Man of God immediately precedes the story of Paul and John.[13] This makes it safe to assume that the two stories belong to the same hagiographical tradition: fifth- or sixth-century, Syriac, Edessene tradition having originated in association with the persona of Rabbula.[14] Thus, it is highly probable that in some later

8. Arneson et al., *Paul and John*, 19.

9. Arneson et al., *Paul and John*, 19–21.

10. Arneson et al., *Paul and John*, 7.

11. The Syriac of this text is edited in A. Amiaud, *La légende syriaque de saint Alexis, l'homme de Dieu* (Paris: É. Bouillon, 1889); an English translation is available in Robert Doran, *Stewards of the Poor: The Man of God, Rabbula and Hiba in Fifth-Century Edessa* (Kalamazoo: Cistercian Publications, 2006), 3–40.

12. Arneson et al., *Paul and John*, 16–17.

13. Arneson et al., *Paul and John*, 20–21.

14. Arneson et al., *Paul and John*, 16ff.

written and/or oral tradition the two stories, that of Paul and John and of the Man of God, converged and were amalgamated.

In Islamic literature an abridged version of the story of Paul and John initially appears in the *Sīra* composed by Ibn Isḥāq. One version of the *Sīra* was edited by Ibn Hishām (d. 833), which enabled the preservation of the story of Paul and John in the Islamic tradition.[15] The conversion of Najrān to Christianity is attributed to two wandering ascetics, whose names are Fīmyūn and Ṣāliḥ. Ibn Isḥāq relates that a pious and ascetic man named Fīmyūn used to live in Syria, where he met his companion Ṣāliḥ. The two men left their village in Syria, and on the way they encountered a tree-dweller, who was waiting for them. After the dendrite passed away, Fīmyūn and Ṣāliḥ were kidnapped by Arabs and taken to Najrān. By uprooting a cultic tree Fīmyūn converted the tree-worshipping pagans of Najrān to the religion of ʿĪsā ibn Maryam. After this, "misfortunes fell upon the people of Najrān." By this Ibn Isḥāq refers to the martyrs of Najrān, an episode known as *aṣḥāb al-ukhdūd* (the People of the Trench) in the Islamic tradition.[16]

Gordon Newby claims that this story in the *Sīra* was derived from the *Apophthegmata Patrum*.[17] As he demonstrates, numerous themes and topoi in the *Apophthegmata* are indeed quite similar to the ones in the story of Fīmyūn and Ṣāliḥ, such as humility, the power to heal, and being taken captive. Harry Norris argues that the romance of Yemeni history probably arose in connection with the Persian occupation of the region in the sixth century.[18] Jürgen Tubach's analysis comes closer

15. The tenth-century Muslim historian Ṭabarī (d.923) provides a slightly longer version of the story in his *Ta'rīkh al-Rusul wal-Mulūk (The History of Prophets and Kings)* on the authority of Ibn Isḥāq. This shows that the story was a part of Ibn Isḥāq's composition and not added by Ibn Hishām to the *Sīra*. C. E. Bosworth, *The History of al-Ṭabarī*, vol. 5. *The Sāsānids, the Byzantines, the Lakhmids and Yemen* (New York: State University of New York Press, 1999).

16. R. Paret, "aṣḥāb al-ukhdūd," in *EI*[2]; Thomas Sizgorich, "'Become infidels or we will throw you into the fire': The Martyrs of Najrān in Early Muslim Historiography, Hagiography and Qur'ānic Exegesis," in *Writing 'True Stories': Historians and Hagiographers in the Late Antique and Medieval Near East*, edited by Arietta Papaconstantinou, 125–148 (Turnhout: Brepols, 2010), 136ff.

17. Gordon Newby, "An Example of Coptic Literary Influence on Ibn Isḥāq's Sīrah," *JNES* 31 (1972): 22–28.

18. Harry T. Norris, "Fables and Legends in pre-Islamic and early Islamic times," in *Arabic Literature to the End of the Umayyad Period*, edited by A. F. L. Beeston et al., 374–386 (Cambridge: Cambridge University Press, 1983), 383; Suleiman Mourad, "Christians and Christianity in the Sīra of Muhammad," in *Christian-Muslim Relations. A Bibliographical History*, vol. 1. *(600-900)*, edited by David Thomas and Barbara Roggema, 57–72 (Leiden, Boston: Brill, 2009), 60 fn. 5. This footnote cites J. Ryckmans, "Le christianisme en Arabie du Sud préislamique," in *Academia Nazionale dei Lincei. Atti del convego internazionale sul tema: L'Oriente cristiano nella storia della civilità* (Rome, 1964), 441–442.

to determining the source, suggesting that *The Man of God* is the origin of the story.[19] However, the story of Fīmyūn and Ṣāliḥ is a redaction of that of *Paul and John*, for many details in the two versions are strikingly parallel to each other, as I will demonstrate in detail below. How did Ibn Isḥāq access the story of Paul and John? The answer to this question lies in the socio-political context of the seventh- and eighth-century Islamic state, the formative period of Islamic historiography, and the elite formation processes of convert families.

Ibn Isḥāq was born in Medina at the beginning of the eighth century. His grandfather, formerly a Christian, was a manumitted slave, who became a *mawlā* (client) during the early Islamic conquests in Iraq; his sons, one of whom was Isḥāq (Ibn Isḥāq's father), were transmitters of *akhbār* (reports).[20] Ibn Isḥāq is known in Islamic historiography to have collected *akhbār* mostly on the authority of transmitters in Egypt and Iraq, a great majority of which were converts, *mawlā*s, and manumitted slaves.[21] In fact, in the *Sīra* Ibn Isḥāq reports the story of Fīmyūn and Ṣāliḥ "on the authority of al-Mughīra b. Abū Labīd, a freedman of al-Akhnas." Al-Bukhārī (d. 870), one of the foremost scholars of *ḥadīth* (tradition particularly of the Prophet), mentions that al-Mughīra transmitted *ḥadīth* from Ibn Sīrīn, a renowned Medinan *ḥadīth* scholar whose father was a manumitted slave of Anas b. Mālik (d. 709), an eminent Companion and traditionist.[22] In addition to his personal connections to converts as sources of historical information, Ibn Isḥāq was also a student of al-Zuhrī (d. 742), another important *ḥadīth* scholar of the Medinan school.[23] Thus, Ibn Isḥāq's access to the story can be contextualized within this wider circle of *akhbār* transmitters and traditionists of the early eighth century,

---

19. Jürgen Tubach, "Das Anfänge des Christentums in Südarabien: Eine Christliche Legende Syrischer Herkunft in Ibn Hišām," *PdO* 18 (1993): 101–111.

20. J. M. B. Jones, "Ibn Isḥāḳ," in *EI*²; Gordon Newby, *The Making of the Last Prophet. A Reconstruction of the Earliest Biography of Muhammad* (Columbia: University of South Carolina Press, 1989), 5–8.

21. Jones, *Ibn Isḥāḳ*.

22. Al-Bukhārī, *Kitāb al-Ta'rīkh al-Kabīr* (Beirut: Dār al-Kutub al-ʿIlmīyah) *bāb mughīra* 1400; T. Fahd, "Ibn Sīrīn," in *EI*².

23. Stephen Judd, *Religious Scholars and the Umayyads. Piety-minded Supporters of the Marwānid Caliphate* (London: Routledge, 2014), 52–61. Note that Maʿmar b. Rāshid (d.770), the author of another eighth-century biography of Muhammad, was also a *mawlā* and a pupil of al-Zuhrī. Sean Anthony, *The Expeditions: An Early Biography of Muhammad* (New York: New York University Press, 2014), xix.

a considerable part of whom were previously-Christian converts and servants, or descendants of these groups.

Ibn Isḥāq was reviled by later Muslim scholars for relying on the authority of descendants of Jews and Christians. Indeed, in the *isnād* (chain of transmission) of the story of Fīmyūn and Ṣāliḥ that Ibn Isḥāq provides, Wahb b. Munabbih (d.732), an *akhbār* transmitter from south Arabia, appears as the origin of the story.[24] Wahb, presumably a first generation Muslim of Persian descent, is often praised as one of the greatest authorities on the traditions of *ahl al-kitāb* (the People of the Book).[25] He served as a judge and had access to courtly libraries, particularly in San'ā' and Egypt. Since many judges in the seventh and eighth centuries were former Christian converts, Wahb's scholarship brings us back to the social milieu of converts, and their importance in transmission of stories between Christianity and Islam. Wahb is also reported to have had access to monastic libraries, where he possibly gathered another great part of his knowledge on pre-Islamic religions and traditions.[26]

Did Wahb read his sources in Arabic, or did he translate them from other languages? Christians in the Near East used the Arabic language in literary production and liturgy starting from late-seventh century, as Sidney Griffith extensively argues.[27] A great corpus of biblical material was translated and circulating in Arabic in written or oral form by that time, and monastic libraries had voluminous works written in Arabic. In the monasteries in Palestine, for instance, numerous saints' lives were written in the eighth century in Arabic.[28] Therefore, it is possible that the story of Paul and John was also translated into Arabic, and that Wahb had access to the text. Nevertheless, instead of merely searching for an *Urtext* of the story in Arabic literature, one should also take into consideration

24. Guillaume, *Life of Muhammad*, 14; Raif Georges Khoury, "Wahb b. Munabbih," in *EI*[2].

25. Raif Georges Khoury, *Wahb B. Munabbih*, pt. 1 (Wiesbaden: Harrassowitz, 1972), 189, 222ff; Tarif Khalidi, *Arabic Historical Thought in the Classical Period* (Cambridge: Cambridge University Press, 1994), 7.

26. Griffith, *Bible in Arabic*, 177.

27. Ibid., 90, 111, 127, 129.

28. Sidney Griffith, "The monks of Palestine and the growth of Christian literature in Arabic," *Muslim World* 78 (1988): 6, 15; Mark Swanson, "Arabic Hagiography," in *The Ashgate Research Companion to Byzantine Hagiography*, vol. 1. *Periods and Places,* edited by Stephanos Efthymiadis, 345–368 (Surray and Burlington: Ashgate, 2011), 345.

oral tradition and the widespread practice of storytelling in the late antique eastern Mediterranean.[29] It is possible that Wahb heard a short version of the story, and both wrote it down *and* narrated it to other people.

The *akhbār* that Wahb transmitted from non-Islamic sources have been preserved in the Muslim tradition through his pupils, family members, and later historians. Whether Wahb encountered the shortened version of the story of Paul and John in Arabic in a written Christian source, or he translated and shortened it, is difficult to ascertain due to the dearth of Wahb's surviving writings.[30] Moreover, we do not know to what extent Wahb wrote the texts that are attributed to him in later Islamic scholarship, or whether he mostly recited his "books," as opposed to writing them down. Nevertheless, with regard to his agency one might comfortably assume that even though there was already a shortened version of the story in Christian sources, Wahb (or his immediate successors in transmitting the story) gave the story an Islamic character.

Wahb and Ibn Isḥāq were Muslims of Jewish and Christian descent, respectively; and al-Mughīra was a freedman. They were members of a significant community in early Islam, namely, converts and manumitted slaves who, regardless of their former occupations, fulfilled important social roles and came to occupy high administrative and judiciary offices under Islam.[31] The *akhbār* that they transmitted constituted the foundation stones of *ḥadīth* (tradition) and *fiqh* (jurisprudence), taking great part in the formation of Islamic discourse

---

29. André Binggeli, "Collections of Edifying Stories," in *The Ashgate Research Companion to Byzantine Hagiography*, vol. 2. *Genres and Contexts*, edited by Stephanos Efthymiadis, 143–160 (Surray and Burlington: Ashgate, 2014), 143ff; Rapp, "Storytelling as Spiritual Communication," 435, 440.

30. Particularly, the loss of *Kitāb al-mulūk al-mutawwaja min Ḥimyar wa-akhbārihim wa-qiṣāṣihim wa-qubūrihim wa-ash'ārihim*, in which Wahb is reported to have narrated the legendary foundation history and possibly the *faḍā'il* of his native land, is unfortunate, for it would have been a key document to shed light on the transmission of stories between Christian, Jewish, and Muslim traditions (Khoury, *Wahb*, 205–206). Nevertheless, extensive quotations from Wahb have been preserved in Ibn Hishām's *Kitāb al-tījān fī mulūk Ḥimyar.*

31. Trimingham, *Christianity among the Arabs*, 260; Wadi Haddad, "Continuity and Change in Religious Adherence: Ninth-Century Baghdad," in *Conversion and Continuity. Indigenous Christian Communities in Islamic Lands, Eighth to Eighteenth Centuries*, edited by Michael Gervers and Ramzi Jibran Bikhazi, 33–54 (Wetteren: Pontifical Institute of Medieval Studies, 1990), 33; Stephen Gerö, "Only a Change of Masters? The Christians of Iran and the Muslim Conquest," in *The Expansion of the Early Islamic State*, edited by Fred Donner, 125–130 (Aldershot: Ashgate, 2008), 129.

and literature as early as the era of the Prophet.[32] Their conversion to Islam entailed another important phenomenon, that is, transmission of biblical and extra-biblical hagiographical stories to the Islamic tradition.[33] These transmissions could have taken place through texts, judicial and monastic libraries being a prominent venue. They more likely could have taken place orally.

Poetry, oration, and storytelling were foundational components of society in pre-Islamic Arabia, and thus, narration and hearing of stories about pre-Islamic prophets, sages, and miracle-workers was a predominant practice in Islamic courts, study circles, and even everyday life.[34] *Quṣṣāṣ* (storytellers) constituted an important social faction in early Islam. Many high officials were also known to be storytellers, and they were, at least in theory, held responsible for "instructing the public in basic beliefs and tenets of Islam."[35] Narrating stories of pre-Islamic prophets and holy men, and the religious authority gained through this practice, was an indispensable component of factionalism and elite formation under the first four caliphs and the Umayyads.[36]

For a Muslim audience, these stories about pre-Islamic prophets and holy men served as highly venerated, edifying accounts; therefore, having access to this sort of knowledge brought the transmitters and narrators a specific sort of religious authority and praise. Nevertheless, because the sources of this information were mostly

32. Claude Gilliot, "On the Origin of the Informants of the Prophet," in *The Hidden Origins of Islam. New Research into its Early History*, edited by Karl-Heinz Ohlig and Gerd-R. Puin, 153–188 (Amherst: Prometheus Books, 2010), 154–160.

33. Roberto Tottoli, *Biblical Prophets in the Qur'ān and Muslim Literature* (London: Routledge, 2002), 86–96.

34. Mourad, "Christians and Christianity," 60; Claude Gilliot, "Christianity and Christians in Islamic Exegesis," in *Christian-Muslim Relations. A Bibliographical History*, vol. 1 *(600-900)*, edited by David Thomas and Barbara Roggema, 31–56 (Leiden, Boston: Brill, 2009), 36–37; Lyall Richard Armstrong, *The Quṣṣāṣ of Early Islam* (Ph.D. Diss., University of Chicago, 2013), esp.143–155; for Christian poets, see Montgomery Watt, "The materials used by Ibn Isḥāq," in *Historians of the Middle East*, edited by Bernard Lewis and P. M. Holt, 23–34 (Oxford: Oxford University Press, 1962), 25; Abdulla El Tayib, "Pre-Islamic Poetry," in *Arabic Literature to the End of the Umayyad Period*, edited by A. F. L. Beeston et al., 27–113 (Cambridge: Cambridge University Press, 1983), 32; R. B. Serjeant, "Early Arabic Prose," in ibid., 122ff; Harry T. Norris, "Fables and Legends in pre-Islamic and early Islamic times," in ibid., 374–375.

35. Robert Hoyland, "History, fiction and authorship in the first centuries of Islam," in *Writing and Representation in Medieval Islam: Muslim Horizons*, edited by Julia Bray, 16–46 (London: Routledge, 2006), 24.

36. Armstrong, *The Quṣṣāṣ of Early Islam*, 241ff; Norris, "Fables and Legends," 385–386; Newby, *Making of the Last Prophet*, 5.

Christians and Jews, these stories and their narrators were perceived and approached with a certain degree of suspicion, particularly by later Muslim historians.[37] They were also used as religio-political tools, as stories about Christians and Christianity helped Muslim historians and scholars build a certain image of Christians for and within the Muslim community.[38] Moreover, in many cases these stories were utilized for qurʾānic exegesis.[39] For a non-Muslim audience, stories of pre-Islamic prophets and holy men in Islamic literature gave a particular message: These servants of God, as opposed to other monotheists that rejected Muhammad's prophethood and message, belonged to the eternal Muslim *umma* (community), a concept to which I will return after analyzing the transformation of the story of Paul and John between Christianity and Islam.

From Paul and John to Fīmyūn and Ṣāliḥ

We have a fifth-century hagiographical text in the Syriac Christian tradition that later, in the eighth century, appears in the Islamic historiographical tradition in a shortened form. There is a period of two centuries between the Syriac story of Paul and John and Ibn Isḥāq's account of the conversion of Najrān. It is highly possible that the story appeared in different versions in both Christian and Islamic oral and written traditions in this interval.[40] Although this intermediate stage is impossible to trace or reconstruct, it is still useful to conduct a close comparative analysis between the Christian version and the earliest known Islamic version, which is in the *Sīra*, in order to have a glimpse of the transmission process. In this section I shall take the narrative of Ibn Isḥāq as the base text and present a comparison of the story with the Syriac version, together with a commentary.[41]

37. Armstrong, *The Quṣṣāṣ of Early Islam*, 103, 110, 115.

38. Mourad, "Christians and Christianity," 70.

39. Armstrong, *The Quṣṣāṣ of Early Islam*, 104–130; Mourad, "Christians and Christianity," 58; for the relationship between *sīra* and Qurʾānic exegesis, see M. J. Kister, "The *Sīrah* literature," in *Arabic Literature to the End of the Umayyad Period*, edited by A. F. L. Beeston et al., 352–67 (Cambridge: Cambridge University Press, 1983), 353–354.

40. It needs no discussion that early Islamic historiography heavily relied on oral tradition. Robinson, *Islamic Historiography*, 25.

41. I fully quote Guillaume's translation of Ibn Isḥāq's version of the story here, with slight corrections. I refer to the Syriac story when I speak about Paul and John.

> Al-Mughīra b. Abū Lābīd, a freedman of al-Akhnas, on the authority of Wahb b. Munabbih the Yamanī told me that the origin of Christianity in Najrān was due to a man named Fīmyūn, who was a righteous, earnest, ascetic man whose prayers were answered.

The Syriac story does not refer to the geographical location in south Arabia as Najrān. It is called the "land of Himyarites," which can be any location in south Arabia. Procopius refers to the Himyarites as *Homeritae*, allies of the Roman Empire together with the Kingdom of Axum, and known for their palm groves.[42] In the letters of the previously-mentioned Simeon of Beth Aršām, the people and language of the city of Najrān are mentioned.[43] There was probably a semantic difference between Najrānites and Himyarites originally; nevertheless, in the context of this conversion narrative it is safe to use the two terms interchangeably.

What is striking about the beginning of the story in the *Sīra* is the name of the holy man, Faymiyūn in Guillaume's translation. Newby suggests that the name can be a transliteration of Apa Poimen, one of the most prominent monastic figures of Egypt in the fifth century, to whom many texts and stories were attributed.[44] Irfan Shahīd similarly states that this name might have come from the Greek word *poimēn* ('shepherd, lord, master'), or be a corruption of the name Pantaenus in the Arabic script.[45] Tubach argues that "Faymiyūn" was the Arabicized version of the Greek name Euphemion/Phemion/Euphemianos and associates Wahb's story with the above-mentioned Man of God, which I find the most plausible.[46] Although the Man of God is anonymous, or identified as Alexius in the later tradition, his father's name is Euphemianus,[47] and this name might have found its way into

42. Dewing, *Procopius. History of the Wars*, I, xix 7–16.

43. Shahīd, *Martyrs of Najrān*, 40, 45.

44. Newby, "Coptic Literary Influence," 27.

45. Shahīd, *Fourth Century*, 87 fn. 47; note that Paul is referred to as a "shepherd of souls" in the Syriac story.

46. Tubach, "Christliche Legende," 108.

47. Doran, *Stewards of the Poor*, 30; for an extensive analysis of the story of Saint Alexis and his father Eufemien in the Old French tradition, see Karl Uitti, *Story, Myth and Celebration in Old French Narrative Poetry, 1050–1200* (Princeton: Princeton University Press, 1973), 3–64.

the story of Paul and John through a chain of transmissions. Considering that the two hagiographical stories are very similar to each other and almost always were placed in sequential order in manuscripts, the story of the Man of God and of Paul and John might have converged at a later time.[48] This explains why the name of the holy man as provided by Ibn Ishāq—*fymywn* (unvoweled)—should be transliterated as Fīmyūn. Nevertheless, the entire section about the conversion of Najrān and other details demonstrate that the story of Fīmyūn and Ṣāliḥ was mostly derived from that of Paul and John, not the story of the Man of God.

Fīmyūn is simply described as a "righteous, earnest and ascetic man" (*wa-kāna rajulan ṣāliḥan mujtahidan zāhidan*). In the Syriac version Paul's description is longer, emphasizing his ecclesiastic title, a bishop, "a shepherd of souls." Paul prays to God and asks Jesus Christ to shine forth from his cross and show him the right way. In his dream God answers him, saying that if he wants to become like a pillar of fire, he should serve the priesthood, with allusion to Exodus 13:21.[49] In the Islamic version this section with strong biblical imagery is cut out, and it is summarized as "whose prayers were answered." This constitutes a clear example of a common practice, which is muting Christian elements during the transmission of hagiographical texts from Christian to the Islamic literature.[50]

— ❖ —

> He used to wander between towns: as soon as he became known in one town he moved to another, eating only what he earned, for he was a builder by trade using mud bricks. He

48. Confluence of stories and saints is a common hagiographical phenomenon. The story of Alexis, for instance, is noted to have also been confused with Saint John Calybite, who was known to have lived in Constantinople, left his parents for his ascetic endeavors, and returned home in disguise, like the Man of God. Uitti, *Story, Myth and Celebration in Old French Narrative Poetry*, 31; Giuseppe Caliò, "Giovanni Calibita," *Bibliotheca Sanctorum*, vol. 6 (Rome, 1961), 640–41; *BHG* 121 (s.v. "Ioannes Calybita").

49. Exodus 13:21: "By day the Lord went ahead of them in a pillar of cloud to guide them on their way and by night in a pillar of fire to give them light, so that they could travel by day or night."

50. Swanson, "Arabic Hagiography," 351; Harry Munt, "Ibn al-Azraq, Saint Marūthā, and the Foundation of Mayyāfāriqīn (Martyropolis)," in *Writing 'True Stories': Historians and Hagiographers in the Late Antique and Medieval Near East*, edited by Arietta Papaconstantinou, 149–174 (Turnhout: Brepols, 2010), 159; Kister, "Sīrah literature," 354–357.

> used to keep Sunday as a day of rest and would not work then. He used to go into a desert place and pray there until evening.

This appears to be a summary of the beginning of the Syriac story. Paul "set out in secret from his city. He thought to himself: 'now I will travel to a distant place where no one knows me.'"[51] Paul came to Edessa and "worked as a day laborer."[52] The Syriac story says he does not work on the holy day of Friday, on which he goes to the desert to find Christ, and help the poor living in the desert. This change in the day on which the holy man takes rest is interesting, for it demonstrates that early Muslim transmitters (Wahb?) made Fīmyūn rest on a Sunday, not on Friday which was a holy day of Jews and Christians in late antiquity and beyond.[53] Other Christian terminology and discourse is also again omitted in the Islamic paraphrase of this section.

— ❖ —

> While he was following his trade in a Syrian village, withdrawing himself from men, one of the people there called Ṣāliḥ perceived what manner of man he was and felt a vehement affection for him, so that unperceived by Fīmyūn he used to follow him from place to place, until one Sunday he went, as his wont was, out into the desert followed by Ṣāliḥ. Ṣāliḥ chose a hiding-place and sat down where he could see him, not wanting him to know where he was.

The story of Paul and John briefly describes John, Paul's companion, as a priest with a desire for monastic life.[54] His encounter with Paul is through work at his house for which he hires Paul as a workman. John one day follows Paul going out and praying on a mountain. Watching the holy man secretly, John sheds tears. The affectionate love of John for Paul finds direct echo in the Islamic version. The onomastic change is also worth elaborating on, for Ṣāliḥ does not appear to

51. Arneson et al., *Paul and John*, 32.

52. Arneson et al., *Paul and John*, 32.

53. C. H. Becker, "On the History of Muslim Worship," in *The Development of Islamic Ritual*, edited by Gerald Hawting, 49–74 (Burlington: Ashgate, 2006).

54. Arneson et al., *Paul and John*, 34.

be an Arabicized version of a foreign word.[55] It has connotations of "good, righteous, pious, God-fearing."[56] It is also the name of a qur'ānic prophet sent to the Arab people of Thamūd.[57] If the name Ṣāliḥ was chosen to replace John at a certain point in the history of transmission of the story, it is difficult to ascertain why and when. Alternatively, Ṣāliḥ might be a direct translation for "man of God," considering the story of Paul and John might have converged with that of Man of God, as mentioned above. In either case, this name choice clearly fits within the attempt to give the story an Islamic/Arabic character.

—❖—

> As Fīmyūn stood to pray, a *tinnīn*, a seven-horned snake, came towards him and when Fīmyūn saw it he cursed it and it died. Seeing the snake but not knowing what had happened to it and fearing for Fīmyūn's safety, Ṣāliḥ could not contain himself and cried out: "Fīmyūn, a *tinnīn* is upon you!" He took no notice and went on with his prayers until he had ended them. Night had come and he departed. He knew that he had been recognized and Ṣāliḥ knew that he had seen him. So Ṣāliḥ said: "Fīmyūn, you know that I have never loved anything as I love you; I want to be always with you and go wherever you go." He replied: "As you will. You know how I live and if you feel that you can bear the life well and good.

The serpent story in the Syriac version is longer, adorned with a speech Paul delivers to John, emphasizing the power given by Christ to the disciples to overcome adversaries.[58] They also recite ten sections of the Psalms together. The dialogue that takes place between them in this scene is heavily laden with allusions to biblical passages. Thereafter they become comrades on the path of Christ and decide to leave Edessa together, which Rabbula approves.

---

55. Bosworth, *History of al-Ṭabarī*, 196 fn. 492.

56. Newby, "Coptic Literary Influence," 25.

57. Andrew Rippin, "Ṣāliḥ," in *EI*^{2}.

58. Arneson et al., *Paul and John*, 38.

—❖—

> So Ṣāliḥ remained with him, and the people of the village were on the point of discovering his secret. For when a man suffering from a disease came in his way by chance Fīmyūn prayed for him and he would be cured; but if Fīmyūn was summoned to a sick man he would not go. Now one of the villagers had a son who was blind and he asked about Fīmyūn and was told that he never came when he was sent for, but that he was a man who built houses for people for a wage. Thereupon the man took his son and put him in his room and threw a garment over him and went to Fīmyūn saying that he wanted him to do some work for him in his house and would he come and look at it, and they would agree on a price. Arrived at the house Fīmyūn asked what he wanted done, and after giving the details the man suddenly whisked off the covering from the boy and said, "O Fīmyūn, one of God's creatures is in the state you see. So pray for him." Fīmyūn did so and the boy got up entirely healed.

This healing story is not mentioned in the Syriac version.[59] Paul and John travel together with an oath of keeping their ecclesiastic titles and identities secret. They do perform healings, but nothing similar to the above story. The story of tricking the saint into healing a child seems to be a later addition.

—❖—

> Knowing that he had been recognized he left the village followed by Ṣāliḥ, and while they were walking through Syria they passed by a great tree and a man called from it, saying, "I've been expecting you," and saying, "When is he coming? until I heard your voice and knew it was you. Don't go until you have prayed over my grave for I am about to die." He did die and Fīmyūn prayed over him until they buried him.

59. Neither is there a similar episode in the story of the Man of God.

This is one of the significant passages in the story that clearly points to the story of Paul and John as the source of the Fīmyūn and Ṣāliḥ story. Although the episode with the dendrite takes place much later in the original story, the Islamic version closely follows the Syriac one in content. On their way back from south Arabia (note that Fīmyūn and Ṣāliḥ have not gone there yet), Paul and John reach a mountain on top of which there was a man dwelling in a tree. Paul and John and the dendrite were all glad upon learning that they were all disciples of Christ, and they converse with each other telling their life stories. The dendrite asks them to stay with him for three days, for he anticipates his imminent death and asks them to bury him. The Islamic version depicts the dendrite as waiting for Fīmyūn, which is not the case in the Syriac story. The two men climb up the tree, bring down the dendrite and prepare a proper burial for him. Paul and John continue their adventures in Syria and northern Mesopotamia, whereas the Islamic version of the story inserts the Najrān episode here.

—❖—

> Then he left followed by Ṣāliḥ until they reached the land of the Arabs who attacked them, and a caravan carried them off and sold them in Najrān. At this time the people of Najrān followed the religion of the Arabs worshipping a great palm-tree there. Every year they had a festival when they hung on the tree any fine garment they could find and women's jewels. Then they sallied out and devoted the day to it. Fīmyūn was sold to one noble and Ṣāliḥ to another.

Paul and John, too, are attacked, taken captive, and brought to the "land of the Ḥimyarites" by *ṭayyāyē* (Arabs).[60] They are bound and put in a tent to be sacrificed for a cultic ritual. The *ṭayyāyē* living in the land of the Himyarites are depicted as tree-worshippers, which, according to the story included human sacrifice (in the Islamic version human sacrifice is omitted and tree worship is referred to as *dīn al-ʿarab*). Before seeing the cultic tree Paul performs numerous healings, all of which are omitted in the Islamic version. Not surprisingly,

60. Arneson et al., *Paul and John*, 50.

the omitted sections are heavily interwoven with biblical imagery and explicitly Christian discourse. To illustrate, Paul, prior to baptizing a possessed young girl, says the following: "Our Lord Jesus Christ, you came to humanity, my Lord, in order to free the children of Adam from the sin that bound them and from the curse that the earth received when Adam transgressed the commandment and when the evil one planted thorns and tares on it."[61]

Upon hearing about their healing and other miracles, and that people began to visit them, the king is enraged, and he sends warriors to oppress their followers and kill the two holy men. Thus, they bring Paul and John to a place where there are many palm trees, one of which was tall and very lush among the others. Right before being killed, John learns that it was the god of the camp, and he petitions the king that their god should fight the god of Paul and John.

—❖—

> Now it happened that when Fīmyūn was praying earnestly at night in a house which his master had assigned to him the whole house was filled with light so that it shone as it were without a lamp. His master was amazed at the sight, and asked him about his religion. Fīmyūn told him and said that they were in error; as for the palm-tree it could neither help nor hurt; and if he were to curse the tree in the name of God He would destroy it, for He was God Alone without companion. "Then do so," said his master, "for if you do that we shall embrace your religion, and abandon our present faith." After purifying himself and performing two *rakʿa*s, he invoked God against the tree and God sent a wind against it which tore it from its roots and cast it on the ground. Then the people of Najrān adopted his religion and he instructed them in the law of ʿĪsā b. Maryam. Afterwards they suffered the misfortunes which befell their co-religionists in every land. This was the origin of Christianity in Najrān in the land of the Arabs. Such is the report of Wahb bin Munabbih on the authority of the people of Najrān.

61. Arneson et al., *Paul and John,* 52.

The conversion episode in the story of Paul and John begins with a conflict with the king of the Himyarites; whereas, Fīmyūn and Ṣāliḥ impress the *sayyid* (master) with their piety. John waves his hand, calls upon Jesus Christ (note that Fīmyūn calls for the help of "God alone without companion," *wa-huwa allāhu wāḥidun lā sharīka lahu*), and uproots the tree. The king converts to Christianity and builds a church for the holy men. Paul and John baptize people, ordain bishops and deacons, and leave for the "mountain of God" (where they would meet the dendrite).[62]

A significant detail in this episode is that Fīmyūn purifies himself and performs two *rak'as* (prostrations) before uprooting the cultic tree. In the Syriac story, Paul and John do not perform any ritual before they destroy the tree, but, in the very next section when they go to the mountain of God, they kneel (*burkā*) there for five days and five nights. The Arabic version says that Fīmyūn performs two *rak'as* (prostrations), another interpolation in the story to attribute an Islamic resonance for the audience of the *Sīra*.[63]

Ibn Isḥāq's version of the story ends with the note that the people of Najrān thus were converted to the 'religion of Jesus, son of Mary, peace be upon him' (*dīn 'Īsā b. Maryam 'alayhi al-salām*), using the standard mode of referring to Jesus in the Islamic tradition.[64] The very last sentence of the story, "afterwards they suffered the misfortunes which befell their co-religionists in every land," possibly refers to the martyrs of Najrān, a Christian community that was persecuted under Jewish kings of Yemen in the early sixth century, as an exegetical note on Sūrat al-Burūj 85:4–8. The latter mentions a certain group of believers who were thrown into a fire pit due to

62. Arneson et al., *Paul and John*, 56.

63. Bowing, kneeling, and prostration were common prayer rituals in the Christian communities in late antiquity, which continued in the Islamic tradition. In the latter, a *rak'a* can refer to prostration (*sajda*) during ritual prayer (*ṣalāt*), or, more comprehensively, it can refer to each part of the *ṣalāt* (including bowing) from the recitation of *sūrat al-fātiḥa* to *sajda*. That Fīmyūn performs two *rak'as* does not seem to be coincidental, however. *Ṣalāt* in the Islamic tradition originally consisted of two *rak'as*, and this number was retained for journeys. It is the most concise form of Islamic ritual prayer. Therefore, even though *rak'a* might have semantically substituted for the Syriac *burkā*, the prayer of Fīmyūn in this part of the story still probably sounded Islamic to the audience. See Fred Donner, *Narratives of Islamic Origins: The Beginnings of Islamic Historical Writing* (Princeton: The Darwin Press, 1998), 73; Guy Monnot, "ṣalāt," in *EI*².

64. G. C. Anawati, "'Īsā," in *EI*²; in the Qur'ān 3:40, 4:169, 19:35.

their unwavering faith.[65] Thus, the narrative returns to the history of Yemeni kings, and the story of Fīmyūn and Ṣāliḥ gets connected to the overarching historical narrative of the *Sīra*.

A teleological God-centered model of history, which depicts pre-Islamic monotheistic religions as precursors of Islam as a result of God's divine plan was a major practice in Islamic historiography.[66] Accordingly, with the prophetic genealogy from Adam to Muhammad, and a brief history of the Yemen, Ibn Isḥāq lays out the historical current that culminates with Muhammad's prophethood and the qur'ānic revelation.[67] With rhetorical tools, prophets become Muhammad's precursors, and particular events having occurred during the reigns of Yemeni kings become contexts of certain qur'ānic verses. In this process Fīmyūn and Ṣāliḥ are integrated into the narrative as Muslim holy men living prior to Muhammad. In fact, immediately after this story Fīmyūn is referred to as a Muslim instructing people in the ways of Islam, and his young disciple as an *imām*.[68]

Regardless of whether there was a short version of the story of Paul and John (or Euphemion and the Man of God) in the Christian tradition, clearly the story was given an Islamic resonance by 1) changing the names of the holy men, especially Ṣāliḥ being a name that is very rare in pre-Islamic usage, 2) Fīmyūn taking the Sunday off (as opposed to Friday) and performing two *rak'as* prior to a miracle, and 3) explicitly calling the holy men Muslims and their followers *imams*. Thus, Paul and John (as Fīmyūn and Ṣāliḥ) became pre-Islamic *yet* Muslim holy men partaking in significant events prefiguring the time

---

65. Sūrat al-Burūj 85:4–8: "Cursed were the companions of the trench containing the fire full of fuel, when they were sitting near it, and they, to what they were doing against the believers, were witnesses. And they resented them not except because they believed in Allah, the Exalted in Might, the Praiseworthy" (all of the Qur'ān translations given in this paper are of Sahih International). *Tafsīr* (qur'ānic exegesis) literature is beyond the scope of this paper, for some examples of the early exegesis of *aṣḥāb al-ukhdūd*, see Aḥmad Farīd, *Tafsīr Muqātil ibn Sulayman* [eighth century] (Beirut: Dār al-Kutub al-'Ilmīyah, 2003), iii, 469; Muhammad Shukrī al-Zāwītī, *Tafsīr al-Ḍaḥḥāk* [eighth century] (Cairo: Dār al-Salām, 1999), ii, 950; Aḥmad Farīd, *Tafsīr Ibn Wahab* [10th cent.] (Beirut: Manshurāt Muhammad 'Alī Bayḍūn, Dār al-Kutub al-'Ilmīyah, 2003), ii, 488.

66. Robinson, *Islamic Historiography*, 129, 135; for historicizing legitimacy, see Donner, *Islamic Origins*, 111–122.

67. Uri Rubin, *The Eye of the Beholder: The Life of Muhammad as Viewed by the Early Muslims* (Princeton: The Darwin Press, 1995), 45; Robinson, *Islamic Historiography*, 129, 135.

68. Guillaume, *Life of Muhammad*, 16–18.

of Muhammad. The story served as a component of the foundation narrative for the Muslim *umma*.

An Eternal Muslim Umma

Islamic tradition is a product of the late antique eastern Mediterranean, a milieu in which Christian monasticism and asceticism were deeply woven into the texture of society.[69] Therefore, Islamic literature situated itself within the wider hagiographical traditions of late antiquity, by partaking in a shared vocabulary of signs, symbols, and forms to present its foundation stories and holy personae, through which it cultivated a specific social memory for the community.[70] Nancy Khalek, for example, demonstrates that the Companions of the Prophet were characterized in Islamic historiography on par with martyrs and holy men in Christianity.[71] Early foundational figures, such as Commander Khālid b. al-Walīd (d. 642), were depicted in hagiographical terms by Muslim historians.[72] This process of building a sanctified Muslim community also extended back in time, incorporating many prophets and holy men and women from the pre-Muhammad history.[73]

History writing was a commemorative practice to create, articulate, revitalize, and sustain a primordial Islamic past that extended back to the creation.[74] As Griffith states, the "Muslim commentators neatly assign[ed] Jesus' true disciples, and therefore the real Christians, to the nascent Muslim community and separate[ed] them from the

69. Nancy Khalek, *Damascus after the Muslim Conquest: Text and Image in Early Islam* (Oxford: Oxford University Press, 2011), 159ff; for general pietism in late antiquity, see Donner, *Islamic Origins*, 64ff; Thomas Sizgorich, "Narrative and Community in Islamic Late Antiquity," *Past & Present* 185 (2004): 22.

70. Sizgorich, "Become Infidels," 144–147; Nancy Khalek, "He was Tall and Slender, and his Virtues were Numerous: Byzantine Hagiographical Topoi and the Companions of Muhammad in al Azdī's Futūḥ al Shām/Conquest of Syria," in *Writing 'True Stories': Historians and Hagiographers in the Late Antique and Medieval Near East*, edited by Arietta Papaconstantinou, 105–123 (Turnhout: Brepols, 2010), 123; Sizgorich, "Narrative and Community," 25.

71. Khalek, "Byzantine Hagiographical Topoi," 106.

72. Sizgorich, "Become Infidels," 146–147.

73. For pre-Muhammad prophets as Muslims, see Sizgorich, "Narrative and Community," 23; Newby, *Making of the Last Prophet*, 23–25.

74. Geoffrey Cubitt, *History and Memory* (Manchester: Manchester University Press, 2007), 214ff.

contemporary Melkites, Jacobites and Nestorians."[75] As a part of the "hermeneutic process whereby the early Muslim community sought to interpret bits and pieces of its recalled primordial past," the memory of Paul and John would be erased only to be replaced by that of Fīmyūn and Ṣāliḥ.[76] The community to which these two holy men belonged was the Muslim *umma* that began with Adam, and extending across generations through prophets and holy men it reached Muhammad and beyond.[77] Christian hagiography was an essential resource for creating the Muslim *umma* in literature, for it provided both semiotic elements for representations of the foundational figures and specific personae, like Paul and John, as members of the ever-existent community.[78]

In this process of integration, the explicitly-Christian features in the story of Paul and John were silenced. Their specific sign value as Christian holy men, previously a bishop and a priest, were transformed and re-elaborated, as a result of which they were depicted as pious, ascetic believers of an almost amorphous monotheist religion which appears as proto-Islam.[79] This was a literary practice sometimes evident in Islamic historiography, another example of which is Ibn al-Azraq's (twelfth century) use of *The Life of Marutha* in his *Ta'rīkh Mayyāfāriqīn*.[80] Harry Munt argues that we should be speaking about cultural appropriation rather than syncretism in such cases.[81] Ibn al-Azraq, he argues, muted the Christian features of his source, because the figure of Marutha *as a Christian* was insignificant for the Muslim historian. Although I agree with the use of the term "adaptation" to refer to the way in which Christian hagiographical vocabulary, themes, and topoi were utilized by Muslim historians, the non-syncretic adaptation approach underestimates the function of Christian holy men in Islamic teleology.

75. Griffith, *Bible in Arabic*, 30. See also Mourad, "Christians and Christianity," 70–71.

76. Sizgorich, "Become Infidels," 126.

77. The oft-cited qur'ānic verse in this context is Sūrat al-Ḥaj 22:78 "It is He who has named you Muslims, both before and in this (Revelation)". See Khalidi, *Arabic Historical Thought,* 8.

78. For use of Christian hagiography in Islamic historiography, see Sizgorich, "Narrative and Community," 11; Robinson, *Islamic Historiography*, 46–49.

79. Sizgorich, "Narrative and Community," 18.

80. Munt, "Ibn al-Azraq."

81. Ibid., 173–4.

Julia Bray refers to Christian holy men as "partners of Muslims" in history, a necessary part of God's plan.[82] The case of Fīmyūn and Ṣāliḥ shows that, beyond being mere *partners*, they were in certain cases depicted as *members* of the ever-existing Muslim *umma*. They were Muslim servants of God prior to Muhammad. Whether stories about them appear in the *qiṣāṣ*, *sīra*, *ta'rīkh*, or other genres, they were described and perceived as primordial Muslim holy men. Fīmyūn was one of them, and he was described as *ṣāliḥan mujtahidan zāhidan,* which underlines the basic features of a holy man in Islamic tradition: a God-fearing and struggling man with ascetic behavior.[83]

While "Islamicizing" pre-Muhammad holy men and women, however, Muslim historians distinguished this community from another important literary trope, namely, the Christian monk.[84] In Islamic literature the latter was a significant topos, an embodiment of wisdom, clairvoyance, and asceticism. Yet, the monk was theoretically an outsider of the *umma*. Stories about monks *qua monks* show that this was a rhetorical tool utilized by Muslim historians mostly for legitimization purposes. The story of Baḥīrā (Sergius), the monk who recognized Muhammad as the imminent last prophet before even Muhammad himself knew it,[85] or the story of the monk who converts to Islam after speaking to Caliph ʿAlī b. Abī Ṭālib (r. 656–661),[86] are among the many examples of the utilization of the monk trope for legitimization of a Muslim holy man or for reinforcing a theological stance in Islamic literature.[87] Moreover, writings about the theory of asceticism and sanctity are explicit in that Muslim theologians drew sharp lines

82. Julia Bray, "Christian King, Muslim Apostate: Depictions of Jabala ibn Al-Ayham in Early Arabic Sources," in *Writing 'True Stories': Historians and Hagiographers in the Late Antique and Medieval Near East*, edited by Arietta Papaconstantinou, 175–204 (Turnhout: Brepols, 2010), 201.

83. Sizgorich, "Narrative and Community," 34–36; Renard, *Friends of God*, 8–9.

84. Sizgorich, "Narrative and Community," 11–12, 27ff; for various types of Christians in Islamic literature, see David Cook, "Christians and Christianity in *Ḥadīth* Works before 900," in *Christian-Muslim Relations. A Bibliographical History*, vol. 1 *(600-900)*, edited by David Thomas and Barbara Roggema, 73–82 (Leiden, Boston: Brill, 2009), 77.

85. Barbara Rogemma, *The Legend of Sergius Baḥīrā: Eastern Christin Apologetics and Apocalyptic in Response to Islam* (Leiden: Brill, 2009).

86. David Bertaina, *Christian and Muslim Dialogues: The Religious Uses of a Literary Form in the Early Islamic Middle East* (Piscataway: Gorgias Press, 2011), 94–99.

87. Mourad, "Christians and Christianity," 62.

between Christian and Muslim modes and practices of asceticism.[88] Monks were still held in high honor most of the time in literature,[89] but they were never a part of the Muslim community in the way Fīmyūn and Ṣāliḥ were.

Conclusion

This paper has analyzed a story that crossed boundaries of language, time period, literary genre, and religious tradition. A section in *The History of the Great deeds of Bishop Paul of Qenṭos and Priest John of Edessa*, a fifth-century Syriac hagiographical text, was transmitted into Islamic historiography as a story narrating the conversion of Najrān to Christianity. In the process in which the story was adapted to Islam, the two ascetics, Bishop Paul and Priest John, were stripped of their ecclesiastic titles and were referred to as Fīmyūn and Ṣāliḥ, two pious, ascetic men. Textual analysis showed that saints' lives were most probably transmitted in oral tradition, at least as much as in written form, and this resulted in many changes and convergences over generations, yielding a complex hagiographical dossier. Muslim historians might have first read or heard a version of the story of Paul and John (possibly with different names) anywhere in the wider hinterland of the eastern Mediterranean. The most probable context for the transmission is the early Islamic religio-political stage in which converts, clients, and manumitted slaves took active part. Converts

88. For the development of the theory of sanctity in Islam, see Sizgorich, "Narrative and Community," 185; Donner, *Islamic Origins*, 92; Khalek, *Damascus after the Muslim Conquest,* 85, 117; Renard, *Friends of God*, 260ff. Muslim theologians frequently referred to the tradition according to which Muhammad asserts that there is no *rahbānīya* (monasticism) in Islam. C. E. Bosworth, "An Early Persian Ṣūfī, Shaykh Abū Saʿīd of Mayhanah," in *Logos Islamikos: Studia Islamica in Honorem Georgii Michaelis*, edited by R. M. Savory and D. A. Agius, 79–96 (Toronto: Pontifical Institute of Medieval Studies, 1984), 79; for another example of such *ḥadīth*, see Alfred Guillaume, *The Traditions of Islam* (Beirut: Khayats, 1966), 142–143. ʿAbd Allāh b. al-Mubārak (d. 797), for instance, in his *ḥadīth* collection *Kitāb al-Jihād,* stated that every community has its own monasticism, and that monks of Islam were the *mujāhidūn* (the ones who struggle). The distinction between holy men of Islam and Christian monks appears to have been established by the time the notion of *awliyā* (friends of God) emerged as a hagiographical category. In *Tadhkirat al-Awliya'* (*Memorial of the Saints*), for instance, monks either convert to Islam, or they are falsely entitled as monks (in fact being Muslims). In either case, they are not members of the community of the friends of God. A. J. Arberry, *Muslim Saints and Mystics: Episodes from the Tadhkirat al-Auliya' (Memorial of the Saints) by Farid al-Din Attar* (Iowa: Omphaloskepsis, 2000), 372, 374.

89. Griffith, *Bible in Arabic,* 30–31; note that the language of the Qur'ān is not unfavorable to monks. The *sūras* mentioning monks are Sūrat al-Mā'ida 5:82, Sūrat al-Tawba 9:31 and 9:34.

from various backgrounds to Islam enabled the Islamic tradition to absorb and adapt pre-Islamic hagiographical traditions, the story of Paul and John being one example of many. Transmission of stories brought converts religious and political authority for being sources of information about exemplary historical figures. Through Islamic historiography, the image of pre-Islamic holy men was utilized in forming images and identities of Christians for the Muslim audience, and they were situated in the Islamic collective memory as members of the eternal Muslim *umma*. Literary analysis, furthermore, showed that Christian hagiographical themes and topoi had nuanced treatments in Islamic hagiography. Holy men prior to Muhammad went through a transition in Islamic tradition to fit into the notion of Islamic sanctity. Even though they were monks or clerics in the original story, they were depicted as ordinary men and women with extreme piety, asceticism, and divine blessing. In contrast, the topos of the monk continued to be employed in Islamic hagiography, serving a different purpose. A monk, whose religious authority was utilized by Muslim historians to attain legitimacy, was an outsider to the *umma*; whereas Fīmyūn and Ṣāliḥ, whose story travelled all the way from Edessa, became primordial holy men of the Muslim community.

Christians in the Islamic World

10. Syriac in the Polyglot Medieval Middle East

Digital Tools and the Dissemination of Scholarship Across Linguistic Boundaries

❖ Thomas A. Carlson

1. Introduction

In the late 1430s, Ulugh Bey, the prince of Samarqand and grandson of the great conqueror Tīmūr Lang (Tamerlane), compiled an astronomical manual in Persian. This *zīj* later became a standard reference work for English merchants in the seventeenth century. In his work, he provided information about several calendars which could be used to convert dates of historical star observations. The second calendar he labeled the Rūmī calendar, better known in English as the Seleucid Era.[1] Among the "notable days" listed for this calendar are festivals whose names clearly derive from Syriac, such as the memorial (*dhukrān*) of Mār Tūmā, the fast (*ṣawm*) of Mārt Maryam, and the "Feast of the Cross" (*ʿīd-i ṣalīb*). The month names for this calendar are all listed with the same names as in Syriac. The date given for the Feast of the Cross on 13 September points even more specifically to the Church of the East,[2] since all other Christian denominations commemorate the discovery

1. Ulug Beigus, *Epochæ Celebriores Astronomis, Historicis, Chronologis, Chataiorum, Syro-Græcorum, Arabum, Persarum, Chorasmiorum, usitatæ ex traditione Ulug Beigi, Indiæ citra extraque Gangem Principis*, ed. Johannes Gravius (London: Jacob Flesher, 1650), 99. This calendar, known in English as the Seleucid era, should not be confused with the Rūmī calendar adopted by the nineteenth-century Ottoman Empire.

2. Ibid., 99, 101.

of the True Cross by Constantine's mother Helena on 14 September. The information on this calendar was clearly derived, at least in part, from an Eastern Syriac Christian, even if the Timurid prince nowhere identified his informant.

This omission points to larger issues. The Muslim prince in Samarqand had access to Christian sources, even in Islamic Central Asia. He either wished not to identify his source or, perhaps more likely, he considered his use of Christian informants to be unremarkable.[3] The use of Syriac information in a Persian astronomical manual makes clear that the achievements of "Islamic civilization" cannot be fully understood by scholars who neglect non-Muslim populations, and correspondingly the legacy of Syriac astronomy is under-represented if it does not take into account Persian texts as well. The failure of a Turkic prince to cite his Syriac source emphasizes to modern scholars that the medieval Middle East was diverse, multi-religious, multi-ethnic, and multi-lingual. This paper will focus on the implications of this last dimension of diversity for Syriac Studies.

The Syriac language has consistently been written in polyglot environments, from competing with Greek and Persian before 600 CE, to medieval Arabic and Armenian, to modern Swedish and Malayalam. While some work in Syriac Studies has taken a longitudinal approach to intra-Syriac questions, other scholars have brought a comparative perspective informed by multiple linguistic and religious traditions. Nevertheless, the study of Syriac sources often remains isolated from scholarship on Persian and Roman antiquity, Islamic Studies, and the modern Middle East. The development of the Digital Humanities provides Syriacists an opportunity to situate their scholarship more broadly and make it more accessible to scholars in additional fields who ought to consider Syriac sources, but who have bypassed them due to linguistic limitations.

This paper has three goals. First, it explores how seeing Syriac in a polyglot context may broaden the range of questions asked of Syriac sources. While this is true of all periods, this paper focuses on the medieval Middle East, which is largely studied under the rubric of Islamic Studies by Arabists and Persianists with no knowledge of

3. T'ovma Mecop'ec'i reports that the same Timurid prince ended Christianity in Samarqand, in response to a "Nestorian" seducing an emir's wife: T'ovma Mecop'ec'i, *Patmagrut'yun*, ed. Levon Xač'ikyan (Yerevan: Magałat, 1999), 34–36.

Syriac. Secondly, the paper suggests that this diversity, far from vitiating the importance of Syriac Studies, makes it integrally important to a wider range of fields of study than it has yet informed. Finally, this paper proposes that digital tools are useful sites for the dissemination of Syriac scholarship to a broader scholarly community and public. This paper is the first scholarly notice of a new Digital Humanities project, the Historical Index of the Medieval Middle East (HIMME), which is inspired by and cooperating with Syriaca.org. It is hoped that digital projects such as Syriaca.org and HIMME, by increasing the visibility of Syriac sources, will correspondingly raise the academic profile of the field of Syriac Studies in other fields.

2. The Polyglot Context

Syriac Studies is one of a range of fields studying the Middle East which divide the subject matter by linguistic and confessional boundaries: Islamic Studies, Judaic Studies, Syriac Studies, Armenian Studies, Coptic Studies, and Christian Arabic Studies. These fields have a certain unity: For the price of learning only one language, scholars can read documents from ancient Edessa, inscriptions from medieval China and Central Asia, and liturgies celebrated in modern American cities. There are certainly longitudinal connections within a language. Authors who composed Syriac texts were more likely to be influenced by earlier Syriac texts than by texts in other languages. Languages therefore tend to act as the channels of tradition and knowledge. Language boundaries are not insuperable barriers, but crossing those boundaries comes at a cost.

But linguistic unity is not the only continuity scholars may wish to consider in approaching the past. The medieval Middle East was a part of the world with a bewildering variety of languages. In the Middle East between 1000 and 1500, most of the rulers spoke a Turkic language, most of the bureaucrats east of Egypt wrote in Persian, most of the Muslim religious leaders and merchants used Arabic, many Jews added some Aramaic or Hebrew to their Arabic, and Christian leaders used Armenian, Syriac, or Coptic in addition to Arabic and/or Persian. Other dialects of Aramaic and various Kurdish languages already existed, but were not yet literary languages. To understand this context, one must reckon with the plurality of languages.

In this context, certain languages acquired specific functions. Someone who composed theology in Syriac might haggle in the market in Arabic and hire a notary to frame a petition in Persian. The linguistic definition of Syriac studies and other fields used to study the medieval Middle East has often resulted in separating the experience of individuals in the past, as scholars have focused on questions which they think will yield meaningful answers in the language in which they work. Thus Islamicists working on the period between 1000 and 1500 CE have primarily asked questions of political history, Arabic Muslim intellectual life, Persian literature, and the economic life of Islamic religious institutions.[4] Most Syriacists of the period have bypassed political and social questions to focus on linguistic, literary, or religious issues, including ecclesiastical structure, monastic life, liturgical development, and theological exposition.[5] Armenologists are more interested in politics, especially international relations with the Crusader States and Western Europe, and in the value of manuscript colophons as sources.[6] Middle Eastern Jewish Studies is still working on digesting the Cairo Geniza, an amazing collection of documents for legal, commercial, and everyday life in Egypt.[7]

4. A good overview of the questions asked by Islamicists, though now somewhat dated, is R. Stephen Humphreys, *Islamic History: A Framework for Inquiry*, Rev. Ed. (Princeton: Princeton University Press, 1991).

5. A sense of the topics which have attracted the greatest attention of Syriacists may be gleaned from the thematic section headings and relative size in Sebastian P. Brock, "Syriac Studies: A Classified Bibliography, 2001–2005," *PdO* 33 (2008): 281–446. These include art, Bible, ecclesiology, exegesis, hagiography, hierarchy, Islam, Judaism, language, law, literature, liturgy, magic, manuscripts, mathematics, medicine, monasticism, music, philosophy, synods, theology, topography, translation, and women, but not economics, ethnicity, family, politics, or society.

6. Compare Brock's thematic headings with those in Robert W. Thomson, "Supplement to A Bibliography of Classical Armenian Literature to 1500 AD: Publications 1993-2005," *Le Muséon* 120 (2007): 207–223. While there is much overlap in the religious headings, Thomson's bibliography includes sections on colophons, folklore, and historiography, while the bibliography's focus on "literature" excludes studies such as Angus Donal Stewart, *The Armenian Kingdom and the Mamluks: War and Diplomacy During the Reigns of Het'um II (1289–1307)*, The Medieval Mediterranean 34 (Leiden: Brill, 2001); Angus Stewart, "The Assassination of King Het'um II: The Conversion of the Ilkhans and the Armenians," *JRAS* 15 (2005): 45–61; Bayarsaikhan Dashdondog, *The Mongols and the Armenians (1220–1335)* (Leiden: Brill, 2010).

7. The starting point remains S. D. Goitein, *A Mediterranean Society; the Jewish Communities of the Arab World as Portrayed in the Documents of the Cairo Geniza*, 6 vols. (Berkeley: University of California Press, 1967). For two more recent studies based on the Geniza, see Marina Rustow, *Heresy and the Politics of Community: The Jews of the Fatimid Caliphate*, Conjunctions of Religion & Power in the Medieval Past (Ithaca: Cornell University Press, 2008); Oded Zinger, *Women, Gender*

There is evidence to address all of these questions, however, in all these various languages. Syriac chronicles provide evidence for Muslim, Armenian, and Crusader dynasties consistently down to the end of the anonymous continuator of Bar 'Ebroyo around 1500.[8] The intellectual culture was likewise not rigidly divided by religious boundaries. A contemporary vita of a late fifteenth-century Syriac Orthodox patriarch of Mardin recorded that he had earlier studied philosophy with a Muslim teacher in the Muẓaffariyya madrasa in the city, returning the compliment that earlier Muslim philosophy students had paid to Christian philosophers like Yaḥyā ibn 'Adī.[9] This Christian patriarch's vita is thus a valuable witness to the "Islamic" intellectual scene in late medieval Mardin. Medieval manuscripts also bear the traces of economic life in notes of restoration or redemption from plundering armies, as well as patronage patterns and endowments recorded in Syriac colophons.[10] An awareness of the studies going on in fields defined by other languages opens up the range of questions which Syriacists might be tempted to ask of Syriac sources and to coordinate those answers with the answers given in other sources. The polyglot context, far from vitiating the value of Syriac Studies, enriches the study of Syriac sources.

3. The Use of Linguistic Diversity for Promoting Syriac Studies

Scholars other than Syriacists likewise profit from recognizing the polyglot dynamic of the medieval Middle East. All who study the region would benefit from the additional sources available in other languages. Thus Syriac sources can shed light on the questions asked by Islamicists, Armenologists, and Geniza scholars. In this academic climate of tight budgets and "interdisciplinarity," the future of Syriac Studies can be somewhat precarious, but the more areas that a field

and Law: Marital Disputes According to Documents of the Cairo Geniza (Ph.D. Diss., Princeton University, 2014).

8. For example, the Ayyūbid ruler of Ḥiṣn-Kayf is named in Jean Baptiste Abbeloos and Thomas Joseph Lamy, *Gregorii Barhebræi Chronicon ecclesiasticum* (Paris: Maisonneuve; Louvain: Peeters, 1872–1877), 813.

9. Ms. Cambridge Dd. 3 (8) 1, f. 83a.

10. For example, on ms. Cambridge BFBS 446, f. 255a. For a later period, Murre-van den Berg analyzed patronage patterns using manuscript colophons: Heleen L. Murre-van den Berg, "Generous Devotion: Women in the Church of the East between 1550 and 1850," *Hugoye* 7 (2004): 11–54.

can inform, the more secure the field itself will be. Publicizing the value of Syriac sources for these parallel fields studying the medieval Middle East will therefore increase the prominence of Syriac Studies among the disciplines.

There is the practical problem, of course, that most Islamicists, Armenologists, and Geniza scholars are not trained to read Syriac. Even if scholars of other fields are taught the rudiments of the Syriac language, they generally do not have the survey knowledge of what sources exist that might help them, or how to access relevant materials. In order for Syriac studies to benefit from the potential to inform other fields, the obstacles posed by disparities of training must be overcome.

4. The Relevance of Digital Tools

Among methods of overcoming such disparities, the developing discipline of Digital Humanities (DH) holds particular potentials. DH projects which maintain a web presence can be indexed by the default scholarly database, Google. For example, an Islamicist who comes across the Arabic name *qlawdhiya* in a primary source may not recognize the toponym. The top Google search result is a link to the Syriac Gazetteer, which includes not only the location, but also a description by Patriarch Afram Barsoum and citations of the *Gorgias Encyclopedic Dictionary of the Syriac Heritage* and David Wilmshurst's *Ecclesiastical Organisation of the Church of the East*.[11] Thus the scholar learns that Claudia was a fortress near Malaṭya in what is today eastern Turkey. The fact that the Syriac Gazetteer contains the Arabic name of this place thus increases the discoverability of the relevance of Syriac Studies to what is called "Islamic" history. In particular, without DH projects like this online, an Islamicist or Armenologist would need to wonder about Syriac sources specifically in order to investigate whether there might be any benefit from consulting such resources. For questions about the origins of Islam and the Umayyad dynasty, scholarship has made this point sufficiently that it will occur to scholars to think of Syriac, but

11. http://syriaca.org/place/63.html is the top Google search result as of 8/4/2015.

probably not for most questions about the period after 750.[12] The fact that Google has indexed Syriaca.org means that non-Syriacists need not investigate Syriac sources specifically, or even consciously consider Syriac, in order to discover the value of Syriac sources for their study. This is a very important barrier to reduce.

But DH projects such as Syriaca.org do not only function as advertising; they also guide skills acquisition and enable collaboration. Scholars who read Arabic can see references to Syriac texts in the Gazetteer and thus can determine whether their research projects would benefit from studying Syriac directly. For Arabists who are too busy to learn Syriac, references to translations of Syriac texts provide direction to sources which they did not know previously. Citations of secondary scholarship on a subject indicates whom the scholar should contact in order to ask specific questions about the Syriac evidence, or even to suggest a team project on a particular aspect of what is being studied. Understanding any polyglot context requires accessing the sources in all of the relevant languages, and where this is infeasible for an individual, then collaboration must happen. This collaboration is made easier to initiate by easily accessible digital discovery tools, such as Syriaca.org.

Such collaboration would be useful in both directions. As Dorothea Weltecke has indicated,[13] some historical questions require consulting sources in a range of languages beyond Syriac. The editors of Syriaca.org will eagerly incorporate data in any language (such as the Arabic name of Claudia) regarding entities in any way related to Syriac Studies. But the methods of Syriaca.org can be employed even more broadly to develop reference tools which integrate Syriac seamlessly into larger disciplines, such as Middle Eastern history. Because Syriaca.org's scope is anything related to Syriac Studies, the search results for a non-Syriacist will often be both too much and too little. For example, an Islamicist who wants to know what monasteries were operating in the medieval Middle East may browse the

12. This awareness of Syriac for the earlier period is largely due to works such as Patricia Crone and Michael Cook, *Hagarism: The Making of the Islamic World* (Cambridge: Cambridge University Press, 1977); Robert G. Hoyland, *Seeing Islam as Others Saw It: A Survey and Evaluation of Christian, Jewish, and Zoroastrian Writings on Early Islam*, Studies in Late Antiquity and Early Islam 13 (Princeton: Darwin Press, 1997). The coverage of the latter work terminates at 750.

13. See pp. 251–275 in this volume.

Syriac Gazetteer by monastery type,[14] but some of the monasteries listed became defunct in antiquity, before the rise of Islam, and others were not founded until the modern period.[15] Some locations are not in the Middle East at all.[16] Furthermore, these are only Syriac monasteries, not Armenian, Coptic, or Greek monasteries. Functionality has been developed to filter these results by a specific time period, though it is imperfect. This would address the first issue, but not the problems of search results outside the Middle East, or missing results from other languages.

From one perspective, this is obvious. People searching the *Syriac* Gazetteer will only get *Syriac* monasteries. One response is to say that for Armenian, Coptic, or Greek monasteries to be discoverable, scholars of those languages should build language-specific Armenian, Coptic, or Greek gazetteers, perhaps along the model of the Syriac Gazetteer. Such a response reinforces the present field divisions, which are demarcated along linguistic and confessional lines, and aims to do the best job that can be done within the existing framework.

In contrast, changing the framework may yield additional opportunities for Syriac scholars. There is currently a large amount of interest in the "Islamic world" and "Islamic history." Most non-specialists in the United States regard "Middle Eastern history" as synonymous with "Islamic history," an identification which implicitly excludes Syriac. The present field divisions grant Islamicists an academic hegemony which often hinders the study of non-Muslims, even though the majority of the Middle Eastern population was not Muslim until sometime later than the year 1000.[17] The way scholars today study the medieval Middle East is representative of modern Middle Eastern demography, specifically a demography that is very different from that before the *Sayfo* of a century ago. The field divisions as

14. http://syriaca.org/geo/browse.html?view=type&type=monastery

15. For example, Barsoum only reported that the monastery of Paʿnūr (http://syriaca.org/place/375) was inhabited between 510 and 575: Ignatius Aphram I Barsoum, *Scattered Pearls: A History of Syriac Literature and Sciences*, trans. Matti Moosa, 2nd ed. (Piscataway: Gorgias Press, 2003), 563. On the other extreme, the monastery of Notre Dame des Semences (http://syriaca.org/place/148) outside Alqosh was not constructed until the middle of the nineteenth century: H. L. Murre-van den Berg, in *GEDSH*, 204.

16. A monastery dedicated to Mor Awgen (http://syriaca.org/place/680) exists in Switzerland: G. A. Kiraz, in *GEDSH*, 100 and S. P. Brock, in *GEDSH*, 120.

17. See, for example, Thomas A. Carlson, "Contours of Conversion: The Geography of Islamization in Syria, 600–1500," *JAOS* 135 (2015): 791–816.

they currently stand sideline Syriac Studies as well as misrepresent the pre-modern Middle East. Yet scholars who build medieval Middle Eastern search tools that cross these field boundaries have the opportunity to demonstrate that Syriac is integrally relevant to "Islamic" history, rather than some extraneous luxury.

For these reasons, a new project aims to augment Syriaca.org by imitating its methods and structures, but defining a new scope across the linguistic divides. The Historical Index of the Medieval Middle East (HIMME) will contain a gazetteer, as well as indices of persons and of practices, that are relevant to the study of the Middle East between approximately 600 and 1500. This will include names in Syriac, Arabic, Armenian, Hebrew, Greek, Latin, Persian, and whatever other languages are relevant for the region in that period. The "practices" to be indexed include, for example, the *jizya* tax and fasting, so that scholars interested in the development of those practices over time will immediately see that they crossed communal boundaries. When HIMME is developed, scholars of the medieval Middle East will be continually confronted with how multilingual the Middle East really was, as they see languages represented that they would not have thought relevant.[18] Any scholars working on the Middle East in the period between 600 and 1500, who wish to publicize specific references to certain persons, places, or practices, are invited to contact the author of this paper.

There may be a couple of objections. Some scholars think that the fact that they do not know all of the relevant languages themselves precludes them from doing this sort of work. This is where collaboration is important. Not many, if any, scholars read Syriac, Arabic, Persian, Coptic, Latin, and Hebrew. Therefore tools like HIMME will require a team of collaborators with different backgrounds to compile them. DH methods encourage collaborative work by necessity. Other scholars may object that, for their research projects, it is more useful to see longitudinal results within Syriac, not results which are more restricted chronologically and perhaps linguistically irrelevant. The answer to this objection is that such researchers are able to continue consulting Syriaca.org's longitudinal data. HIMME is not a replacement for Syriaca.org. Instead, the ability to copy digital records for nearly nothing

18. For an Uyghur inscription in an Iraqi monastery, see H. Pognon, "Note," *JA* 8.19 (1892): 153–155; J. Halévy, "Déchiffrement et interprétation de l'inscription ouïgoure, découverte par M. Pognon," *JA* 8.20 (1892): 291–92.

makes it very easy for projects with overlapping scope to share data that is of interest to both projects. Anything in HIMME which has a Syriac connection will also be entered into Syriaca.org. But having an alternate aggregator of results will integrate Syriac into a broader study of the medieval Middle East. Thus multiple DH tools with overlapping scope can raise the profile of Syriac Studies in the multiple fields and disciplines which Syriacists also inhabit.

5. Conclusion

This paper started by noticing an omission, and it ends by calling attention to a mistake. In 1262, Chinggis Khan's grandson Hülegü, as the new Mongol ruler of Persia, sent a letter in Latin to Louis IX of France. The letter has a number of Mongol words that are glossed by Latin phrases, such as "Mengutengri (id est dei uiui)."[19] The phrase *Möngke Tenggeri* means "eternal sky," while *dei uiui* means "the living God." Clearly the scribe who supplied the glosses had an agenda other than theological precision. The editor of the Latin document enlisted the help of the eminent Turkologist Francis Cleaves to deal with the unfamiliar "Mongol" terms, but one term eluded both scholars. In the greeting of the letter, the Mongol ruler wished the French king "Barachmar (id est salutem)."[20] Cleaves suggested it might represent Persian *bi-raḥmat*, an abbreviation of *bi-raḥmat Allah* ("by God's mercy"), but the Latin editor remarked that the letters were sufficiently clear as they stood.[21] This difficulty was left unresolved.

The "Mongol" term in question is actually Syriac. Hülegü's chief wife, Doquz Khatun, was a member of the Church of the East, and the Mongol ruler cultivated rumors that he himself was a Christian.[22] According to Bar 'Ebroyo, he endowed a Syriac Christian courtier with extensive land in and near his capital of Maragha, from which

19. P. Meyvaert, "An Unknown Letter of Hulagu, Il-Khan of Persia, to King Louis IX of France," *Viator* 11 (1980): 253.

20. Ibid.

21. Ibid., 253, fn. 42.

22. Peter Jackson, "Mongols and the Faith of the Conquered," in *Mongols, Turks, and Others: Eurasian Nomads and the Sedentary World*, edited by Reuven Amitai and Michal Biran, Brill's Inner Asian Library 11, 245-290 (Leiden: Brill, 2005), 273.

his Latin letter to Louis IX was sent.[23] There was even a church-tent within the royal encampment, where Christian liturgies were frequently celebrated.[24] One of the most frequently repeated phrases of the Eastern Syriac liturgy is "Bless, O my Lord" (*barekh mār*). Chinggis Khan's grandson, the Mongol ruler of Persia, used a Syriac liturgical acclamation as a "Christian-y" greeting in a letter to the Christian king of France, Louis IX. In order for this usage to make sense, and for it to be discoverable by scholars, Syriacists need to make their expertise more widely available and reduce the currently rather high barriers to discovering and accessing Syriac sources. Digital Humanities projects, especially ones designed to cross linguistic boundaries, may be a useful tool to accomplish those goals, not only for the medieval Middle East, but for every period, region, and discipline into which Syriac scholarship reaches.

23. Paul Bedjan, *Gregorii Barhebræi Chronicon Syriacum e codd. mss. emendatum ac punctis vocalibus adnotationibusque locupletatum* (Paris: Maisonneuve, 1890), 512; Meyvaert, "Unknown Letter of Hulagu," 259.

24. Robert Thomson, "The Historical Compilation of Vardan Arewelc'i," *DOP* 43 (1989): 217.

11. Christian Arabic Historiography at the Crossroads between the Byzantine, the Syriac, and the Islamic Traditions

❖ Maria Conterno

Christian Arabic studies is a relatively young research field, with large areas still unexplored and with a lack of systematic research on many topics.[1] Nevertheless, the origins of Christian Arabic literary production have received increasing attention in the last decades. The arabicization of Christians under Islamic rule and the adoption of Arabic as a liturgical and literary language between the ninth and tenth centuries have been thoroughly investigated by Sidney Griffith.[2] The emerging role of Christian Arab intellectuals and the development of Christian theology, apologetics, and philosophy in Arabic have been studied in the wider context of the interactions between Christian and Muslim cultures in early Abbasid

* Part of the research leading to this publication has received funding from the European Research Council under the European Union's Seventh Framework Programme (FP/2007–2013) / ERC Grant, agreement n. 313153. The research project discussed in the paper will be funded by an FWO (Funds Wetenschappelijk Onderzoek) post-doctoral fellowship.

1. Samir Khalil Samir, "La tradition arabe chrétienne. État de la question, problèmes et besoins," in *Actes du premier congrès international d'études arabes chrétiennes, Goslar septembre 1980*, OCA 218, edited by S. K. Samir, 21-120 (Rome: Edizioni Orientalia Christiana, 1982); Samir Khalil Samir, "L'avenir des études arabes chrétiennes," *PdO* 24 (1999): 21-44.

2. Sidney H. Griffith, *Arabic Christianity in the monasteries of ninth-century Palestine*, Collected Studies Series 380 (Brookfield, Vermont: Variorum, 1992); idem, "Melkites, Jacobites and the christological controversies in Arabic in third/ninth century Syria," in *Syrian Christians under Islam. The first thousand years*, edited by D. Thomas, 9-55 (Leiden: Brill, 2001); idem, *The beginnings of Christian theology in Arabic: Muslim-Christian encounters in early Islamic period*, Collected Studies Series 746 (Aldershot-Burlington: Ashgate, 2002).

times,[3] with particular attention being paid to the figures involved in the so-called "Graeco-Arabic translation movement."[4] Research on this specific topic is mature enough to allow the first monographic syntheses to appear.[5] Yet, one fundamental aspect of early Christian Arabic culture remains conspicuously understudied, namely, the beginnings of Christian historical writing in Arabic.

The very first Christian historical works in Arabic are regrettably lost. We know for instance that Qusṭā ibn Lūqā (d. ca. 912), a Melkite physician active at the Abbasid court as a philosopher and translator, wrote a historical text entitled *The Paradise*,[6] and a world history is recorded among the books authored by Ḥunayn ibn Isḥāq (ca. 808–873).[7] The earliest preserved texts date from the tenth and early eleventh centuries, and they are of Melkite and East-Syrian origin: Agapius of Mabbug's *Kitāb al-ʿunwān* (Melkite, mid tenth cent.);[8] Eutychius of

---

3. Bénédicte Landron, *Chrétiens et musulmans en Irak: Attitudes nestoriennes vis-à-vis de l'Islam* (Paris: Cariscript, 1994); Sidney Griffith, "Answering the Call of the Minaret: Christian Apologetics in the World of Islam," in *Redefining Christian Identity. Cultural Interaction in the Middle East since the Rise of Islam*, edited by J. J. van Ginkel, H. L. Murre-van den Berg, and T. M. van Lint, 91–126 (Louvain: Peeters, 2005); Sandra Toenies Keating, *Defending the 'People of Truth' in the Early Islamic period. The Christian apologies of Abū Rā'iṭah* (Leiden: Brill, 2006).

4. Dimitri Gutas, *Greek thought, Arabic culture: The Graeco-Arabic translation movement in Baghdad and early 'Abbasid society (2nd–4th/8th–10th c.)* (London: Routledge, 1998); John W. Watt, "The Strategy of the Baghdad Philosophers. The Aristotelian Tradition as a Common Motif in Christian and Islamic Thought," in J. J. van Ginkel, H. L. Murre-van den Berg, and T. M. van Lint, eds., *Redefining Christian Identity*, 151–65; idem, "Christianity in the renaissance of Islam. Abū Bishr Mattā, al-Fārābī and Yaḥyā Ibn ʿAdī," in *Christians and Muslims in dialogue in the Islamic Orient of the Middle Ages*, edited by M. Tamcke, 92–112 (Würzburg: Ergon, 2007); Sidney H. Griffith, "From Patriarch Timothy I to Ḥunayn ibn Isḥāq: Philosophy and Christian apology in Abbasid times; reason, ethics and public policy," in M. Tamcke, ed., *Christians and Muslims in dialogue*, 75–98.

5. Sidney H. Griffith, *The Church in the Shadow of the Mosque: Christians and Muslims in the World of Islam* (Princeton: Princeton University Press, 2010).

6. The work is listed by both Ibn al-Nadīm and Ibn Abī Uṣaybiʿa: G. Flügel, *Kitāb al-Fihrist* (Leipzig: Vogel, 1872), 2.295; B. Dodge, *The Fihrist of Ibn al-Nadīm. A 10th century AD survey of Islamic culture* (New York: Columbia University Press, 1970), 695; A. Müller, *Kitāb ʿuyūn al-anbāʾ fī ṭabaqāt al-aṭibbāʾ* (Köningsberg: Selbstverlag, 1884), 244–5; L. Kopf, *Ibn Abu Usaibiʿah. History of Physicians* (Jerusalem: The Hebrew University, Institute of Asian and African Studies, 1971), 469–472. The anonymous author of the *Chronicle of Seert* mentions Qusṭā ibn Lūqā as a source four times, for events related to Constantine the Great. Although he does not say it explicitly, the quotes refer most likely to Qusṭā's historical work, see Louis Sako, "Les sources de la chronique de Séert," *PdO* 14 (1987): 155–166.

7. Müller, *Kitāb ʿuyūn al-anbāʾ fī ṭabaqāt al-aṭibbāʾ*, 200; Kopf, *Ibn Abu Usaibiʿah. History of Physicians*, 384.

8. A. Vasiliev, *Kitab al-ʿUnvan. Histoire universelle écrite par Agapius (Mahboub) de Menbidj*, PO 5.4, 7.4, 8.3, 11.1 (Paris: Societas Jesu, 1906–1916); L. Cheikho, *Agapius episcopus Mabbugensis: Historia universalis*, CSCO 65 (Louvain: Peeters 1912).

Alexandria's universal history, or Annals (Melkite, mid tenth cent.);[9] the continuation of the latter produced by Yaḥyā al-Anṭākī (Melkite, ca. 1028);[10] the two anonymous ecclesiastical histories known as *Chronicle of Seert* (East-Syrian, tenth/eleventh cent.),[11] *Mukhtaṣār al-akhbār al-bī'iyya* (East-Syrian, early eleventh cent.),[12] and Elias of Nisibis' Syriac-Arabic chronicle (East-Syrian, ca. 1018).[13] To this list one should add also the Arabic translation and continuation of Orosius' *Historiae adversus paganos* (produced, as it seems, at Córdoba in the second half of the tenth century)[14] and, if the philological reconstruction proposed by Bo Holmberg is correct, the historical section of the longer (seven-chapter) version of the *Kitāb al-majdal.*[15] Remarkably, we have no knowledge of Syriac Orthodox historiography in Arabic before the thirteenth century,[16] and the Copts translated and continued their *History of the Patriarchs of Alexandria* in Arabic only from the second half of the eleventh century.[17]

9. M. Breydy, *Das Annalenwerk des Eutychios von Alexandrien. Ausgewählte Geschichten und Legenden kompiliert von Said ibn Batriq um 935 AD*, CSCO 471–472 (Louvain: Peeters, 1985); L. Cheikho, *Eutychii Patriarchae Alexandrini Annales I*, CSCO 50 (Paris: Poussielgue, 1906).

10. L. Cheikho, B. Carra de Vaux, and H. Zayyat, *Eutychii Patriarchae Alexandrini Annales II: Accedunt Annales Yahia ibn Said Antiochensis*, CSCO 51 (Paris: Poussielgue, 1909); I. Kratchkowsky, *Histoire de Yahya Ibn Sa'id d'Antioche continuateur de Sa'id Ibn Bitriq*, PO 18.5, 23.3, 47.4 (Turnhout: Brepols, 1924, 1932, 1997).

11. A. Scher, *Histoire Nestorienne Inédite (Chronique de Séert)*, PO 4.3, 5.2, 7.2, 13.4 (Paris: Societas Jesu, 1907–1918).

12. B. Haddad, *Mukhtasar al-akhbār al-bī'iyya* (Baghdad: Al-Diwan, 2000).

13. E. W. Brooks and J.-B. Chabot, *Eliae metropolitae Nisibeni Opus chronologicum*, CSCO 62–63 (Paris: Poussielgue, 1909–1910).

14. Giorgio Levi Della Vida, "La traduzione araba delle Storie di Orosio," *Al-Andalus* 19 (1954): 257–93; Christian C. Sahner, "From Augustine to Islam: Translation and History in the Arabic Orosius," *Speculum* 88/4 (2013): 905–931; Mayte Penelas, *Kitāb Hurūshiyūsh (Traduccíon árabe de las Historiae adversus paganos de Orosio)*, Fuentes Arábico-Hispanas 26 (Madrid: Consejo Superior de Investigaciones Científicas, 2011).

15. Which, according to Holmberg, was composed at the beginning of the eleventh century by 'Amr ibn Mattā, see Bo Holmberg, "A reconsideration of the *Kitāb al-mağdal*," *PdO* 18 (1993): 255–273. In Graf's traditional view, the seven-chapter version of this theological compendium was composed in the middle of the twelfth century by Mārī ibn Sulaymān, whereas the five-chapter version was written by 'Amr ibn Mattā two hundred years later, and plagiarized by 'Amr's contemporary Ṣalībā ibn Yūḥannā. Both works are still unpublished, but their chapters on the history of the East-Syrian patriarchs have been published separately: E. Gismondi, *Maris Amri et Slibae De patriarchis nestorianorum commentaria* (Rome: De Luigi, 1896–1899).

16. To my knowledge, the first Syriac Orthodox work of history in Arabic is Bar Hebraeus' (d. 1286) *Mukhtaṣār fī al-duwal.*

17. Johannes Den Heijer, *Mawhub ibn Mansur ibn Mufarrig et l'historiographie copto-arabe. Étude sur la composition de l'Histoire des Patriarches d'Alexandrie*, CSCO 513 (Louvain: Peeters, 1989).

Available in modern editions, the above-mentioned texts are often exploited as sources of factual information by historians of the Medieval Near East. As yet, however, they have been rather neglected as an object of study per se, and they have not been suitably analyzed as products of new emerging cultures, as expressions of social and cultural identities in development, which indeed they are. Most research so far has been source critical. After Louis Sako's concise survey,[18] a broader source-critical analysis of the *Chronicle of Seert* has been proposed by Philip Wood, who looked at the text as a testimony of the complex stratification of East-Syrian historical writing through the centuries.[19] Likewise, Antoine Borrut pointed out the traces of lost Umayyad historiographical works in Elias of Nisibis.[20] Herman Teule has investigated the relation between the *Chronicle of Seert* and the *Mukhtasar al-akhbār al-bīʿiyya*, opening the path for future source-critical studies on the latter.[21] Agapius of Mabbug has come lately to the fore in the debate over the transmission of Theophilus of Edessa's lost History,[22] but no relevant study on his chronicle itself has so far been produced. The work of Eutychius of Alexandria (or Saʿīd ibn Baṭrīq), with its later recensions, is the one that has received by far more attention, with the thorough philological study by Michel Breydy,[23] and the reading of the text in relation to its social, cultural, and denominational context proposed by Sidney Griffith and Uriel Simonsohn.[24]

18. Louis Sako, "Les sources de la chronique de Séert," *PdO* 14 (1987): 155–166.

19. Philip Wood, "The sources of the Chronicle of Seert: Phases in the writing of history and hagiography in late antique Iraq," *OC* 96 (2012): 106–48; idem, *The Chronicle of Seert: Christian historical imagination in late antique Iraq* (Oxford: Oxford University Press, 2013).

20. Antoine Borrut, "La circulation de l'information historique entre les sources arabo-musulmanes et syriaques: Élie de Nisibe et ses sources," in *L'historiographie syriaque*, ÉS 6, edited by M. Debié, 137–159 (Paris: Geuthner, 2009).

21. Herman Teule, "L'abrégé de la chronique ecclésiastique (*Muḫtaṣār al-aḫbār al-bīʿiyya*) et la chronique de Séert: Quelques sondages," in M. Debié, ed., *L'historiographie syriaque*, 161–177.

22. Robert G. Hoyland, *Theophilus of Edessa's Chronicle and the circulation of historical knowledge in Late Antiquity and Early Islam*, TTH 57 (Liverpool: Liverpool University Press, 2011); idem, "Agapius, Theophilus and Muslim sources," in *Studies in Theophanes*, Travaux et Mémoires 19, edited by F. Montinaro and M. Jankowiak, 355–364 (Paris: Éditions de l'IHEAL, 2015); Maria Conterno, *La 'descrizione dei tempi' all'alba dell'espansione islamica. Un' indagine sulla storiografia greca, siriaca e araba fra VII e VIII secolo*, Millennium Studien 47 (Berlin: De Gruyter, 2014); eadem, "Theophilos, 'the more likely candidate'? Towards a reappraisal of Theophanes' 'Oriental Source(s)'," in F. Montinaro and M. Jankowiak, eds., *Studies in Theophanes*, 383–400.

23. Michel Breydy, *Études sur Said ibn Batriq et ses sources*, CSCO 450 (Louvain: Peeters, 1983).

24. Sidney Griffith, "Apologetics and historiography in the annals of Eutychios of Alexandria:

A comprehensive, cross-denominational study of the beginnings of Christian historical writing in Arabic, involving all the above-mentioned sources, is still among the *desiderata*. The way a community keeps record of the past and builds up its own memory is a fundamental test to understand how it deals with its present, and the choice of language often entails identity issues. Scholars of the medieval West have demonstrated that historical and cognate texts can and must be studied as "identity markers," investigating the deep connections between the processes of memory building and identity formation, and testing socio-political, anthropological, and literary theories in their sources.[25] Analogue studies have been recently proposed for Byzantine, Syriac, and Islamic sources as well.[26] But the formation of Christian Arabic identities in Egypt, Syria, Mesopotamia, and Persia, and the role of the earliest Christian Arabic historiographical works in this process, has not received comparable attention. No answer yet has been given to the question of why Melkite and East-Syrian Christians adopted Arabic for memory-keeping almost at the same time, whereas the Syro-Orthodox stuck to Syriac four centuries longer. In addition, the emergence of Christian historiographical works in Arabic has not been deeply investigated in connection to the rest of early

Christian self-definition in the world of Islam," in *Studies on the Christian Arabic heritage: In honour of Father Prof. dr. Samil Khalil Samir S.I. at occasion of his sixty-fifth birthday*, ECS 5, edited by R. Y. Ebied, 65–89 (Louvain: Peeters 2005); Uriel Simonsohn, "The biblical narrative in the Annales of Saʿīd ibn Baṭrīq and the question of medieval Byzantine-Orthodox identity," *ICMR* 22 (2011): 37–55; idem, "Motifs of a South-Melkite affiliation in the Annales of Saʿīd ibn Baṭrīq," in *Cultures in contact: Transfer of knowledge in the Mediterranean context*, Series Syro-Arabica 1, edited by S. Torallas Tovar and J. P. Monferrer-Sala, 243–255 (Cordoba – Beirut: CNERU – CEDRAC, 2013).

25. James Fentress and Chris Wickham, *Social memory* (Oxford: Blackwell, 1992); Patrick J. Geary, *Phantoms of remembrance. Memory and oblivion at the end of the First Millennium* (Princeton: Princeton University Press, 1994); Gabrielle M. Spiegel, *The past as text. The theory and practice of Mediaeval historiography* (Baltimore: John Hopkins University Press, 1997).

26. For Byzantine sources, see Teresa Shawcross, *The Chronicle of Morea. Historiography in Crusader Greece* (Oxford: Oxford University Press, 2009); Ruth Macrides, *History as literature in Byzantium. Papers from the Fortieth Spring Symposium of Byzantine Studies, University of Birmingham, April 2007* (Aldershot: Ashgate, 2010). For Syriac sources, see Bas ter Haar Romeny, *Religious origins of nations? The Christian communities of the Middle East* (Leiden: Brill, 2010), in particular the chapters by Muriel Debié and Dorothea Weltecke, entitled respectively "Syriac Historiography and Identity Formation" (92–114) and "Michael the Syrian and Syriac Orthodox Identity" (115–25); Philip Wood, *"We have no king but Christ": Christian political thought in greater Syria on the eve of the Arab conquest (c.400–585)* (Oxford: Oxford University Press, 2010). For Islamic sources, see Tarif Khalidi, *Arabic historical thought in the classical period*, Cambridge Studies in Islamic Civilization (Cambridge: Cambridge University Press, 1994); Konrad Hirschler, *Medieval Arabic historiography. Authors as actors*, SOAS/Routledge Studies on the Middle East (London: Routledge, 2006).

Christian cultural production in Arabic, in connection to the activity and role of Christian intellectuals at the caliphal court and in the main centers of knowledge and teaching, nor, most importantly, in connection to the agendas set by the different Christian communities in their daily confrontation with one another and with the increasingly islamicized society in which they lived. Nor has the interaction with the flourishing Muslim production been studied in any detail, mainly because of disciplinary boundaries. The very place of early Christian Arabic historiography in the history of late antique and medieval historical writing is still to be understood and defined. In this respect, it is telling that Christian Arabic historiography did not deserve its own section in the second volume of the recent Oxford History of Historical Writing—an otherwise highly commendable work—but it has been dealt with together with Syriac historiography, in a chapter entitled "Syriac and Syro-Arabic Historical Writing."[27]

The absence of such a study is therefore a substantial gap in the history of medieval historiography in the East, and in the history of the Near East in the Middle Ages as well. In this paper I will present some preliminary remarks concerning an ongoing research project that aims to fill precisely this gap, by producing a comprehensive study on the origins of Christian historical writing in the language of Islam. The research I am carrying out is based on the six earliest preserved Christian Arabic historiographical works (Agapius' *Kitāb al-ʿunwān*, Eutychius' *Annals* and their Antiochene version by Yaḥyā al-Anṭākī, the *Chronicle of Seert*, the *Mukhtaṣar al-akhbār al-bīʿiyya*, and Elias of Nisibis' *Chronicle*),[28] and it entails a study of both the texts and their contexts. I am starting with a prosopographical survey of Christian intellectuals within the Caliphate from the ninth to

27. Muriel Debié and David Taylor, "Syriac and Syro-Arabic Historical Writing," in *The Oxford History of Historical Writing*, vol. 2 *400-1400*, edited by S. Foot and C. F. Robinson, 155–179 (Oxford: Oxford University Press, 2012).

28. Although Holmberg's hypotheses have been greeted favorably (see Mark N. Swanson, "Kitāb al-majdal," in *Christian-Muslim Relations. A Bibliographical History*, vol. 2. *[900-1050]*, edited by D. Thomas, A. Mallet, and B. Roggema, 627–632 [Leiden: Brill, 2010]), further philological research is needed in order to assess the dating and the mutual relation of the two texts that go under the title of *Kitāb al-majdal*. Therefore, I am not including the *De patriarchis nestorianorum commentaria* in my study. The texts, though, will be taken into account with regard to the *Chronicle of Seert* and the *Mukhtaṣar al-akhbār al-bīʿiyya*, as they share many a common source. Likewise, the Arabic Orosius will be referred to as an important testimony of the circulation of historical material across the Mediterranean, but, since the main focus of my research is the Eastern Mediterranean, it is not to be included in the core of the research.

the early eleventh centuries, an investigation which will provide the background for the more specific study of the authors of the mentioned texts (leaving aside, of course, the two anonymous ones) but will also serve the purpose of contextualizing the very first two Christian Arabic historical works we know of, and of retrieving information on the possible existence of other early texts that have not come down to us. Furthermore, since this overview of Christian intellectual networks will include also the Copts and the Syro-Orthodox, it will eventually help to elucidate the reasons why these two communities started writing history in Arabic only later on. The work on the texts themselves consists of a study of their sources and their composition, aimed at detecting which kind of materials the authors had at their disposal and how they used it and reworked it, unlocking thus their communication codes, their rhetorical strategies and, consequently, their ideological agendas. The purpose of this analysis is not to draw a neat *stemma fontium*, nor to unearth lost texts, but to assess to which historiographical traditions the authors are indebted and to outline broad lines of intercultural transmission.

The following step will be to recognize distinct features, common trends, and possible influences in terms of genres, formats, and more broadly historical vision, in order to situate the emerging Christian Arabic historical writing in the wider context of late antique and early medieval historiography—with an eye to Byzantium, Islam, and Syriac Christianity first. Agapius' *Kitāb al-ʿunwān*, Eutychius' *Annals*, and Yaḥya al-Anṭākī's continuation of the latter must be analyzed against the backdrop of Byzantine and Islamic universal histories, which in the ninth and tenth centuries were burgeoning (or re-flourishing, in the first case) and presented significant similar traits. George Synkellos' (ca. 745–810) *Ecloga chronographica* and its continuation, Theophanes Confessor's (ca. 760–818) *Chronographia*, George the Monk's (ca. 830–875) *Chronikon syntomon,* the chronicles of Symeon the Logothete (ca. 925–990) and of the Pseudo-Symeon (d. after 978); al-Yaʿqūbī's (d. ca. 897/8) *Al-kāmil fī al-taʾrīkh*, Khalīfa ibn Khayyāṭ's (777–854) *Kitāb al-taʾrīkh*, al-Masʿūdī's (897–957) *Murūj al-dhahab*, al-Ṭabarī's (839–923) *Taʾrīkh al-rusul wal-mulūk*: All these universal chronicles present themselves in the form of large, even monumental, collections of excerpts from previous sources, sewn together with (apparently) no personal intervention on the part of the compiler.

On the Byzantine side, this is one of the many manifestations of what Paul Lemerle had called "encyclopaedism" and was lately, more accurately, labelled "the culture of the sylloge," or "la culture du receuil":[29] a way of "storing" old and at the same time producing new knowledge that is peculiar to the middle-Byzantine period. On the Islamic side, it is a consequence of the deep influence the traditionists had on every layer of early Islamic culture, where *isnāds* of authoritative "transmitters" determined the trustworthiness, and therefore the legitimacy, of legal, religious, and historical traditions as well.[30] In both cases, the final result is the almost total disappearance from the text of the original voice of the author, which must be looked for less in explicit personal statements than in the way the various sources were selected, reworked, and assembled. In addition to assessing whether the three Christian Arabic universal chronicles were influenced by one or the other of these contexts,[31] I will have to pay attention to the presence and configuration of other features of monotheist universal history, such as the role of chronology (which assumed a specific apologetic function in the Christian texts)[32] and of geography (more developed in the Islamic ones). Finally, Agapius' and Eutychius' works enable a test of the connection between "universal empire" and "universal history." The assumption that the idea of a monotheist universal empire is central to the very concept of monotheist universal history presumes

29. Paul Lemerle, *Le premier humanisme byzantin: Notes et remarques sur enseignement et culture à Byzance des origines au Xᵉ siècle* (Paris: Presses Universitaires de France, 1971), 267–300; Paolo Odorico, "La cultura della Sylloge," *BZ* 83 (1990): 1–21; idem, "'Parce-que je suis ignorant'. Imitatio/variatio dans la chronique de George le Moine," in *Imitatio – aemulatio – variatio: Akten des internationalen wisseschaftelichen Syposium zur byzantinische Sprache und Literatur (Wien, 22–25 Oktober 2008)*, edited by A. Rhoby and E. Schiffer, 209–216 (Wien: Verlag der Österreichischen Akademie der Wissenschaften, 2010); idem, "Cadre d'exposition/cadre de pensée – la culture du recueil," in *Encyclopedic trends in Byzantium? Proceedings of the International Conference held in Leuven, 6–8 May 2009*, OLA 212, edited by P. Van Deun and C. Macé, 89–108 (Louvain: Peeters, 2011). For a discussion of the controversial term "encyclopaedism" applied to this Byzantine practice, see Paul Magdalino, "Byzantine encyclopaedism of the ninth and tenth centuries," in *Encyclopaedism from Antiquity to the Renaissance*, edited by J. König and G. Woolf, 219–231 (Cambridge: Cambridge University Press, 2013).

30. Chase F. Robinson, *Islamic Historiography* (Cambridge: Cambridge University Press, 2003), 83–103.

31. An influence of the traditionists of Fustat on Eutychius has been postulated by Michel Breydy, see Breydy, *Études sur Said ibn Batriq*, 1–10. Agapius, in contrast, is more likely indebted to the Byzantine tradition, and a blend of the two may be discernible in the Antiochene recension(s) of Eutychius' *Annals*, produced in Syria during the Byzantine reconquest.

32. Brian Croke, "The origins of the Christian World Chronicle," in *History and Historians in Late Antiquity*, edited by B. Croke and A. M. Emmett, 116–131 (Sidney: Pergamon Press, 1983).

of course one and the same monotheist religion behind the two.[33] But Agapius and Eutychius, as Christian historians living under Muslim rule, wrote universal history within the wrong universal empire, so to speak, and they thus provide a valuable case to study the evolution of this historiographical genre in a socio-political context at odds with its supposed intrinsic nature. In this respect, a comparison is called for with the view and approach of their Syriac peers who also wrote Christian universal histories within the Islamic empire, such as the anonymous chronicler of Zuqnin, John of Phenek, and, later on, Michael the Syrian and the chronicler of 1234.

The Syriac traditions come on stage when it comes to studying the reception of Greek historiographical models by Christian Arabic authors, the Eusebian model in particular. But the perpetuation in the early Christian Arabic texts of trends that are peculiar to Syriac historiography deserves as much attention, and this applies especially to the two East-Syrian ecclesiastical histories, the *Chronicle of Seert* and the *Mukhtaṣār al-akhbār al-bīʿiyya*. In an insightful article of 2010, entitled "Writing history as 'histories': The biographical dimension of East-Syriac historiography,"[34] Muriel Debié pointed out what she called the "biographical dimension" as a main feature of East-Syriac historiography. Debié draws a cogent comparison between works such as Barḥadbshabba ʿArbaya's *History of the holy fathers who were persecuted for the sake of the truth*, the *History of Karka of Beth Slokh*, the *History of Arbela*, the *Book of Chastity*, and the genre of the "collective biographies," widely attested in the Christian hagiographical tradition but also in Latin and Greek ancient literature. Contrary to a collection of lives, a collective biography is written by a single author with the precise intent of producing a coherent text and with a strong underlying purpose of moral edification. Just like collective biographies, these East-Syriac historiographical texts are structured not as an outline of events in chronological order but as a series of portraits of relevant figures in a certain region, or institution. Contrary to history proper and to chronicles, the principle of organization of these

33. Andrew Marsham, "Universal Histories in Christendom and the Islamic World, c.700–c.1400," in S. Foot and C. F. Robinson, eds., *The Oxford History of Historical Writing*, vol. 2 *400–1400*, 431–456.

34. Muriel Debié, "Writing history as 'histoires': The biographical dimension of East Syriac historiography," in *Writing "true stories". Historians and hagiographers in the Late Antique and Medieval Near East*, Cultural Encounters in Late Antiquity and the Middle Ages 9, edited by A. Papacostantinou, M. Debié, and H. Kennedy, 43–77 (Turnhout: Brepols, 2010).

texts is not the chronological aspect but the idea of succession, from teacher to disciple, or from an abbot/bishop/patriarch to his follower.

It is certainly worth assessing the possible influence of such a model of composition on Christian Arabic historiography, even though two aspects urge us to consider this as a main feature, and not the main feature, of East-Syriac historiography. First, some of the preserved texts do not fit the picture—the *Khuzistan chronicle*, John of Phenek's *Rish Mellē*, Elias of Nisibis' *Chronicle*, for instance—and they are accordingly marked as noticeable exceptions by Debié. Second, there are a fair number of lost works, mostly mentioned in the sources as "ecclesiastical histories," about whose structure and contents we hardly know anything. This said, one cannot deny that East-Syriac historiographers—Elias of Nisibis being the only exception we know of—lacked the concern for chronological accuracy that most West-Syriac texts show, and had rather a predilection for narrative nuclea assembled in a framework of loose, mostly relative, chronology. In a bird's-eye view, also the *Chronicle of Seert* and the *Mukhtaṣar al-akhbār al-bīʿiyya* look as if they had been built up according to the "story model" delineated by Debié. The narrative seems to proceed story after story, and most of these stories deal with the life or deeds of relevant figures. If one looks only at the table of contents, these texts are indeed garlands of *akhbār* and *qiṣaṣ*. Such an impression, though, is fostered by the partition in the modern editions, and a few caveats are called for. The contents of the chapters, in fact, do not always match the titles, and after a heading such as "Story of So-and-so" we find very often a much more developed and varied narrative than we would expect. This suggests that either the partition and the headings are the work of a later hand, or the text itself outgrew the straightjacket of the "story model." What is also striking in these two texts is that sometimes they provide different versions of the same story one after the other, clearly drawing them from different sources, without any attempt at producing a uniform narrative, nor at explaining away or fixing the inconsistencies (it happens, for instance, with the stories of Constantine the Great and Julian the Apostate). The effect is very much the same as in the Muslim world chronicles, with the difference that, just like in the Byzantine world chronicles, the sources are not explicitly mentioned. Contrary to the East-Syriac texts analyzed by Debié, therefore, these East-Syrian Arabic works do not seem to be altogether comparable to collective biographies. My task will be to assess how the biographical dimension, which to some extent is still discernible, is combined in them with elements coming from other traditions (such as the Islamic *ṭabaqāt*, prosopographical compilations organized by generations), or with new peculiar features, to ascertain whether the idea of succession survives as the main principle of organization and to see how the "story model" evolves in a context of "narrative agglutination" which has strong Islamic and Byzantine echoes. My working hypothesis is that early Christian Arabic historiography saw the convergence of different historiographical trends, whose features may coexist in the same text, attesting thus to the porosity of cultural, religious, and linguistic barriers.

I will conclude with some remarks on Elias of Nisibis, who, oddly enough, is considered solely as a Syriac historian. The reason is probably that his chronicle has been published in the series *Scriptores Syri* of the Corpus Scriptorum Christianorum Orientalium, based on the assumption that the Syriac text came first, whereas the Arabic one, which at times is incomplete, was a translation produced by Elias' collaborators.[35] Yet it is worth looking at the chronicle also from a Christian Arabic perspective. First of all, this text is a unique example of the switch from Syriac to Arabic in historical writing: because it is bilingual, of course, and because its author was deeply concerned with the "language issue," as clearly evidenced by other works of his.[36] But it also represents the very first—and as far as I know, the only—example of a full Eusebian chronicle in Arabic. And by full, I mean including both the chronology and the canons. Looked at from the Syriac side, Elias' chronicle has often been pointed out as an exception in East-Syriac historiography, or as the most Western of East-Syriac historiographical works,[37] and it has been thoroughly

35. Friedrich Baethgen, *Fragmente syrische und arabische Historiker*, AKM 8.3 (Leipzig: Brockhaus, 1884); Robert G. Hoyland, *Seeing Islam as Others Saw It. A Survey and Evaluation of Christian, Jewish and Zoroastrian Writings on Early Islam* (Princeton: The Darwin Press, 1997), 421–422. Such a view—suggested also by the fact that the Syriac part of the only surviving manuscript is written by a unique hand, whereas the Arabic one by at least three—still needs to be corroborated by a deeper study of the text, especially of the entries based on Islamic sources.

36. His Syriac-Arabic dictionary and his treatise on Syriac grammar, for instance. But also one of the *Sessions with the Vizier al-Maghribi*, see David Bertaina, "Science, syntax, and superiority in eleventh-century Christian-Muslim discussion: Elias of Nisibis on the Arabic and Syriac languages," *ICMR* 22 (2011): 197–207.

37. Debié, "Writing history as 'histoires,'" 58 and 72.

studied as a testimony to the reception of the Eusebian model in the Syriac tradition. Since the Eusebian model has left the earliest and most apparent traces in West-Syriac historiography, it is of course there that one should start looking for what might have influenced Elias. An old study by Keseling shows that the Eusebian material in Elias is very close to that attested in the *Zuqnin Chronicle* and in the *Chronicle of 724* but not enough to allow to say for sure that it came down the very same transmission line.[38] Furthermore, at the origin of this branch of the Syriac Eusebian tradition there might have been an East-Syriac translation, namely the one produced by Simeon of Beth Garmai, mentioned by Abdishoʿ in his catalogue of Syriac writers[39] and possibly quoted by Elias himself under the name of Simeon Barqaya.[40] To this, one must add what Witakowski has concluded as regards Elias' use of Jacob of Edessa's chronicle: although quoting him as a source, Elias did not borrow from Jacob the structure of his chronicle.[41] Jacob's chronicle was in fact more faithful to the original Eusebian model, whereas Elias' one presents some innovation: The chronological columns are simplified and the so-called "fila regnorum," containing the relative chronology of the various kingdoms, are replaced by a single column where the sources are mentioned instead. This simplification might have been a feature of the Syriac translation used by Elias but also a change brought about by Elias himself, on his own initiative or in imitation of some other model. Here, as well, it is worth considering a possible Islamic influence, if not in the very idea of writing an annalistic chronicle, at least in the meticulous mention of the sources, possibly introduced to live up to the standards of accuracy of the Muslim traditionists.

In this presentation of my work in progress I have outlined some of the issues I am going to address in the study of early Christian Arabic historiography, some of the questions that I will try to answer.

38. Paul Keseling, "Die Chronik des Eusebius in der syrischen Überlieferung," *OC* 3.1 (1927): 23–48, 223–241; 3.2 (1927): 33–56.

39. Giuseppe S. Assemani, *Bibliotheca Orientalis Clementino-Vaticana* (Rome: Typis Sacrae Congregationis de Propaganda Fide, 1719–28), vol. 3.1, 168.

40. J.-B. Chabot, *Eliae metropolitae nisibeni opus chronologicum II,* CSCO 62 (Paris: Poussielgue, 1910), 99.

41. Witold Witakowski, "Elias Barshenaya's Chronicle," in *Syriac Polemics. Studies in honour of Gerrit Jan Reinink*, OLA 170, edited by W. J. van Bekkum, J. W. Drijvers, and A. C. Klugkist, 219–237 (Louvain: Peeters, 2007).

I will conclude drawing the readers' attention to an intriguing passage of Elias of Nisibis', which brings back some of the points touched upon in the previous pages. It appears that Elias was planning to write (or was writing?) an ecclesiastical history as well, at least according to what he himself says toward the end of the chronological section of his chronicle:

> And if God grants [us] a bit of life, I am describing his[42] virtues and the virtues of the fathers who [came] before him, and the stories of the kings, the governors, the metropolitans, the bishops, the teachers, the monks, the learned men/secretaries, and the faithful who [lived] from the days of Mar Abraham the catholicos up to this time of ours, in a book of ecclesiastical [history] whose start I am putting as a continuation to what Elias bishop of al-Anbar composed, if God will.[43]

Such a work, if he ever really composed it, would make Elias the real heir of Eusebius in the Syriac and Christian Arabic traditions. And the intention of resuming the narrative from the point where another work stopped, besides evoking the practice of the early Byzantine historians, associates him also to another great Syriac historiographer, Dionysius of Telmaḥre, who in his prologue claimed he would continue Cyrus of Batna's work.[44] In this respect, it is worth noticing that in writing his chronicle, too, Elias could have continued either Jacob of Edessa, or directly Eusebius, as Jacob did, but he chose instead to start anew from the very beginning, and the reasons behind this choice are to be investigated as well. Regardless, reading this passage we burn with curiosity to know whether Elias actually wrote his ecclesiastical history or not, and if he did, what the work looked like: like Barḥadbshabba's *History of the holy fathers*, like the *Chronicle of Seert*, or more like Dionysius' *History*? The passage seems to suggest a focus on relevant figures, therefore the principle of composition might well

42. I.e., the catholicos John VI (1012–1016).

43. E. W. Brooks, *Eliae metropolitae nisibeni opus chronologicum I*, CSCO 62 (Paris: Poussielgue, 1910), 70 (Syriac text), 72 (Arabic text).

44. The preface of Dionysius' lost *History* is reported in full by Michael the Syrian, see J.-B. Chabot, *Chronique de Michel le Syrien, Patriarch Jacobite d'Antioche (1166–1199)* (Paris: Ernest Lerous éditeur, 1899–1905), 2.357–358.

have been the "story model," or the "biographical model," and we should observe that in the Arabic text the word *manāqib* ("virtues", "deeds") is used, an almost technical term that appears very often in the title of Islamic laudatory biographies. Still, he mentions a rather wide range of disparate characters, and this description of the work might as well be just rhetorical.[45] But another, major, question arises spontaneously: In which language did he write or was he planning to write? Syriac? Arabic? Or once again both?

The answers to these and other questions will be material for a future paper, but I hope I was able, with this brief presentation of my work in progress, to show that the origins of Christian historical writing in the language of Islam need and deserve to be studied per se, and to be approached from many diverse angles.

45. We find a similar list at the very beginning of the *Chronicle of the Year 1234*, which is definitely not built as a collection of biographies, see J.-B. Chabot, *Anonymi Auctoris Chronicon ad annum Christi 1234 pertinens I*, CSCO 81 (Paris: Bibliopola, 1937), 26.

12. Seeing to be Seen

Mirrors and Angels in John of Dalyatha

❖ Zachary Ugolnik

This paper will analyze the relationship between angels and mirrors in John of Dalyatha's *Letters* and *Homilies.*[1] Angels or "Watchers" (*'irē*) play an important role in John's inward metaphysical journey and so does the mirror (*maḥzitā*) in the soul, in which such angels are often seen. In the Syriac tradition, the illuminated mirror in the heart or soul, as has been argued by Robert Beulay and Sebastian Brock, demonstrates humanity's creation in the image of God and intimacy with divine light.[2] Yet the mirror also maintains the transcendence of what is reflected or, in John's words, unity with divine glory (*šubḥā*) not divine nature (*kyānā*). I elaborate upon these conclusions by highlighting the pervasive importance of divine reflection in John's understanding of humanity, angels, and Christ.

To situate John's corpus in its historical context, I discuss common themes in the works of earlier authors, such as Pseudo-Dionysius, Gregory of Nyssa, Evagrius, and Pseudo-Macarius, that may have influenced

---

1. The extant works of John include a collection of letters, homilies, and a few chapters on spiritual knowledge. This article is based on his *Letters* and *Homilies*. For an updated list of his translations, see Alexander Treiger, "Could Christ's Humanity See His Divinity? An Eighth-Century Controversy Between John of Dalyatha and Timothy I, Catholicos of the Church of the East," *JCSSS* 9 (2009): 3–21.

2. See Sebastian Brock, "The Imagery of the Spiritual Mirror in the Syriac Literature," *JCSSS* 5 (2005): 4; Robert Beulay, *L'enseignement spirituel de Jean de Dalyatha, mystique syro-oriental du VIIIe siècle* (Paris: Beauchesne, 1993), 445.

John's thought. Though it is difficult to trace a direct line between all of these thinkers and John of Dalyatha, it is clear that their transmission into Syriac exerted influence upon the East Syriac tradition, of which John was a part. I will also incorporate a phenomenological approach when analyzing the role of angels and mirrors in hopes of better understanding their function in John's spiritual program.

I will argue that for John of Dalyatha both the mirror in the soul and the angels met there allow for an interiorized encounter and a continual shift between "seeing" and "being seen." This dialectic foreshadows the dynamic quality of John's later stage of contemplation when experiencing the light of the Holy Trinity. The final vision of the Holy Trinity in John of Dalyatha is not an event of complete union, even at its farthest stages, but an encounter amidst unity or a "mingling" (*ḥlṭ*) between unity and multiplicity, where the ascetic alternates between visions of glory and stages of "wonder" (*temhā*). Overwhelmed by light, even the self is periodically forgotten. Both a mirror and a choir of angels within the heart—emphasized in John's earlier stages of contemplation—express this paradox and the continual shift between seeing and being seen (or knowing and not-knowing). Both angels and humans encounter the divine in a similar process.

John as the Elder and the Heretic

The little information we have of John's life comes to us from two main sources: Išoʿdnaḥ of Baṣra's *Book of the Chastity* (*Ktābā d-Nakputā*) and a fifteenth-century manuscript from Mardin.[3] John was born in the village of Ardāmuth in Northern Iraq near the present-day border with Turkey, most likely around 690.[4] John's monastic life began north of this region, known in Syriac as Beth-Nuhadrā, in the Qardu Mountains at the monastery of Mār Yuzādaq. John went on to compose most of his writings further north in the mountains of the region (*Beh-Dalyāthā*) from which he earned his name "of Dalyatha," meaning "of grapevines" or "of the vine branches."[5] Though not at the site of the monastery of

3. See note seven in Treiger, "Could Christ's Humanity," 15. See also Brian Colless, "The Biographies of John Saba," *PdO* 3 (1972): 45–63.

4. Treiger, "Could Christ's Humanity," 5.

5. Ibid.

Mār Yuzādaq, he still may have been affiliated with that community.[6] John later ended his ascetical life in the region where he started in Qardu, where disciples gravitated around him and formed a monastic community in the renovated ruins of an old monastic structure.[7] He was most likely buried there around 780, though Treiger dates his death a few years later. He is often referred to as John "the Elder" (John Sābā) or, in Arabic, as the "Spiritual Elder" (*al-Šayk al-rūhānī*).[8]

In the Christological climate of this period in the Church of the East, it makes sense that John would emphasize vision of the divine as seeing a *reflection* rather than the object itself. According to this church's traditional Christology, simply put, there is a sharp distinction between Christ's human and divine nature to such a degree that each cannot participate in the other's properties. Jesus the man could not "see" Christ the God even within himself. Thus ascetics, despite their level of perfection, cannot see the divine in their own human nature. John of Dalyatha, however, seems to have emphasized the medium of the mirror within the human intellect in order to argue that the purified ascetic can see reflections of divine glory. Furthermore, in order to perhaps stretch the distinction between Christ's human and divine nature, John identifies the Son as the "knowledge" (*ida'tēh*) of the Father as well as of all rational beings (*mallālē*).[9] The intellect of these rational beings—humans and angels alike, as we shall see—possesses the potential to reflect divine glory. For John, the reflexive nature of a purified intellect or its "mirror" not only *reflects* the image of Christ but *emulates* Christ's own likeness to his Father. These statements, though, seem to have been problematic for Catholicos Timothy I (r. 780–823), who accused John of Sabellian and Messalian tendencies.

According to the ninth-century *Book of the Chastity* (*Ktābā d-Nakputā*), Catholicos Timothy I anathematized John of Dalyatha at the council of 786–787 for claiming that "our Lord's humanity could see His divinity."[10] These allegations are elaborated upon in Timothy's letter

6. Mary Hansbury, *The Letters of John of Dalyatha* (Piscataway: Gorgias Press, 2006), vii.

7. Treiger, "Could Christ's Humanity," 4.

8. Treiger also notes that he is referred to as "Spiritual Elder" (*Arägawi mänfäsawi*) in Ethiopic translations. Ibid., 3.

9. Ms. Vat. Syr. 124, ff. 332v–333r.

10. Treiger, "Could Christ's Humanity," 6. Joseph Ḥazzāyā and John of Apamea were also condemned at this council. The Syriac text and French translations of Išoʿdnaḥ of Baṣra's *Book of the Chastity*

to a later council, preserved in ʿAbdishoʿ bar Brikhā's *Nomocanon* (IX 6), where among errors, John is said to believe that "a created being can see its Creator."[11] As Brian Colless reminds us, though Timothy's successor Catholicos Ishoʿ bar Nun (r. 823–827) attempted to resuscitate John's reputation, John's writings are preserved for us only by West Syriac or Chalcedonian sources.[12] Thus his writings may have been edited to remove his more "heretical" statements, first perhaps by members of the Church of the East and later by West Syriac scribes. Nonetheless, we find a spiritual path articulated in imagery that resonates with Evagrius, Gregory of Nyssa, Pseudo-Macarius, and Pseudo-Dionysius. John's treatment of angels and mirrors, however, is particularly unique and captivating.[13]

Angels and Mirrors in Pseudo-Dionysius

Mary Hansbury, in the introduction to her volume on John of Dalyatha's *Letters*, points out that many of John's descriptions of

(*Ktābā d-Nakputā*) is available in J.-M. Chabot, *Le Livre de la chasteté composé par Jésusdenah, évêque de Baçrah* (Rome: École française de Rome, 1896).

11. As quoted in Treiger, "Could Christ's Humanity," 8; see the French translation in Robert Beulay, *La lumière sans forme: Introduction à l'étude de la mystique chrétienne syro-orientale* (Chevetogne: Editions de Chevetogne, 1987), 229.

12. Brian Colless, "The Mysticism of John Saba," *OCP* 39 (1973): 84. For example, Colless points to the presence of "Theotokos" (*Yāldat Alāhā*) in John's *Homilies* (ibid.). On the possible resuscitation of John in the early ninth century, see Alexander Treiger, "Al-Ghazālī's 'Mirror Christology' and Its Possible East-Syriac Sources," *The Muslim World* 101 (2011): 711.

13. Sebastian Brock, in his article that surveys mirror imagery throughout the Syriac tradition, points to a change in the use of mirror imagery that occurs in the seventh to eighth century in contrast to earlier writers, exemplified by Ephrem: "Whereas Ephrem was more concerned with the eye of the heart seeing the divine world reflected in the mirror of Nature and of Scripture situated *outside* itself, the monastic writers of the seventh and eighth century speak of an interior mirror that is to be found *within* the human person" (Brock, "Imagery of the Spiritual Mirror," 10). This change in emphasis is most apparent in Simon of Ṭaybuthēh and John of Dalyatha and, according to Brock, is due to the increased familiarity with Greek authors (most notably Athanasius, Gregory of Nyssa, Dionysius the Areopagite, and Abba Isaiah) among Syriac writers beginning in the fifth century. Particularly, Brock points to the Syriac translation of Gregory of Nyssa's *Commentary on the Song of Songs* around 500 (Ibid., 11). Robert Beulay also points to Nyssa as a principle influence upon John of Dalyatha's mirror imagery, though he cites Evagrius to a lesser extent, whose writings were translated into Syriac in the fifth and sixth century (Beulay, *L'enseignement spiritual*, 445). As possible sources for the turn towards the internalization of divine vision in the Syriac traditions, Beulay cites Pseudo-Macarius' emphasis on the brilliance of the glory of God present in the heart, Evagrius' emphasis on the contemplation of God in the intellect, and Gregory of Nyssa's emphasis on the presence of the God in the soul (Beulay, *La lumière sans forme*, 137). For more on the possible transmission of this theme into Islam, see Daniel De Smet, Meryem Sebti, and Godefroid De Callataÿ, eds., *Miroir et savior: La transmission d'un thème platonicien, des Alexandrins, à la philisophie arabo-musulmane* (Leuven: Leuven University Press, 2008).

angels can be found in Pseudo-Dionysius (ca. 500).[14] She quotes the following passages from *Celestial Hierarchy* that find resonances in John of Dalyatha: "their beauty similar to God and united with his Glory" (CH 165A); "their simplicity and their ability to be in whatever place they desire" (CH 333B); and "their multitudes" (CH 321A).[15] I hope to add to this list their ability to act as reflections of the divine.

The role of angels as *mirrors* is not necessarily explicit in John of Dalyatha, unlike John's description of the human soul. For this reason, when surveying the Syriac mystics of the seventh and eighth century (among which John of Dalyatha would be included), Brock points out that we do not find explicit images of angels, in his words, "serving as mirrors."[16] Brock notes that one might have expected these mystics to develop the following imagery found in Pseudo-Dionysius' *Divine Names*: "The Angel is an image of God. He is a manifestation of the hidden light. He is a mirror, pure bright, untarnished, unspotted, receiving, in one may say, the full loveliness of the divine goodness and purely enlightening within itself as far as possible the goodness of the silence in the inner sanctuaries."[17] I illustrate in this paper, however, that we find imagery of reflection running through—much a like a ray of light—John of Dalyatha's anthropology, angelology, and Christology. Angels do not necessarily serve the function of mirrors in themselves of the divine (though they do at times), but they often act as conduits of divine light, through which the image of God can be seen in the mirror of the human soul. Furthermore, every human contains a mirror through which we see angels that contain Christ who contains his Father. The act of seeing in each of these successive

14. Hansbury, *Letters of John of Dalyatha,* xvii. Hansbury's English translation with Syriac on the opposing pages is based on Robert Beulay's critical edition of the Syriac text in *La collection des lettres de Jean de Dalyatha,* PO 39.3 (Turnhout: Brepols, 1978). The writings of Dionysius were translated into Syriac relatively quickly after their composition in the beginning of the sixth century and again in the late seventh century. See Treiger, "Could Christ's Humanity," 5b; Beulay, *Lumière sans forme,* 158–183. Adam Becker speculates that, because the writings of Pseudo-Dionysius were used early on to defend West Syrian arguments, he may have been associated with West Syrian authors and thus not used initially by East Syrian monastic writers. However, according to Becker, he began to exert influence upon East Syrian writers by the late seventh century. Adam Becker, *Fear of God and the Beginning of Wisdom: The School of Nisibis and the Development of Scholastic Culture in Late Antique Mesopotamia* (Philadelphia: University of Pennsylvania Press, 2006), 178.

15. Hansbury, *Letters of John of Dalyatha,* xvii.

16. Brock, "Imagery of the Spiritual Mirror," 15.

17. Ibid, referencing *Divine Names,* 4:22, Colm Luibheid, *Pseudo-Dionysius: The Complete Works* (Mahwah: Paulist Press, 1987), 89.

interior journeys involves reflection. I will begin with John's understanding of vision in his anthropology, before progressing to how this is paralleled in his conception of angels and Christ.

The Eye of Light

Vision is important for John of Dalyatha. His monastic program begins and ends with discussions of seeing and not seeing. He begins his rule for novices that appears in letter eighteen, and in a similar form in homily ten, with the following warning: "Let a man's eyes not look here and there, but only be looking in front of him."[18] This restriction of earthy vision in all its fragmented forms is equated with the constant contemplation of the divine and the heavenly vision of unity that is revealed in oneself. John then ends his rule for novices: "If you observe all of these admonitions and engage at all times in thinking about God, truly in a short time your soul will be able to see the light of Christ in itself and never again will it become blind."[19] Interestingly, despite the prominence of the "Face of God" in his ultimate divine vision, John recommends that a novice should "look at everyone with modesty and not focus his eyes on a man's face."[20] In order to better understand these warnings, we must also understand John's conception of the mechanics of the eye and light.

John does not dwell on or explain the human eye, as does Plato, Gregory of Nyssa, and, as Nadira Khayyat illustrates, Philoxenus of

18. Letter 18:2 (Hansbury, *Letters of John of Dalyatha,* 88, Syriac on opposing page). All translations of John's *Letters* are cited from this volume, unless otherwise noted. Hansbury points out that this line also appears in Abba Isaiah's *Logos* X, 4 (see notes one and two in Hansbury, *Letters of John of Dalyatha,* 88). See also John's Homily 10, ms. Vat. Syr. 124, f. 311r. All translations of John's *Homilies* are my own and based on ms. Vat. Syr. 124, though I am in debt to Brian Colless' dissertation, which I consulted: Brian Colless, *The Mysticism of John Saba* (Ph.D. Diss., University of Melbourne, 1969). Colless' dissertation includes an English translation of twenty-five of John's homilies arranged according to their spiritual program. Colless prefers the term "discourse" rather than "homily" and plans on publishing a critical edition along with translation soon. The first fifteen homilies are available in Syriac with a French translation on the opposing page in Nadira Khayyat, *Jean de Dalyatha. Les homélies I–XV* (Université Antonine, Liban: Centre d'Études et de Recherches Orientales, 2007). Khayyat plans to publish the remaining homilies soon. My numbering of the homilies follows ms. Vat. Syr. 124 and Nadira Khayyat's numbering. However, for those wishing to consult Colless' translation, when citing John's *Homilies* I have also included the "discourse" in which the citation appears.

19. Letter 18:47 (Hansbury, *Letters of John of Dalyatha,* 96). See also Homily 10 (Discourse 1), ms. Vat. Syr. 124, f. 313v.

20. Letter 18:22 (Hansbury, *Letters of John of Dalyatha,* 90). See also Homily 10 (Discourse 1), ms. Vat. Syr. 124, f. 312r.

Mabbug (d. 523).[21] However, like many Christian thinkers before him, he demonstrates evidence of a hybrid "extramission" (the eye acting upon the object) and "intromission" (the object acting upon the eye) theory of vision. The debates concerning whether the eye acts upon the object or vice-versa, that had dominated Greek scientific treatises in earlier centuries, were no longer a major question by the second century when Christian theologians began employing optical metaphors for philosophical purposes.[22] Plato, himself, though famous for his emphasis on the visual fire or light that the eye emits, had already syncretized earlier optical debates. According to his *Timaeus,* vision consists of the light of the eye meeting the light of day to form a homogenous stream that then interacts with a material efflux or ray from the object and is somehow transmitted back to the eye.[23] For Aristotle, the eye (likened to water) has a much more passive role, and the properties of an object travel through the medium of air, made transparent by light, where there are imprinted into the eye.[24] For Plato, assimilation occurs in the meeting of the light of the eye with light of the day, and for Aristotle, it occurs in the eye receiving rays or color from outside it through a medium. But in both cases, vision is very tactile and includes assimilation through contact. Many early Christian writers in the eastern Mediterranean and Near East, despite other advances in geometric theories of vision, tended to revert to Plato's and Aristotle's understanding of vision, which were often not treated as being in conflict with another.[25] We thus see, in John of Dalyatha and other later Syriac writers, optical theories that

21. See Nadira Khayyat, "Le visage du Christ resplendissant dans le miroir du cœur," in *Le visage de Dieu dans le patrimoine oriental: Patrimoine syriaque actes du colloque VII,* edited by Rita Tohmé and Chawki El-Ramy, 77-87 (Université Antonine, Antélias-Liban: Centre d'Études et de Recherches Orientales, 2001), 82.

22. Mark Smith, *From Sight to Light: The Passage From Ancient to Modern Optics* (Chicago: University of Chicago Press, 2015), 131–132.

23. See *Timaeus* 45c–d. For a commentary on this passage, see David C. Lindberg, *Theories of Vision From Al-Kindi to Kepler* (Chicago: University of Chicago Press, 1981), 5. Lindberg points to Plato's *Thaetetus,* 156d–e, for a more explicit reference to how an object's emanations act upon the eye.

24. See *De Anima* II.7 and *De Sensu* 2 and 7. For a summary of Aristotle's theory of vision, see Lindberg, *Theories of Vision,* esp. 6–9.

25. According to Mark Smith, by the fourth century, the schools of Plato and Aristotle had been largely synergized especially in philosophical approaches to optics, thanks, in part, to the work of Porphyry. Mark Smith, *From Sight to Light,* 131–132. What appeared contradictory only needed to be "coaxed" into cohesion (ibid., 132).

demonstrate both the internal light of the eye extending outward and external light acting upon the eye.[26]

Vision is both an act of emitting and receiving light. Though the sun occupies the privileged position, the beholder's role is not passive. Rays of light form a "physical" connection between a person's eyes and the thing within one's gaze. Ascetics, concerned with purifying their hearts, should thus be careful with what they allow within reach of their eyes. Letter eleven of John of Dalyatha hints at this understanding of vision: "Since the outer sun of your pupils has been darkened by the violence of the adversities, all at once you will receive in exchange the place whose sun is the Creator. And this sun will gladden your face with a light without shadow."[27] John describes the pupil of the eyes as a sun, connoting a sense of the eye as emitting its own light. Yet this same sun is "darkened" through its exposure to the adversities it has had to endure. Thus the eye both emits light and has the capacity to receive light, regardless of the light's nature. For instance, in letter five, John compares humanity's turning away from divine things to the eye that does not see despite the light that shines in it: "Your light shines in the pupils of the eyes and we do not want to see."[28] Though John does not make any explicit reference to impressions or particles from objects entering the eye, he may have in fact subscribed to this theory. Nonetheless, the light that is received in the eye is often described in terms of daylight.

This dialectic can best be understood as a process of sympathy or mimesis. The eye, containing its own light, is attracted to the light of day and is transformed through its exposure to the sun, becoming more sun-like. Similarly, humans, as made in the image of God, are drawn towards the divine and in our exposure to God become more Godlike. This understanding of mimesis is not limited to vision. John writes: "The mouth of the pure in soul speaks at every hour about his Creator and listens to him gladly, taking on his likeness."[29] Listening to the divine just as seeing the divine enables one to emulate

26. For Ephrem's understanding of vision, which differs from John of Dalyatha's in a few respects, see Ute Possekel, *Evidence of Greek Philosophical Concepts in the Writings of Ephrem the Syrian*, CSCO 580 (Louvain: Peeters, 1999), chapter 8.2.2.

27. Letter 11:2 (Hansbury, *Letters of John of Dalyatha*, 48).

28. Letter 5:4 (Hansbury, *Letters of John of Dalyatha*, 36).

29. Homily 23 (Discourse 2), ms. Vat. Syr. 124, f. 346r.

what one receives, much like a mirror. One must point the mirror of one's soul in the right direction, so as to reflect the appropriate image. Through this process of emulation, in the case of vision, one's own light becomes united with the light that it encounters. John describes this process in the following passage:

> Just as the physical eye has power over all that is in existence because the created sun has the power to pass by it with its radiance, and its own view is extended without hindrance: so also it is for the spiritual eye which has obtained sight from Christ by means of purity, in that God is its Sun and He is stretched over all and in all without hindrance; likewise its own sight when it has acquired union with Him is stretched out over all and in all and above all, and all is a clear place for it. Who is able to prepare remedies for the eyes yielding light such as this?[30]

Just as the light of the sun allows the eye to see into the distance or "extend" without hindrance (a possible reference to Plato's "homogenous stream"), the spiritual eye once united with the light of Christ is able to view all that this spiritual light touches. This "yielding" of divine light within the spiritual eye, however, is a cause for caution.

Though John uses the mechanics of the eye and light as a source of analogy when describing his spiritual program, he is clear on the distinction between the physical and spiritual eye and thus promotes a divide between bodily and spiritual senses. That is, bodily senses must be interrupted before spiritual senses can be employed. In homily twelve, he prescribes "the ordering of senses" (*ṭukkās regšē*) "in discernment" (*pārošutā*) as the first step in being reborn as a Son of God.[31] He recommends "withholding" (*klā*) your sight from temporal beauty; "restraining" (*ḥsak*) your hearing of amusing sounds; "abstinence" (*ḥsikutā*) from pleasurable smells; and "curbing" (*pagged*) your tongue from vain words.[32] This watchfulness of

30. Letter 40:1 (Hansbury, *Letters of John of Dalyatha,* 174).

31. Homily 12 (Discourse 12), ms. Vat. Syr. 124, f. 321r.

32. Homily 12 (Discourse 12), ms. Vat. Syr. 124, f. 321r–321v.

bodily senses leads to an upwelling of spiritual delight. As we saw in his rule for novices, John often contrasts earthly blindness with celestial revelation.

His emphasis on the "turning off" of bodily senses maintains the transcendence of spiritual experiences, a point John may have been keen to stress to his audience of potential critics. The distinction between the physical and spiritual eye is mapped onto the type of light each enjoys, whether of the "created sun" or the "Sun the Creator."

However, when John describes the operations of these types of light, the relationship between physical and spiritual light appears to be more than mere metaphor.

Just as light illuminates the size of a dark room, John often describes light in terms of its ability to increase the spatial range of one's vision, materially or otherwise. In homily six he describes "divine light" as that which "is worn (*lbiš*) by all and passes through all unhindered."[33] While created light shines only on physical creation, divine light pervades all things material and spiritual. Thus, when the mind sees divine light, it is able to "observe in it all the boundaries of creation and beyond the boundaries and above every heaven, and the seas and the depths and all that is in them."[34] The human soul and angels are "visible" in this light, similar to the relationship between physical forms and the light of the sun. When discussing divine light, John writes: "In this light, the soul sees every soul. This is contemplation. And within it, the soul sees angels in their place, in their nature, and in their spirituality just as the eyes of the body see corporeal natures (*knāyē*) in their nature by means of created light. It also sees demons and the deeds performed by them."[35] But yielding to such light creates an issue of scale. How can a human grasp such a large perspective? How can something so big fit into something so small as the spiritual eye or soul? John solves this issue with the image of the mirror.

33. Homily 6 (Discourse 13), ms. Vat. Syr. 124, f. 296v. Also found in Khayyat, *Jean de Dalyatha*, 166.

34. Ibid.

35. Ibid.

The Mirror of the Intellect

The mirror in the soul allows a human being to bear divine light through reflection. John often uses the mirror as a device that maintains the transcendence of the divine image. For instance, John writes: "Blessed is the soul that knows itself to be a mirror (*maḥzitā*), and gazing intently on it sees the brightness of the One who is hidden from all."[36] In this case, one sees "the brightness" of the divine rather than the divine itself. We see the same contrast between immanence and transcendence in letter fourteen: "He is revealed then to the few who gaze intently within themselves: those who make of themselves a mirror in which the invisible is seen."[37] Through the watchfulness of one's passions, what was hidden or invisible becomes revealed in the reflection of a purified soul. As Brock points out, John goes on in this letter to stress this internal aspect of vision by slightly altering, or shall we say, "playing with," the sixth beatitude of Matthew 5:8. We read in the Peshiṭta, a verse with which John's readers would have been familiar: "Blessed are those who are pure in their hearts for they shall see God." John's version begins with the same chorus but perhaps surprises his readers with its last verse: "Blessed are those who are pure, for in their hearts, they shall see God."[38]

Gregory of Nyssa interprets this line of scripture in a similar fashion in his commentary on the beatitudes. Though he does not go so far as to locate the vision of God "in the heart" when quoting the beatitude, he clearly thinks this is where such vision occurs. And like John, he compares the heart to a mirror in order to maintain the transcendence of what is seen and reconcile this line of scripture with

36. Letter 7:3 (Hansbury, *Letters of John of Dalyatha,* 40).

37. Letter 14:2 (Hansbury, *Letters of John of Dalyatha,* 68).

38. Letter 14:2 (Hansbury, *Letters of John of Dalyatha,* 68, translation slightly altered to reflect word order). See Brock, "Imagery of the Spiritual Mirror," 14b and 17b. Brock also notes the similar association between Mt 5:8 and 2 Corinthians 4:18 in the Syriac *Book of Steps* (Memrā 18:3) and Clement of Alexandria (*Stromateis* I.94.6, V.40.1; VI.102.2; VII.57.1). On Clement, see R. Mortley, "The Mirror of 1 Cor. 13:12 and the epistemology of Clement of Alexandria," *VC* 30 (1976): 109–20. Gregory of Nyssa also references Paul and invokes the image of the "mirror" when reading this beatitude. As Beulay notes, Gregory of Nyssa's reading of Paul may have influenced John, though it is difficult to draw a direct line of transmission (see note 13). The clearest source of John's mirror imagery is Paul himself, as he cites him repeatedly. On Paul, see Norbert Hugedé, *La métaphore du miroir dans les Epîtres de saint Paul aux Corinthiens* (Neuchâtel, Switzerland: Delachaux & Niestlé, 1957). On Gregory of Nyssa, see G. Horn, "Le 'miroir,' la 'nuée' deux manières de voir dieu d'après S. Grégoire De Nysse," *Revue d'ascetique et de mystique* 8 (1927): 113–131.

those it seemingly contradicts, such as: "no one may see me and live" (Exodus 33:20).[39] Athanasius also invokes the mirror image in his commentary on the sixth beatitude in his *Contra Gentes.*[40] Despite the beatitude's clarity, even for those purest of heart to see God is impossible. Such a vision would circumscribe what cannot be limited and exceed humanity's ability to bear such an experience. But to see a *reflection* of God in a purified heart is possible and, in fact, a worthy goal.

This emphasis on the light of the divine as the object of vision rather the divine itself means that the divine source is not limited by such a vision. Gregory of Nyssa famously writes, when commenting on this beatitude: "He who is by nature invisible becomes visible in his operations (*energeias*)."[41] And John is clear that he is speaking of seeing divine "glory" (*šubḥā* or *tešboḥtā*) not divine "nature" (*kyānā*).[42] Thus both thinkers, in very simplistic terms, foreshadow Gregory of Palamas' distinction between God's essence (*ousia*) and energies (*energeiai*).[43] John, however, rather than employing phil-

39. Gregory of Nyssa writes in his commentary to this beatitude: "He does not seem to me to be offering God as an instant vision of the one whose spiritual eye is purified, but what the grandeur of the text proposes to us is that which the Word sets out more directly also to others, when he says that the kingdom of God is within us (Luke 17:21) so that we might learn that the person who has purged his heart of every tendency to passion perceives in his own beauty the reflection of the divine nature." (Homily VI: 4, cited according to Hubertus R. Drobner and Alberto Viciano, *Gregory of Nyssa. Homilies on the Beatitudes* [Leiden: Brill, 2000], 70). Gregory then compares purifying the heart of passions to the stripping of iron of rust, and continues: "Just as those who observe the sun in a mirror, though they do not gaze directly at the sky itself, none the less see the sun in the light beaming from the mirror of those who do look at the sun's own disc, so, he says, you also, even though you are too feeble to understand the unapproachable light, yet if you go right back to the grace of the image which was built into you from the first, you possess in yourselves what you seek."

40. Athanasius writes in *Contra Gentes* 2: 32–35: "Indeed the purity of the soul is able to contemplate even God through itself as in a mirror (*katoptrizesthai*), as the Lord himself said: Blessed are the pure in heart, for they shall see God" (according to Robert W. Thomson, *Athanasius: Contra Gentes and De Incarnatione* [Oxford: Clarendon Press, 1971], 6–8 [Greek], 7–9 [translation]). I have translated *di eautīs katoptrizesthai* as "through itself as in a mirror" rather than Thomas' translation "by itself" (7).

41. Homily VI: 3, Gregory of Nyssa, *Homilies on the Beatitudes,* 69 (*PG* 44.1269).

42. For example, John writes: "But as children resemble their begetter, so the sons which are of your Spirit are transformed into your likeness, not by nature (*kyānā*) but by glory (*šubḥā*)," Letter 51:12 (Hanbury, 252). As Berti Vittorio argues, Timothy I agreed with John of Dalyatha on the distinction between divine nature and glory but not on the qualities of that glory as an object of vision and the degree to which it transformed human ontology ("Le débat sur la vision de Dieu et la condamnation des mystiques par Timothée I: La perspective du patriarche," in *Les Mystiques Syriaques,* edited by Alain Desreumaux, 151-176 [Paris: Geuthner, 2011], 172).

43. See Beulay, *L'enseignement spirituel,* 460–464. For a treatment of Gregory of Nyssa and Gregory of Palamas on this question, see Alexis Torrance, "Precedents for Palamas' Essence-Energies Theology in the Cappadocian Fathers," *VC* 63 (2009): 47–70.

osophical vocabulary, often grounds his discussion by referring to God as simply light.

For John, the mirror in the human being maintains the transcendence of God not only in abstract terms but also spatially through the bending of divine light. John writes in letter twenty-five in response to a fellow brother who asks him the following question: "How God is wholly in every place while not being limited by the place."[44] When reading John's response, the importance of the mirror in the soul become apparent:

> Concerning the glorious and most blessed Nature which has created all and dwells in all without limits, being completely in every place while all the worlds together do not limit it, listen to what the Word says about this ineffable Nature: "He dwells in his saints." And in each of them He dwells totally with reflections (*ṣemḥē*) of light from his bosom, his ineffable powers; there He activates and shows forth all his power without being limited.[45]

The mirror in the soul of saints thus allows the glory of God's nature to "dwell totally with reflections of light" but not be limited by the "place" of the soul's body. We find a similar association of a purified intellect and limitlessness in Evagrius' famous description of the state of the mind at the time of prayer: "When the spirit has put off the old man to replace him with the new man, created by charity, then he will see that his own state at the time of prayer resembles that of a sapphire; it is as clear and bright as the very sky. This is what Scripture describes as the 'place of God'—what was seen by the ancients on Mt. Sinai."[46] Drawing from the Septuagint, Evagrius associates the "place of God" with sapphire light and equates this experience to Moses' vision of Mt. Sinai.[47] For both Evagrius and John, however, this

44. Letter 25:1 (Hansbury, *Letters of John of Dalyatha,* 118).

45. Letter 25:3 (Hansbury, *Letters of John of Dalyatha,* 120).

46. John Eudes Bamberger, *Evagrius Ponticus: The Praktikos & Chapters on Prayer* (Kalamazoo: Cistercian Publications, 1981), xci; *Peri logismōn* 39 and *PG* 40: 1244 A. Harmless and Fitzgerald point out that this exact quote is found in the Syriac version of the *Skemmata* but not in the Greek (William Harmless and Raymond R. Fitzgerald, "The Sapphire Light of the Mind: The Skemmata of Evagrius Ponticus," *JTS* 62 [2001]: 518).

47. Bamberger, *Evagrius Ponticus*, xci.

experience is internal. We thus find examples of reflexive vision, or the act of seeing oneself, in their descriptions of the spiritual states that accompany prayer. As in the example above, Evagrius periodically uses the image of the blue sapphire gem to describe this vision of the purified mind or *nous*. He compares the depths of the purified human to the limitless sky with which the sapphire shares its color. In John's description of this highest state, he often compares the depth encountered in the soul to the abyss of the ocean.[48] Though John also uses the image of a sapphire periodically, he more often uses the image of the mirror, among other metaphors.[49] Both images, though, include the reflecting or refracting of light and thus the unhindered extension of the light's rays. In this way, the mind or soul acts as a lens, whether in the image of a sapphire or a mirror, through which the limitless "place of God" can be experienced in the "container" of the created being. For John, angels—whose own "subtle" bodies could perhaps be described in terms of a collection of light similar to a sapphire or a mirror—participate in divine light through a similar process.

Angels as Mirrors

John is clear on the presence of angels within a purified individual. Angels populate the "place of God" seen within the human person. At times, John describes the "location" of this vision as the "intellect":

48. Among other examples, see Letter 40: 12–13 (Hansbury, *Letters of John of Dalyatha,* 184); Letter 37:3 (Hansbury, *Letters of John of Dalyatha,* 156); Letter 43:12 (Hansbury, *Letters of John of Dalyatha,* 201).

49. For examples of mirror references, see Hansbury, *Letters of John of Dalyatha,* 311 and fn. 47. John uses the sapphire image on rare occasions, for example: "So then in the vision of the sapphire, with the eternal eye, let us gaze on the Master of the house in the universal bosom. And outside it, let us exalt the many-splendored One and in this mystery may we find Him who effaces everything, even if we become ignorant of ourselves" (Letter 17:2 [Hansbury, *Letters of John of Dalyatha,* 84]). 'Universal bosom' *('ubbā kullānāyā)* most likely refers to the shared image of Christ within each human person. However, there is also a sense that Christ acts as the bosom of the Father. John prays: "Glorious radiance that shines forth to us from the bosom of the Father, through your desirable beauty, you captivate the desire of those who love you towards you from all else" (Homily 3 [Discourse 8], ms. Vat. Syr. 124, f. 284r; also found in Khayyat, *Jean de Dalyatha,* 122). Though this may also be a reference the Holy Spirit, the bosom imagery demonstrates a clear divine interiority. We find a similar reference to Christ, the only-begotten one, as the bosom of the Father in Aphrahaṭ's sixth demonstration: "The solitary (*iḥidāyā*) from the bosom of his Father gives pleasure to all the solitaries (*iḥidāyē*)." Aphrahat, *Demonstrations,* edited by D. Ioannes Parisot, *Aphraatis Sapientis Persae Demonstrationes I–XXII,* PS 1.1 (Paris: Firmin-Didot, 1894), 1, col. 269; as quoted in Adam Becker, *Fear of God,* 24.

"When the intellect has been purified of the obscurity of error, it becomes a heaven for the angels of light."[50] Similar to the vision of divine light, we can assume angels, as beings of light, are also visible through the medium of a mirror. John describes this device as the "mirror of the mind" but also the "mirror of the heart."[51] But as Brock notes, we can interpret the purified mind and heart as referring to the same thing.[52] The first stage of contemplation only begins after this purification has occurred. The soul, through repentance and God-centered prayer, must first remove its passions before it can reflect the light of the divine. In these beginning stages of encountering divine light, John describes the vision of the soul and the vision of angels. In the following series of questions that John poses to the reader—their presentation as questions perhaps hinting at the speculative and mysterious nature of the subject—John conflates throne and mirror imagery in his description of the human person as the locus of divine presence:

> When will all the kings reverence you and all the tongues praise you because you have become the holy throne of the King, the eternal King? When will you see in yourself the new heavens (Isaiah 65:17, 66:22; 2 Peter 3:13; Revelation 21:1) proclaiming in you the "Holy" of the Hidden One, in the order of their ranks? When will you see within you the mirror of the Light of the One who sees all, that you might see in it the things which are his and examine in it all that belongs to yourself?[53]

In this case, we can interpret "all that belongs to yourself" as a vision of one's soul and "the things which are his" as a vision of angels (among other possibilities), all of which is made visible by the mirror within the intellect. In addition, we also see the importance of praise in this program. The hosts of angels, as congregants in a liturgy within the

50. Letter 19:6 (Hansbury, *Letters of John of Dalyatha,* 102).

51. For instance, John equates the soul (*napšā*) with a mirror in Letter 7:3 (Hansbury, *Letters of John of Dalyatha,* 40); he describes the mirror of the "person" (*qnomā*) in Letter 51:13 (Hansbury, *Letters of John of Dalyatha,* 255); and he describes the mirror of the "intellect" or "mind" (*hawnā*) in Homily 24 ([Discourse 17], ms. Vat. Syr. 124, f. 349r).

52. Brock, "Imagery of the Spiritual Mirror," 14.

53. Letter 15:1 (Hansbury, *Letters of John of Dalyatha,* 70).

soul, sing "Holy, Holy, Holy." They are praying and participating in divine "glory" (*šubḥā*), the term John uses to explain what can be seen in the human person.

This intellect is something shared by humans and angels, and thus we can expect the "intellect" of spiritual beings to serve a similar function in the encountering of divine light. John begins homily twenty-four by comparing angels, in this case "holy powers" (*ḥaylē*), with humans: "Just as your holy powers are more abundant than the sand (*ḥālā*) in the seas, humans also are without number who are sanctified for your indwelling."[54] Despite these multitudes, John explains the paradox of intimacy that is felt by each, as if God dwelled within each alone:

> And although in each, you are seen in your entirety. Nothing is equal to your limit without limits. But each bears confidence and assurance in themselves that you—without alternation—are imprinted on the mirror of their minds. And thus each sees you within himself completely. Glory to you, many splendored star from Jacob, that rises from the heart and is seen in the mind of those above just as in those below.[55]

John's reference to the vision of light within the mind of "beings above as well as below" hints at the presence of a "mirror"—through which such light is seen—within the intellect of humans as well as angels. Though God is "without limits" he is imprinted on this mirror. We see here again the mirror functioning as a device that allows for the convergence of limitlessness, much like seeing the expanse of the horizon in a car's rearview mirror. Both angels and humans paradoxically contain the divine through such reflection of godly light. This imagery of angelic reflection is thus evocative of Pseudo-Dionysius' description of angels in *Divine Names*.[56]

This mirror also allows for an interiorized encounter. In this same homily, John describes angels and humans as recipients of a "seal"

---

54. Homily 24 (Discourse 17), ms. Vat. Syr. 124, f. 349r.

55. Homily 24 (Discourse 17), ms. Vat. Syr. 124, f. 349r–349v.

56. *Divine Names* 4:22. See fn. 18 above.

(*ṭabʿā*) of the divine image.[57] Similar to a mirror, once the seal is purified, Christ can be seen within it gazing back at the viewer. Both the viewer and Christ occupy passive and active roles in this process and serve as objects and subjects of vision. John describes Christ initiating this experience: "He makes all marvel at his indwelling, heavenly beings and humans alike who are pure, receiving the seal of his beloved image within themselves and gazing upon the beauty of his lordship in their hidden being insatiably."[58] Much like the simultaneous act of seeing and being seen when viewing a person looking at you through a mirror, John describes the vision of Christ's beauty within one's inner being. It is clear, for John, that Christ makes himself present internally for both humans and angels. John is very explicit that the mirror of the mind allows this to occur within the human person, but he also hints at a similar process within celestial beings.

The Angelic Threshold

We thus see the role of emulating angels in John's spiritual program. To encounter an angel is to become like an angel. John often describes angels as helping ascetics along the path of praise.[59] For example, John prays to Christ that angels may instruct him in their ways: "may your Spirit teach me their language so as to extol with them inaudible praise of You."[60] This assistance can include, it seems, replacing bad thoughts with good thoughts in the mind of the postulant. Angels, according to John, "lead men of diligence and illuminate their minds until they bring them toward them to see God, while extinguishing their passionate impulses and transforming their base thoughts into virtuous contemplation (*hergā*)."[61] Here, as in many other cases, the vision to which angels lead ascetics is associated with divine meditation. John writes that when the pure mind beholds the divine mysteries and other such things that shine forth from angels it is "drawn

57. Homily 24 (Discourse 17), ms. Vat. Syr. 124, f. 349r–349v.

58. Homily 24 (Discourse 17), ms. Vat. Syr. 124, f. 348r–349v.

59. For instance, John relates the testimony of another monk: "I was seeing the angel who clothed and covered me and my body was like fire from the activity of the angel" (Homily 6 [Discourse 5], ms. Vat. Syr. 124, f. 300a; also found in Khayyat, *Jean de Dalyatha*, 178).

60. Letter 5:3 (Hansbury, *Letters of John of Dalyatha*, 36).

61. Homily 11 (Discourse 21), ms. Vat. Syr. 124, f. 316r. Also found in Khayyat, *Jean de Dalyatha*, 226.

by them within them and is absorbed into God and captivated by the vision of his beauty."[62] John seems to be describing a series of inner sanctuaries beginning with the soul of the person and leading through the interior sanctum of angelic beings. Thus the ascetic, through the mirror of the soul, sees angels, who lead him or her further into the depths of their own celestial being, where one encounters the glory of God, all the while participating in God's glorification.[63]

We find angels playing a similar role of praise in Macarius, who clearly influenced John. Macarius begins his fifty spiritual homilies with Ezekiel's vision of the chariot and describes the Cherub with many wings "so that one could not discern any front or posterior parts."[64] He continues, "their backs were full of eyes and likewise their breasts were covered with eyes so that there was no place that was not completely covered with eyes."[65] He goes on to describe the ascent of the soul in similar angelic terms:

> For the soul that is deemed to be judged worthy to participate in the light of the Holy Spirit by becoming his throne and habitation, and is covered with the beauty of ineffable glory of the Spirit, becomes all light, all face, all eye. There is no part of the soul that is not full of the spiritual eyes of light. That is to say, there is no part of the soul that is covered with darkness but is totally covered with spiritual eyes of light. For the soul has no imperfect part but is in every part on all sides facing forward and covered with the beauty of the ineffable glory of the light of Christ, who mounts and rides upon the soul.[66]

62. Homily 11 (Discourse 21), ms. Vat. Syr. 124, f. 316r. Also found in Khayyat, *Jean de Dalyatha*, 226.

63. John, however, is not systematic in his treatment of angels. In other cases, he seems to draw a contrast between humanity's vision of God and the divine vision of angels: "The Cherubim and the Seraphim look modestly at the glory of his Greatness, but the pure soul sees this glory within itself without a veil. When the intellect has been purified of the obscurity of error, it becomes a heaven for the angels of light" (Letter 19:6 [Hansbury, *Letters of John of Dalyatha,* 102]). This notion of "modesty" (*knikutā*) can also be translated "dignity" or "reverence," thus John can also be describing an appropriate way of encountering divine glory.

64. George Maloney, *Pseudo-Macarius: The Fifty Spiritual Homilies and the Great Letter* (New York: Paulist Press, 1992), 33.

65. Ibid.

66. Ibid.

Interestingly, the beatified soul, like the cherub, is "all eyes." For Macarius, this seems to symbolize the soul's constant God-centered or "forward" gaze. The soul, like the cherub, lacks any distinguishing features between its front and back; it is all eyes, all face. There is no part of soul that is not fully focused on and participating in the divine. The soul, Macarius continues, "is privileged to be the dwelling-place and the throne of God, all eye, all light, all face, all glory and all spirit."[67]

We see here the imagery of the soul as the "dwelling place" of divine epiphany populated with angels, a theme we also find in John. John repeatedly refers to the highest stage of vision as a "place" (*atrā*), or the "place of no-place."[68] Bamberger explains this as a move by the Septuagint that, rather than describe a vision of God, which would be impossible, it describes where such a vision would occur (Ex 24:10; Is 24:15).[69]

Macarius and John also describe the notion of angelic "vision" as God-centered concentration or pure prayer. There is no aspect of one's being that is not praising God, that is not completely contemplating the divine and absorbed in its light. John describes this light as "holy, from which is filled the minds of your holy powers gazing upon its radiances without ceasing."[70] It thus makes sense that we find angels referred to in the Syriac tradition, drawing from Daniel, as "Watchers." For example, John compares the ascetic way of life to the path of angels: "our way of life is not casual but resembles that of the exalted Watchers."[71] He then goes on to play with the similarities between the terms "Watcher" (*'irā*) and the ascetic practice of watching one's consciousness (*'irutā*): "Watchfulness makes it a companion to the Seraphim."[72] Filtering out thoughts that are not of the divine leads to experiences of angelic or celestial vision. Watchfulness, in this sense, is associated with constant prayer, praise, and vision: the way of the angels. "Speaking briefly," John writes, "prayer without

67. Ibid.

68. Homily 15 (Discourse 15), ms. Vat. Syr. 124, f. 326v. Translation in agreement with Colless, "Mysticism," 191 (translation), 59 (Syriac). Also found in Khayyat, *Jean de Dalyatha*, 267.

69. Bamberger, *Evagrius Ponticus,* xci.

70. Homily 20 (Discourse 16), ms. Vat. Syr. 124, f. 332r.

71. Letter 3.4 (Hansbury, *Letters of John of Dalyatha,* 22).

72. Ibid.

ceasing is heartfelt praise or peering into God and amazement (*temhā*) at him."[73]

While Macarius describes this vigilance in terms of being "all eyes, all face," John describes this process as encountering angels in a mirror, before being absorbed in a cloud of light and darkness, where one forgets one's own being.[74] In both cases, however, we find a focus on divine presence to such a degree that there is dissolution of the subject and object. Amidst this encounter, it is as important that one is seen as it is that one sees.

In the Likeness of the Son

Just as divine light is found inwardly within the human intellect and within angelic beings, John often describes Christ's relationship with his Father in similar terms of interiority. John disagreed with Timothy I, however, on the degree to which Christ, as a human, participated in his divine nature. For John, when the Logos became incarnate, the human nature it assumed was able to see its divine nature. Referring to those who disagreed with him, John writes: "What shall we say to those lying prone in blindness, who rave and say that the human nature that was assumed from us does not see the nature of he that assumed it and united it to himself."[75] As Treiger points out in his commentary on this passage, the logic of this statement rests on John's description of the Son as the "mind" (*hawnā*) and "knowledge" of the Father.[76] All must approach the Father through this knowledge. John is clear that he is not speaking about the Logos only but the incarnate Son. Since the Son is united to the Father's divine nature, his human nature has access to the riches of his other half. Thus the

73. Homily 11 (Discourse 21), ms. Vat. Syr. 124, f. 318r–318v. Also found in Khayyat, *Jean de Dalyatha*, 232.

74. See my conclusion and Homily 6 (Discourse 13), ms. Vat. Syr. 124, f. 297v. Also found in Khayyat, *Jean de Dalyatha*, 170–172.

75. Homily 20 (Discourse 16), ms. Vat. Syr. 124, f. 332v–333r.

76. Homily 20 (Discourse 16), ms. Vat. Syr. 124, f .332r. It was this imagery that Catholicos Timothy I, eager to preserve his Trinitarian theology amidst Muslim and Miaphysite critic, found evocative of Sabellianism. For detailed discussion of Timothy's council, see Treiger, "Could Christ's Humanity." As Treiger notes, this description of Christ as the mind (*hawnā*) of the Father, however, is also found in East Syriac writings considered orthodox by Timothy (see ibid., 9b–10a). Treiger also speculates this homily may have been written by John in reaction to Timothy's anti-Messalian campaign of 782, thus placing John's death sometime thereafter (ibid., 11).

humanity of Christ knows and sees what the Father sees. In addition, drawing from Evagrian notions of the mind (*nous*) at the time of prayer, John often describes the human soul as seeing its own being and nature in its ascent towards the divine. If we map this onto Christ, Christ is able to see his own nature, a nature that is both human and divine.

Because Christ's human and divine natures are united, his being does not *reflect* the divine but *is* the divine in perfect likeness. John writes of the Son: "You are in the likeness of your Father without change or alternation."[77] This allows John to describe Christ as hidden in the Father and the Father as hidden in Christ. John's presentation of this paradox is similar to the way in which he discusses the mystery of divine presence within the human person and celestial beings. John writes in Homily twenty-four:

> You are hidden in your Father in incomprehensibility from all. While your Father alone is equal to your quantity (*mānāyutā*), you alone, also, are equal to his quiddity (*aykānāyutā*). Christ, the beauty of the Father, through you is opened to us the gate of the mysteries of your Father that were concealed in you from eternity, grant that we might enter through you the temple of our souls. And within it, that we might see you, the hidden treasure of life.[78]

John, here, compares the concealment of the Father's mysteries within Christ to the concealment of Christ within the temple of the human soul. A similar mimesis that exists between the Son and the Father can exist between humans and Christ. However, rather than the small containing the big (as we find when humans and angels bear the divine), Christ is equal to the Father. Ascetics, nonetheless, strive after emulation of Christ in seeking divine union. But rational creatures require a purified being capable of receiving divine light in order to bear the full quantity of this light, while Christ's divine nature is the light's very source.

77. Homily 24 (Discourse 17), ms. Vat. Syr. 124, f. 350r.

78. Homily 24 (Discourse 17), ms. Vat. Syr. 124, f. 350r.

Conclusion: Blinding Reflections

Just as Evagrius states that one must reach a stage of dispassion (*apatheia*), Dalyatha asserts that one's mind must be "naked" (*'arṭellāyā*) and "limpid" (*šapyā*) in order to contemplate the Trinity.[79] Similar to Pseudo-Dionysius' phases of repentance, illumination, and perfection, John of Dalyatha demonstrates three levels of contemplation that also map easily onto 'Abdisho' (Joseph) Ḥazzāyā's "corporeal," "psychical," and "spiritual" stages.[80] And similar to Evagrius' *praktikē* and *theoria*, John's later stages are characterized by "light without form" (*nuhrā dlā dmū*).[81]

In homily eight, John describes three stages of a spiritual program: the contemplation (*te'oriyā*) of "bodies," the contemplation of "intellectual natures" (including angels), and the "vision of the Holy Trinity."[82] John makes a distinction between the different levels of light encountered throughout this process, beginning with created light and ascending unto the light of the Holy Trinity. In this final stage of wonder, the light of Christ and the Trinity "effaces everything," even the awareness of the self.[83]

However, as Beulay and Nadira Khayyat describe in detail, these stages of form and formlessness are not always described in succession but rather are often experienced in alternating sequence much like waves on a shore.[84] For the purposes of this article, I only wish to highlight this dialectic between the positive and negative ways of experiencing divine light. That is, it can be experienced positively through seeing the soul illuminated and the angelic bodies. And it can also be experienced negatively as a blinding light or dark cloud, into which one can no longer gaze and within which one forgets even oneself.[85] John summarizes this last stage in the following pas-

79. Treiger, "Could Christ's Humanity," 4b.

80. Colless, "The Mysticism of John Saba," 96. See also Beulay, *L'enseignement spirituel*, 33–51; Colless, "The Mysticism of John Saba," 93–97; Khayyat, *Jean de Dalyatha*, 43–57.

81. See Beulay, *L'enseignement Spirituel*, 393–395.

82. Homily 8 (Discourse 22), ms. Vat. Syr. 124, f. 306r–307r; also found in Khayyat, *Jean de Dalyatha*, 200–204.

83. Letter 17:2 (Hansbury, *Letters of John of Dalyatha*, 84).

84. See Khayyat, *Jean de Dalyatha*, 48 and 62–63; Beulay, *L'enseignement spirituel*, 390.

85. The light that emerges from such paradoxically luminous but dark clouds seems to permit an appropriate type of vision, where the light of one's own eyes is unable to fully penetrate and

sage that warrants an extended quote:

> Until now, the mind is directed by the hand of the angels; From here and within he is led, like them, through the operations of the spirit. While meeting a dark cloud of light and awestruck, he forgets himself, the vision of spirits, and the vision of his existence. And within it, from this cloud of unapproachable light in which it is said God dwells, rays of lights shine—upon the mind deemed worthy through mercy—of a glory of grandeur in their beauty that surpasses the vision of that light of the cloud, just as that (light) surpassed the radiance of the sun. Blessed is the one who is deemed worthy of entering here and seeing this. Here the soul sees the face of its Lord and is astonished.[86]

The highest stage seems to alternate between "visions" and "stupor," leading to higher and higher stages of glory.[87] For John, this state of wonder is privileged and the role of the mirror in the soul is no longer emphasized. However, ontologically, the mirror always remains.[88] We can perhaps describe this last stage as a mirror polished without any traces of tarnish or blemish. When reflecting such intense spiritual light there are moments when the distinction between the source of the light and the mirror itself (whether within the viewer or within other beings) no longer becomes recognizable.

Khayyat, in her article on mirror imagery in John of Dalyatha, briefly points to this intersubjective quality of the mirror in John's spiritual program. On the phenomenological level, the mirror points to, in her words: "the interaction between the knower and the known, between the subject and the object, of the sort that the knowledge is

---

"understand" what one is seeing. For instance, John describes this type of light in Letter 51: "And because the vision is not able to expand in the light, driven back by its powerful reflections (*ṣemḥē*), they say that You are clouds and thick darkness, and that luminous clouds surround you and block the sight of those who love You from gazing in a disorderly way, seeking to see your hidden Nature" (Letter 51:8 [Hansbury, *Letters of John of Dalyatha,* 250]).

86. Homily 6 (Discourse 13), ms. Vat. Syr. 124, f. 297v. Also found in Khayyat, *Jean de Dalyatha,* 170–172.

87. See fn. 80 above.

88. See Beulay, *L'enseignement spirituel,* 447; Hansbury, *Letters of John of Dalyatha,* xii; Khayyat, "Le visage du Christ," 81.

marked by the qualities of the one and the other."[89] Khayyat, borrowing a phrase from the eighth-century Joseph Ḥazzāyā, characterizes this image as a "living mirror." She relates this to the relationship of Paul with Christ, when Paul writes: "It is no longer I, but he, who lives in me" (Gal 2:20).[90]

Above all others, Paul—a writer read by many others—is the clearest influence on John's mirror imagery. But we can point to several sources that may have been in the ether of the eighth-century East Syrian milieu. The works of Pseudo-Dionysius not only influenced—perhaps indirectly—John's negative theology but also, very likely, influenced his depiction of angels. John of Dalyatha's mirror and angel imagery also resonates with Gregory of Nyssa, Evagrius, and Macarius. Like Pseudo-Dionysius, angels act as mirrors of divine light and, like Gregory of Nyssa, John emphasizes the mirror within the human intellect. Though Evagrius describes the state of the mind in prayer as a sapphire, John's description of the mind or soul as a mirror also allows for the unhindered extension of divine light. And like Macarius, in the highest stages of contemplation, only praise and light remain.

Based on John's theory of vision and his understanding of light, turning one's gaze inward, for both humans and angels, rather than extending outward, hints at John's notion of spiritual "non-vision." The mirror within one's being allows for the yielding of such spiritual light. Humans were made in the image of God (Genesis 1:27), that is, in the image of the Christ, who, according to John, is a pure likeness of his Father. The polished mirror within the human person not only *reflects* this image but also emulates Christ's own divine mimesis. This dialectic of reflection runs throughout John's spiritual program. In the earlier stages, divine light is seen in the mirror of the soul and within the angels seen there, "visions" that also seem to reoccur later amidst waves of "wonder" (*temhā*). Both of these early experiences, though, foreshadow the quality of vision in the final stage. Angels and mirrors cast a returning gaze; seeing personified light in a mirror or in an angel involves "being seen" as much as it involves "seeing." And encountering a reflection, whether in the human person or in a celestial being, retains the transcendence of what is seen.

89. Khayyat, "Le visage du Christ," 81.

90. Ibid.

In John's vision of the Holy Trinity, like Macarius' vision of the heavens, there is only light to such a degree that it becomes too difficult to distinguish between the seer and the seen. Here, in a stage of stupor and mingling between unity and multiplicity, there is only divine presence; there is only the Face of a Triune God. John is clear that humans must polish the mirror within their intellect to experience this vision, while angels encounter divine light in a similar process. John of Dalyatha perhaps attempted to defend his descriptions of seeing the divine by emphasizing vision as an awareness of presence and encounter rather than an understanding of what one is seeing.

13. On Sources for the Social and Cultural History of Christians during the Syriac Renaissance

❖ Dorothea Weltecke

"Back to the sources" is a very welcome motto for the historian. Two avenues to approach it present themselves. First, some analytical questions will be examined regardless of whether sources for their treatment are known or even available. Second, some groups of sources shall be discussed from the point of view of social and cultural history.

I

The Period: The Age of the Syriac Renaissance

The term "renaissance" as an analytical designation for medieval cultures was formed in the early 20th century. Charles Homer Haskins, for example, published his monograph on the renaissance of the 12th century in the Medieval Latin world.[1] In his influential portrayal of the period, Haskins stressed elements like revival and reform movements, the transfer of philosophy and science from Arabic into Latin, and the birth of the universities. Haskins strove to correct the image of the Middle Ages as a dark age of ignorance. Similar cultural features were

1. Charles H. Haskins, *The Renaissance of the Twelfth Century* (Cambridge: Harvard University Press, 1927). It is impossible to present an adequate bibliographical documentation of the point made in this overview; I confine myself to works mentioned in the text and to some more recent publications.

observed elsewhere and also labelled as "renaissance." For the Muslim world, for example, the rule of the Buyyids (930–1060) has been called a "renaissance" as well.[2] Accordingly, the period of Syriac literature from the eleventh to the thirteenth century was conceptualized in this vein.[3] These concepts reflect the scholarly tradition of classical modernity. On this foundation, the Warburg school and the renaissance studies of the following decades changed the concepts again and constructed the cultural movement of the renaissance of the fourteenth to the seventeenth century as the decisive watershed of European history.[4]

In light of the Warburgian concept, the term does not seem to be appropriate any longer, but it has remained in use,[5] and it was recently supported again by a number of publications by and under the auspices of Herman Teule.[6] The "Syriac renaissance" is seen today as one strand of similar revival movements all over Eastern Christian worlds, like the Coptic renaissance,[7] and cultural revivals in Armenian, Melkite, or Georgian cultures. Consequently, Mat Immerzeel suggested the term "Christian renaissance" as a common denominator.[8] Viewed together, a cross-continental cultural drive becomes apparent that included Eastern and Western Christians, as well as Muslim and Jewish cultures in the West and in the East.[9]

2. Adam Mez, *Die Renaissance des Islam* (Heidelberg: C. Winter, 1922); English translation by Salahuddin Khudi Bakhsh and D. S. Margoliouth as *The Renaissance of Islam* (Patna: Jubilee Printing & Publishing House, 1937).

3. Anton Baumstark, *Geschichte der syrischen Literatur mit Ausschluss der christlich-palästinensischen Texte* (Bonn: A. Marcus, E. Weber und A. Ahn, 1922), 285–326.

4. Raymond Klibansky, Erwin Panofsky, and Fritz Saxl, *Saturn and Melancholy. Studies in the History of Natural Philosophy, Religion and Art* (Nendeln—Liechtenstein: Kraus, 1964, rep. 1979).

5. Joel Kraemer, *Humanism in the Islamic Renaissance* (Leiden: Brill, 1993); Stefan Heidemann, *Die Renaissance der Städte in Nordsyrien und Nordmesopotamien. Städtische Entwicklungen und wirtschaftliche Bedingungen in ar-Raqqa und Ḥarrān von der Zeit der benuinischen Vorherrschaft bis zu den Seldschuken* (Leiden: Brill, 2002); Peter Kawerau, *Die jakobitische Kirche im Zeitalter der syrischen Renaissance. Idee und Wirklichkeit* (Berlin: Akademie-Verlag, 1960); Jules Leroy, "La renaissance de l'église syriaque au XIIe–XIIIe siècles," *Cahiers de civilisation médiévale* 14 (1971): 131–148; 239–255.

6. See, for example, Herman Teule, "Gregory Barhebraeus and his Time. The Syrian Renaissance," *JCSSS* 3 (2003): 21–43; Herman Teule, Carmen Fotescu Tauwinkl, Bas ter Haar Romeny, and Jan J. van Ginkel, eds., *The Syriac Renaissance*, ECS 9 (Louvain: Peeters, 2010).

7. Adel Sidarus, "La Renaissance copte arabe du Moyen Âge," in H. Teule et al., eds., *The Syriac Renaissance*, 311–340.

8. Mat Immerzeel, "Medieval wall paintings in Lebanon: Donors and Artists," *Chronos* 10 (2004): 7–47, at 13–15.

9. Norman A. Stillman, *The Jews of Arab lands. A history and source book* (Philadelphia: The Jewish Publication Society of America, 1979); Shelomo Dov Goitein, *A Mediterranean Society* (Berkeley:

Two contradicting forces complicated political conditions at the time. There were imperial tendencies, for example, those of the Eastern (Byzantine) and Western Roman Empire, the Seljuqid Sultans, and the Mongols. At the same time political structures disintegrated and localized, and small principalities emerged on the area of former empires like the kingdoms of the Artuqids, the Atabegs of Mosul, the Latin crusader principalities, or the Armenian principalities in Cilicia. The period witnessed countless minor and major wars, rapid shifts of military borders and of secular rule.

Yet at the same time this was also a period of general economic development, of arts and crafts, of trade. Medieval cultures created surplus and even wealth which manifested itself, for example, in monumental new religious and secular buildings from Iran to the British Isles. In these centuries multiple economic and cultural relations between Asia, Europe, and Northern Africa formed an interconnected space as large as the ancient empires. The period from the eleventh to the thirteenth century is a dynamic and momentous period in history. With all due caution and reserve, the term "renaissance" might nevertheless be justified to promote the study of the history of the Syrian Christians at that time, at least for as long as it is still in the shadow of earlier periods.

Social and cultural history of Syrian Christians

As to a social and cultural history of the Syrian Christians during this period, there is no comprehensive presentation available.[10] History is not the academic discipline most active in Syriac studies. Consequently, early programs did not translate into empirical research and methodological refinement beyond initial stages. The visionary design of the chapters on the Eastern churches developed by Bertold Spuler for the *Handbuch der Orientalistik*[11] was employed in the thesis of his pupil Peter Kawerau on the Syriac Orthodox

University of California Press, 1967–1993); Johann Arnason, "Parallels and Divergences: Perspectives on the Early Second Millennium," *Medieval Encounters* 10 (2004): 13–40, and the other articles in this number.

10. Herman Teule, "The Syriac Renaissance," in Teule et al., eds., *The Syriac Renaissance*, 1–30, at 2.

11. Bertold Spuler, "Die nestorianische Kirche, Die westsyrische (monophsyitische/jakobitische) Kirche, Die Maroniten, Die Thomas-Christen in Süd-Indien, Die armenische Kirche, Die koptische Kirche, Die Äthiopische Kirche," in *Handbuch der Orientalistik* 1, vol. 8, edited by Bertold Spuler, 120–324 (Leiden: Brill, 1961).

church. Both aimed at understanding the structure of the church with all its institutions and social groups, and the church's interaction with other communities.[12] This was also true for contemporary historians of Jewish history, like Shelomo Goitein and his magisterial work on the social history of the Mediterranean Jews.

Goitein covers the same period and developed his design also in the 1960s. These years were the peak phase of writing social history in the US and Europe.[13] Obvious discrepancies between the short and the monumental size left aside, there are interesting differences in the design of both works of historiography. Kawerau saw the heart of the Syriac Orthodox history in the structure of its ecclesiastical hierarchy, as traditional church historians tended to. For Goitein the foundation of Jewish society was economy and the working people, men and women. In Syriac studies, in contrast, the life of the lay people in the Middle Ages is not taken much notice of.

At that time, broad representations of the social and economic history of Medieval Europe, including Latin, Byzantine, and Slavonic regions, were also written.[14] They display a special interest in the natural environment and conditions of human life; in the details of social strata, starting with the aristocracy; and in economic theory along with a historical study of crafts, trades, and money. In medieval studies a long and lively controversy on the structure of social order (traditionally labelled "feudalism") and the so-called estates accompanied and still accompanies the scholarly debate, and calls attention to the virtual absence of any such discussions on social strata in the history of Syriac Christians.[15]

In comprehensive histories of Islamic culture, sociological theories also seem to be less frequently employed. Instead, state and community formation, religious thought, and institutions once

12. Kawerau, *Die jakobitische Kirche im Zeitalter der syrischen Renaissance*; Dorothea Weltecke, "60 years after Peter Kawerau. Remarks on the Social and Cultural History of Syriac-Orthodox Christians from the XIth to the XIIIth Century," *Le Muséon* 121 (2008): 311–335.

13. Peter N. Stearns, "Social History," in *Encyclopedia of Social History*, 806–811 (London: Routledge, 1993).

14. See, for example, Jan A. van Houte, ed., *Handbuch der europäischen Wirtschafts- und Sozialgeschichte*, vol. 2. *Europäische Wirtschafts- und Sozialgeschichte im Mittelalter* (Stuttgart: Klett-Cotta, 1980).

15. See, for example, Georges Duby, *The Three Orders: Feudal Society Imagined* (Chicago: University of Chicago Press, 1981); Richard Abels, "The Historiography of a Construct: 'Feudalism' and the Medieval Historian," *History Compass* 7 (2009): 1008–1031.

more take center stage. The emergence of the so-called Islamic society is the main focus, rather than social inequality. Non-Muslims in these social histories often take the role of mere "minorities," which is as little adequate as the usual treatment of Jews in Latin history.[16] However, here, too, the impact of socio-historical methods and interests are clearly felt.[17]

For a long time, social history has faced the challenges of other methodological perspectives, among them new cultural history.[18] Cultural history is less interested in the hard facts, statistics, and social structures than it is in how and by which means people made sense of them and who dominated this process. These and other approaches can be taken as complementary. While classical social history may seem somewhat old-fashioned today, the foundation of a future cultural history of Syriac Christians from the eleventh to the thirteenth century should be a clearer understanding of social strata and access to resources, of those who worked and those who ruled.

Churches and political power

One crucial condition for the existence of the Syriac communities was their respective relation to political powers. As we have seen, there were different and rapidly changing political structures. The impact of the political structures, Byzantine, Latin, Muslim Shiʿa and Sunni, has not been studied in a comparative and systematic way, nor the impact of the moving military frontiers. For example, secular rulers, Christian and Muslim alike, frequently interfered with the jurisdiction of the patriarchs and imposed the investiture of bishops. The strategies of both sides, the agency of the churches and the calculations of the secular rulers in these relations, are part of the political frame of Christian life.[19]

Concerning the impact of political entities, two primary—and

16. Alfred Haverkamp, "Europas Juden im Mittelalter. Zur Einfühung," in *Europas Juden im Mittelalter. Beiträge des internationalen Symposiums in Speyer vom 20.–25. Oktober 2002*, edited by Christoph Cluse, 13–29 (Trier: Kliomedia, 2004).

17. P. M. Holt, Ann K.S. Lambton, and Bernard Lewis, eds., *The Cambridge History of Islam* (Cambridge: Cambridge University Press, 1970).

18. See, for example, Peter Burke, *What Is Cultural History* (Cambridge: Polity, 2004).

19. For example, Alessandro Orengo and Pier Giorgio Borbone, "Stato e chiesa nell'Iran ilkhanide. La chiesa alla corte di Arghon nelle fonti siriache e armene," *EVO* 29 (2006): 325–337.

contradictory—tendencies involving the Syriac Christians present themselves. Because of the asymmetrical position of Muslims and Dhimmis and because of the shifting political allegiances, the situation for Syriac Christian communities was always potentially dangerous. Christians, beside their affiliation to the churches, were also locally attached and integrated. Thus, political conflicts and wars had a destabilizing effect on the social cohesion of the churches. The Western and Eastern part of the Armenian hierarchy drifted apart, and the Syriac Orthodox church experienced schisms more or less along the Eastern crusade frontier.

In contrast to that, there were the small but culturally active courts of Latin Antioch, the Armenian principality of Cilicia, of the Artuqids,[20] of the Atabegs of Mosul especially in the period of Badr al-Din Lu'lu' (1211–1259),[21] and of the Mongols. Positive relations between non-Christian rulers and Christians resulted in the flourishing of Syriac Christian culture, writings, and art.[22] The city of Mardin, for example, was promoted to a Syriac Orthodox metropolis at the end of the eleventh century. The new status was only possible with the approval of the Artuqids.[23]

On the level of making sense of the world, Syriac poets and historiographers commented on and integrated the dramatic events into their own memorial culture.[24] It is interesting to see that Syriac historical writings often deliberately ignore political borders and designations but keep using traditional designations. Consequently, for both the Church of the East and the Syriac Orthodox Church, the ancient Roman–Persian demarcation remained very present even 500 years after its dissolution. The ancient border continued to define

20. Ray Jabre Mouawad, "The Syriac Renaissance Viewed from Ḥesnō Ziad (Kharpūt), near Melitene," in Teule et al, eds., *The Syriac Renaissance*, 265–292.

21. Bas Snelders, *Identity and Christian-Muslim Interaction: Medieval Art of the Syrian Orthodox from the Mosul Area* (Louvain: Peeters, 2010), 99–104.

22. Charles Burnett, "Antioch as a Link between Arabic and Latin Culture in the Twelfth and Thirteenth Century," in *Occident et Proche-Orient: Contacts scientifiques au temps des Croisades. Actes du colloque de Louvain-la-Neuve, 24 et 25 Mars 1997*, edited by Draelants Tihon Abeele and Isabelle Anne van Baudouin, 1–78 (Turnhout: Brepols, 2000).

23. Jean-Maurice Fiey, *Pour un Oriens Christianus Novus. Répertoire des diocèses syriaques orientaux et occidentaux* (Stuttgart: Steiner, 1993), 233–238.

24. Alessandro Mengozzi, "A Syriac Hymn on the Crusades from a Warda Collection," *EVO* 33 (2010): 187–203.

Syriac Orthodox identity as either "Westerners" or "Easterners."[25]

Ultimately only a combination of Syriac and non-Syriac sources will provide an adequate basis to understand the two strategies of loyalty and autonomy concerning political rule, borders, and landscape at that time of heightened religious awareness in Muslim as well as in Christian quarters.

Rural cultures

Syriac Christians lived rural lives in West and Central Asia, and their agricultural products were one element that kept the societies going. So far there have been no systematic studies of rural life for our period. Syriac sources such as chronicles and law books can yield more information on rural life than has hitherto been drawn from them. On the basis of these sources, I argue that there were powerful families among the Christian population. Village populations were sometimes ruled by Syriac Christian leaders, who resided in fortified places, or by monasteries, which were also often fortified and defended by militia. There was personal bondage like slavery, and apparently something similar to servitude.[26] As the picture is not very clear yet, it would also be useful to look elsewhere for information, to Byzantine and Islamic studies as well as to sociological and anthropological sources of the present.[27] Elizabeth Campbell, for example, has analyzed Muslim geographers and their books on monasteries in order to reconstruct medieval Muslim interpretations of their own world as urban, in contrast to a rural Christian culture.[28] These writings

25. Dorothea Weltecke, "Bar 'Ebroyo on Identity: Remarks on his historical writing," *Hugoye* 19 (2016): 303-332.

26. Dorothea Weltecke, "Contacts between Syriac Orthodox and Latin Military Orders," in *East and West in the Crusader States. Context - contacts - confrontations, III. Acts of the congress held at Hernen in September 2000*, OLA 125, edited by Krijnie Ciggaar and Herman Teule, 53–77 (Louvain: Peeters, 2003); Weltecke, "60 years after Peter Kawerau," 318.

27. See, for example, Société Jean Bodin pour L'histoire Comparative des Institutions, ed., *Les communautés rurales*, pt. 3. *Asie et Islam*, vol. 3. *Recueils de la Société Jean Bodin pour l'histoire comparative des institutions,* vol. 42. (Paris: Dessain et Tolra, 1982), although it entirely fades out non-Muslim minorities.

28. Elizabeth Campbell, *A Heaven of Wine: Muslim-Christian encounters at monasteries in the early Islamic Middle East* (Ph.D. Diss., University of Washington, 2009).

were edited and translated almost a century ago,[29] but Campbell uses them with new methods of cultural history that produce important and fresh insights into the structure of the worlds Christians and Muslims shared. Yāqūt al-Rūmī (1179–1229), in his geographical dictionary of the thirteenth century, registers a large number of monasteries.[30] Whereas he added descriptions of their natural products, Syriac Christian texts highlighted the spiritual importance of the monasteries. In this respect, the book by the thirteenth-century Coptic priest Abū al-Makārim on the "History of the churches and monasteries of Egypt and some neighbouring countries" even reads like a Christian answer to the Muslim geographers and what must have seemed a distortion of monastery life to Christian readers. His work deals with parts of Western Asia and is thus relevant for the study of Syriac Christians.[31]

Urban cultures

While Muslim conceptions of urban culture tended to ignore the Dhimmis,[32] Dhimmis were present in the cities of the Levant and the Mediterranean, in Central Asia, in the ports along the Arabian Gulf, and all the way to China. One of the medieval changes shown by Goitein was the urbanization of Jewish culture; Christians, as well, strove for presence, representation, and participation in the city.[33]

In modern scholarship, too, the medieval cities under Muslim rule are unvaryingly labelled as "Islamic cities." Even if this concept

29. Eduard Sachau, *Vom Klosterbuch des Šâbuštî* (Berlin: Verlag der Akademie der Wissenschaften, 1919).

30. Ferdinand Wüstenfeld, *Yāqūt Ibn-ʿAbdallāh ar-Rūmī. Kitāb Muʿǧam al-Buldān* (Leipzig: F. A. Brockhausin Comm., 1866–1873).

31. Clara ten Hacken, "The Description of Antioch in Abū al-Makārim's History of the Churches and Monasteries of Egypt and some Neighbouring Countries," in *East and West in the Medieval Eastern Mediterranean: Antioch from the Byzantine Reconquest until the End of the Crusader Principality*, vol. 3. *Acts of the Congress held at Hernen in May 2003*, OLA 269, edited by Krijnie Nelly Ciggaar, David Michael Metcalf, and Herman Teule, 185–216 (Louvain: Peeters, 2006); Basil T. A. Evetts (with Alfred J. Butler), *The Churches and Monasteries of Egypt and Some Neighbouring Countries Attributed to Abu Salih the Armenian* (Oxford: Clarendon Press, 1895, rep. 1969, 2001).

32. Some categories of Muslim geographers are presented in Paul Wheatley, *The Places where Men pray together. Cities in Islamic Lands, Seventh through the Tenth Centuries* (Chicago: University of Chicago Press, 2001).

33. Goitein, *A Mediterranean Society*; Samuel N. C. Lieu et al., eds., *Medieval Christian and Manichean Remains from Quanzhou (Zayton)*, vol. 2. (Turnhout: Brepols, 2012); Hamad M. Bin Seray, "The Arabian Gulf in Syriac Sources," *NAS* 4 (1997): 205–232.

has been under scrutiny for a while, integrated multi-religious models for these cities are so far lacking.[34] In the urban spaces, religious interaction, competition, and exchange were inevitable. One would like to know more about the occupations and trades in which Syriac Christians were active. The municipal authorities had to administrate taxes and fees across religious demarcations and either actively structured the social, ethnic, and religious topography of the city or accepted its uncontrolled growth. Often a division into quarters in the Islamic city is taken for granted. And it is true, some of these cities, such as Jerusalem, are known for their more pronounced segregation along the lines of religious affiliation. In Aprah (Farah), Kharijites and Sunni lived in separate neighbourhoods;[35] Damascus had quarters;[36] Maypherkaṭ and Mosul had Jewish areas.[37] Samosata (Sumaysat), when it was under Armenian rule in the thirteenth century, accordingly had an Armenian Quarter.[38] Edessa, in contrast, was not religiously segregated;[39] neither was Tiberias, as Israeli excavations have shown.[40]

Concerning the sources for the study of cities, Syriac literature, epigraphy, chronicles, and law contain information on the organization of the communities, their leaders, and the different social and ethnic groups within the communities. But often no more than the name of a bishop has come down to us that proves the existence of a

34. See, for example, Janet L. Abu-Lughod "The Islamic City – Historic Myth, Islamic Essence, and Contemporary Relevance," *IJMES* 19 (1987): 155–176; Gregory Aldous, "The Islamic City Critique: Revising the Narrative," *JESHO* 56 (2013): 471–493.

35. Guy Le Strange, *The Lands of the Eastern Caliphate: Mesopotamia, Persia, and Central Asia from the Moslem Conquest to the Time of Timur*, Cambridge Geographical Series (Cambridge: University Press, 1905), 341.

36. Dorothée Sack, *Damaskus. Entwicklung und Struktur einer orientalisch-islamischen Stadt* (Mainz: Zabern, 1989); eadem, "Die Topographie der historischen Stadt Damaskus," in *Damaskus – Aleppo. 5000 Jahre Stadtentwicklung in Syrien*, Beiheft der Archäologischen Mitteilungen aus Nordwestdeutschland, edited by Mamoun Fansa, Heinz Gaube, and Jens Windelberg, 83–86 (Mainz: Zabern, 2000).

37. Ariel I. Ahram, "Mosul," in *Encyclopedia of Jews in the Islamic World*, edited by Norman A. Stillman (Leiden: Brill, 2015), accessed October 2, 2015.

38. Le Strange, *The Lands of the Eastern Caliphate*, 108; Hellenkemper Hansgerd, *Burgen der Kreuzritterzeit in der Grafschaft Edessa und im Königreich Kleinarmenien. Studien zur historischen Siedlungsgeographie Südost-Kleinasiens*, Geographica Historica (Bonn: Habelt, 1976), 73–77.

39. Judah B. Segal, *Edessa. The Blessed City* (Oxford: Oxford University Press, 1970).

40. David Stacey, *Excavations at Tiberias, 1973–1974: The Early Islamic Periods* (Jerusalem: Israel Antiquities Authority, 2004); Amos Harif, "A crusader church in Tiberias," *PEQ* 116 (1984): 103–109.

bishopric. In order to understand the fabric of Syriac Orthodox life, many sources should be added: writings of non-Syriac origin, local Muslim sources, geographical and travel accounts, Latin and Byzantine sources, and, wherever possible, archaeology.

II

Epigraphy and Archaeology

In the second part of this contribution, some genres of sources will be highlighted. Inscriptions, even if they consist only of crosses or names on tombstones, contribute greatly to the study of social and cultural history.[41] At least they inform us about the existence of Christians, as well as of their linguistic and, sometimes, social and cultural affiliation. There are a number of recent publications on Christian inscriptions from the Asian West,[42] from India,[43] or from the Church of the East in Central Asia[44] and China—for example, from the busy port of Quanzhou (Zayton)[45] on the Pacific coast. Inscriptions display the multi-ethnic character of the churches of the Syriac tradition in this period; apart from Syriac, they are written in Greek, Arabic, Turkish, Uighur, or Chinese. Syriac identity and the social composition of the Syriac churches were two different things at that time. The Chinese inscriptions also prove that the Church of the East was present in China even after the persecution at the end of the Tang dynasty in the ninth and tenth centuries, before Christians during the Yuan dynasty (1276–1368) flocked back into China.[46]

41. Wassilios Klein, *Das nestorianische Christentum an den Handelswegen durch Kyrgyzstan bis zum 14. Jahrhundert* (Turnhout: Brepols, 2000).

42. Amir Harrak, *Recueil des inscriptions syriaques*, vol. 2. *Syriac and Garshuni Inscriptions of Iraq* (Paris: De Boccard, 2010); Francoise Briquel Chatonnet, and Alain Desreumaux, "Syriac Inscriptions in Syria," *Hugoye* 14 (2011): 27–44; Andrew Palmer, "How the Village of M'arre, Christian in 1800, Became Largely Muslim before 1911: Archives, Travellers' Tales and Oral Traditions," in *Christsein in der islamischen Welt: Festschrift für Martin Tamcke zum 60. Geburtstag*, edited by S. H. Griffith and S. Grebenstein, 439-478 (Wiesbaden: Harrassowitz, 2015).

43. Françoise Briquel Chatonnet, Alain Desreumaux, and Jacob Thekeparampil, *Recueil des inscriptions syriaques*, vol. 1. *Kérala* (Paris: De Boccard, 2008), also for further references.

44. Pier Giorgio Borbone, "Some Aspects of Turco-Mongol Christianity in the Light of Literary and Epigraphic Syriac Sources," *JAAS* 19 (2005): 5–20.

45. Lieu et al., *Medieval Christian and Manichean Remains from Quanzhou (Zayton).*

46. Lieu et al., *Medieval Christian and Manichean Remains from Quanzhou (Zayton)*, 30–32; Ken Parry, "The Iconography of the Christian Tombstones from Zayton," in *From Palmyra to Zayton:*

For over a hundred years, the huge archaeological projects in Western Asia have not only taken no interest in medieval settlements, but even cleared their remnants away in order to reach the Roman or the Ancient Near Eastern strata. Settlement research of cities and villages would be helpful in understanding social history, but such research is rarely undertaken.[47] In this respect, the study by Ronnie Ellenblum should be mentioned, who analysed rural crusader settlements and found, to the surprise of the academic community, that the crusaders lived in villages in populations mixed with local Syrian Christians, usually Melkites. Thus, the theory based on written sources, that the Latins were an urban group isolated from the population of the land, had to be radically corrected.[48]

Art History

One important feature of the Syriac Renaissance was the revival of church building and the arts. Several new important studies on art and archaeology in Lebanon have been published during the last years.[49] Still, many areas are only superficially known. Entire strands of art history have not been established in terms of dating, influence, style, and iconography. Important segments of the artistic heritage have been lost, for example, the medieval secular architecture and art. And many of the findings of recent years are rural in character rather than part of the urban culture. In the cities, only fragments

Epigraphy and Iconography, Silk Road Studies, edited by Iain Gardner, Samuel N. C. Lieu, and Ken Parry, 229-246 (Turnhout: Brepols, 2005), 243–244.

47. See, for example, Sack, *Damaskus. Entwicklung und Struktur einer orientalisch-islamischen Stadt.*

48. Ronnie Ellenblum, *Frankish Rural Settlement in the Latin Kingdom of Jerusalem* (Cambridge: Cambridge University Press, 1998).

49. See the journal *Eastern Christian Art* 1 (2000) and following for ongoing research projects and the most eminent contributors to the field, as well as for book reviews. See also Andrea Schmidt and Stephan Westphalen, eds., *Christliche Wandmalereien in Syrien. Qara und das Kloster Mar Yakub*, SKCO 14 (Wiesbaden: Reichert, 2005); Stephan Westphalen "Deir Mar Musa: Die Malschichten 1–3," *ECA* 4 (2007): 99–126; Nada Hélou, *La fresque dans les anciennes églises du Liban* (Mansourié: Editions Aleph, 2007–2008); eadem, *L'icône dans le patriarcat d'Antioche (VIe–XIXe siècles)* (Mansourié: Editions Aleph, 2007); Mat Immerzeel, *Identity Puzzles. Medieval Christian Art in Syria and Lebanon* (Louvain: Peeters, 2009), to mention just one of his many publications; Mouawad, "The Syriac Renaissance Viewed from Ḥesnō Ziad (Kharpūt), near Melitene"; Snelders, *Identity and Christian-Muslim Interaction*, etc.

have survived, as in Nisibis or Mosul—which are under great threat today or already destroyed, respectively.[50]

Concerning the use of the extraordinary new findings and documentations, Bas Snelders' observation still holds true that the results of archaeological and art historical studies of these medieval centuries are largely neglected by historians.[51] One of the results I would like to highlight for social and cultural history is the regional character of artistic styles. There were, for example, Western stylistic patterns in works of art of the Levant which were interrelated with the Byzantine world through relations, taste, patronage, or workshops; Latin crusaders also took part in this common language of styles and motives.[52] Artistic styles were regional in character, but they were not denominationally determined.[53] The studies by Immerzeel, Snelders, and others even showed a fluidity of styles and motives between Christians and Muslims.[54] They reconstructed common use of Muslim or Christian workshops and artists as well as the crossover of motives and form that were appreciated by both groups at the time.

The regional rather than denominational character of art teaches the historian that there must have been local areas with some kind of cultural cohesion. They determined one's outlook on life, one's tastes, and one's social interaction. Certainly, artistic motives and styles could be used to highlight political or religious allegiance and to make polemic points. Very often, however, art is no reliable marker of religious difference. Shared motives and styles thus first and foremost open up a perspective written sources are silent about, on a shared

50. For Nisibis, see Justine Gaborit, Gérard Thébault, and Abdurrahman Oruç, "L'église Mar-Ya'qub de Nisibe," in *Les églises en monde syriaque*, ÉS 10, edited by Françoise Briquel Chatonnet, 289–330 (Paris: Geuthner, 2013). For bibliographical documentation of Mosul, see Snelders, *Identity and Christian-Muslim Interaction.*

51. Snelders, *Identity and Christian-Muslim Interaction*, 70.

52. Lucy-Anne Hunt, *Byzantium, Eastern Christendom and Islam. Art at the Crossroads of the Medieval Mediterranean* (London: Pindar Press, 1998); Maria Georgopoulou, "The Artistic World of the Crusaders and Oriental Christians in the Twelfth and Thirteenth Centuries," *Gesta* 43 (2004): 115–128; Jaroslav Folda, *Crusader Art. The Art of the Crusaders in the Holy Land, 1099–1291* (Aldershot: Lund Humphries Publishers, 2008); Maja Kominko, "Byzantine, Syriac, Armenian and Latin: A Note on Artistic Interaction in Eastern Mediterranean Manuscripts," *ECA* 7 (2010): 59–70.

53. Immerzeel, *Identity Puzzles. Medieval Christian Art in Syria and Lebanon.*

54. Immerzeel, *Identity Puzzles. Medieval Christian Art in Syria and Lebanon*; Snelders, *Identity and Christian-Muslim Interaction*, 414–420; Eva R. Hoffman, "Christian-Islamic Encounters on Thirteenth-Century Ayyubid Metalwork: Local Culture, Authenticity, and Memory," *Gesta* 43 (2004): 129–142.

world beyond cultural, religious, and political boundaries. In contrast, the historian could use the geographical distribution of artistic styles and motives as markers for areas of close social relations within the Middle and Central East. Interestingly enough, these areas are not congruent with the political entities mentioned above. They form an independent and sometimes very stable level of cultural networks,[55] as did Gothic styles in Europe, for example.

Material culture and art as a historical source have become very important for Western medieval studies in recent years, because they tell us something about what people enjoyed, their fantasies and fears, where they went shopping, which trade routes and connections were open to them, how affluent or poor they were, and how they interpreted their world. If artistic elements are shared across religious boundaries, we are not limited to objects that can be identified as of Syriac Christian patronship in order to use art for social and cultural questions in Syriac studies.

Instead, we might go back to the art historians of the Muslim world as well as to Christian archaeology to learn about objects, of whichever religious patronage; for example, about luxurious brass objects like the incense burners from Syria of the thirteenth century. The secular use of incense as an item of luxury, purification, and fragrance was one of the important common features of cultures from Iran to Al-Andalus in this period. These objects and their use are particularly interesting because they lead us to the lay culture of which so little is known.

A group of such thirteenth-century brass incense burners from Iraq, with golden and silver inlays, kept today in the British Museum, show very similar shapes (Image 3). They have a lid with a knob and would have had a handle to carry them. One of these burners displays a series of figures marked as Christian with liturgical items in their hands, including a cross and censer (Image 4).[56] It is true that Rachel Ward, unlike Eva Baer, suggested a Christian patron for this incense burner because of these motifs.[57] However, Ward herself pointed towards another object with Christian motifs clearly commissioned by

55. Schmidt and Westphalen, *Christliche Wandmalereien in Syrien. Qara und das Kloster Mar Yakub*; Glenn Peers, "The Church at the Jerusalem Gate in Crusader Ascalon: A Rough Tolerance of Byzantine Culture?" *ECA* 6 (2009): 67–86.

56. Rachel Ward, *Islamic Metalwork* (London: British Museum Press, 1993), 83, fig. 61; 84, fig. 63.

57. Eva Baer, *Ayyubid Metalwork with Christian Images* (Leiden: Brill, 1989).

Image 3. Incense burner, Syria, British Museum

a Muslim ruler.[58] Indeed, objects with Christian motifs were not exclusively made for Christians but also made for Muslims, and vice versa; thus, the specialists often consider a clear distinction infeasible.[59] The so-called brass Freer Canteen in Washington is a case in point. From the same period and of Syrian or Palestinian origin, it combines Muslim and Christian motifs and so far defies definitive interpretations, which vary from Muslim triumphalism, to religious tolerance, to crusading ideology.[60] In any case, it tells something about the local world Christians and Muslims shared.

As we know from the written records, Syriac Christians (for example, of Edessa) worked as silk merchants and wore silk garments.[61] Colorful silk dresses are also depicted in the frescos in Christian

58. Ward, *Islamic Metalwork,* 85.

59. Hoffman, "Christian-Islamic Encounters on Thirteenth-Century Ayyubid Metalwork," 132.

60. On the canteen, see Baer, *Ayyubid Metalwork*; Nuha N. N. Khoury, "Narratives of the Holy Land: Memory, Identity and inverted Imagery in the Freer Basin and Canteen," *Orientations* 29, 5 (1998): 63–69; Hoffman, "Christian-Islamic Encounters on Thirteenth-Century Ayyubid Metalwork"; Heather Ecker and Teresa Fitzherbert, "The Freer Canteen reconsidered," *Ars Orientalis* 42 (2012): 176–193; Teresa Fitzherbert, "The Freer Canteen: Jerusalem or Jazira?," in *Islamic Art, Architecture and Material Culture: New Perspectives*, edited by Margaret S. Graves, 1–6 (Oxford: Archaeopress, 2012).

61. Weltecke, "60 years after Peter Kawerau," 327.

Image 4. Incense burner, Syria, British Museum, 1878, 1230.679

Churches.[62] While the field of Syriac studies has so far not taken up this topic, silk specimens of this time are extant, and specialists study these objects as well as their production. Renewed activities of Syrian Christians in silk route centers like Merv and generally in Khorasan during the eleventh century to the Mongol conquests may be considered together with more general information on Syriac Christians'

62. Erica Cruikshank Dodd, *The Frescoes of Mar Musa al-Habashi. A Study in Medieval Painting in Syria* (Toronto: Pontifical Institute of Mediaeval Studies, 2001); Stephan Westphalen, "Deir Mar Musa: Die Malschichten 1–3," *ECA* 4 (2007): 99–126.

occupation in this trade.[63] Thus new patterns in social history become visible. While the concept of "Islamic art" excludes the contribution of non-Muslims to the material world, and also of the colonizing use made of them and their culture by the ruling religion, Syriac studies should not mirror this image.

The stunning beauty and the refinement of the artistic endeavours of this period in so many different fields constantly reminds us that we deal with people of taste, of some affluence, of optimism, of leisure. While the art and archaeology of the period are indispensable to correct the image of a gloomy period full of crisis, war, and decay, shared cultural spaces should not be misinterpreted as tolerance or inter-religious harmony. Just as art corrects the image the written sources present, the latter balances out overtly positive interpretations of the material heritage.

Intellectual heritage

There is no need here to emphasise the importance of the written heritage. Intellectuals of the period like Jacob bar Shakko (d. 1241), Bar ʿEbroyo (1226–1286), Gewargis Warda (fl. thirteenth century), or ʿAbdishoʿ Bar Brikha (d. 1318) are well known, and more of their works are continually being edited. These writers of Syriac dominated their communities' cultural process of making sense of life, the universe, and everything. Socially, however, these scholar-clerics and scholar-prelates are not representative of the use of learning and intellectual activities of their time. Ecclesiastical schools did not systematically provide higher studies at the time; thus, young men who became professionals, physicians, secretaries, astrologers, or teachers usually studied and worked outside the church. They spent their time in earning their livelihood and did not necessarily leave written works—or else, their writings, poems, letters, and stories as well as their libraries are lost today.[64]

Herman Teule highlighted the following aspects of the written culture of this time: a rise of awareness of the Syriac language; openness towards and ample use of the cultural achievements of Islam,

63. Jean-Maurice Fiey, "Chrétientés syriaques du Horāsān et du Ségestān," *Le Muséon* 86 (1973): 75–104.

64. On some sources and references, see Weltecke, "60 years after Peter Kawerau."

which changed dramatically the form and content of Syriac writings on philosophy, grammar, science, poetry, and even theology;[65] and last but not least, an awareness of the past and the fathers of old.[66] Within their social frame, these features of the Syriac renaissance may be characterised in a slightly different phrasing. Science certainly was, like art and even theology to some extent, not divided by religious demarcations.[67] The scholar-clerics known to us through the written heritage were not the spearheads of the absorption of recent scientific developments. Rather, the anonymous professionals, who depended on secular relations and a good education to make successful careers, were the ones who studied these developments in Arabic and Persian.[68] The scholar-clerics then reacted to the laity's appreciation of secular culture. If it were not a *contradictio in adiectu*, one could say they were innovative traditionalists or, rather, visionary realists. They integrated Arabic learning into their tradition, summarizing it in encyclopaedic overviews, reshaping and adapting it into Syriac literature attractive for their communities to turn to. This treasure lasts until today. This is also true of poetry. Helen Younansardaroud has studied the works of 'Abdisho' bar Brikha,[69] who used an Arabic genre for his poetry, the *maqamāt*, because he was acutely aware of its popularity among his flock. He resolutely took up the challenge to produce something equal to prove Syriac poetic creativity.

The historiography of this period is clearly unique. The work by Eliya of Nisibis (975–1046) of the East Syrian tradition, and especially the three monumental chronicles of the Syriac Orthodox Church—the chronicle by Michael the Great (1126–1199), the anonymous chronicle to the year 1234, and the chronicle by Bar 'Ebroyo—display

65. Teule, "The Syriac Renaissance," 23–28.

66. Teule, "The Syriac Renaissance," 29–30.

67. For example, Herman G. B. Teule, "Barhebraeus' Ethicon, al-Ghazâlî and Ibn Sina," *Islamochristiana* 18 (1992): 73–86.

68. Samir Khalil Samir, "Les Suryan et la civilisation arabo-musulmane: Conférence inaugurale," *PdO* 30 (2005): 31–61.

69. Helen Younansardaroud, "Sogenannte Neologismen in 'Aḇdīšō's Paradies von Eden," in *Geschichte, Theologie, Liturgie und Gegenwartslage der syrischen Kirchen. Beiträge zum sechsten deutschen Syrologen-Symposium in Konstanz, Juli 2009*, edited by Dorothea Weltecke, 53–58 (Wiesbaden: Harrassowitz, 2012); eadem, "'Abdīšō' bar Brīkā's († 1318) Book of the Paradise of Eden: A Literary Renaissance?," *ECS* 9 (2010): 195–204; eadem, "A list of the known Manuscripts of the Syriac Maqāmat of 'Abdīšō' bar Brīkā's († 1318): Paradise of Eden," *JAAS* 20: (2006): 28–41.

a level of complex historical writing and thought that was never reached before or after this period. These writers constructed entire new universal narratives, each different from the other.[70] While the chronicles obviously were a product of intensive interreligious discourse, the authors stood firmly on the ground of their own identity at the same time. They were reluctant to name sources outside of their religious affiliation while making ample use of them, because of which these outside sources are largely unknown. Fortunately, the last ten years have seen important publications in this field.[71] As mentioned above, the chronicles are productive sources for social history—about, for example, scholars and professionals,[72] slips of everyday life, crafts and merchants, trade routes and connections, and Syriac Christians at war as auxiliary troops in Muslim and Latin armies.[73]

However, the prelate-writers often explained the calamities of the period by the sins of the people and their own, not by the general political and economic conditions of the time.[74] This negative bias towards their own society has been taken at face value and led to unfavorable historical narratives by Western scholars, the impact of which is still felt. At the same time, these attempts at explanation and reason preserve valuable information about the sentiments of the hierarchy and the people, and their distress with persecution and war. Thus, they are a significant counterbalance against any of the romanticising tendencies mentioned above.

70. Dorothea Weltecke, "Les trois grandes chroniques syro-orthodoxes des XIIe et XIIIe siècles," in *L'historiographie syriaque*, ÉS 6, edited by Muriel Debié, 107–135 (Paris: Geuthner, 2009).

71. Andy Hilkens, *The Anonymous Syriac Chronicle up to the Year 1234 and Its Sources* (Gent: Universiteit Gent, 2014); Pier Giorgio Borbone, "Barhebraeus and Juwayni: A Syriac Chronicler and his Persian Source," *Acta Mongolica* 9 (2009): 147–168; Samir Khalil Samir, *Foi et culture en Irak au XIe siècle: Élie de Nisibe et l'Islam* (Aldershot: Variorum, 1996); Antoine Borrut, "La circulation de l'information historique entre les sources arabo-musulmanes et syriaques: Elie de Nisibe et ses sources," in Debié, ed., *L'historiographie Syriaque,* 137–160.

72. Susanne Regina Todt, "Die syrische und die arabische Weltgeschichte des Bar Hebraeus – Ein Vergleich," *Der Islam* 65 (1988): 60–80.

73. Weltecke, "Contacts between Syriac Orthodox and Latin Military Orders," 69–74.

74. Dorothea Weltecke, "Überlegungen zu den Krisen der syrisch-orthodoxen Kirche im 12. Jahrhundert," in *Syriaca. Zur Geschichte, Theologie, Liturgie und Gegewartslage der syrischen Kirchen, 2. Deutsches Syrologen-Symposium (Juli 2000, Wittenberg)*, SOK 17, edited by Martin Tamcke, 125–145 (Münster: Lit, 2002).

Legal material

Legal material of the period originates from the same twofold strategy of preserving tradition while also allowing for innovation, in the face of the challenges of the non-Christian environment.[75] This part of the heritage displays the same negative bias as historiography with the same effect on modern scholars as canons inform us about all sorts of deviances. They, however, also contain data on everyday life, commerce and marriage, urban markets, ruins and playgrounds, slavery and schools. For this wealth of information, legal material is and has always been studied by historians of the medieval period, and this research has gained momentum in our time.[76] Likewise, editions of Syriac legal sources date from the beginning of Syriac studies in the West and continue to be published to the present day, as manuscripts containing legal material are continually being discovered.[77]

There are three main groups of legislation from this period. The first are the canons of synods, either of the entire church or of local meetings, which were then compiled into collections. The second group is formed by ordinances gathered by named bishops, metropolitans, and the heads of the churches either as simple collections or as concise law books. Small collections or rather mere lists of canons, often without any indication as to the author, concentrating more or less on one subject, form the third group of legal

75. See Hubert Kaufhold, "Sources of Canon Law in the Eastern Churches," in *The History of Byzantine and Eastern Canon Law to 1500*, edited by Wilfried Hartmann and Kenneth Pennington, 215–342 (Washington: The Catholic University of America Press, 2012).

76. Karl Ubl, *Inzestverbot und Gesetzgebung: Die Konstruktion eines Verbrechens (300–1100)* (Berlin: De Gruyter, 2008); see the ongoing ERC-project RelMin and its publications, for example, John Tolan, *Jews in Early Christian Law: Byzantium and the Latin West, 6th–11th Centuries*, RLMCMS 2 (Turnhout: Brepols, 2014); David M. Freidenreich, *Foreigners and Their Food: Constructing Otherness in Jewish, Christian, and Islamic Law* (Berkeley: University of California Press, 2011); Uriel I. Simonsohn, *A Common Justice. The Legal Allegiances of Christians and Jews under Early Islam* (Philadelphia: University of Pennsylvania Press, 2011).

77. For bibliographical references, see Walter Selb and Hubert Kaufhold, *Das syrisch-römische Rechtsbuch*, vol. 1. *Einleitung* (Wien: Verlag der Österreichischen Akademie der Wissenschaften, 2002); Walter Selb, *Orientalisches Kirchenrecht*, vol. 1. *Die Geschichte des Kirchenrechts der Nestorianer*; vol. 2, *Die Geschichte des Kirchenrechts der Westsyrer (von den Anfängen bis zur Mongolenzeit)* (Wien: Verlag der Österreichischen Akademie der Wissenschaften, 1981–1989); Hubert Kaufhold, "Eine unbekannte syrische Kanonessammlung," in *Synaxis katholikė. Beiträge zu Gottesdienst und Geschichte der fünf altkirchlichen Patriarchate für Heinzgerd Brakmann zum 70. Geburtstag*, Orientalia - Patristica - Oecumenica 6.1-2, edited by Diliana Atanassova and Tinatin Chronz, 317–340 (Münster: LIT, 2014) and other publications by Kaufhold.

texts.[78] The multi-religious city and the city residence of the bishops is the *Sitz im Leben*, the setting, of these sources. The bishops and the metropolitans were the experts of law and the ones to practice it as judges, not only in ecclesiastical matters, but also in civil conflicts and even criminal matters.[79]

We know from other sources that a wealth of legal material once existed, but very little of it has survived. The canons of the synods of the eleventh to thirteenth century led by the patriarchs of the time, like, for example, Patriarch Michael, are all lost, as are many local collections.[80] There is a cycle of canons by Metropolitan Yuḥanon of Mardin (d. 1165) from 1153[81] and fragments of lists by the Metropolitan Dionysius bar Ṣalibi (d. 1171),[82] both of whom are well-known personalities of the Syriac reform movement of the twelfth century. In the thirteenth century, Maphrian Bar 'Ebroyo wrote a concise law book, which is the only one extant in the Syriac Orthodox tradition.[83] 'Abdisho' bar Brikha of the Church of the East also wrote a law book, adding to the existing ones in his tradition.

Yet the preparation of Syriac legal material for the purposes of historical analysis turns out to be a slow process. The compelling enthusiasm of Arthur Vööbus,[84] when he published his groundbreaking works on Syriac Church law, is little felt today. For Vööbus, canons, especially of the synods, were an excellent source, because they are datable and can be localised. In his view, legislation answered to direct challenges of a specific moment in time and thus may help to reconstruct these realities.[85] This was also the assumption upon which Kawerau acted when he used legal sources for his study; he simply took them as reflections of reality.

78. Kaufhold, "Eine unbekannte syrische Kanonessammlung," 317.

79. Hubert Kaufhold, "Der Richter in den syrischen Rechtsquellen. Zum Einfluß islamischen Rechts auf die Christlich-Orientalische Rechtsliteratur," *OC* 68 (1984): 91–113.

80. Arthur Vööbus, *Syrische Kanonessammlungen. Ein Beitrag zur Quellenkunde*, vol. 1. *A.–B.* (Louvain: Secrétariat du CSCO, 1970), 71–88.

81. Vööbus, *Syrische Kanonessammlungen*, 104–121.

82. Vööbus, *Syrische Kanonessammlungen*, 240–253.

83. See Kaufhold, "Sources of Canon Law in the Eastern Churches," for references.

84. Arthur Vööbus, *The Synodicon in the West Syrian Tradition*, CSCO 368 (Louvain: Sécrétariat du CSCO, 1974), 1: "This fact alone stamps these records as first-rate sources. They constitute material to be treated with confidence"; Teule, "The Syriac Renaissance," 29.

85. See also Vööbus, *Syrische Kanonessammlungen*, 2–3.

Since then, professional lawyers and historians of law like Walter Selb[86] and Hubert Kaufhold,[87] who added critical editions, have called for caution, as have others.[88] To begin with, the material is so fragmentary that it is very difficult to evaluate the quality of the extant sources. Furthermore, so little can be said about the societies of the time that there are no reliable categories to decide whether a canon reflects reality or not, such as whether a deviant practice mentioned existed at all or whether the correcting norm was ever put into practice. Besides, the vocabulary of the legal collections is very specific, and the subjects the canons deal with are often cryptic. Thus it is no surprise that there is no critical edition and modern academic translation of the law book by Bar ʿEbroyo.

In a collection of canons of the late-twelfth- or early-thirteenth-century, Patriarch Michael is quoted as author of the following ordinance: "It is not right for the priests, deacons, and believers to eat meat at vigils, like it is the pagan practice of the priests of evil spirits (*kumrē d-šidē*) as they do before their gods."[89] What kind of priests and what kind of gods does this canon refer to? And again, what exactly was in Bar ʿEbroyo's mind, when he quoted a canon that prohibited the following occupations for a good Syriac Orthodox boy: Fire eater, chariot driver, instructor of gladiators, lyre player, dancer, wine chandler, dream reader, magician, astrologer, or amulet maker?

Law is a conservative discipline, and legal specialists of the Middle Ages repeated and collected canons for reasons other than practical use. Scholars have noticed, for example, that Christian law books contain material that had no everyday value for the prelates, like rules for the distribution of spoils of war or regulations for the visitation of prisoners in jail.[90] These unpractical canons, one taken from Byz-

86. Selb, *Orientalisches Kirchenrecht.*

87. Selb and Kaufhold, *Das syrisch-römische Rechtsbuch*; Kaufhold, "Sources of Canon Law in the Eastern Churches"; idem, "Eine unbekannte syrische Kanonessammlung." On works of Kaufhold, see also Peter Bruns and Heinz Luthe, eds., *Orientalia Christiana. Festschrift für Hubert Kaufhold zum 70. Geburtstag* (Wiesbaden: Harrassowitz, 2013).

88. Johannes Pahlitzsch, *Der arabische Procheiros Nomos. Untersuchung und Edition der Übersetzung eines byzantinischen Rechtstextes* (Frankfurt: Löwenklau-Gesellschaft e.V. Frankfurt am Main, 2014).

89. Kaufhold, "Sources of Canon Law in the Eastern Churches"; idem, "Eine unbekannte syrische Kanonessammlung," 329.

90. Carlo Alfonso Nallino, "Il diritto musulmano nel Nomicanone siricaco cristaino di Barhebreo," *RSO* 9 (1921–1923): 512–580, at 534; Johannes Pahlitzsch, "The Translation of the Byzantine Procheiros Nomos into Arabic: Techniques and Cultural Context," *Byzantinoslavica* 65 (2007): 19–29,

antine and the other from Muslim sources, serve political purposes: The prelates claimed legal authority in their communities against their many competitors. They acted in a situation of rivalry between the different denominations in the city, between the levels of church hierarchy on the one hand and non-Christian legal institutions on the other, the latter of which were also frequented by Christians, legal prohibitions notwithstanding.[91] The prelates thus strove to produce something on an equal level with, if not superior to, their Christian competitors and the rich legal traditions of Islam and Judaism.[92] The polemical attacks by Muslims and also by Jews against Christian law were acutely felt and explicitly answered by, for example, ʿAbdishoʿ bar Brikha[93] as well as by his contemporary Bar ʿEbroyo.

In his chronicle, Bar ʿEbroyo states: "Concerning the books of their Law [of the Muslims], that is to say, canons of marriages, and offerings, and ablutions, and the manner of [saying] prayers, and the amount of alms, and the various kinds of merchandise, and loans, and the division of inheritances, and the liberation of slaves—all these matters they [the Muslims] have dilated upon to such a degree that not one of them, even though he has studied [the subject] during the whole period of his life, is able to decide finally questions and answers concerning them in a fitting manner."[94] Bar ʿEbroyo clearly wanted to surpass the Muslims in view of clarity and conciseness. Therefore, almost every chapter in his law book contains one or more *Huddoye*, decisions by himself, which comment on the quoted sources and provide a definitive answer as to how to react to a specific problem. He reports in the proem to his law book that he included in his *Huddoye*

at 27; Hubert Kaufhold, "Der Richter in den syrischen Rechtsquellen. Zum Einfluß islamischen Rechts auf die christlich-orientalische Rechtsliteratur," *OC* 68 (1984): 91–113, at 109.

91. Simonsohn, *A Common Justice*, for our period see the canons quoted by Vööbus, *Syrische Kanonessammlungen*, I A. p. 110, I. B., p. 389.

92. For example, the introduction by Hubert Kaufhold, *Syrische Texte zum islamischen Recht. Das dem nestorianischen Katholikos Johannes V. bar Abgarē zugeschriebene Rechtsbuch* (München: Beck, 1971).

93. Teule, "The Syriac Renaissance," 26–27, quoting Jacques Marie Vosté, *Ordo iudiciorum ecclesiasticorum, ordinatus et compositus a Mar Abdišo. Latine interpretatus est notis illustravit* (Rome: Typis Poliglottis Vaticanis, 1940), 24.

94. Paul Bedjan, *Gregorii Barhebraei Chronicon Syriacum* (Paris: Maisonneuve, 1890), 98 (textus); Ernest A. Wallis Budge, *The Chronography of Gregory Abû'l Faraj, the son of Aaron, the Hebrew physician, commonly known as Bar Hebraeus being the first part of his political history of the world* (Oxford: Oxford University Press, 1932), 92 (English translation).

well-known practices. In fact, these are often quotations from his Muslim source that he was not inclined to name. Yet they were possibly indeed well-known to his people from their appearance in Muslim courts.[95]

Bar ʿEbroyo also intended his book for practical use by the prelate-judges, as he stated explicitly. His law book is particularly interesting because it contains the largest collection of secular material of all the law books with known authors. Although the purpose of many canons is obscure for now, the intended conciseness and practical use serve as a lever to open up the collection for analysis, taking up each canon separately. Three groups of canons in particular seem to be useful starting points for analysis: First, the *Huddoye* must reflect Bar ʿEbroyo's world and his intentions. Secondly, there are some canons which Bar ʿEbroyo quoted from elsewhere and adapted to his world. They also directly relate to his intentions. Finally, there are some canons referring to contemporary situations that are well established historically.[96]

One example shall be mentioned, taking us into the bustling cities of the Middle East: Bar ʿEbroyo's statements on the taking of interest in money lending. According to the traditional Christian legal collections of the Byzantine and the Eastern world, the taking of interest was licensed.[97] Bar ʿEbroyo rejected the practice and even explicitly refuted older Christian law.[98] Economical justice was a question of great social and religious brisance.[99] In his eyes, obviously, only the complete renouncement of interest could take Christian merchants

95. On the sources of Bar ʿEbroyo's law book, see Hanna Khadra, *Le Nomocanon de Barhebraeus: Son importance juridique entre les sources chrétiennes et les sources Musulmanes* (Rome: Pontificia Università Lateranense, 2005).

96. For a more detailed discussion, see Dorothea Weltecke, "Zum syrisch-orthodoxen Leben in der mittelalterlichen Stadt und zu den Hūddōyē (dem Nomokanon) des Bar ʿEbrōyō," in *Orientalia Christiana. Festschrift für Hubert Kaufhold zum 70. Geburtstag,* edited by Peter Bruns and Heinz Luther, 586–613 (Wiesbaden: Harrassowitz, 2013).

97. Nallino, "Il diritto musulmano nel Nomicanone siricaco cristaino di Barhebreo," 547ff, on sources; Vööbus, *Syrische Kanonessammlungen,* 549–551, Fabian Wittreck, *Interaktion religiöser Rechtsordnungen. Rezeptions- und Translationsprozesse dargestellt am Beispiel des Zinsverbots in den orientalischen Kirchenrechtssammlungen* (Berlin: Duncker & Humblot, 2009).

98. Bar ʿEbrōyō, Nomokanon, XI, 5, in print, for example, as Paul Bedjan, *Nomocanon Gregorii Barhebraei* (Paris: Harrasowitz, 1898); translated by Vööbus, *Syrische Kanonessammlungen,* 549; Wittreck, *Interaktion religiöser Rechtsordnungen,* 140–144.

99. See for example Hans-Jörg Gilomen, "Wucher und Wirtschaft im Mittelalter," *HZ* 250 (1990): 265–301.

and moneylenders out of the firing line of Muslim polemics. In fact, Metropolitan Yuḥanon of Mardin's synod in the year 1153 also called for the abolition of the practice:[100] Clerics as well as laymen should abstain from taking interest, and clerics should be suspended from office if they acted against this canon. It seems that some of the clerics, probably the deacons, who earned their living outside the church as trained professionals, were active in money commerce. These canons most likely did not have the intended effect. Besides ignoring or circumventing the prohibitions, Muslims delegated money lending to the Dhimmis, in the same way that the Latin Christians (until the fifteenth century) passed it on to the Jews. Commercial activities depended on loans.[101]

As much as legislation, like any other learning, travelled between religions, law was also very much used for religious demarcation. Demarcation and social separation seemed a necessary precondition for the integrity of one's identity. The relation between the different realms of cultural expression like law and art should, however, not be defined as one between norm and reality. Rather, these are two contradicting strategies employed at the same time.

Conclusion

This contribution advocates for a period that has tended to be overlooked, and even dismissed, in previous scholarship. In the first part, I took the opportunity to highlight the use of social history in addition to cultural studies. After all, without an understanding of the societies and worlds Syriac Christians lived in, their written heritage remains isolated, and its *Sitz im Leben* unexplored. Theology and piety formed only a part of the lives of Syriac Christians. A set of sociologically-informed questions may guide the search for the other realities, for social structures and inequality, for urban and rural life, economy and politics, local affiliations and rivalries, as well as the overarching cohesion of the churches. Results from neighbouring medieval studies could help to construct historical models. Also, for this set of questions, non-Christian and non-Syriac sources are vital for the analysis

100. Can. 37: Vööbus, *Syrische Kanonessammlungen*,111.

101. For sources and references, see Joseph Schacht, "Riba," in *EI*², accessed September 29, 2015; Phillip I. Ackerman-Lieberman, "Banks and Banking, Historical," in *EI*³, accessed September 29, 2015.

alongside the Syriac material. In the second part, some genres of Syriac sources served to show that specimens of art history and archaeology, literature and law, each provide different perspectives and thus counterbalance and complement each other. Traditional histories of Syriac Christians tend to obscure their religious, ethnic, and cultural entanglement with the peoples around them. They follow the historical narratives of the communities themselves, which were often deliberately silent about those with whom they interacted. Contradicting evidence of the written heritage, art and archaeology points towards a particularly lively exchange and common cultural participation in a culture which is usually known by its exclusive label "Islamic." Both perspectives reflect different strategies employed by Christians within a world of potentially disadvantageous power structures, which was nevertheless their home. They had to cope with domination and colonization, choose to counteract them, develop spaces of autonomy as well as of participation, preserve their identity, and thus strike the balance between separation and interaction, and between tradition and innovation.

Postscript: This contribution was last updated in September 2016, and so a number of more recent publications and research developments are not featured, such as Bärbel Beinhauer-Köhler, *Spielräume religiöser Pluralität: Kairo im 12. Jahrhundert* (Stuttgart: Verlag W. Kohlhammer, 2018) and Jack Tannous, *The Making of the Medieval Middle East: Religion, Society, and Simple Believers* (Princeton: Princeton University Press, 2018).

Epilogue

14. Syriac Studies in the Contemporary Academy

Some Reflections

❖ Kristian S. Heal

This essay aims to briefly reflect on what it means to work in Syriac studies in the contemporary academy.[1] It originates in a conversation I had at my first meeting of the North American Patristics Society. When asked what I work on, I answered confidently, "Syriac literature." "What, all of it?" the questioner countered. I don't recall what I said next, but I do remember the experience, because it accidently exposed my own perception of what it means to work in Syriac studies. As a student of Sebastian Brock and David Taylor, I cannot help but feel that to work in Syriac studies is to take on the combined roles of scholar, curator, and ambassador for, yes, all of Syriac literature—all periods, all genres, all topics.[2] Though one cannot hope to work expertly over such a vast period, or hope to control all the sources together with an increasingly substantial secondary literature, to work in Syriac

* This essay has been improved by valuable comments from Thomas Carlson (Oklahoma State University) and extended discussion with, and valuable comments and suggestions from, Carl Griffin (Brigham Young University).

1. Much of what I say here echoes the wise words of Gilbert Murray's inaugural lecture: *The Interpretation of Ancient Greek Literature: An Inaugural Lecture Delivered before the University of Oxford, January 27 1909* (Oxford: The Clarendon Press, 1909).

2. As exemplified in Sebastian P. Brock and David G. K. Taylor, *The Hidden Pearl: The Syrian Orthodox Church and its Ancient Heritage*, 3 vols. (Florence: Octavo Press, 2001).

studies means not wholly sacrificing breadth in the worthy quest for depth of knowledge and competence.

There is a dynamic synergy that emerges from striving to be open to broad intellectual stimulation while maintaining narrower personal research boundaries.[3] Working in Syriac studies means that one must focus in order to attain competence, and focus certainly requires establishing boundaries. An anecdote from Helen Vendler, the renowned Harvard scholar of English poetry, illustrates one aspect of this process. "I only once," she confessed, "in want of money, agreed to review a novel; and although I don't think the review was mistaken, I felt such guilt at falsifying my competence that I never again consented to write on fiction."[4] Syriac studies needs researchers who are willing to be similarly focused and self-aware. However, when there are relatively few laborers in a given field, maintaining such impermeable boundaries is often not possible, or even desirable. In fact, working in Syriac studies means being constantly invited to falsify our competence, especially in community endeavors, such as book reviews and contributions to encyclopedias, handbooks, and collected volumes. The field still demands and encourages the splendid extravagance of the dilettante. For many this is part of its attraction. But it must be done responsibly. Indeed, by responsibly drawing attention to the opportunities in Syriac studies we can continue to attract new laborers to the field, thereby moving Syriac studies to the center of early Christian, late antique, and medieval studies.

We can no longer agree with Franz Rosenthal's 1978 observation that "Syriac, the best-attested Aramaic dialect with its large literature and all the important topics it offers for study, is not being accorded the attention it deserves."[5] In quantitive terms, Syriac studies is flourishing as never before. Yes, Syriac studies publication rates plateaued

3. See, for example, David Brakke, "The Early Church in North America: Late Antiquity, Theory, and the History of Christianity," *CH* 71 (2002): 473–491; Peter Brown, "A Life of Learning: Charles Homer Haskins Lecture for 2003," *American Council of Learned Societies Occasional Paper*, No. 55.

4. Helen Vendler, "A Life of Learning: Charles Homer Haskins Lecture for 2001," *American Council of Learned Societies Occasional Paper*, No. 50.4.

5. Franz Rosenthal, "Aramaic Studies during the Past Thirty Years," *JNES* 37 (1978): 81–91, at 82. A decade earlier the British scholar Robert Murray similarly lamented, "At the beginning of this century England probably led the learned world in Syriac studies, but is now surpassed by France, Germany, Italy, Belgium, Holland and even Dom Leloir's Luxembourg—the Six! Will England join?" (Robert Murray, "Syriac Studies To-day," *Eastern Churches Review* 1 [1966–1967]: 370–373, at 373).

in the first half of the twentieth century and, naturally, dropped during the 1940s. However, by the time Rosenthal wrote in 1978, Syriac studies was once again flourishing and has continued to do so at increased rates.[6] Syriac Studies is now well established as a vibrant field, especially in North America. In fact, it is the very fecundity of Syriac studies that suggests the need to return to Rosenthal's 1978 statement and consider the implicit question in qualitative rather than in quantitive terms. What kind of attention do Syriac sources deserve in the contemporary academy? I will consider this question under three headings suggested as valuable by Sebastian Brock: "(1) the publication and translation of texts, (2) the task of interpretation and synthesis, and (3) the work of responsible *haute vulgarisation*."[7]

Editing and Translating Syriac Texts

Philology has made something of a comeback.[8] However, philology is an oft misunderstood term, as Hans Ulrich Gumbrecht rightly notes. Philology is not, says Gumbrecht, "synonymous with any study of language," but rather "narrowly circumscribed to mean a historical text curatorship."[9] This, he argues, primarily involves "the identification and restoration of texts from [their] cultural past." These tasks require three basic philological practices: "Identifying fragments, editing texts and writing historical commentary." Gumbrecht goes on to observe that, "For these practices and their underlying scholarly competence to be used, however, we have to presuppose, beyond the three basic philological skills, an awareness of the differences between different historical periods and cultures, that is, the capacity of historicizing."[10]

6. The invaluable *Comprehensive Bibliography on Syriac Christianity* informs us, for example, that nearly twice as much has been published on Syriac topics in the past four decades as in the preceding four centuries. 6640 items were published up to 1978; 10974 items from 1978–2015 (checked on 6/21/2015).

7. Sebastian P. Brock, "Syriac Studies in the Last Three Decades: Some Reflections," in *SymSyr* VI, 29.

8. The philological turn was already being made in medieval studies in the 1980s as is clear from Lee Patterson, "The Return to Philology," in *The Past and Future of Medieval Studies*, edited by John Van Engen, 231–244 (Notre Dame: University of Notre Dame Press, 1994); and Stephen G. Nichols, "Philology and Its Discontents," in *The Future of the Middle Ages: Medieval Literature in the 1990s*, edited by William D. Paden, 113–141 (Gainesville: University Press of Florida, 1994).

9. Hans Ulrich Gumbrecht, *The Powers of Philology: Dynamics of Textual Scholarship* (Urbana-Champaign: University of Illinois Press, 2003), 2.

10. Gumbrecht, *The Powers of Philology*, 3.

Working in Syriac studies means being engaged in these primary and interrelated philological activities. However, should not these activities receive some scholarly attention in their own right? One may point to the obvious need for a guide to editing Syriac texts. Scholars editing classical texts can turn to Maas and West.[11] Arabists enjoy guidance from the lectures of Bergsträsser.[12] Biblical scholars work under a set of clearly defined editorial principles.[13] Yet no such handbook exists for the editing of Syriac texts. Indeed, the few attempts that have been made to articulate a methodological approach to editing Syriac texts either pertain to a specific corpus or are fraught with problems.[14] As a result, even in the major series there is no clear and consistent methodological approach.[15] A handbook is certainly needed. The brief but excellent recent article by Alessandro Mengozzi suggests, too, that there are many opportunities for further study of the history and process of Syriac text editing.[16]

Working in Syriac studies also means being responsibly involved in the related activity of translation. In part, this means addressing the practice and function of translation more rigorously, especially given the importance of modern-language translations of Syriac texts for

11. Paul Maas, *Textual Criticism* (Oxford: Clarendon Press, 1958); Martin L. West, *Textual Criticism and Editorial Technique: Applicable to Greek and Latin Texts* (Stuttgart: Teubner, 1973). See also, R. B. C. Huygens, *Ars Edendi: A Practical Introduction to Editing Medieval Latin Texts* (Turnhout: Brepols, 2000).

12. G. Bergsträsser, *Uṣūl naqd al-nuṣūṣ wa-nashr al-kutub* (Cairo: Matba'at Dar al-Kutub, 1969) (delivered in Arabic in Cairo in 1931–1932).

13. For example, Ronald Hendel, "The Oxford Hebrew Bible: Prologue to a New Critical Edition," *VT* 58 (2008): 324–351.

14. On the editing of the Leiden Peshiṭta, see Moshe H. Goshen-Gottstein, "Prolegomena to a Critical Edition of the Peshitta," *Scripta Hierosolymitana* 8 (1961): 26–67. An editorial method from the then-editor of the Syriac series of the CSCO is given in René Draguet, "Une method d'édition des texts Syriaques," in *A Tribute to Arthur Vööbus*, edited by Robert H. Fischer, 13–18 (Chicago: The Lutheran School of Theology at Chicago, 1977).

15. Alessandro Bausi, "Current Trends in Ethiopian Studies: Philology," in *Proceedings of the XVth International Conference of Ethiopian Studies*, edited by Siegbert Uhlig, 542–551 (Wiesbaden: Harrasowitz, 2006).

16. Alessandro Mengozzi, "Past and Present Trends in the Edition of Classical Syriac Texts," in *Comparative Oriental Manuscript Studies: An Introduction*, edited by Alessandro Bausi (general editor) et al., 435–439 (Hamburg: COMSt, 2015). Rather than producing editions, graduate students may be best advised to cut their teeth by engaging with known manuscripts and existing editions. For two excellent recent examples of this kind of work, see Philip Michael Forness, "Narrating History through the Bible in Late Antiquity: A Reading Community for the Syriac Peshitta Old Testament Manuscript in Milan (Ambrosian Library, B. 21 inf.)," *Le Muséon* 127 (2014): 41–76 and Dina Boero, "The Context of Production of the Vatican Manuscript of the Syriac Life of Symeon the Stylite," *Hugoye* 18 (2015): 319–359.

both Syriac studies and other disciplines. We might ask whether the preparation of an accompanying translation should be seen as integral to the text editing process. Might translations be, in fact, as valuable as the editions themselves? If so, why is the work of translation generally undervalued and not considered to be an essential scholarly activity? We recognize that translation is not simply a mechanistic activity. It requires a thorough knowledge of the thought, vocabulary, corpus, and world of the author being treated. But, how important is it to achieve fluency of diction and elegance of style in the target language?

These and other important questions all need to be considered, especially now, when there are so many translation projects underway. In a recent interview, Sebastian Brock expressed his concern about the contemporary state of editing and translating Syriac texts. "What is so sad," he said "is if something gets badly edited, badly translated. That, in a way, ruins that particular text for quite a long time until someone gets down to redoing it."[17] Brock expands on this thought by saying, "One wants to impress on people that if you are going to undertake to edit and translate a text you need to really know the language well, and be fully familiar with the author's works and so on."[18] Moreover, as Gilbert Murray said of tackling an edition and translation, "all should of course work carefully at understanding every word of the text."[19] Certainly, if we are to give Syriac texts the attention they deserve, then the theory, practice, and results of translation require further consideration.

Interpretation and Synthesis

Gordon Teskey is right to observe that, "Philology, in the broad sense of the term, is where criticism starts from, but not where it ends."[20] As Brock notes, without further critical engagement the "significance [of Syriac sources] may remain unrecognized."[21] It is not enough to describe or sympathetically recount the contents of our texts, though

17. Sebastian Brock, interview by Timothy Michael Law, *Marginalia Review of Books*, July 8, 2014, at 28:42 (http://marginalia.lareviewofbooks.org/coffee-table-talk-with-sebastian-brock/).

18. Sebastian Brock, interview with T. M. Law, at 29:16.

19. Murray, *Interpretation*, 6.

20. Gordon Teskey, *The Poetry of John Milton* (Cambridge: Harvard University Press, 2015), xi.

21. Brock, "Syriac Studies in the Last Three Decades," 28.

this is an important element of the interpretative process.[22] Working in Syriac studies requires that we expose the significance of our texts through interpretation and synthesis. Unfortunately, only a very few texts have been critically edited, with translation and historical commentary. Many more have been critically edited with a modern translation, though the majority of Syriac literature is only available in minor editions or directly from manuscripts. This makes working in Syriac studies both more difficult and more interesting, since works of interpretation and synthesis will often require preliminary philological activity.

Exposing the significance of Syriac sources may actually become more difficult as the field establishes its own venues for academic exchange, achieving a kind of academic self-sustenance. It is important that the success of Syriac studies does not actually marginalize discussions of the Syriac sources. We must continually work to demonstrate the significance of Syriac sources to the broader academic community. We need to be asking the kind of interesting questions that engage the broader academy, and then work to answer those questions through serious philological engagement, interpretation, and synthesis. In doing so we will raise the intellectual capital of Syriac studies in the broader academy.

Responsible *haute vulgarisation*

Responsible *haute vulgarisation* aspires to engage not only a broad non-specialist audience but also scholars working in other related academic fields. It serves the field by making Syriac studies interesting.[23] Indeed, Syriac studies will only be regarded as significant to the degree that it is seen to be interesting. Syriac studies has long been considered potentially significant simply because it is filled with underutilized sources relevant to a broad variety of research

22. "The intelligent description of the work of art in its own terms is the endeavor of which Derrida speaks when, in one of his least frequently repeated comments, he describes 'doubling commentary' as that essential 'recognition and respect' without which criticism 'would risk developing in any direction at all and authorize itself to say almost anything.'" (Paul Strohm, *Theory and the Premodern Text* [Minneapolis: University of Minnesota Press, 2000], xii).

23. A point well made by Peter Brown in his Festschrift chapter, "To Make Byzantium Interesting: Our Debt to Averil Cameron," in *From Rome to Constantinople: Studies in Honour of Averil Cameron*, edited by Hagit Amirav and Bas ter Haar Romeny, 1–9 (Louvain: Peeters, 2007).

questions.[24] However, we have much work to do in demonstrating its inherent interest. We need work that demonstrates the significant intellectual force of particular authors and texts. We need work that uses Syriac sources to illustrate unknown or unrecognized aspects of late antique or medieval society. We need work that exposes the compelling aspects of Syriac manuscript culture. We need work that shows how Syriac sources contribute to and illuminate the most urgent questions of the contemporary academy.[25] To do this we must keep pace with contemporary disciplinary approaches and research questions which will illuminate new distinctives in our sources, and better place us in conversation with researchers in other disciplines and fields.

Conclusion

When thinking about the contribution of Syriac studies to the broader academy, it is worth considering the comment of Jacob Neusner on Jewish Studies. "I believe," said Neusner "that section meetings in the history of Judaism [at the American Academy of Religion] should be so planned as to interest scholars in diverse areas of religious studies. If these [section] meetings do not win the attention and participation of a fair cross section of scholars in the field as a whole, then they will not materially contribute to the study of religion in this country." This statement is cited in an article by Jonathan Z. Smith, who then goes on to add, "This, I would submit, is a new voice and a new confidence. It is that of the study of Judaism come of age! To accomplish such an agendum, it is axiomatic that careful attention must be given to matters of description and comparison—even more, that description be framed in light of comparative interests in such a way as to further comparison."[26]

24. As shown, for example, by Sebastian P. Brock, "Syriac Sources and Resources for Byzantinists," in *Proceedings of the 21st International Congress of Byzantine Studies (London, 21–26 August 2006)*, edited by E. Jeffreys, 193–210 (Aldershot: Ashgate, 2006).

25. For example, William Adler, "The Kingdom of Edessa and the Creation of a Christian Aristocracy," in *Jews, Christians, and the Roman Empire: The Poetics of Power in Late Antiquity*, edited by Natalie B. Dohrmann and Annette Yoshiko Reed, 43–62 (Philadelphia: University of Pennsylvania Press, 2013).

26. Jonathan Z. Smith, *Imagining Religion: From Babylon to Jonestown* (Chicago: University of Chicago Press), 19–20.

According to this model, our most important work is done in conversation with scholars working in other fields with shared historical interests, or disciplinary and methodological approaches. To paraphrase Smith and Neusner, we may say that the most valuable work in Syriac studies will not only contribute to scholars asking questions in related fields. It will also have the capacity to enrich their work and illuminate their fields with new perspectives and compelling questions.

Bibliography

Abbeloos, Jean Baptiste and Thomas Joseph Lamy. *Gregorii Barhebræi Chronicon ecclesiasticum.* Paris: Maisonneuve; Louvain: Peeters, 1872–1877.

Abels, Richard. "The Historiography of a Construct: 'Feudalism' and the Medieval Historian." *History Compass* 7 (2009): 1008–1031.

Abu-Lughod, Janet L. "The Islamic City – Historic Myth, Islamic Essence, and Contemporary Relevance." *IJMES* 19 (1987): 155–176.

Adler, William. "The Kingdom of Edessa and the Creation of a Christian Aristocracy." In *Jews, Christians, and the Roman Empire: The Poetics of Power in Late Antiquity*, edited by Natalie B. Dohrmann and Annette Yoshiko Reed, 43–62. Philadelphia: University of Pennsylvania Press, 2013.

Aejmelaeus, A. "Translation Technique and the Intention of the Translator." In *VII Congress of the International Organization for Septuagint and Cognate Studies*, edited by C. E. Cox, 23–36. Atlanta: Scholars Press, 1989.

Ahram, Ariel I. "Mosul." In *Encyclopedia of Jews in the Islamic World*, edited by Norman A. Stillman. Leiden: Brill, 2015.

Al-Bukhārī. *Kitāb al-Ta'rīkh al-Kabīr.* Beirut: Dār al-Kutub al-'Ilmīyah.

Aldous, Gregory. "The Islamic City Critique: Revising the Narrative." *JESHO* 56 (2013): 471–493.

Alter, Robert. "Biblical Type-Scenes and the Uses of Convention." *Critical Inquiry* 5 (1978): 355–368.

Alter, Robert. *The Art of Biblical Narrative.* New York: Basic Books, 1981.

Amar, Joseph P. "Byzantine Ascetic Monasticism and Greek Bias in the *Vita* Tradition of Ephrem the Syrian." *OCP* 58 (1992): 123–156.

Amar, Joseph P. "An Unpublished *Karšûnî* Arabic Life of Ephrem the Syrian." *Le Muséon* 106 (1993): 119–144.

Amar, Joseph P. *A Metrical Homily on Holy Mar Ephrem by Mar Jacob of Sarug*, PO 47.1. Turnhout: Brepols, 1995.

Amar, Joseph P. "An Encomium on Edessa attributed to Ephrem the Syrian." *Orientalia Christiana Analecta* 58 (2008): 120–162.

Amar, Joseph P. *The Syriac Vita Tradition of Ephrem the Syrian*, CSCO 629. Louvain: Peeters, 2011.

Amiaud, A. *La légende syriaque de saint Alexis, l'homme de Dieu.* Paris: É. Bouillon, 1889.

Amirav, Hagit. *Rhetoric and Tradition: John Chrysostom on Noah and the Flood*, TEG 12. Louvain: Peeters, 2003.

Annas, Julia. *An Introduction to Plato's Republic.* Oxford: Clarendon Press, 1981.

Anthony, Sean. *The Expeditions: An Early Biography of Muhammad.* New York: New York University Press, 2014.

Antonelli, Nicholas. *Sancti patris nostri Jacobi Episcopi Nisibeni Sermones cum praefatione, notis, & differatione de Ascetis.* Rome: Sacrae Congregationis de Propoganda Fide, 1756.

Arberry, A. J. *Muslim Saints and Mystics: Episodes from the Tadhkirat al-Auliya' (Memorial of the Saints) by Farid al-Din Attar.* Ames: Omphaloskepsis, 2000.

Armstrong, Lyall Richard. *The Quṣṣāṣ of Early Islam.* Ph.D. Diss., University of Chicago, 2013.

Arnason, Johann. "Parallels and Divergences: Perspectives on the Early Second Millennium." *Medieval Encounters* 10 (2004): 13–40.

Arneson, Hans, Emanuel Fiano, Christine Luckritz Marquis, and Kyle Smith. *The History of the Great Deeds of Bishop Paul of Qenṭos and Priest John of Edessa.* Piscataway: Gorgias Press, 2010.

Arzhanov, Yury. "A Syriac Collection of Sentences of Diogenes, Socrates, Plato and Aristotle." *Simvol* 61: *Syriaca • Arabica • Iranica* (Paris-Moscow, 2012): 238–257.

Arzhanov, Yury. "Das Florilegium in der Hs. *Vat. Sir.* 135 und seine griechisch-arabischen Parallelen." in *Geschichte, Theologie und Kultur des syrischen Christentums: Beiträge zum 7. Deutschen Syrologie-Symposium in Göttingen, Dezember 2011*, edited by M. Tamcke and S. Grebenstein, 35–48. Wiesbaden: Harrassowitz, 2014.

Arzhanov, Yury. "Abba Platon und Abba Evagrius." In *Begegnungen in Vergangenheit und Gegenwart: Beiträge dialogischer Existenz,* edited by C. Rammelt, C. Schlarb, and E. Schlarb, 75–82. Berlin: LIT, 2015.

Arzhanov, Yury. “Plato in Syriac Literature.” *Le Muséon* 132 (2019): 1–36.

Arzhanov, Yury. *Syriac Sayings of Greek Philosophers: A Study in Syriac Gnomologia with Edition and Translation,* CSCO 669. Louvain: Peeters, 2019.

Assemani, J. S. *Bibliotheca Orientalis Clementino-Vaticana.* Rome: Typis Sacrae Congregationis de Propaganda Fide, 1719–1728.

Assemani, J. S. and S. E. Assemani. *Biblioteca apostolica vaticana* (Reprint). Paris: Maisonneuve frères, 1926.

Assemani, S. E. *Acta Sanctorum et Martyrum,* I–II. Rome: Typis J. Collini, 1748.

Assfalg, Julius. *Syrische Handscriften,* Verzeichnis der Orientalischen Handschriften in Deutschland 5. Wiesbaden: Franz Steiner, 1963.

Baer, Eva. *Ayyubid Metalwork with Christian Images.* Leiden: Brill, 1989.

Baethgen, Friedrich. *Fragmente syrische und arabische Historiker,* AKM 8.3. Leipzig: Brockhaus, 1884.

Bahr, Arthur. *Fragments and Assemblages: Forming Compilations of Medieval London.* Chicago: University of Chicago Press, 2013.

Barnes, T. D. “Constantine and the Christians of Persia.” *JRS* 75 (1985): 126–136.

Barr, James. *The Typology of Literalism in Ancient Biblical Translations,* Mitteilungen des Septuaginta-Unternehmens der Akademie der Wissenschaft in Göttingen 15. Göttingen: Vandenhoeck & Ruprecht, 1979.

Barsoum, Ignatius Aphram I. *Scattered Pearls: A History of Syriac Literature and Sciences,* trans. Matti Moosa, 2nd ed. Piscataway, Gorgias Press, 2003.

Barthold, Claudia. *De viris illustribus = Berühmte Männer / Hieronymus, mit umfassender Werkstudie herausgegeben, übersetzt und kommentiert.* Mülheim: Carthusianus, 2010.

Baumstark, Anton. *Geschichte der syrischen Literatur mit Ausschluss der christlich-palästinensischen Texte.* Bonn: A. Marcus, E. Weber und A. Ahn, 1922.

Bausi, Alessandro. “Current Trends in Ethiopian Studies: Philology.” In *Proceedings of the XVth International Conference of Ethiopian Studies,* edited by Siegbert Uhlig, 542–551. Wiesbaden: Harrassowitz, 2006.

Beck, Edmund. *Die Theologie des hl. Ephräm in seinen Hymnen über den Glauben*, Studia Anselmiana 21. Rome: Libreria Vaticana, 1949.

Beck, Edmund. *Des Heiligen Ephraem des Syrers Hymnen de Fide*, CSCO 154–155. Louvain: Peeters, 1955.

Beck, Edmund. *Des Heiligen Ephraem des Syrers Hymnen de Paradiso und Contra Julianum*, CSCO 174–175. Louvain: Peeters, 1957.

Beck, Edmund. *Des heiligen Ephraem des Syrers Hymnen de nativitate (Epiphania)*, CSCO 82–83. Louvain: Peeters, 1959.

Beck, Edmund. "Ephrem le Syrien." *Dictionnaire de Spiritualité* 4 (1960): 788–822.

Beck, Edmund. *Des Heiligen Ephraem des Syrers Sermones de Fide*, CSCO 212. Louvain: Peeters, 1961.

Beck, Edmund. *Des Heiligen Ephraem des Syrers Carmina Nisibena*, I–II, CSCO 218–219, 240– 241. Louvain: Peeters, 1961, 1963.

Beck, Edmund. *Des heiligen Ephraem des Syrers Hymnen de Virginitate*, CSCO 222–223. Louvain: Peeters, 1962.

Beck, Edmund. *Des Heiligen Ephraem des Syrers Hymnen de Ieiunio*, CSCO 246–247. Louvain: Peeters, 1964.

Beck, Edmund. *Des Heiligen Ephraem des Syrers Paschahymnen (De Azymis, De Crucifixone, De Resurrectione)*, CSCO 248–249. Louvain: Peeters, 1964.

Beck, Edmund. *Des Heiligen Ephraem des Syrers Sermo de Domino Nostro*, CSCO 270. Louvain: Peeters, 1966.

Beck, Edmund. *Ephraem des Syrers Hymnen auf Abraham Kidunaya und Julianos Saba*, CSCO 322. Louvain: Peeters, 1972.

Becker, Adam H. "Anti-Judaism and Care of the Poor in Aphrahat's *Demonstration* 20." *JECS* 10 (2002): 305–327.

Becker, Adam H. "Beyond the Spatial and Temporal *Limes*: Questioning the 'Parting of the Ways' Outside the Roman Empire." In *The Ways That Never Parted*, edited by A. H. Becker and A. Y. Reed, 373–392. Tübingen: Mohr Siebeck, 2003.

Becker, Adam H. *Fear of God and the Beginning of Wisdom: The School of Nisibis and the Development of Scholastic Culture in Late Antique Mesopotamia*. Philadelphia: University of Pennsylvania Press, 2006.

Becker, Adam H. "The Discourse on Priesthood (BL Add 18295 137b–140b): An Anti-Jewish text on the Abrogation of the Israelite Priesthood." *JSS* 51 (2006): 85–115.

Becker, Adam H. *Sources for the Study of the School of Nisibis*, TTH 50. Liverpool: Liverpool University Press, 2008.

Becker, Adam H. "Martyrdom, Religious Difference, and 'Fear' as a Category of Piety in the Sasanian Empire: The Case of the *Martyrdom of Gregory* and the *Martyrdom of Yazdpaneh*." *JLA* 2 (2009): 300–336.

Becker, Adam H. *Revival and Awakening: American Evangelical Missionaries and the Origins of Assyrian Nationalism*. Chicago: University of Chicago Press, 2015.

Becker, Adam H. "Mar Addai Scher and the Recovery of East Syrian Scholastic Culture." In *Griechische Wissenschaft und Philosophie bei den Ostsyrern: Zum Gedenken an Mār Addai Scher (1867-1915)*, edited by Matthias Perkams and Alexander Schilling, 13–28. Berlin: De Gruyter, 2020.

Becker, C. H. "On the History of Muslim Worship." In *The Development of Islamic Ritual*, edited by Gerald Hawting, 49–74. Burlington: Ashgate, 2006.

Bedjan, Paul. *Acta martyrum et sanctorum*. Paris: Via dicta de Sèvres, 1890–1897.

Bedjan, Paul. *Gregorii Barhebræi Chronicon Syriacum e codd. mss. emendatum ac punctis vocalibus adnotationibusque locupletatum*. Paris: Maisonneuve, 1890.

Bedjan, Paul. *Histoire de Mar-Jabalaha et trois autres Patriarches, d'un prêtre et deux laïques nestoriens*. Paris–Leipzig: Harrassowitz, 1895.

Bedjan, Paul. *Nomocanon Gregorii Barhebraei*. Paris: Harrassowitz, 1898.

Bedjan, Paul and Sebastian P. Brock. *Homilies of Jacob of Sarug*. Piscataway: Gorgias Press, 2006.

Beeston, A. F. L. et al., eds. *Arabic Literature to the End of the Umayyad Period*. Cambridge: Cambridge University Press, 1983.

Beigus, Ulug (ed. Johannes Gravius). *Epochæ Celebriores Astronomis, Historicis, Chronologis, Chataiorum, Syro-Græcorum, Arabum, Persarum, Chorasmiorum, usitatæ ex traditione Ulug Beigi, Indiæ citra extraque Gangem Principis*. London: Jacob Flesher, 1650.

Bekkum, Wout van. "The Aqedah and its Interpretation in Midrash and Piyyut." In *The Sacrifice of Isaac: The Aqedah (Genesis 22) and its Interpretations*, edited by E. Noort and E. J. Tigchelaar, 86–95. Leiden: Brill, 2002.

Benin, Stephen D. "Commandments, Covenants and the Jews in Aphrahat, Ephrem and Jacob of Sarug." In *Approaches to Judaism in Medieval Times*, edited by David R. Blumenthal, 135–156. Chico: Scholars Press, 1985.

Benz, Ernst. *Der gekreuzigte Gerechte bei Plato, im Neuen Testament und in der alten Kirche*, Akademie der Wissenschaften und der Literatur in Mainz; Abhandlungen der geistes- und sozialwissenschaftlichen Klasse, Nr. 12, 1031–1074. Wiesbaden: F. Steiner, 1950.

Bergsträsser, G. *Uṣūl naqd al-nuṣūṣ wa-naš al-kutub*. Cairo: Matbaʿat Dar al-Kutub, 1969.

Bertaina, David. *Christian and Muslim Dialogues: The Religious Uses of a Literary Form in the Early Islamic Middle East*. Piscataway: Gorgias Press, 2011.

Bertaina, David. "Science, syntax, and superiority in eleventh-century Christian-Muslim discussion: Elias of Nisibis on the Arabic and Syriac languages." *ICMR* 22 (2011): 197–207.

Beulay, Robert. *La collection des lettres de Jean de Dalyatha*, PO 39.3. Turnhout: Brepols, 1978.

Beulay, Robert. *La lumière sans forme: Introduction à l'étude de la mystique chrétienne syro-orientale*. Chevetogne: Editions de Chevetogne, 1987.

Beulay, Robert. *L'enseignement spirituel de Jean de Dalyatha, mystique syro-oriental du VIIIe siècle*. Paris: Beauchesne, 1993.

Beyer, Klaus (translated by John F. Healey). *The Aramaic Language: Its Distribution and Subdivisions*. Göttingen: Vandenhoeck & Ruprecht, 1986.

Bidez, J. and L. Parmentier. *Evagrius, Ecclesiastical History*. London: Methuen & Co., 1898.

Bin Seray, Hamad M. "The Arabian Gulf in Syriac Sources." *NAS* 4 (1997): 205–232.

Binggeli, André. "Collections of Edifying Stories." In *The Ashgate Research Companion to Byzantine Hagiography*, vol. 2. *Genres and Contexts*, edited by Stephanos Efthymiadis, 143–160. Surrey and Burlington: Ashgate, 2014.

Binggeli, André, ed. *L'hagiographie syriaque*, ÉS 9. Paris: Paul Geuthner, 2012.

Binggeli, André. "Les collections de vies de saints dans les manuscrits syriaques." In *L'hagiographie syriaque*, ÉS 9, edited by André Binggeli, 49–75. Paris: Paul Geuthner, 2012.

Blanchard, Monica. "Moses of Nisibis (fl. 906–943) and the Library of Deir Suriani." In *Studies in the Christian East in Memory of Mirrit Boutros Ghali*, edited by L. S. B. MacCoull, vol. 1, 13–24. Washington: The Society for Coptic Archaeology, 1995.

Bloch, Joshua. "A Critical Examination of the Text of the Syriac Version of the Song of Songs." *AJSLL* 38 (1922): 103–139.

Bloom, Allan. *The Republic of Plato*, 2nd ed. New York: Basic Books, 1991.

Bloom, Harold. *The Anxiety of Influence: A Theory of Poetry*. New York: Oxford University Press, 1997.

Boero, Dina. "The Content of Production of the Vatican Manuscript of the Syriac Life of Symeon the Stylite." *Hugoye* 18 (2015): 319–359.

Book of Crumbs [*ktābonā d-partutē*]. Urmia: Archbishop of Canterbury's Mission, 1898.

Booth, Phil. *Crisis of Empire: Doctrine and Dissent at the End of Late Antiquity*. Berkeley: University of California Press, 2013.

Borbone, Pier Giorgio. "Some Aspects of Turco-Mongol Christianity in the Light of Literary and Epigraphic Syriac Sources." *JAAS* 19 (2005): 5–20.

Borbone, Pier Giorgio. "Barhebraeus and Juwayni: A Syriac Chronicler and his Persian Source." *Acta Mongolica* 9 (2009): 147–168.

Borrut, Antoine. "La circulation de l'information historique entre les sources arabo-musulmanes et syriaques: Élie de Nisibe et ses sources," in *L'historiographie syriaque*, ÉS 6, edited by M. Debié, 137–159. Paris: Geuthner, 2009.

Bosworth, C. E. "An Early Persian Ṣūfī, Shaykh Abū Saʿīd of Mayhanah." In *Logos Islamikos: Studia Islamica in Honorem Georgii Michaelis*, edited by R. M. Savory and D. A. Agius, 79–96. Toronto: Pontifical Institute of Medieval Studies, 1984.

Bosworth, C. E. *The History of al-Ṭabarī*, vol. 5. *The Sāsānids, the Byzantines, the Lakhmids and Yemen*. New York: State University of New York Press, 1999.

Bovon, François. *Luke 2: A Commentary on the Gospel of Luke 9:51–19:27*. Translated by Donald S. Deer and edited by Helmut Koestler. Minneapolis: Fortress Press, 2013.

Bowersock, G. W. *Hellenism in Late Antiquity*. Ann Arbor: University of Michigan Press, 1990.

Boyarin, Daniel. "An Unimagined Community. Against The Legends of the Jews." In *Louis Ginzberg's Legends of the Jews*, edited by

Galit Hasan-Rokem and Ithamar Gruenwald, 49–63. Detroit: Wayne State University Press, 2014.

Boyarin, Daniel. *Dying for God: Martyrdom and the Making of Christianity and Judaism.* Stanford: Stanford University Press, 1999.

Brakke, David. "The Early Church in North America: Late Antiquity, Theory, and the History of Christianity." *CH* 71 (2002): 473–491.

Braun, Oscar. *Das Buch der Synhados oder Synodicon Orientale.* Stuttgart and Vienna: s.n., 1900; repr. Amsterdam: Philo Press, 1975.

Braun, Oscar. *Ausgewählte Akten persischer Märtyrer.* Kempten and Munich: Verlag der Jos Köselschen, 1915.

Braund, S. M. *Juvenal and Persius*, LCL 91. Cambridge: Harvard University Press, 2004.

Bray, Julia. "Christian King, Muslim Apostate: Depictions of Jabala ibn Al-Ayham in Early Arabic Sources." In *Writing 'True Stories': Historians and Hagiographers in the Late Antique and Medieval Near East*, edited by Arietta Papaconstantinou, 175–204. Turnhout: Brepols, 2010.

Breydy, Michel. *Études sur Said ibn Batriq et ses sources*, CSCO 450. Louvain: Peeters, 1983.

Breydy, Michel. *Das Annalenwerk des Eutychios von Alexandrien. Ausgewählte Geschichten und Legenden kompiliert von Said ibn Batriq um 935 AD*, CSCO 471–472. Louvain: Peeters, 1985.

Briquel Chatonnet, Françoise, ed. *Les églises en monde syriaque*, ÉS 10. Paris: Geuthner, 2013.

Briquel Chatonnet, Françoise and Alain Desreumaux, "Syriac Inscriptions in Syria." *Hugoye* 14 (2011): 27–44.

Briquel Chatonnet, Françoise, Alain Desreumaux, and Jacob Thekeparampil. *Recueil des inscriptions syriaques*, vol. 1. *Kérala*. Paris: De Boccard, 2008.

Brock, Sebastian P. Review of G. Wiessner, *Untersuchungen zur syrischen Literaturgeschichte*, *JTS n.s.* 19 (1968): 300–309.

Brock, Sebastian P. *The Syriac Version of the Pseudo-Nonnos Mythological Scholia*. Cambridge: Cambridge University Press, 1971.

Brock, Sebastian P. "An Early Syriac Life of Maximus the Confessor." *AB* 91 (1973): 299–346.

Brock, Sebastian P. "A Martyr at the Sasanid Court under Vahran II: Candida." *AB* 96 (1978): 167–181.

Brock, Sebastian P. "Aspects of Translation Technique in Antiquity." *GRBS* 20 (1979): 69–87.
Brock, Sebastian P. "Genesis 22 in Syriac Tradition." In *Mélanges Dominique Barthélemy: Études bibliques offertes à l'occasion de son 60e anniversaire*, edited by Pierre Casetti, Keel Othman, and Adrian Schenker, 1–30. Göttingen: Vandenhoeck & Ruprecht, 1981.
Brock, Sebastian P. "Christians in the Sassanian Sasanian Empire: A Case of Divided Loyalties." In *Religious and National Identity: Papers Read at the Nineteenth Summer Meeting and the Twentieth Winter Meeting of the Ecclesiastical History Society*, Studies in Church History 18, edited by Stuart Mews, 1–19. Oxford: Basil Blackwell, 1982.
Brock, Sebastian P. "From Antagonism to Assimilation: Syriac Attitudes to Greek Learning." In *East of Byzantium: Syria and Armenia in the Formative Period*, ed. Nina Garsoian, Thomas Mathews, and Robert Thompson, 17–34. Washington: Dumbarton Oaks, 1982.
Brock, Sebastian P. *Syriac Perspectives on Late Antiquity*. London: Variorum Reprints, 1984.
Brock, Sebastian P. "Towards a History of Syriac Translation Technique." In *SyrSym* III, 1–14.
Brock, Sebastian P. "Two Syriac Verse Homilies on the Binding of Isaac." *Le Muséon* 99 (1986): 61–129.
Brock, Sebastian P. *St. Ephrem the Syrian. Hymns on Paradise*. Crestwood: St. Vladimir's Seminary Press, 1990.
Brock, Sebastian P. "The Syriac Background to Ḥunayn's Translation Techniques." *ARAM* 3 (1991): 139–162.
Brock, Sebastian P. *The Luminous Eye: The Spiritual World Vision of Saint Ephrem*. Kalamazoo: Cistercian Publications, 1992.
Brock, Sebastian P. "Eusebius and Syriac Christianity." In *Eusebius, Christianity, and Judaism*, edited by Harold W. Attridge and Gohei Hata, 212–234. Detroit: Wayne State University Press, 1992.
Brock, Sebastian P. "To Revise or Not to Revise: Attitudes to Jewish Biblical Translation." In *Septuagint, Scrolls and Cognate Writings, Papers Presented to the International Symposium on the Septuagint and its Relations to the Dead Sea Scrolls and Other Writings, Manchester, 1990*, Septuagint and Cognate Studies Series 3, edited by G. J. Brooke and B. Lindars, 301–338. Atlanta: Scholars Press, 1992.

Brock, Sebastian P. "Syriac Studies in the Last Three Decades: Some Reflections." In *SymSyr* VI, 13–29.

Brock, Sebastian P. "The Scribe Reaches Harbour." *BF* 21 (1995): 195–202.

Brock, Sebastian P. "The Transmission of Ephrem's *madrashe* in the Syriac Liturgical Tradition." *SP* 33 (1997): 490–505.

Brock, Sebastian P. "St. Ephrem in the Eyes of Later Syriac Liturgical Tradition." *Hugoye* 2 (1999): 5–25.

Brock, Sebastian P. "Stomathalassa, Dandamis and Secundus in a Syriac monastery anthology." In *After Bardaisan: Studies on continuity and change in Syriac Christianity in Honour of Professor Han J. W. Drijvers*, edited by G. Reinink and A. Klugkist, OLA 89, 35–50. Louvain: Peeters, 1999.

Brock, Sebastian P. "Syriac translations of Greek popular philosophy." In *Von Athen nach Bagdad: Zur Rezeption griechischer Philosophie von der Spätantike bis zum Islam*, edited by P. Bruns, 9–28. Bonn: Borengässer, 2003.

Brock, Sebastian P. "Without Mushē of Nisibis, Where Would We Be? Some Reflections on the Transmission of Syriac Literature." *Journal of Eastern Christian Studies* 56 (2004): 15–24.

Brock, Sebastian P. *Spirituality in the Syriac Tradition*. Kottayam: St. Ephrem Ecumenical Research Institute, 2005.

Brock, Sebastian P. "The Imagery of the Spiritual Mirror in the Syriac Literature." *JCSSS* 5 (2005): 3–17.

Brock, Sebastian P. "Syriac Sources and Resources for Byzantinists." In *Proceedings of the 21st International Congress of Byzantine Studies (London, 21–26 August 2006)*, edited by E. Jeffreys, 193–210. Aldershot: Ashgate, 2006.

Brock, Sebastian P. *History of Mar Ma'in, with a Guide to the Persian Martyr Acts*. Piscataway: Gorgias Press, 2008.

Brock, Sebastian P. "Saints in Syriac: A Little-Tapped Resource." *JECS* 16 (2008): 181–196.

Brock, Sebastian P. "Syriac Studies: A Classified Bibliography, 2001–2005." *PdO* 33 (2008): 281–446.

Brock, Sebastian P. "Abbot Mushe of Nisibis, Collector of Syriac Manuscripts." In *Gli studi orientalistici in Ambrosiana nella cornice del IV centenario, 1609–2009: Pimo dies academicus, 8–10 novembre 2010*, Orientalia Ambrosiana 1, edited by Carmela Baffioni, Rosa

Bianca Finazzi, Anna Passoni Dell'Acqua, and Emidio Vergani, 15–32. Rome: Bulzoni / Milan: Biblioteca Ambrosiana, 2012.

Brock, Sebastian P. "Some Syriac Pseudo-Platonic Curiosities." In *Medieval Arabic Thought: Essays in Honour of F. Zimmermann*, edited by R. Hansberger, M. A. al-Akiti, and C. Burnett, 19–26. London: Warburg Institute, 2012.

Brock, Sebastian P. "Charting the Hellenization of a Literary Culture: The Case of Syriac." In *New Horizons in Graeco-Arabic Studies*, edited by D. Gutas, S. Schmidtke, and A. Treiger, 98–124. Leiden: Brill, 2015.

Brock, Sebastian P., Aaron M. Butts, George A. Kiraz, and Lucas Van Rompay, eds. *Gorgias Encyclopedic Dictionary of the Syriac Heritage*. Piscataway: Gorgias Press, 2011.

Brock, Sebastian P. and David G. K. Taylor. *The Hidden Pearl: The Syrian Orthodox Church and its Ancient Heritage*, 3 vols. Florence: Octavo Press, 2001.

Brockelmann, Carl. *Lexicon Syriacum*, 2nd ed. Göttingen: W. Fr. Kaestner, 1928.

Brooks, E. W. *Eliae metropolitae nisibeni opus chronologicum I*, CSCO 62. Paris: Poussielgue, 1910.

Brooks, E. W. *James of Edessa. The Hymns of Severus of Antioch and Others*, PO 7.5. Paris: Firmin-Didot, 1911.

Brooks, E. W. and J.-B. Chabot. *Eliae metropolitae Nisibeni Opus chronologicum*, CSCO 62–63. Paris: Poussielgue, 1909–1910.

Brown, Peter. "A Life of Learning: Charles Homer Haskins Lecture for 2003." *American Council of Learned Societies Occasional Paper*, No. 55.

Brown, Peter. "To Make Byzantium Interesting: Our Debt to Averil Cameron." In *From Rome to Constantinople: Studies in Honour of Averil Cameron*, edited by Hagit Amirav and Bas ter Haar Romeny, 1–9. Louvain: Peeters, 2007.

Bruns, Peter and Heinz Luthe, eds. *Orientalia Christiana. Festschrift für Hubert Kaufhold zum 70. Geburtstag*. Wiesbaden: Harrassowitz, 2013.

Bruns, Peter. "Antizoroastrische Polemik in den syro-persischen Märtyrerakten." In *Jews, Christians and Zoroastrians: Religious Dynamics in a Sasanian Context*, edited by Geoffrey Herman, 47–65. Pisacataway: Gorgias Press, 2014.

Budge, Ernest A. Wallis. *The Chronography of Gregory Abû'l Faraj, the son of Aaron, the Hebrew physician, commonly known as Bar Hebraeus being the first part of his political history of the world.* Oxford: Oxford University Press, 1932.

Buell, Denise. *Why this New Race: Ethnic Reasoning in Early Christianity.* New York: Columbia University Press, 2005.

Burgess, Richard W. and Raymond Mercier. "The Dates of the Martyrdom of Simeon bar Sabba'e and the 'Great Massacre.'" *AB* 117 (1999): 9–66.

Burke, Peter. *What Is Cultural History.* Cambridge: Polity, 2004.

Burnett, Charles. "Antioch as a Link between Arabic and Latin Culture in the Twelfth and Thirteenth Century." In *Occident et Proche-Orient: Contacts scientifiques au temps des Croisades. Actes du colloque de Louvain-la-Neuve, 24 et 25 Mars 1997*, edited by Draelants Tihon Abeele and Isabelle Anne van Baudouin, 1–78. Turnhout: Brepols, 2000.

Butts, Aaron Michael. "Embellished with Gold: The Ethiopic Reception of Syriac Biblical Exegesis." *OC* 97 (2013/2014): 137–159.

Butts, Aaron Michael and Simcha Gross. *The History of the "Slave of Christ": From Jewish Child to Christian Martyr.* Piscataway, Gorgias Press, 2016.

Caliò, Giuseppe. "Giovanni Calibita." *Bibliotheca Sanctorum*, vol. 6, 640–641. Rome: Instituto Giovanni XXIII nela Pontifica Università lateranense, 1961.

Cameron, Averil. *Christianity and the Rhetoric of Empire: The Development of Christian Discourse.* Berkeley: University of California Press, 1991.

Cameron, Averil. "Blaming the Jews: The Seventh Century Invasions of Palestine in Context." *Travaux et Mémoires* 14 (2002): 57–78.

Campbell, Elizabeth. *A Heaven of Wine: Muslim-Christian encounters at monasteries in the early Islamic Middle East.* Ph.D. Diss., University of Washington, 2009.

Carbajosa, Ignacio. *The Character of the Syriac Version of Psalms. A Study of Psalms 90–150 in the Peshitta*, MPI 17. Leiden: Brill, 2008.

Carlson, Thomas A. "Contours of Conversion: The Geography of Islamization in Syria, 600–1500." *JAOS* 135 (2015): 791–816.

Carpentier, E. "Martyrium Sancti Arethae et Sociorum in Civitate Negran." *Acta Sanctorum* October X (1869): 721–759.

Cassingena-Trévedy, François. *Éphrem de Nisibe: Hymnes pascales*, SC 502. Paris: Cerf, 2006.

Castelli, Elizabeth. *Martyrdom and Memory: Early Christian Culture Making*. New York: Columbia University Press, 2004.

Ceriani, A. M. *Translatio Syra Pescitto Veteris Testamenti ex Codice Ambrosiano sec. fere 6., photolithographice edita*. Milan: della Croce, 1876.

Chabot, J.-B. "Notice sur les manuscrits syriaques conservés dans la bibliothèque du patriarcat grec orthodoxe de Jérusalem." *JA* 9.3 (1894): 92–134.

Chabot, J.-B. *Le Livre de la chasteté composé par Jésusdenah, évêque de Baçrah*. Rome: École française de Rome, 1896.

Chabot, J.-B. "Histoire de Jésus-Sabran écrite par Jésus-Yab d'Adiabène." *Nouvelles archives des missions scientifiqueset littéraires* 7 (1897): 485–584.

Chabot, J.-B. *Chronique de Michel le Syrien, Patriarch Jacobite d'Antioche (1166–1199)*. Paris: Ernest Lerous éditeur, 1899–1905.

Chabot, J.-B. *Synodicon Orientale*. Paris: Imprimerie Nationale, 1902.

Chabot, J.-B. *Eliae metropolitae nisibeni opus chronologicum II*, CSCO 62. Paris: Poussielgue, 1910.

Chabot, J.-B. *Anonymi Auctoris Chronicon ad annum Christi 1234 pertinens I*, CSCO 81. Paris: Bibliopola, 1937.

Chadwick, H. "John Moschos and his friend Sophronios the Sophist." *JTS* 25 (1974): 47–49.

Charles, R. H. *The Chronicle of John of Nikiu*. London: Williams & Norgate, 1916.

Charlesworth, James H. *The Odes of Solomon*. Missoula: Scholars Press, 1977.

Cheikho, L. *Eutychii Patriarchae Alexandrini Annales I*, CSCO 50. Paris: Poussielgue, 1906.

Cheikho, L. *Agapius episcopus Mabbugensis: Historia universalis*, CSCO 65. Louvain: Peeters, 1912.

Cheikho, L., B. Carra de Vaux, and H. Zayyat. *Eutychii Patriarchae Alexandrini Annales II: Accedunt Annales Yahia ibn Said Antiochensis*, CSCO 51. Paris: Poussielgue, 1909.

Ciancaglini, Claudia. *Iranian Loanwords in Syriac*. Wiesbaden: Reichert, 2008.

Coakley, James F. "The Explanations of the Feasts of Moše bar Kepha." In *SymSyr* IV, 403–410.

Colless, Brian. *The Mysticism of John Saba*. Ph.D. Diss., University of Melbourne, 1969.

Colless, Brian. "The Biographies of John Saba." *PdO* 3 (1972): 45–63.

Colless, Brian. "The Mysticism of John Saba." *OCP* 39 (1973): 83–102.

Connolly, R. Hugh. *Didascalia Apostolorum: The Syriac version translated and accompanied by the Verona Latin fragments*. Oxford: Oxford University Press, 1929.

Conterno, Maria. *La 'descrizione dei tempi' all'alba dell'espansione islamica. Un' indagine sulla storiografia greca, siriaca e araba fra VII e VIII secolo*, Millennium Studien 47. Berlin: De Gruyter, 2014.

Conterno, Maria. "Theophilos, 'the more likely candidate'? Towards a reappraisal of Theophanes' 'Oriental Source(s).'" In *Studies in Theophanes*, Travaux et Mémoires 19, edited by F. Montinaro and M. Jankowiak, 383–400. Paris: Éditions de l'IHEAL, 2015.

Conybeare, F. C. *The Apology and Acts of Apollonius and Other Monuments of Early Christianity*. New York: Macmillan, 1894.

Cook, David. "Christians and Christianity in *Ḥadīth* Works before 900." In *Christian-Muslim Relations. A Bibliographical History*, vol. 1. *(600–1500)*, edited by David Thomas, 73–82. Leiden: Brill, 2009.

Coope, Jessica A. *The Martyrs of Cordoba: Community and Family Conflict in an Age of Mass Conversion*. Lincoln: University of Nebraska Press, 1995.

Cribiore, Raffaella. *The School of Libanius in Late Antique Antioch*. Princeton: Princeton University Press, 2007.

Croke, Brian. "The origins of the Christian World Chronicle." In *History and Historians in Late Antiquity*, edited by B. Croke and A. M. Emmett, 116–131. Sydney: Pergamon Press, 1983.

Crone, Patricia and Michael Cook. *Hagarism: The Making of the Islamic World*. Cambridge: Cambridge University Press, 1977.

Cubitt, Geoffrey. *History and Memory*. Manchester: Manchester University Press, 2007.

Cureton, William. *Spicilegium Syriacum: Containing Remains of Bardesan, Meliton, Ambrose and Mara Bar Serapion*. London: Rivingtons, 1855.

Cureton, William. *History of the Martyrs in Palestine*. London: Williams and Norgate, 1861.

Cureton, William. *Ancient Syriac Documents*. London: Williams and Norgate, 1864.

Dashdondog, Bayarsaikhan. *The Mongols and the Armenians (1220–1335).* Leiden: Brill, 2010.

Davies, W. D. and Dale C. Allison. *Matthew: A Shorter Commentary.* New York: T&T Clark, 2004.

De Smet, Daniel, Meryem Sebti, and Godefroid De Callataÿ, eds. *Miroir et savior: La transmission d'un thème platonicien, des Alexandrins, à la philisophie arabo-musulmane.* Leuven: Leuven University Press, 2008.

Debié, Muriel. "Devenir chrétien dans l'Iran sassanide: La conversion à la lumière des récits hagiographiques." In *Le problème de la chistianisation du monde antique*, edited by Hervé Inglebert, Sylvain Destephen, and Bruno Dumézil, 329–358. Paris: Picard, 2010.

Debié, Muriel. "Syriac Historiography and Identity Formation." In *Religious origins of nations? The Christian communities of the Middle East*, edited by Bas ter Haar Romeny, 92–114. Leiden: Brill, 2010.

Debié, Muriel. "Writing history as 'histoires': The biographical dimension of East Syriac historiography." In *Writing "true stories". Historians and hagiographers in the Late Antique and Medieval Near East*, Cultural Encounters in Late Antiquity and the Middle Ages 9, edited by A. Papaconstantinou, M. Debié, and H. Kennedy, 43–77. Turnhout: Brepols, 2010.

Debié, Muriel and David Taylor. "Syriac and Syro-Arabic Historical Writing." In *The Oxford History of Historical Writing*, vol. 2. *The Oxford History of Historical Writing: 400–1400*, edited by S. Foot and C. F. Robinson, 155–179 (Oxford: Oxford University Press, 2012).

Delehaye, H. *Les versions grecques des martyrs persans sous Sapor II*, PO 2.4. Paris: Firmin-Didot, 1907.

Demandt, Alexander. *Sokrates antwortet.* Zürich: Artemis & Winkler, 1992.

Den Heijer, Johannes. *Mawhub ibn Mansur ibn Mufarrig et l'historiographie copto-arabe. Étude sur la composition de l'Histoire des Patriarches d'Alexandrie*, CSCO 513. Louvain: Peeters, 1989.

Des Places, Édouard. "Un thème platonicien dans la tradition patristique: Le juste crucifié (Platon, *République*, 361e4–362a2)." *SP* IX.3, TU 94, edited by F. L. Cross, 30–40. Berlin: Akademie-Verlag, 1966.

Detoraki, Marina. *Le Martyre de Saint Aréthas et de ses compagnons, Bibliotheca Hagiographica Graeca 166.* Paris: Association des amis du Centre d'histoire et civilization de Byzance, 2007.

Detoraki, Marina. "Greek *Passions* of the Martyrs in Byzantium." In *The Ashgate Research Companion to Byzantine Hagiography*, vol. II. *Genres and Contexts*, edited by Stephanos Efthymiadis, 61–101. Farnham: Ashgate, 2014.

Devos, Paul. "Abgar, hagiographe perse méconnu (début du Ve siècle)." *AB* 83:3–4 (1965): 303–328.

Devos, Paul. "Les martyrs persans à travers leurs actes syriaques." In *Atti del Convegno sul tema: La Persia e il mondo greco-romano (Roma 11–14 aprile 1965)*, Accademia Nazionale dei Lincei 363, Problemi attuali di scienza e di cultura 76, 213–225. Rome: Accademia Nazionale dei Lincei, 1966.

Dewing, Henry Bronson. *Procopius. History of the Wars*. London: W. Heinemann; New York: Macmillan, 1914–1940.

Dirksen, P. B. "The Peshitta and Textual Criticism of the Old Testament." *VT* 42 (1992): 376–390.

Dodd, Erica Cruikshank. *The Frescoes of Mar Musa al-Habashi. A Study in Medieval Painting in Syria*. Toronto: Pontifical Institute of Mediaeval Studies, 2001.

Dodge, B. *The Fihrist of Ibn al-Nadīm. A 10th century AD survey of Islamic culture*. New York: Columbia University Press, 1970.

Donner, Fred. *Narratives of Islamic Origins: The Beginnings of Islamic Historical Writing*. Princeton: The Darwin Press, 1998.

Doran, Robert. *Stewards of the Poor: The Man of God, Rabbula and Hiba in Fifth-Century Edessa*. Kalamazoo: Cistercian Publications, 2006.

Draguet, René. "Une method d'édition des texts syriaques." In *A Tribute to Arthur Vööbus*, edited by Robert H. Fischer, 13–18. Chicago: The Lutheran School of Theology at Chicago, 1977.

Drijvers, H. J. W. "Christians, Jews and Muslims in Northern Mesopotamia in Early Islamic Times." In *La Syrie de Byzance a l'Islam*, edited by P. Canivet and J.-P. Rey-Coquais, 67–74. Damas: Institut Français de Damas, 1992.

Drobner, Hubertus R. and Alberto Viciano. *Gregory of Nyssa. Homilies on the Beatitudes*. Leiden: Brill, 2000.

Duby, Georges. *The Three Orders: Feudal Society Imagined*. Chicago: University of Chicago Press, 1981.

Duffy, John. "Passing remarks on three Byzantine texts." *Palaeoslavica* 10 (2002): 54–64.

Duffy, John. "The Jewish Boy Legend and the 'Western Twist.'" In *Byzantine Religious Culture: Studies in Honor of Alice-Mary Talbot*, edited by D. Sullivan, E. Fisher, and S. Papaioannou, 313–322. Leiden: Brill, 2012.

Dyk, Janet W. and Percy S. F. van Keulen. *Language System, Translation Technique, and Textual Tradition in the Peshitta of Kings*, MPI 19. Leiden: Brill, 2013.

Ebach, Jürgen. *Genesis 37–50*, Herders Theologischer Kommentar zum Alten Testament. Freiburg: Herder, 2007.

Ecker, Heather and Teresa Fitzherbert. "The Freer Canteen reconsidered." *Ars Orientalis* 42 (2012): 176–93.

Efthymiadis, Stephanos. "Introduction." In *The Ashgate Research Companion to Byzantine Hagiography*, vol. 1. *Periods and Places*, edited by Stephanos Efthymiadis, 1–14. Surrey and Burlington: Ashgate, 2011.

El Tayib, Abdulla. "Pre-Islamic Poetry." In *Arabic Literature to the End of the Umayyad Period*, edited by A. F. L. Beeston et al., 27–113. Cambridge: Cambridge University Press, 1983.

Ellenblum, Ronnie. *Frankish Rural Settlement in the Latin Kingdom of Jerusalem*. Cambridge: Cambridge University Press, 1998.

Esbroeck, M. van. "Abraham le confesseur (Ve s.), traducteur des passions des martyrs perses: À propos d'un livre recent." *AB* 95 (1977): 169–179.

Evetts, Basil T. A. (with Alfred J. Butler). *The Churches and Monasteries of Egypt and Some Neighbouring Countries Attributed to Abu Salih the Armenian*. Oxford: Clarendon Press, 1895.

Farīd, Aḥmad. *Tafsīr Ibn Wahab*. Beirut: Manshurāt Muhammad ʿAlī Bayḍūn, Dār al-Kutub al-ʿIlmīyah, 2003.

Farīd, Aḥmad. *Tafsīr Muqātil ibn Sulayman*. Beirut: Dār al-Kutub al-ʿIlmīyah, 2003.

Fentress, James and Chris Wickham. *Social memory*. Oxford: Blackwell, 1992.

Fiey, Jean-Maurice. "Aônès, Awun et Awgin." *AB* 80 (1962): 52–81.

Fiey, Jean-Maurice. "Encore ʿAbdulmasīḥ de Singăr." *Le Muséon* 77 (1964): 215–223.

Fiey, Jean-Maurice. "L'apport de Mgr Addaï Scher (†1915) à l'hagiographie orientale." *AB* 83 (1965): 121–142.

Fiey, Jean-Maurice. "Notulae de littérature syriaque: La Démonstration XIV d'Aphraate." *Le Muséon* 81 (1968): 449–454.

Fiey, Jean-Maurice. *Jalons pour une histoire de l'église en Iraq*, CSCO 310. Louvain: Peeters, 1970.

Fiey, Jean-Maurice. "Chrétientés syriaques du Horāsān et du Ségestān." *Le Muséon* 86 (1973): 75–104.

Fiey, Jean-Maurice. *Pour un Oriens Christianus Novus. Répertoire des diocèses Syriaques orientaux et occidentaux.* Stuttgart: Steiner, 1993.

Fiey, Jean-Maurice. *Saints syriaques.* Edited by Lawrence I. Conrad. Studies in Late Antiquity and Early Islam 6. Princeton: Darwin Press, 2004.

Fiorenza, Elisabeth Schüssler. *But She Said: Feminist Practices of Biblical Interpretation.* Boston: Beacon Press, 1992.

Fitzherbert, Teresa. "The Freer Canteen: Jerusalem or Jazira?" In *Islamic Art, Architecture and Material Culture: New Perspectives*, edited by Margaret S. Graves, 1–6. Oxford: Archaeopress, 2012.

Flügel, G. *Kitāb al-Fihrist.* Leipzig: Vogel, 1872.

Flusin, B. *Saint Anastase le Perse et l'histoire de la Palestine au début du VIIe siècle.* Paris: Centre national de la recherche scientifique, 1992.

Folda, Jaroslav. *Crusader Art. The Art of the Crusaders in the Holy Land, 1099–1291.* Aldershot: Lund Humphries Publishers, 2008.

Forness, Philip Michael. "Narrating History through the Bible in Late Antiquity: A Reading Community for the Syriac Peshitta Old Testament Manuscript in Milan (Ambrosian Library, B. 21 inf.)." *Le Muséon* 127 (2014): 41–76.

Fowden, Elizabeth Key. *The Barbarian Plain: Saint Sergius between Rome and Iran.* Berkeley: University of California Press, 1999.

Francisco, Hector Ricardo. "Corpse Exposure in the Acts of the Persian Martyrs and its Literary Models." *Hugoye* 19 (2016): 193–235.

Freidenreich, David M. *Foreigners and Their Food: Constructing Otherness in Jewish, Christian, and Islamic Law*. Berkeley: University of California Press, 2011.

Gaborit, Justine, Gérard Thébault, and Abdurrahman Oruç. "L'église Mar-Ya'qub de Nisibe." In *Les Églises en Monde Syriaques*, ÉS 10, edited by Françoise Briquel Chatonnet, 289–330. Paris: Geuthner, 2013.

Gafni, Isaiah. "Babylonian Rabbinic Culture." In *Cultures of the Jews*, edited by David Bialle, vol. 1, 23–265. New York: Schocken Books, 2002.

Garitte, G. "La passion géorgienne de sainte *Golindouch*." *AB* 74 (1956): 405–40.

Garitte, G. "La passion géorgienne de saint ʿAbd al-Masīh." *Le Muséon* 79 (1966): 187–237.

Geary, Patrick J. *Phantoms of remembrance. Memory and oblivion at the end of the First Millennium*. Princeton: Princeton University Press, 1994.

Georgopoulou, Maria. "The Artistic World of the Crusaders and Oriental Christians in the Twelfth and Thirteenth Centuries." *Gesta* 43 (2004): 115–128.

Gerö, Stephen. "Only a Change of Masters? The Christians of Iran and the Muslim Conquest." In *The Expansion of the Early Islamic State,* edited by Fred Donner, 125–130. Aldershot: Ashgate, 2008.

Gignoux, Philippe. "À la frontière du syriaque et de l'iranien: Quelques confluences tirées des Actes des martyrs perses." *Semitica et Classica* 3 (2010): 189–193.

Gignoux, P., F. Julien, and C. Julien. *Noms propres syriaques d'origine iranienne*. Vienna: Verlag der Österreichischen Akademie der Wissenschaften, 2009.

Gilliot, Claude. "Christianity and Christians in Islamic Exegesis." In *Christian-Muslim Relations: A Bibliographical History*, vol. 1 *(600-900),* edited by David Thomas and Barbara Roggema, 31–56. Leiden, Boston: Brill, 2009.

Gilliot, Claude. "On the Origin of the Informants of the Prophet." In *The Hidden Origins of Islam. New Research into its Early History*, edited by Karl-Heinz Ohlig and Gerd-R. Puin, 153–188. Amherst: Prometheus Books, 2010.

Gilomen, Hans-Jörg. "Wucher und Wirtschaft im Mittelalter." *HZ* 250 (1990): 265–301.

Gismondi, E. *Maris Amri et Slibae De patriarchis nestorianorum commentaria*. Rome: De Luigi, 1896–1899.

Goitein, Shelomo Dov. *A Mediterranean Society*. Berkeley: University of California Press, 1967–1993.

Goodblatt, David. *Rabbinic Instruction in Sasanian Babylonia*. Leiden: Brill, 1975.

Goshen-Gottstein, Moshe H. "Prolegomena to a Critical Edition of the Peshitta." *Scripta Hierosolymitana* 8 (1961): 26–67.

Graf, George. *Geschichte der christlichen arabischen Literatur*. Vatican City: Biblioteca apostolica vaticana, 1944–1952.

Gray, Louis. "Two Armenian Passions from the Sasanian Period." *AB* 67 (1949): 361–376.

Greisiger, Lutz. "Saints populaires d'Édesse." In *L'hagiographie syriaque*, ÉS 9, edited by André Binggeli, 171–200. Paris: Paul Geuthner, 2012.

Griffith, Sidney H. "Ephrem, the Deacon of Edessa, and the Church of the Empire." In *Diakonia. Studies in Honor of Robert T. Meyer*, edited by T. Halton and J. P. Williman, 22–52. Washington: The Catholic University of America Press, 1986.

Griffith, Sidney H. "Jews and Muslims in Christian Syriac and Arabic Texts of the Ninth Century." *Jewish History* 3 (1988): 65–94.

Griffith, Sidney H. "The monks of Palestine and the growth of Christian literature in Arabic." *Muslim World* 78 (1988): 1–28.

Griffith, Sidney H. "A Spiritual Father for the Whole Church: The Universal Appeal of St. Ephrem the Syrian." *Hugoye* 1 (1998): 1–33.

Griffith, Sidney H. *Arabic Christianity in the monasteries of ninth-century Palestine*, Collected Studies Series 380. Brookfield, Vermont: Variorum, 1992.

Griffith, Sidney H. "The Monk in the Emir's Majlis: Reflections on a Popular Genre of Christian Literary Apologetics in Arabic in the Early Islamic Period." In *The Majlis: Interreligious Encounters in Medieval Islam*, edited by Hava Lazarus-Yafeh et al., 13–65. Wiesbaden: Harrassowitz, 1999.

Griffith, Sidney H. "Melkites, Jacobites and the christological controversies in Arabic in third/ninth century Syria." In *Syrian Christians under Islam. The first thousand years*, edited by D. Thomas, 9–55. Leiden: Brill, 2001.

Griffith, Sidney H. *The beginnings of Christian theology in Arabic: Muslim-Christian encounters in early Islamic period*, Collected Studies Series 746. Aldershot – Burlington: Ashgate, 2002.

Griffith, Sidney H. "Answering the Call of the Minaret: Christian Apologetics in the World of Islam." In *Redefining Christian Identity. Cultural Interaction in the Middle East since the Rise of Islam*, edited by J. J. van Ginkel, H. L. Murre van den Berg, and T. M. van Lint, 91–126. Louvain: Peeters, 2005.

Griffith, Sidney H. "Apologetics and historiography in the annals of Eutychios of Alexandria: Christian self-definition in the world of Islam." In *Studies on the Christian Arabic heritage: In honour of Father Prof. dr. Samil Khalil Samir S.I. at occasion of his sixty-fifth birthday*, ECS 5, edited by R. Y. Ebied, 65–89. Louvain: Peeters 2005.

Griffith, Sidney H. "From Patriarch Timothy I to Ḥunayn ibn Isḥāq: Philosophy and Christian apology in Abbasid times; reason, ethics and public policy." In *Redefining Christian Identity. Cultural Interaction in the Middle East since the Rise of Islam*, edited by J. J. van Ginkel, H. L. Murre van den Berg, and T. M. van Lint, 75–98. Louvain: Peeters, 2005.

Griffith, Sidney H. *The Church in the Shadow of the Mosque: Christians and Muslims in the World of Islam*. Princeton: Princeton University Press, 2010.

Griffith, Sidney H. *The Bible in Arabic*. Princeton: Princeton University Press, 2013.

Gross, Simcha. "A Persian Anti-Martyr Act: The Death of Rabbah Bar Naḥmani." In *The Aggada of the Bavli and its Cultural World*, edited by G. Herman and J. L. Rubenstein, 211–242. Providence: Brown Judaic Studies, 2018.

Guidi, Ignazio. "Mosè di Aghel e Simone Abbato." *Rendiconti della Reale Accademia dei Lincei, Classe di scienze morali, storiche e filologiche*, ser. 4, vol. 2 (1886): 545–556.

Guidi, Ignazio. *Chronica Minora I*, CSCO 1–2. Louvain: Peeters, 1903.

Guillaume, Alfred. *The Life of Muhammad: Translation of Isḥāq's Sīrat Rasūl Allāh*. Oxford: Oxford University Press, 1955.

Guillaume, Alfred. *The Traditions of Islam*. Beirut: Khayats, 1966.

Gullotta, D. N. "Among Dogs and Disciples: An Examination of the Story of the Canaanite Woman (Matthew 15:21–28) and the Question of the Gentile Mission within the Matthean Community." *Neotestamentica* 48 (2014): 327–329.

Gumbrecht, Hans Ulrich. *The Powers of Philology: Dynamics of Textual Scholarship*. Urbana-Champaign: University of Illinois Press, 2003.

Gutas, Dimitri. *Greek thought, Arabic culture: The Graeco-Arabic translation movement in Baghdad and early 'Abbasid society (2nd–4th/8th–10th c.)*. London: Routledge 1998.

Gutas, Dimitri. "Platon - Tradition arabe." In *Dictionnaire des philosophes antiques*, edited by R. Goulet, vol. 5/1, 845–863. Paris: CNRS, 2012.

Gutas, Dimitri. "Graeco-Arabic Studies from Amable Jourdain through Franz Rosenthal to the Future." In *New Horizons in Graeco-Arabic Studies*, edited by D. Gutas, S. Schmidtke, and A. Treiger, 1–14. Leiden: Brill, 2015.

Gutas, D., S. Schmidtke, and A. Treiger, eds. *New Horizons in Graeco-Arabic Studies*. Leiden: Brill, 2015.

Hacken, Clara ten. "The Description of Antioch in Abū al-Makārim's History of the Churches and Monasteries of Egypt and some Neighbouring Countries." In *East and West in the Medieval Eastern Mediterranean: Antioch from the Byzantine Reconquest until the End of the Crusader Principality*, vol. 3. *Acts of the Congress held at Hernen in May 2003*, OLA 269, edited by Krijnie Nelly Ciggaar, David Michael Metcalf, and Herman Teule, 185–216. Louvain: Peeters, 2006.

Haddad, B. *Mukhtasar al-akhbār al-bī'iyya*. Baghdad: Al-Diwan, 2000.

Haddad, Wadi. "Continuity and Change in Religious Adherence: Ninth-Century Baghdad." In *Conversion and Continuity. Indigenous Christian Communities in Islamic Lands, Eighth to Eighteenth Centuries*, edited by Michael Gervers and Ramzi Jibran Bikhazi, 33–54. Wetteren: Pontifical Institute of Medieval Studies, 1990.

Halévy, J. "Déchiffrement et interprétation de l'inscription ouïgoure, découverte par M. Pognon." *JA* 8.20 (1892): 291–292.

Halton, Thomas P. *Dialogue with Trypho*, Selections from the Fathers of the Church 3. Washington: Catholic University of America Press.

Hamilton, Victor P. *The Book of Genesis: Chapters 18–50*, The New International Commentary on the Old Testament. Grand Rapids: William B. Eerdmans, 1995.

Hannah, Robert. *Time in Antiquity*, Sciences of Antiquity. Abingdon: Routledge, 2008.

Hansbury, Mary. *The Letters of John of Dalyatha*. Piscataway: Gorgias Press, 2006.

Hansgerd, Hellenkemper. *Burgen der Kreuzritterzeit in der Grafschaft Edessa und im Königreich Kleinarmenien. Studien zur historischen Siedlungsgeographie Südost-Kleinasiens*, Geographica Historica. Bonn: Habelt, 1976.

Harif, Amos. "A crusader church in Tiberias." *PEQ* 116 (1984): 103–09.

Harmless, William and Raymond R. Fitzgerald. "The Sapphire Light of the Mind: The Skemmata of Evagrius Ponticus." *JTS* 62 (2001): 498–529.

Harrak, Amir. "Piecing Together the Fragmentary Account of the Martyrdom of Cyrus of Ḥarrān." *AB* 121 (2003): 297–328.

Harrak, Amir. *Acts of Mar Mari the Apostle.* Atlanta: Society of Biblical Literature, 2005.

Harrak, Amir. *The Acts of Mar Mari the Apostle.* Leiden: Brill, 2005.

Harrak, Amir. *Recueil des inscriptions syriaques*, vol. 2. *Syriac and Garshuni Inscriptions of Iraq*. Paris: De Boccard, 2010.

Harrington, Daniel J. *The Gospel of Matthew.* Collegeville: Liturgical Press, 1991.

Harvey, Susan Ashbrook. "Embodiment in Time and Eternity: A Syriac Perspective." *St. Vladimir's Theological Quarterly* 43 (1999): 105–130.

Harvey, Susan Ashbrook. "Spoken Words, Voiced Silence: Biblical Women in Syriac Tradition." *JECS* 9 (2001): 105–131.

Harvey, Susan Ashbrook. "Why the Perfume Mattered: The Sinful Woman in Syriac Exegetical Tradition." In *In Dominico Eloquio, In Lordly Eloquence: Essays on Patristic Exegesis in honor of Robert Louis Wilken,* edited by Paul M. Blowers et al., 69–89. Grand Rapids: W. B. Eerdmans Publishers, 2002.

Harvey, Susan Ashbrook. *Song and Memory: Biblical Women in Syriac Tradition.* Milwaukee: Marquette University Press, 2010.

Haskins, Charles H. *The Renaissance of the Twelfth Century.* Cambridge: Harvard University Press, 1927.

Haverkamp, Alfred. "Europas Juden im Mittelalter. Zur Einfühung." In *Europas Juden im Mittelalter. Beiträge des internationalen Symposiums in Speyer vom 20.–25. Oktober 2002*, edited by Christoph Cluse, 13–29. Trier: Kliomedia, 2004.

Hayman, A.P. *The Disputation of Sergius the Stylite against a Jew*, CSCO 338–339. Louvain: Peeters, 1973.

Hayman A. P. "The Image of the Jew in the Syriac Anti-Jewish Polemical Literature." In "*To See Ourselves as Others See Us*": *Christians, Jews, and "Others" in Late Antiquity*, edited by J. Neusner and S. Frerichs, 423–441. Chico: Scholars Press, 1985.

Heidemann, Stefan. *Die Renaissance der Städte in Nordsyrien und Nordmesopotamien. Städtische Entwicklungen und wirtschaftliche Bedingungen in ar-Raqqa und Ḥarrān von der Zeit der benuinischen Vorherrschaft bis zu den Seldschuken*. Leiden: Brill, 2002.

Heil, G., A. van Heck, E. Gebhardt, and A. Spira. *Sermones, Pars I*, GNO 9. Leiden: Brill, 1992.

Hélou, Nada. *L'icône dans le patriarcat d'Antioche (VIe–XIXe siècles)*. Mansourié: Editions Aleph, 2007.

Hélou, Nada. *La fresque dans les anciennes églises du Liban*. Mansourié: Editions Aleph, 2007–2008.

Hendel, Ronald. "The Oxford Hebrew Bible: Prologue to a New Critical Edition." *VT* 58 (2008): 324–351.

Henten, Jan Willem van and Friedrich Avemarie. *Martyrdom and Noble Death: Selected Texts from Graeco-Roman, Jewish and Christian Antiquity*. London: Routledge, 2002.

Herman, Geoffrey. "Note on the Recently Published *Discourse on the Priesthood* (BL Add. 18295, ff. 137B–140B)." *JSS* 54 (2009): 389–391.

Herman, Geoffrey. "'Bury My Coffin Deep!' Zoroastrian Exhumation in Jewish and Christian Sources." In *Tiferet Leyisrael: Jubilee Volume in Honor of Israel Francus*, edited by Joel Roth, Menahem Schmelzer, and Yaacov Francus, 31–59. New York: The Jewish Theological Seminary of America, 2010.

Herman, Geoffrey. "The Passion of Shabur, Martyred in the 18th Year of Yazdgird with a Fragment of the Life of Mar Aba Catholicos." *JSS* 58 (2013): 121–130.

Herman, Geoffrey. "The Last Years of Yazdgird I and the Christians," in *Jews, Christians and Zoroastrians: Religious Dynamics in a Sasanian Context*, edited by Geoffrey Herman, 67–90. Pisacatway: Gorgias Press, 2014.

Herman, Geoffrey. *Persian Martyr Acts under King Yazdgird I*. Piscataway: Gorgias Press, 2016.

Herman, Geoffrey. "'In Honor of the House of Caesar': Attitudes to the Kingdom in the Aggada of the Babylonian Talmud and Other Sasanian Sources." In *The Aggada of the Bavli and its Cultural World*, edited by G. Herman and J. L. Rubenstein, 103–124. Providence: Brown Judaic Studies, 2018.

Hespel, Robert and René Draguet. *Theodore bar Konai. Livre des scolies. Recension de Séert*, vol. 2. *Mimrè VI–XI*, CSCO 432. Louvain: Peeters, 1982.

Hilgenfeld, Heinrich. *Ausgewählte Gesänge des Giwargis Wards von Arbel.* Leipzig: Harrassowitz, 1904.

Hilkens, Andy. *The Anonymous Syriac Chronicle up to the Year 1234 and Its Sources.* Gent: Universiteit Gent, 2014.

Hinterberger, Martin. "Byzantine Hagiography and its Literary Genres. Some Critical Observations." In *The Ashgate Research Companion to Byzantine Hagiography*, vol. 2. *Genres and Contexts*, edited by Stephanos Efthymiadis, 25–60. Surrey and Burlington: Ashgate, 2014.

Hirschler, Konrad. *Medieval Arabic historiography: Authors as actors.* SOAS/Routledge Studies on the Middle East. London: Routledge, 2006.

Hoffman, Eva R. "Christian-Islamic Encounters on Thirteenth-Century Ayyubid Metalwork: Local Culture, Authenticity, and Memory." *Gesta* 43 (2004): 129–142.

Hoffman, Georg. *Auszüge aus syrischen Akten persischer Märtyrer.* Leipzig: Brockhaus, 1880.

Holm, Tawny L. "The Fiery Furnace in the Book of Daniel and the Ancient Near East." *JAOS* 128 (2008): 85–104.

Holmberg, Bo. "A reconsideration of the *Kitāb al-maǧdal.*" *PdO* 18 (1993): 255–273.

Holt, P. M., Ann K.S. Lambton, and Bernard Lewis, eds. *The Cambridge History of Islam.* Cambridge: Cambridge University Press, 1970.

Honigmann, Ernest. *Le couvent de Barsaumā et le patriarcat Jacobite d'Antioche et de Syrie.* Louvain: L. Durbecq, 1954.

Horn, Cornelia B. "Children as Pilgrims and the Cult of Holy Children in the Early Syriac Tradition: The Cases of Theodoret of Cyrrhus and the Child-Martyrs Behnām, Sarah, and Cyriacus." *ARAM* 19 (2007): 439–462.

Horn, G. "Le 'miroir,' la 'nuée' deux manières de voir dieu d'après S. Grégoire De Nysse." *Revue d'ascetique et de mystique* 8 (1927): 113–131.

Houte, Jan A. van, ed. *Handbuch der europäischen Wirtschafts- und Sozialgeschichte*, vol. 2. *Europäische Wirtschafts- und Sozialgeschichte im Mittelalter.* Stuttgart: Klett-Cotta, 1980.

Howard, George. *The Teaching of Addai*. The Society of Biblical Literature Texts and Translations. Chico: Scholars Press, 1981.

Hoyland, Robert G. "Arabic, Syriac and Greek Historiography in the First Abbasid Century: An Inquiry into Inter-Cultural Traffic." *ARAM* 3 (1991): 211–233.

Hoyland, Robert G. *Seeing Islam as Others Saw It: A Survey and Evaluation of Christian, Jewish, and Zoroastrian Writings on Early Islam*. Studies in Late Antiquity and Early Islam 13. Princeton: Darwin Press, 1997.

Hoyland, Robert G. "Agapius, Theophilus and Muslim sources." In *Studies in Theophanes*, Travaux et Mémoires 19, edited by F. Montinaro and M. Jankowiak, 355–364. Paris: Éditions de l'IHEAL, 2015.

Hoyland, Robert G. "History, fiction and authorship in the first centuries of Islam." In *Writing and Representation in Medieval Islam: Muslim Horizons*, edited by Julia Bray, 16–46. London: Routledge, 2006.

Hoyland, Robert G. *Theophilus of Edessa's Chronicle and the circulation of historical knowledge in Late Antiquity and Early Islam*, TTH 57. Liverpool: Liverpool University Press, 2011.

Hugedé, Norbert. *La métaphore du miroir dans les Epîtres de saint Paul aux Corinthiens*. Neuchâtel, Switzerland: Delachaux & Niestlé, 1957.

Hugonnard-Roche, Henri. "Platon syriaque." In *Pensée grecque et sagesse d'orient: Hommage à Michel Tardieu*, Bibliothèque de l'École des Hautes Études, Sciences religieuses 142, edited by M. A. Amir-Moezzi, J.-D. Dubois, C. Jullien, and F. Jullien, 307–322. Turnhout: Brepols, 2009.

Huizenga, Leroy Andrew. "The Aqedah at the End of the First Century of the Common Era: *Liber Antiquitatum Biblicarum, 4 Maccabees,* Josephus' *Antiquities, 1 Clement*." *JSP* 20 (2010): 105–133.

Humfress, Caroline. "Roman Law, Forensic Argument and the Formation of Christian Orthodoxy." In *Orthodoxie, christianisme, histoire*, edited by S. Elm, E. Rebillard and A. Romano, 125–147. Rome: École Française de Rome, 2000.

Humphreys, R. Stephen. *Islamic History: A Framework for Inquiry*, Rev. Ed. Princeton: Princeton University Press, 1991.

Hunt, Lucy-Anne. *Byzantium, Eastern Christendom and Islam. Art at the Crossroads of the Medieval Mediterranean.* London: Pindar Press, 1998.

Huygens, R. B. C. *Ars Edendi: A Practical Introduction to Editing Medieval Latin Texts.* Turnhout: Brepols, 2000.

Ihssen, Brenda Llewellyn. *John Moschos'* Spiritual Meadow: *Authority and Autonomy at the End of the Antique World.* Farnham: Ashgate, 2014.

Immerzeel, Mat. "Medieval wall paintings in Lebanon: Donors and Artists." *Chronos* 10 (2004): 7–47.

Immerzeel, Mat. *Identity Puzzles. Medieval Christian Art in Syria and Lebanon.* Louvain: Peeters, 2009.

Isaac, Benjamin. "The Meaning of the Terms *Limes* and *Limitanei.*" *JRS* 78 (1988): 125–147.

Jackson, Glenna. *Have Mercy on Me: The Story of The Canaanite Woman in Matthew 15:21–28.* London: Sheffield Academic Press, 2002.

Jackson, J. *Tacitus: Annals 13–16*, LCL 322. Cambridge: Harvard University Press, 1937.

Jackson, Peter. "Mongols and the Faith of the Conquered." In *Mongols, Turks, and Others: Eurasian Nomads and the Sedentary World*, Brill's Inner Asian Library 11, edited by Reuven Amitai and Michal Biran, 245–290. Leiden: Brill, 2005.

Jansma, T. "Ephrem's Commentary on Exodus: Some Remarks on the Syriac Text and the Latin Translation." *JSS* 17 (1972): 203–212.

Jansma, T. "The Provenance of the Last Sections in the Roman Edition of Ephrem's Commentary on Exodus." *Le Muséon* 85 (1972): 155–169.

Jonge, M. de. *The Testaments of the Twelve Patriarchs: A Critical Edition of the Greek Text.* Leiden: Brill, 1978.

Jonge, M. de. "Again: 'To Stretch out the Feet' in the Testaments of the Twelve Patriarchs." *JBL* 99 (1980): 120–121.

Judd, Stephen. *Religious Scholars and the Umayyads. Piety-minded Supporters of the Marwānid Caliphate.* London: Routledge, 2014.

Jullien, Christelle. "Martyrs en Perse dans l'hagiographie syro-orientale: le tournant du VIe siècle." In *Juifs et Chrétiens en Arabie aux Ve et VIe siècles. Regards croisés sur les sources*, Centre de Recherche d'Histoire et Civilisation de Byzance, Monographies 32; Le massacre de Najrân 2, edited by Joëlle Beaucamp,

Françoise Briquel Chatonnet, and Christian Julien Robin, 279–290. Paris: Association des amis du Centre d'histoire et civilisation de Byzance, 2010.

Jullien, Christelle. "Les Actes des martyrs perses: Transmettre l'histoire." In *L'hagiographie syriaque*, ÉS 9, edited by André Binggeli, 127–140. Paris: Paul Geuthner, 2012.

Jullien, Florence. *Histoire de Mār Abba, catholicos de l'Orient. Martyres de Mār Grigor, général en chef du roi Khusro Ier et de Mār Yazd-panāh, juge et gouverneur*, CSCO 658–659. Louvain: Peeters, 2015.

Kalimi, Isaac. "The Land of Moriah, Mount Moriah, and the Site of Solomon's Temple in Biblical Historiography." *HTR* 83 (1990): 345–362.

Kalmin, Richard. *Migrating Tales: The Talmud's Narratives and Their Historical Context*. Berkeley: University of California Press, 2014.

Kaufhold, Hubert. *Syrische Texte zum islamischen Recht. Das dem nestorianischen Katholikos Johannes V. bar Abgarē zugeschriebene Rechtsbuch*. München: Beck, 1971.

Kaufhold, Hubert. "Der Richter in den syrischen Rechtsquellen. Zum Einfluß islamischen Rechts auf die christlich-orientalische Rechtsliteratur." *OC* 68 (1984): 91–113.

Kaufhold, Hubert. "Sources of Canon Law in the Eastern Churches." In *The History of Byzantine and Eastern Canon Law to 1500*, edited by Wilfried Hartmann and Kenneth Pennington, 215–342. Washington: Catholic University of America Press, 2012.

Kaufhold, Hubert. "Eine unbekannte syrische Kanonessammlung." In *Synaxis katholiké. Beiträge zu Gottesdienst und Geschichte der fünf altkirchlichen Patriarchate für Heinzgerd Brakmann zum 70. Geburtstag*, Orientalia - Patristica - Oecumenica 6.1–2, edited by Diliana Atanassova and Tinatin Chronz, 317–340. Münster: LIT, 2014.

Kawerau, Peter. *Die jakobitische Kirche im Zeitalter der syrischen Renaissance. Idee und Wirklichkeit*. Berlin: Akademie-Verlag, 1960.

Kayser, C. *Die Canones Jacob's von Edessa übersetzt und erläutert*. Leipzig: J. C. Hinrichs, 1886.

Kazan, S. "Isaac of Antioch's Homily against the Jews." *OC* 45 (1961): 30–53; 46 (1962): 87–98; 47 (1963): 89–97; 49 (1965): 57–78.

Keating, Sandra Toenies. *Defending the 'People of Truth' in the Early Islamic period. The Christian apologies of Abū Rā'iṭah.* Leiden: Brill, 2006.

Kennedy, D. L. "The Garrisoning of Mesopotamia in the Late Antonine and Early Severan Periods." *Antichthon* 21 (1987): 57–66.

Keseling, Paul. "Die Chronik des Eusebius in der syrischen Überlieferung." *OC* 3.1 (1927): 23–48, 223–241; 3.2 (1927): 33–56.

Kessel, Grigory M. "A Note on One Borrowing from Aphrahat." *PdO* 31 (2006): 295–307.

Kessel, Grigory M. "A Manuscript Tradition of Dadīšō' Qaṭrāyā's Work 'On Stillness' (*'al šelyā*) in the Syrian Orthodox Milieu." In *Geschichte, Theologie und Kultur des syrischen Christentums: Beiträge zum 7. Deutschen Syrologie-Symposium in Göttingen, Dezember 2011*, Göttinger Orientforschungen: Reihe 1, Syriaca 46, edited by Martin Tamcke and Sven Grebenstein, 103–122. Wiesbaden: Harrassowitz, 2014.

Kessel, Grigory M. "Syriac monastic miscellanies." In *Comparative Oriental Manuscript Studies: An Introduction*, edited by Alessandro Bausi (general editor) et al., 439–443. Hamburg: COMSt, 2015.

Khadra, Hanna. *Le Nomocanon de Barhebraeus: Son importance juridique entre les sources chrétiennes et les sources Musulmanes.* Rome: Pontificia Università Lateranense, 2005.

Khalek, Nancy. "He was Tall and Slender, and his Virtues were Numerous: Byzantine Hagiographical Topoi and the Companions of Muhammad in al Azdī's Futūḥ al Shām/Conquest of Syria." In *Writing 'True Stories': Historians and Hagiographers in the Late Antique and Medieval Near East*, edited by Arietta Papaconstantinou, 105–123. Turnhout: Brepols, 2010.

Khalek, Nancy. *Damascus after the Muslim Conquest: Text and Image in Early Islam.* Oxford: Oxford University Press, 2011.

Khalidi, Tarif. *Arabic historical thought in the classical period.* Cambridge Studies in Islamic Civilization. Cambridge: Cambridge University Press, 1994.

Khalidi, Tarif. *The Muslim Jesus: Sayings and Stories in Islamic Literature.* Cambridge: Harvard University Press, 2001.

Khayyat, Nadira. "Le visage du Christ resplendissant dans le miroir du cœur." In *Le visage de Dieu dans le patrimoine oriental: Patrimoine syriaque actes du colloque VII*, edited by Rita Tohmé and

Chawki El-Ramy, 77–87. Antélias-Liban: Centre d'Études et de Recherches Orientales, 2001.

Khayyat, Nadira. *Jean de Dalyatha. Les homélies I–XV*. Antélias-Liban: Centre d'Études et de Recherches Orientales, 2007.

Khoury, Nuha N. N. "Narratives of the Holy Land: Memory, Identity and inverted Imagery in the Freer Basin and Canteen." *Orientations* 29.5 (1998): 63–69.

Khoury, Raif Georges. *Wahb B. Munabbih*, pt. 1. Wiesbaden: Harrassowitz, 1972.

Kiperwasser, Reuven. "Zoroastrian Proselytes in Rabbinic and Syriac Christian Narratives: Orality-related markers of cultural identity." *History of Religions* 51 (2012): 203–235.

Kiperwasser, Reuven and Serge Ruzer. "To Convert a Persian and Teach him the Holy Scriptures: A Zoroastrian Proselyte in Rabbinic and Syriac Christian Narratives." In *Jews, Christians and Zoroastrians: Religious Dynamics in a Sasanian Context*, edited by Geoffrey Herman, 101–138. Piscatway: Gorgias Press, 2014.

Kister, M. J. "The *Sīrah* literature." In *Arabic Literature to the End of the Umayyad Period*, edited by A. F. L. Beeston et al., 352–367. Cambridge: Cambridge University Press, 1983.

Klancher, Nancy. *The Taming of the Canaanite Woman: Constructions of Christian Identity in the Afterlife of Matthew 15:21–28*. Berlin: De Gruyter, 2013.

Klein, Wassilios. *Das nestorianische Christentum an den Handelswegen durch Kyrgyzstan bis zum 14. Jahrhundert*. Turnhout: Brepols, 2000.

Klibansky, Raymond, Erwin Panofsky, and Fritz Saxl. *Saturn and Melancholy. Studies in the History of Natural Philosophy, Religion and Art*. Nendeln—Liechtenstein: Kraus, 1964, rep. 1979.

Klostermann, Erich. *Das Markusevangelium*, Handbuch zum Neuen Testament 3, 4th ed. Tübingen: Mohr Siebeck, 1950.

Klostermann, Erich. *Das Lukansevangelium*, Handbuch zum Neuen Testament 5, 3rd ed. Tübingen: Mohr Siebeck, 1975.

Kmosko, Michael. *S. Simeon Bar Ṣabbaʿe: Martyrium et Narratio*, PS 1.2. Paris: Firmin-Didot, 1907.

Koltun-Fromm, Naomi. "Yokes of the Holy Ones: The Embodiment of a Christian Vocation." *HTR* 94 (2001): 205–218.

Koltun-Fromm, Naomi. *Hermeneutics of Holiness. Ancient Jewish and*

Christian Notions of Sexuality and Religious Community. Oxford: Oxford University Press, 2010.

Kominko, Maja. "Byzantine, Syriac, Armenian and Latin: A Note on Artistic Interaction in Eastern Mediterranean Manuscripts." *ECA* 7 (2010): 59–70.

Kopf, L. *Ibn Abu Usaibiʿah. History of Physicians*. Jerusalem: The Hebrew University, Institute of Asian and African Studies, 1971.

Kraemer, Joel. *Humanism in the Islamic Renaissance*. Leiden: Brill, 1993.

Kratchkowsky, I. *Histoire de Yahya Ibn Saʿid d'Antioche continuateur de Saʿid Ibn Bitriq*, PO 18.5, 23.3, 47.4. Turnhout: Brepols, 1924, 1932, 1997.

Krueger, Derek. *Symeon the Holy Fool: Leontius's Life and the Late Antique City*. Berkeley: University of California Press, 1996.

Krueger, Derek. "The Unbounded Body in the Age of Liturgical Reproduction." *JECS* 17 (2009): 267–279.

Krusch, B. *Passiones vitaeque sanctorum aevi merovingici*. Hannover: Impensis Bibliopolii Hahniani, 1910.

Krusch B. and W. Levison. *Gregorii Turonesis opera*, pt. 2. *Miracula et opera minora*, Scriptores Rerum Merovingicarum 1. Hannover: Impensis Bibliopolii Hahniani, 1885; repr. 1969 with new pagination and revised index, 1988.

Kurth, G. *Études franques*. Paris: H. Champion; Brussels: A. Dewit, 1919.

Labourt, Jérôme. *Le christianisme dans l'empire perse, sous la dynastie sassanide (224–632)*. Paris: V. Lecoffre, 1904.

Lafontaine, Guy. *La version arménienne des œuvres d'Aphraate le Syrien*, CSCO 382–383, 405–406, 432–424. Louvain: Peeters, 1977, 1979, 1980.

Lagrange, F. *Les Actes des martyrs d'Orient*. Paris: Eugène Belin, 1852.

Landron, Bénédicte. *Chrétiens et musulmans en Irak: Attitudes nestoriennes vis-à-vis de l'Islam*. Paris: Cariscript, 1994.

Lang, David Marshall. *Lives and Legends of the Georgian Saints*. Crestwood: St. Vladimir's Seminary Press, 1976.

Lange, Christian. *The Portrayal of Christ in the Syriac Commentary on the Diatessaron*, CSCO 616. Louvain: Peeters, 2005.

Le Boulluec, Allain. *Clément d'Alexandrie. Les Stromates: Stromate* V, t. 1, SC 278. Paris: Cerf, 1981.

Le Strange, Guy. *The Lands of the Eastern Caliphate: Mesopotamia, Persia, and Central Asia from the Moslem Conquest to the Time of Timur*. Cambridge Geographical Series. Cambridge: Cambridge University Press, 1905.

Leemans, Johan, ed. *More than a Memory: The Discourse of Martyrdom and the Construction of Christian Identity in the History of Christianity*. With the collaboration of Jurgen Mettepenningen. Louvain: Peeters, 2005.

Leloir, Louis. *Saint Ephrem. Commentaire de l'Évangile concordant. Version arménienne*, CSCO 137, 145. Louvain: Peeters, 1953–1954.

Leloir, Louis. *Saint Éphrem: Commentaire de l'Évangile concordant. Texte syriaque (manuscript Chester Beatty 709). Folios additionnels*. Louvain: Peeters, 1990.

Lemerle, Paul. *Le premier humanisme byzantin: Notes et remarques sur enseignement et culture à Byzance des origines au Xe siècle*, 267–300. Paris: Presses Universitaires de France, 1971.

Lequeux, Xavier. "La Passion grecque (BHG 2245) inédite de Mamelchta, mystérieuse martyre en Perse." *AB* 131 (2013): 268–275.

Leroy, Jules. "La renaissance de l'église syriaque au XIIe–XIIIe siècles." *Cahiers de civilisation médiévale* 14 (1971): 131–148; 239–255.

Levi Della Vida, Giorgio. "La traduzione araba delle Storie di Orosio." *Al-Andalus* 19 (1954): 257–293.

Levine, Amy-Jill. *The Social and Ethnic Dimensions of Matthean Salvation History*. Lewiston: Edwin Mellen Press, 1988.

Levine, Amy-Jill. "Matthew's Advice to a Divided Readership." In *The Gospel of Matthew in Current Study: Studies in Memory of William G. Thompson, S.J.*, edited by David E. Aune, 22–41. Grand Rapids: William B. Eerdmans Publishing Company, 2001.

Lieu, Samuel N. C. et al., eds. *Medieval Christian and Manichean Remains from Quanzhou (Zayton)*, vol. 2. Turnhout: Brepols, 2012.

Lindberg, D. C. *Theories of Vision From Al-Kindi to Kepler*. Chicago: University of Chicago Press, 1981.

Luibheid, Colm. *Pseudo-Dionysius: The Complete Works*. Mahwah: Paulist Press, 1987.

Lund, Jerome A. *The Influence of the Septuagint on the Peshitta: A Re-evaluation of Criteria in Light of Comparative Study of the Versions in Genesis and Psalms*. Ph.D. Diss., Hebrew University, Jerusalem, 1988.

Lund, Jerome A. "Genesis in Syriac." In *The Book of Genesis: Composition, Reception, and Interpretation,* Supplements to Vetus Testamentum 152, edited by Craig A. Evans, Joel N. Lohr, and David L. Petersen, 537–560. Leiden: Brill, 2012.

Luz, Ulrich. *Matthew: A Commentary 8–20.* Trans. by James E. Crouch and edited by Helmut Koester. Hermeneia: A Critical and Historical Commentary on the Bible. Minneapolis: Fortress Press, 2001.

Maas, Paul. *Textual Criticism.* Oxford: Clarendon Press, 1958.

Macrides, Ruth. *History as literature in Byzantium. Papers from the Fortieth Spring Symposium of Byzantine Studies, University of Birmingham, April 2007.* Aldershot: Ashgate, 2010.

Macuch, Rudolf. *Geschichte der spät- und neusyrischen Literatur.* Berlin: de Gruyter, 1976.

Magdalino, Paul. "Byzantine encyclopaedism of the ninth and tenth centuries." In *Encyclopaedism from Antiquity to the Renaissance,* edited by J. König and G. Woolf, 219–231. Cambridge: Cambridge University Press, 2013.

Maier, Paul. *Eusebius. The Church History: A New Translation with Commentary.* Grand Rapids: Kregel Publications, 1999.

Malech, George David. *History of the Syrian Nation and the Old Evangelical-Apostolic Church of the East: From Remote Antiquity to the Present Time.* Minneapolis: s.n., 1910.

Maloney, George. *Pseudo-Macarius: The Fifty Spiritual Homilies and the Great Letter.* New York: Paulist Press, 1992.

Manna, Jacques Eugène. *Morceaux choisis de littérature araméenne.* Mosul: Dominican Press, 1901–1902.

Marcovitch, Miroslav. *Iustini Martyris Dialogus cum Tryphone,* PTS 47. Berlin: De Gruyter, 1997.

Marsham, Andrew. "Universal Histories in Christendom and the Islamic World, c.700–c.1400." In *The Oxford History of Historical Writing,* vol. 2. *400–1400,* edited by S. Foot and C. F. Robinson, 431–456. Oxford: Oxford University Press, 2012.

Matthews, Edward G. "The Vita Tradition of Ephrem the Syrian, the Deacon of Edessa." *Diakonia* 22 (1988–1989): 15–42.

Matthews, Edward G., Jr., and Joseph P. Amar. *St. Ephrem the Syrian: Selected Prose Works.* Washington: The Catholic University of America Press, 1994.

McCarthy, Carmel. *Saint Ephrem's Commentary on Tatian's Diatessaron: An English Translation of Chester Beatty Syriac MS 709.* Oxford: Oxford University Press, 1993.

McCollum, Adam Carter. "The Martyrdom of Theonilla in Syriac." *AB* 128 (2010): 312–328.

McCollum, Adam Carter. *The Story of Mar Pinḥas.* Piscataway: Gorgias Press, 2013.

McCollum, Adam Carter. "Greek Literature in the Christian East: Translations into Syriac, Georgian and Armenian." In *New Horizons in Graeco-Arabic Studies,* edited by D. Gutas, S. Schmidtke, and A. Treiger, 15–66. Leiden: Brill, 2015.

McDonough, Scott J. "A Question of Faith? Persecution and Political Centralization in the Sasanian Empire of Yazdgard II (438–457 CE)." In *Violence in Late Antiquity. Perceptions and Practices,* edited by H. A. Drake, 69–81. Aldershot: Ashgate, 2006.

McDonough, Scott J. "A Second Constantine? The Sasanian King Yazdgard in Christian History and Historiography." *JLA* 1 (2008): 127–140.

McVey, Kathleen E. *Ephrem the Syrian: Hymns.* New York: Paulist Press, 1989.

McVey, Kathleen E. "A Fresh Look at the Letter of Mara Bar Serapion to his Son." In *SymSyr* V, 263–270.

McVey, Kathleen E. *George, Bishop of the Arabs. A Homily on Blessed Mar Severus, Patriarch of Antioch,* CSCO 531. Louvain: Peeters, 1993.

Melki, J. "S. Ephrem le Syrien, un bilan de l'édition critique." *PdO* 11 (1983): 3–88.

Mengozzi, Alessandro. "A Syriac Hymn on the Crusades from a Warda Collection." *EVO* 33 (2010): 187–203.

Mengozzi, Alessandro. "Past and Present Trends in the Edition of Classical Syriac Texts." In *Comparative Oriental Manuscript Studies: An Introduction,* edited by Alessandro Bausi (general editor) et al., 435–439. Hamburg: COMSt, 2015.

Menze, Volker L. *Justinian and the Making of the Syrian Orthodox Church.* Oxford: Oxford University Press, 2008.

Meyvaert, P. "An Unknown Letter of Hulagu, Il-Khan of Persia, to King Louis IX of France." *Viator* 11 (1980): 245–260.

Mez, Adam. *Die Renaissance des Islam*. Heidelberg: C. Winter, 1922.
Mez, Adam. *The Renaissance of Islam*. Trans. by Salahuddin Khudi Bakhsh and D. S. Margoliouth. Patna: Jubilee Printing & Publishing House, 1937.
Mingana, Alphonse. *Narsai doctoris syri homiliae et carmina*, I–II. Mosul: Typis Fratrum Praedicatorum, 1905.
Mingana, Alphonse. *Sources syriaques*, vol. 1. Leipzig: Harrassowitz, 1908.
Mingana, Alphonse. *Catalogue of the Mingana Collection of Manuscripts*. Cambridge: Heffer and Sons, 1933.
Minov, Sergey. *Syriac Christian Identity in Late Sasanian Mesopotamia: The* Cave of Treasures *in Context*. Ph. D. Diss., Hebrew University of Jerusalem, 2013.
Mioni, E. "Il Pratum Spirituale di Giovanni Mosco: Gli episodi inediti del cod. Marciano greco II.21." *OCP* 17 (1951): 61–94.
Mioni, Elpidio. "Jean Moschus Moine." *Dictionnaire de Spiritualité* 7 (1973), cols. 632–640.
Mitchell, C. W., et al. *S. Ephraim's Prose Refutations of Mani, Marcion, and Bardaisan*. London: Williams and Norgate, 1912–1921.
Moberg, Axel. *The Book of the Ḥimyarites: Fragments of a Hitherto Unknown Syriac Work*. Oxford: Oxford University Press, 1924.
Morony, Michael. *Iraq After the Muslim Conquest*. Princeton: Princeton University Press, 1984.
Morrison, Craig E. *The Character of the Syriac Version of the First Book of Samuel*, MPI 11. Leiden: Brill, 2001.
Mortley, R. "The Mirror of 1 Cor. 13.12 and the epistemology of Clement of Alexandria." *VC* 30 (1976): 109–120.
Moss, Candida. *The Other Christs: Imitating Jesus in Ancient Christian Ideologies of Martyrdom*. Oxford: Oxford University Press, 2010.
Mouawad, Ray Jabre. "The Syriac Renaissance Viewed from Ḥesnō Ziad (Kharpūt), near Melitene." In *The Syriac Renaissance*, ECS 9, edited by Herman Teule, Carmen Fotescu Tauwinkl, Bas ter Haar Romeny, and Jan J. van Ginkel, 265–292. Louvain: Peeters, 2010.
Mourad, Suleiman. "Christians and Christianity in the Sīra of Muhammad." In *Christian-Muslim Relations. A Bibliographical History*, vol. 1 *(600-900)*, edited by David Thomas and Barbara Roggema, 57–72. Leiden, Boston: Brill, 2009.

Mras, Karl and Édouard des Places. *Eusebius Werke,* vol. 8. *Die Preparatio Evangelica,* pt. 2. *Die Bücher XI bis XV,* GCS 43/1. 2nd ed. Berlin: Akademie-Verlag, 1983.

Mulder, M. J. "The Use of The Peshitta in Textual Criticism." In *La Septuaginta en la investigacion contemporánea (V congreso de la IOSCS),* Textos y estudios "Cardenal Cisneros" 34, edited by Natalio Fernández Marcos, 37–53. Madrid: Instituto Arias Montano, 1985.

Müller, A. *Kitāb ʿuyūn al-anbāʾ fī ṭabaqāt al-aṭibbāʾ.* Köningsberg: Selbstverlag, 1884.

Munt, Harry. "Ibn al-Azraq, Saint Marūthā, and the Foundation of Mayyāfāriqīn (Martyropolis)." In *Writing 'True Stories': Historians and Hagiographers in the Late Antique and Medieval Near East,* edited by Arietta Papaconstantinou, 149–174. Turnhout: Brepols, 2010.

Murray, Gilbert, *The Interpretation of Ancient Greek Literature: An Inaugural Lecture Delivered before the University of Oxford, January 27 1909.* Oxford: The Clarendon Press, 1909.

Murray, Robert. "Syriac Studies To-day." *Eastern Churches Review* 1 (1966–1967): 370–373.

Murray, Robert. *Symbols of Church and Kingdom: A Study in Early Syriac Tradition,* Rev. Ed. London: T&T Clark International, 2004.

Murre-van den Berg, Heleen L. "Generous Devotion: Women in the Church of the East between 1550 and 1850." *Hugoye* 7 (2004): 11–54.

Murre-van den Berg, Heleen L. "Paul Bedjan, Missionary for Life (1838–1920)." In *Homilies of Mar Jacob of Sarug,* vol. 6, edited by Paul Bedjan, with additional material by Sebastian P. Brock, 339-369. Piscataway: Gorgias Press, 2006.

Musurillo, Herbert. *Acts of the Christian Martyrs.* Oxford: Clarendon Press, 1972.

Nagel, P. *Die Motivierung der Askese in der alten Kirche und der Ursprung des Mönchtums,* TUCL 95. Berlin: Akademie-Verlag, 1966.

Nallino, Carlo Alfonso. "Il diritto musulmano nel Nomicanone siriaco cristaino di Barhebreo." *RSO* 9 (1921–1923): 512–580.

Nau, François. "Hagiographie syriaque." *ROC* 15 (1910): 56–60.

Nau, F. *Jean Rufus, évêque de Maïouma. Plérophories,* PO 8.1. Paris: Firmin-Didot, 1912.

Nau, F. *Martyrologes et ménologes orientaux, I–XIII. Un martyrologie et douze ménologes syriaques édités et traduits*, PO 10.1. Paris: Firmin-Didot, 1912.

Nau, F. *La second partie de l'histoire de Barhadbešabba 'Arbaïa*, Patrologia Orientalis 9.5. Paris: Firmin-Didot, 1913.

Nedungatt, George. "The Authenticity of Aphrahat's Synodal Letter." *OCP* 46 (1980): 62–88.

Newby, Gordon. "An Example of Coptic Literary Influence on Ibn Isḥāq's Sīrah." *JNES* 31 (1972): 22–28.

Newby, Gordon. *The Making of the Last Prophet. A Reconstruction of the Earliest Biography of Muhammad.* Columbia: University of South Carolina Press, 1989.

Nichols, Stephen G. "Philology and Its Discontents." In *The Future of the Middle Ages: Medieval Literature in the 1990s*, edited by William D. Paden, 113–141. Gainesville: University Press of Florida, 1994.

Nissen, Th. "Unbekannte Erzählungen aus dem Pratum Spirituale." *Byzantinische Zeitschrift* 38 (1938): 351–376.

Nissen, Th. "Zu den ältesten Fassungen der Legende vom Judenknaben." *Zeitschrift für französische Sprache und Literatur* 62 (1939): 393–403.

Nolland, John. *The Gospel of Matthew: A Commentary on the Greek Text.* Grand Rapids: William B. Eerdmans Publishing Company, 2005.

Norman, A. F. *Antioch as a Centre of Hellenic Culture as Observed by Libanius*, TTH 34. Liverpool: Liverpool University Press, 2000.

Norris, Harry T. "Fables and Legends in pre-Islamic and early Islamic times." In *Arabic Literature to the End of the Umayyad Period*, edited by A. F. L. Beeston et al., 374–386. Cambridge: Cambridge University Press, 1983.

O'Sullivan, Shaun. "Anti-Jewish Polemic and Early Islam." In *The Bible in Arab Christianity*, edited by David R. Thomas, 49–68. Leiden: Brill, 2007.

Odorico, Paolo. "La cultura della Sylloge." *BZ* 83 (1990): 1–21.

Odorico, Paolo. "'Parce-que je suis ignorant'. Imitatio/variatio dans la chronique de George le Moine." In *Imitatio – aemulatio – variatio: Akten des internationalen wisseschaftelichen Syposium zur byzantinische Sprache und Literatur (Wien, 22–25 Oktober 2008)*, edited by A. Rhoby and E. Schiffer, 209–216. Wien: Verlag der Österreichischen Akademie der Wissenschaften, 2010.

Odorico, Paolo. "Cadre d'exposition/cadre de pensée – la culture du recueil." In *Encyclopedic trends in Byzantium? Proceedings of the International Conference held in Leuven, 6–8 May 2009*, OLA 212, edited by P. Van Deun and C. Macé, 89–108. Louvain: Peeters, 2011.

Olster, David M. *Roman Defeat, Christian Response, and the Literary Construction of the Jew*. Philadelphia: University of Pennsylvania Press, 1994.

Oppenheimer, Aharon. *Between Rome and Babylon. Studies in Jewish Leadership and Society*, TSAJ 108. Tübingen: Mohr Siebeck, 2005.

Oppenheimer, Aharon, Benjamin H. Isaac, and Michael Lecker. *Babylonia Judaica in the Talmudic Period*. Wiesbaden: L. Reichert, 1983.

Orengo, Alessandro and Pier Giorgio Borbone. "Stato e chiesa nell' Iran ilkhanide. La chiesa alla corte di Arghon nelle fonti siriache e armene." *EVO* 29 (2006): 325–337.

Outtier, Bernard. "Saint Éphrem d'après ses biographies et ses œuvres." *PdO* 4 (1973): 11–34.

Outtier, Bernard. "Contribution à l'étude de la préhistoire des collections d'hymnes d'Ephrem." *PdO* 6–7 (1975–1976): 49–61.

Overman, J. Andrew. *Matthew's Gospel and Formative Judaism: The Social World of the Matthean Community*. Minneapolis: Fortress Press, 1990.

Pahlitzsch, Johannes. "The Translation of the Byzantine Procheiros Nomos into Arabic: Techniques and Cultural Context." *Byzantinoslavica* 65 (2007): 19–29.

Pahlitzsch, Johannes. *Der arabische Procheiros Nomos. Untersuchung und Edition der Übersetzung eines byzantinischen Rechtstextes*. Frankfurt: Löwenklau-Gesellschaft e.V. Frankfurt am Main, 2014.

Palmer, Andrew. "How the Village of M'arre, Christian in 1800, Became Largely Muslim before 1911: Archives, Travellers' Tales and Oral Traditions." In *Christsein in der islamischen Welt: Festschrift für Martin Tamcke zum 60. Geburtstag*, edited by S. H. Griffith and S. Grebenstein, 439–478. Wiesbaden: Harrassowitz, 2015.

Panaino, Antonio C. D. "References to the Term Yašt and Other Mazdean Elements in the Syriac and Greek Martyrologia, with a

Short Excursus on the Semantic Value of the Greek Verb μαγεύω." In *Proceedings of the 5th Conference of the Societas Iranologica Europæa, Held in Ravenna, 6–11 October 2003*, vol. 1. *Ancient & Middle Iranian Studies*, edited by Antonio C. D. Panaino and Andrea Piras, 167–182. Milan: Mimesis, 2006.

Panaino, Antonio C. D. "The 'Persian' Identity in the Religious Controversies: Again on the Case of the 'Divided Loyalty' in Sasanian Iran." In *Iranian Identity in the Course of History: Proceedings of the Conference Held in Rome, 21–24 September 2005*, Serie Orientale Roma 105, Orientalia Romana 9, edited by Carlo G. Cereti, 227–239. Rome: Istituto italiano per l'Africa e l'Oriente, 2010.

Papaconstantinou, Arietta. "Historiography, Hagiography, and the Making of the Coptic 'Church of the Martyrs' in Early Islamic Egypt." *DOP* 60 (2006): 65–86.

Papaconstantinou, Arietta. *Writing 'True Stories': Historians and Hagiographers in the Late Antique and Medieval Near East*. Turnhout: Brepols, 2010.

Parisot, D. Ioannes. *Aphraatis Sapientis Persae Demonstrationes I–XXI*, PS 1.1. Paris: Firmin-Didot, 1894.

Parisot, D. Ioannes. *Aphraatis Sapientis Persae Demonstrationes XXIII*. PS 1.2. Paris: Firmin-Didot, 1907.

Parry, Ken. "The Iconography of the Christian Tombstones from Zayton." In *From Palmyra to Zayton: Epigraphy and Iconography*, Silk Road Studies, edited by Iain Gardner, Samuel N. C. Lieu, and Ken Parry, 229–246. Turnhout: Brepols, 2005.

Pattenden, Philip. "The Text of the Pratum Spirituale." *JTS* 26 (1975): 38–54.

Patterson, Lee. "The Return to Philology." In *The Past and Future of Medieval Studies*, edited by John Van Engen, 231–244. Notre Dame: University of Notre Dame Press, 1994.

Payne Smith, R. *Thesaurus Syriacus*. Oxford: Clarendon Press, 1868–1897.

Payne, Richard E. *A State of Mixture: Christians, Zoroastrians, and Iranian Political Culture in Late Antiquity*. Berkeley: University of California Press, 2015.

Payne, Richard. "Les polémiques syro-orientales contre le zoroastrisme et leurs contexts politiques." In *Les controversies religieuses en syriaque*, ÉS 13, edited by Flavia Ruani, 239–260. Paris: Geuthner, 2016.

Peers, Glenn. "The Church at the Jerusalem Gate in Crusader Ascalon: A Rough Tolerance of Byzantine Culture?" *ECA* 6 (2009): 67–86.

Peeters, Paul. "Une passion arménienne des ss. Abdas, Hormisdas, Šâhîn (suenes) et Benjamin." *AB* 28 (1909): 399–415.

Peeters, Paul. *Bibliotheca Hagiographica Orientalis*. Brussels: Société des Bollandistes, 1910.

Peeters, Paul. "Sainte *Golindouch*, martyre perse († 13 juillet 591)." *AB* 62 (1944): 74–125.

Pelikan, Jaroslav. *Whose Bible Is It? The History of the Scriptures Through the Ages*. New York: Viking, 2005.

Penelas, Mayte. *Kitāb Hurūshiyūsh (Traduccíon árabe de las Historiae adversus paganos de Orosio)*, Fuentes Arábico-Hispanas 26. Madrid: Consejo Superior de Investgaciones Científicas, 2011.

Penn, Michael. *Envisioning Islam: Syriac Christians and the Early Muslim World*. Philadelphia: University of Pennsylvania Press, 2015.

Pierre, Marie-Joseph. "Un synode contestataire à l'époque d'Aphraate le sage Persan." In *La controverse religieuse et ses formes*, edited by Alain Le Boulluec, 243–279. Paris: Cerf, 1995.

Pognon, H. "Note." *JA* 8.19 (1892): 153–155.

Possekel, Ute. *Evidence of Greek Philosophical Concepts in the Writings of Ephrem the Syrian*, CSCO 580. Louvain: Peeters, 1999.

Preuschen, Erwin. *Origenes Werke*, vol. 4. *Commentarius in Iohannem*, GCS 10. Leipzig: Hinrichs, 1903.

Price, R. M. *Cyril of Scythopolis. Lives of the Monks of Palestine*. Kalamazoo: Cistercian Publications, 1991.

Rajak, Tessa. "Dying for the Law: The Martyrs Portrait in Jewish-Greek Literature." In *Portraits: Biographical Representation in the Greek and Latin Literature of the Roman Empire*, edited by M. J. Edwards and Simon Swain, 39–67. Oxford: Clarendon Press, 1997.

Rapp, Claudia. "Storytelling as Spiritual Communication in early Greek Hagiography: The Use of *diegesis*." *JECS* 6 (1998): 431–448.

Ratzinger, Joseph. *Einführung in das Christentum*. Munich: E. Beck, 1968.

Ratzinger, Joseph. *Introduction to Christianity*, 2nd ed. San Francisco: Ignatius Press, 2004.

Reinink, G. J. "Babai the Great's Life of George and the Propagation of Doctrine in the Late Sasanian Empire." In *Portraits of Spiritual Authority: Religious Power in Early Christianity, Byzantium & the Christian Orient*, edited by J. W. Drijvers and J. W. Watt, 171–193. Leiden: Brill, 1999.

Renard, John. *Friends of God: Islamic Images of Piety, Commitment and Servanthood.* Berkeley: University of California Press, 2008.

Richardson, E. C. *Hieronymous. Liber de Viris Inlustirbus*, Texte und Untersuchungen 14. Leipzig: J. C. Hinrichs, 1896.

Riginos, Alice S. *Platonica: The Anecdotes concerning the Life and Writings of Plato.* Leiden: Brill, 1976.

Rignell, Lars G. *Briefe von Johannes dem Einsiedler mit kritischem Apparat, Einleitung und Übersetzung.* Lund: H. Ohlsson, 1941.

Rigolio, Alberto. "From 'Sacrifice to the Gods' to the 'Fear of God': Omissions, Additions and Changes in the Syriac Translations of Plutarch, Lucian and Themistius." *SP* 64 (2013): 133–143.

Rist, Josef. "Geschichte und Geschichten: Die Christenverfolgungen in Edessa und ihr populäres Echo in den syrischen Märtyrerakten." In *Volksglaube im antiken Christentum*, edited by Heike Grieser and Andreas Merkt, 157–175. Darmstadt: Wissenschaftliche Buchgesellschaft, 2009.

Robinson, Chase F. *Islamic Historiography.* Cambridge: Cambridge University Press, 2003.

Robinson, P. A. "To Stretch out the Feet: A Formula for Death in the Testaments of the Twelve Patriarchs." *JBL* 97 (1978): 369–374.

Roggema, Barbara. *The Legend of Sergius Baḥīrā: Eastern Christin Apologetics and Apocalyptic in Response to Islam.* Leiden: Brill, 2009.

Romeny, B. ter Haar. "Techniques of Translation and Transmission in the Earliest Text Forms of the Syriac Version of Genesis." In *The Peshitta as a Translation: Papers Read at the II Peshitta Symposium Held at Leiden 19–21 August 1993*, MPI 8, edited by P. B. Dirksen and A. van der Kooij, 177–185. Leiden: Brill, 1995.

Romeny, Bas ter Haar. *Religious origins of nations? The Christian communities of the Middle East.* Leiden: Brill, 2010.

Rosen, F. and J. Forshall. *Catalogus codicum manuscriptorum orientalium qui in Museo Britannico asservantur.* London: British Museum, 1838.

Rosenthal, Franz. "On the knowledge of Plato's philosophy in the Islamic world." *Islamic Culture* 14/15 (1940): 387–422.

Rosenthal, Franz. "Aramaic Studies during the Past Thirty Years." *JNES* 37 (1978): 81–91.

Rouët de Journel, M.-J. *Le pré spirituel*, SC 12. Paris: Cerf, 1946.

Rouwhorst, G. A. M. *Les hymnes pascales d'Ephrem de Nisibe. Analyse théologique et recherche sur l'evolution de la fête pascale chrétienne à Nisibis et à Edesse et dans quelques églises voisines au qautrième siècle*, vol. 1, Supplements to Vigiliae Christianae 7. Leiden: Brill, 1989.

Rubenstein, Jeffrey. "Martyrdom in the Persian Martyr Acts and in the Babylonian Talmud." In *The Aggada of the Bavli and its Cultural World*, edited by G. Herman and J. L. Rubenstein, 175–210. Providence: Brown Judaic Studies, 2018.

Rubin, Miri. *Gentile Tales: The Narrative Assault on Late Medieval Jews*. Philadelphia: University of Pennsylvania Press, 1999.

Rubin, Uri. *The Eye of the Beholder: The Life of Muhammad as Viewed by the Early Muslims*. Princeton: The Darwin Press, 1995.

Ruiten, Jacques T. A. G. M. van. *Abraham in the Book of Jubilees: The Rewriting of Genesis 11:26–25:10 in the Book of Jubilees 11:14–23:8*. Leiden: Brill, 2012.

Rustow, Marina. *Heresy and the Politics of Community: The Jews of the Fatimid Caliphate*. Conjunctions of Religion & Power in the Medieval Past. Ithaca: Cornell University Press, 2008.

Ryckmans, J. "Le christianisme en Arabie du Sud préislamique." In *Academia Nazionale dei Lincei. Atti del convego internazionale sul tema: L'Oriente cristiano nella storia della civilità*, 413–454. Rome: Accademia Nazionale dei Lincei, 1964.

Sabatier, Petrus. *Vetus Latina. Die Reste der altlateinischen Bibel*, vol. 2. *Genesis*. Freiburg: Herder, 1951.

Sachau, Eduard. *Inedita Syriaca: Eine Sammlung syrischer Übersetzungen von Schriften griechischer Profanliteratur*. Wien: Verlag der Buchhandlung des Waisenhauses in Halle, 1870.

Sachau, E. *Verzeichnis der syrischen Handschriften der Königlichen Bibliothek zu Berlin*. Berlin: A. Asher, 1899.

Sachau, Eduard. *Syrische Rechtsbücher*, vol. 2. Berlin: Verlag von Georg Reimer, 1907.

Sachau, Eduard. *Vom Klosterbuch des Šâbuštî*. Berlin: Verlag der Akademie der Wissenschaften, 1919.

Sack, Dorothée. *Damaskus. Entwicklung und Struktur einer orientalisch-islamischen Stadt.* Mainz: Zabern, 1989.

Sack, Dorothée. "Die Topographie der historischen Stadt Damaskus." In *Damaskus – Aleppo. 5000 Jahre Stadtentwicklung in Syrien*, Beiheft der Archäologischen Mitteilungen aus Nordwestdeutschland, edited by Mamoun Fansa, Heinz Gaube, and Jens Windelberg, 83–86. Mainz: Zabern, 2000.

Sahner, Christian C. "From Augustine to Islam: Translation and History in the Arabic Orosius." *Speculum* 88/4 (2013): 905–931.

Sahner, Christian. "Old Martyrs, New Martyrs, and the Coming of Islam: Writing Hagiography after the Conquests." In *Cultures in Motion: Studies in the Medieval and Early Modern Periods*, edited by Adam Izdebski and Damian Jasiński, 89–112. Krakow: Jagiellonian University Press, 2014.

Saint-Laurent, Jeanne-Nicole Mellon and Kyle Smith. *The History of Mar Behnam and Sarah.* Piscataway: Gorgias Press, 2017.

Sako, Louis. "Les sources de la chronique de Séert." *PdO* 14 (1987): 155–166.

Saldarini, Anthony J. *Matthew's Christian-Jewish Community.* Chicago: University of Chicago Press, 1994.

Samir, Samir Khalil. "La tradition arabe chrétienne. État de la question, problèmes et besoins." In *Actes du premier congrès international d'études arabes chrétiennes, Goslar septembre 1980*, OCA 218, edited by S. K. Samir, 21–120. Rome: Edizioni Orientalia Christiana, 1982.

Samir, Samir Khalil. *Foi et culture en Irak au XIe siècle: Élie de Nisibe et l'Islam.* Aldershot: Variorum, 1996.

Samir, Samir Khalil. "L'avenir des études arabes chrétiennes." *PdO* 24 (1999): 21–44.

Samir, Samir Khalil. "Les Suryan et la civilisation arabo-musulmane: Conférence inaugurale." *PdO* 30 (2005): 31–61.

Sarna, Nahum. *The JPS Torah Commentary: Genesis.* Philadelphia: Jewish Publication Society, 1989.

Scafi, Alessandro. *Mapping Paradise. A History of Heaven and Earth.* Chicago: The University of Chicago Press, 2006.

Schäfer, Peter. *Jesus in the Talmud.* Princeton: Princeton University Press, 2007.

Schäfer, Peter. *The Jewish Jesus. How Judaism and Christianity Shaped Each Other.* Princeton: Princeton University Press, 2012.

Schatkin, Margaret and Paul Harkins. *Saint John Chrysostom: Apologist*. Washington: The Catholic University of America Press, 1985.
Scher, Addai. "Notice sur les manuscrits syriaques et arabes conserves à l'archevêché chaldéen de Diarbékir." *JA* 10.10 (1907): 331–362, 385–431.
Scher, Addai. *Histoire nestorienne inédite (Chronique de Séert)*, PO 4.3, 5.2, 7.2, 13.4. Paris: Firmin-Didot, 1907–1919.
Scher, Addai. *Mar Barhadbšabba ʿArbaya, Cause de la fondation des écoles*, PO 4.4. Paris: Firmin-Didot, 1908.
Scher, Addai. *Theodorus Bar Kōnī. Liber scholiorum*, vol. 2, CSCO 69. Louvain: Peeters, 1912.
Schmidt, Andrea and Stephan Westphalen, eds. *Christliche Wandmalereien in Syrien. Qara und das Kloster Mar Yakub*, SKCO 14. Wiesbaden: Reichert, 2005.
Scholten, Clemens. *Theodoret. De Graecarum affectionum curatione*. Leiden: Brill, 2015.
Schwartz, Daniel L. "Religious Violence and Eschatology in the *Syriac Julian Romance*." *JECS* 19 (2011): 565–587.
Schwartz, E. *Kyrillos von Skythopolis*. Leipzig: J. C. Hinrichs, 1939.
Segal, Judah B. *Edessa 'The Blessed City'*. Oxford: Clarendon Press, 1970.
Selb, Walter. *Orientalisches Kirchenrecht*, vol. 1. *Die Geschichte des Kirchenrechts der Nestorianer*; vol. 2. *Die Geschichte des Kirchenrechts der Westsyrer (von den Anfängen bis zur Mongolenzeit)*. Wien: Verlag der Österreichischen Akademie der Wissenschaften, 1981–1989.
Selb, Walter and Hubert Kaufhold. *Das syrisch-römische Rechtsbuch*, vol. 1. *Einleitung*. Wien: Verlag der Österreichischen Akademie der Wissenschaften, 2002.
Serjeant, R. B. "Early Arabic Prose." In *Arabic Literature to the End of the Umayyad Period*, edited by A. F. L. Beeston et al. 114–153. Cambridge: Cambridge University Press, 1983.
Shahīd, Irfan. *Martyrs of Najrān: New Documents*. Brussels: Société des Bollandistes, 1971.
Shahīd, Irfan. *Byzantium and the Arabs in the Fourth Century*. Washington: Dumbarton Oaks, Trustees for Harvard University, 1984.
Shaked, Shaul. *Dualism in Transformation: Varieties of Religion in Sasanian Iran*. London: SOAS, 1994.

Shapira, Dan. "Gleanings on Jews of Greater Iran under the Sasanians (According to the Oldest Armenian and Georgian Texts)." *Iran and the Caucasus* 12 (2008): 202–209.
Sharf, A. *Byzantine Jewry from Justinian to the Fourth Crusade*. London: Routledge, 1971.
Shawcross, Teresa. *The Chronicle of Morea. Historiography in Crusader Greece*. Oxford: Oxford University Press, 2009.
Shepardson, Christine. "'Exchanging Reed for Reed': Mapping Contemporary Heretics onto Biblical Jews in Ephrem's Hymns on Faith." *Hugoye* 5 (2002): 15–33.
Shepardson, Christine. *Anti-Judaism and Christian Orthodoxy: Ephrem's Hymns in Fourth Century Syria*. Washington: The Catholic University of America Press, 2008.
Shepardson, Christine. *Controlling Contested Places: Late Antique Antioch and the Spatial Politics of Religious Controversy*. Berkeley: University of California Press, 2014.
Sidarus, Adel. "La Renaissance copte arabe du Moyen Âge." In *The Syriac Renaissance*, ECS 9, edited by Herman Teule, C. Fotescu Tauwinkl, Bas ter Haar Romeny, and Jan J. van Ginkel, 311–340. Louvain: Peeters, 2010.
Simonsohn, Uriel I. *A Common Justice. The Legal Allegiances of Christians and Jews under Early Islam*. Philadelphia: University of Pennsylvania Press, 2011.
Simonsohn, Uriel. "The biblical narrative in the Annales of Saʿīd ibn Baṭrīq and the question of medieval Byzantine-Orthodox identity." *ICMR* 22 (2011): 37–55.
Simonsohn, Uriel. "Motifs of a South-Melkite affiliation in the Annales of Saʿīd ibn Baṭrīq." In *Cultures in contact: Transfer of knowledge in the Mediterranean context*, Series Syro-Arabica 1, edited by S. Torallas Tovar and J. P. Monferrer-Sala, 243–255. Cordoba – Beirut: CNERU – CEDRAC, 2013.
Sims-Williams, Nicholas. *The Christian Soghdian Manuscript C2*. Berlin: Akademie, 1985.
Sizgorich, Thomas. "Narrative and Community in Islamic Late Antiquity." *Past & Present* 185 (2004): 9–42.
Sizgorich, Thomas. "'Become infidels or we will throw you into the fire': The Martyrs of Najrān in Early Muslim Historiography, Hagiography and Qur'ānic Exegesis." In *Writing 'True Stories':*

Historians and Hagiographers in the Late Antique and Medieval Near East, edited by Arietta Papaconstantinou, 125–148. Turnhout: Brepols, 2010.

Smith Lewis, Agnes. *Select Narratives of Holy Women: From the Syro-Antiochene or Sinai Palimpsest.* London: Cambridge University Press, 1900.

Smith, Jennifer Nimmo. *Pseudo-Nonniani in IV Orationes Gregorii Nazianzeni Commentarii*, CCSG 27, Corpus Nazianzenum 2. Turnhout: Brepols, 1992.

Smith, Jennifer Nimmo. *The Christian's Guide to Greek Culture: The Pseudo-Nonnus* Commentaries *on* Sermons *4, 5, 39 and 43 by Gregory of Nazianzus*, TTH 37. Liverpool: Liverpool University Press, 2001.

Smith, Jonathan Z. *Imagining Religion: From Babylon to Jonestown.* Chicago: University of Chicago Press.

Smith, Kyle. "Constantine and Judah the Maccabee: History and Memory in the Acts of the Persian Martyrs," *JCSSS* 12 (2012): 16–33.

Smith, Kyle. *The Martyrdom and the History of Blessed Simeon bar Ṣabba'e.* Piscataway: Gorgias Press, 2014.

Smith, Kyle. *Constantine and the Captive Christians of Persia: Martyrdom and Religious Identity in Late Antiquity.* Berkeley: University of California Press, 2016.

Smith, Mark. *From Sight to Light: The Passage From Ancient to Modern Optics.* Chicago: University of Chicago Press, 2015.

Snelders, Bas. *Identity and Christian-Muslim Interaction: Medieval Art of the Syrian Orthodox from the Mosul Area.* Louvain: Peeters, 2010.

Société Jean Bodin pour L'histoire Comparative des Institutions, ed. *Les communautés rurales,* pt. 3. *Asie et Islam,* vol. 3. *Recueils de la Société Jean Bodin pour* L'*histoire Comparative des* Institutions, vol. 42. Paris: Dessain et Tolra, 1982.

Sokoloff, Michael. *A Syriac Lexicon: A translation from the Latin; correction, expansion, and update of C. Brockelmann's Lexicon Syriacum.* Winona Lake: Eisenbrauns, 2012.

Spiegel, Gabrielle M. *The past as text. The theory and practice of Mediaeval historiography.* Baltimore: John Hopkins University Press, 1997.

Spiegel, S. *The Last Trial. On the Legends and Lore of the Command to Abraham to Offer Isaac as a Sacrifice: The Akedah.* Trans.

by J. Goldin. Philadelphia: The Jewish Publication Society of America, 1967.

Spuler, Bertold. "Die nestorianische Kirche, Die westsyrische (monophsyitische/jakobitische) Kirche, Die Maroniten, Die Thomas-Christen in Süd-Indien, Die armenische Kirche, Die koptische Kirche, Die Äthiopische Kirche." In *Handbuch der Orientalistik* 1, vol. 8, edited by Bertold Spuler, 120–324. Leiden: Brill, 1961.

Stacey, David. *Excavations at Tiberias, 1973–1974: The Early Islamic Periods*. Jerusalem: Israel Antiquities Authority, 2004.

Stanzel, Karl-Heinz. *Dicta Platonica: Die unter Platons Namen überlieferten Aussprüche*. Darmstadt, 1987.

Starr, Joshua. *The Jews in the Byzantine Empire, 641–1204*. New York: B. Franklin, 1970.

Stearns, Peter N. "Social History." In *Encyclopedia of Social History*, 806–811. London: Routledge, 1993.

Stern, Sacha. "Near Eastern Lunar Calendars in the Syriac Martyr Acts." *Le Museon* 117 (2004): 447–472.

Stern, Sacha. *Calendars in Antiquity: Empires, States, and Societies*. Oxford: Oxford University Press, 2012.

Sternbach, Leo. *Gnomologium Vaticanum: E Codice Vaticano Graeco 743*. Berlin: De Gruyter, 1963.

Stewart, Angus Donal. *The Armenian Kingdom and the Mamluks: War and Diplomacy During the Reigns of Het'um II (1289–1307)*, The Medieval Mediterranean 34. Leiden: Brill, 2001.

Stewart, Angus Donal. "The Assassination of King Het'um II: The Conversion of the Ilkhans and the Armenians." *JRAS* 15 (2005): 45–61.

Stewart-Sykes, Alistair. *The Didascalia Apostolorum: An English Version with Introduction and Annotation*. Studia Traditionis Theologiae: Explorations in Early and Medieval Theology 1. Turnhout: Brepols, 2009.

Stillman, Norman A. *The Jews of Arab lands. A history and source book*. Philadelphia: The Jewish Publication Society of America, 1979.

Stone, Michael. "An Armenian Tradition Relating to the Death of the Three Companions of Daniel." *Le Muséon* 86 (1973): 111–123.

Stone, Michael. *Armenian Apocrypha Relating to Adam and Eve*. Leiden: Brill, 1996.

Strohm, Paul. *Theory and the Premodern Text*. Minneapolis: University of Minnesota Press, 2000.

Swanson, Mark N. "Kitāb al-majdal." In *Christian-Muslim Relations. A Bibliographical History*, vol. 2 *(900–1500)*, edited by D. Thomas and A. Mallet, 627-632. Leiden: Brill, 2010.
Swanson, Mark. "Arabic Hagiography." In *The Ashgate Research Companion to Byzantine Hagiography*, vol. 1. *Periods and Places*, edited by Stephanos Efthymiadis, 345–368. Surrey and Burlington: Ashgate, 2011.
Takeda, Fumihiko. "Monastic Theology of the Syriac Version of the Life of Antony." *SP* 35 (2001): 148–157.
Takeda, Fumihiko. "The Syriac Version of the Life of Antony: A Meeting Point of Egyptian Monasticism with Native Syriac Asceticism." in *SymSyr* VII, 185–194.
Tannous, Jack. "L'hagiographie syro-occidentale à la période islamique." In *L'hagiographie syriaque*, ÉS 9, edited by André Binggeli, 225–245. Paris: Paul Geuthner, 2012.
Tannous, Jack. "You Are What you Read: Qenneshre and the Miaphysite Church in the Seventh Century." In *History and Identity in the Late Antique Near East*, edited by Philip Wood, 83–102. Oxford: Oxford University Press, 2013.
Tardy, René. *Najrān: Chrétiens d'Arabie avant l'islam*. Beirut: Dar el-Machreq Éditeurs, 1999.
Taylor, Richard A. *The Peshitta of Daniel*, MPI 7. Leiden: Brill, 1994.
Tcherikover, Victor A., Alexander Fuchs, and Menahem Stern. *Corpus Papyrorum Judaicarum*, vol. 3. Cambridge: Harvard University Press, 1964.
Teskey, Gordon. *The Poetry of John Milton*. Cambridge: Harvard University Press, 2015.
Teule, Herman "Barhebraeus' Ethicon, al-Ghazâlî and Ibn Sina." *Islamochristiana* 18 (1992): 73–86.
Teule, Herman. "Gregory Barhebraeus and his Time. The Syrian Renaissance." *JCSSS* 3 (2003): 21–43.
Teule, Herman. "L'abrégé de la chronique ecclésiastique (*Muḫtaṣār al-aḫbār al-bī'iyya*) et la chronique de Séert: Quelques sondages." in *L'historiographie syriaque*, ÉS 6, edited by M. Debié, 161–177. Paris: Geuthner, 2009.
Teule, Herman. "The Syriac Renaissance." In *The Syriac Renaissance*, ECS 9, edited by Herman Teule, Carmen Fotescu Tauwinkl, Bas ter Haar Romeny, and Jan J. van Ginkel, 1–30. Louvain: Peeters, 2010.

Teule, Herman, Carmen Fotescu Tauwinkl, Bas ter Haar Romeny, and Jan J. van Ginkel, eds. *The Syriac Renaissance*, ECS 9. Louvain: Peeters, 2010.

Thomas, Christine M. *The Acts of Peter, Gospel Literature, and the Ancient Novel: Rewriting the Past.* Oxford: Oxford University Press, 2003.

Thomson, Robert W. *Athanasius: Contra Gentes and De Incarnatione.* Oxford: Clarendon Press, 1971.

Thomson, Robert W. "The Historical Compilation of Vardan Arewelc'i." *DOP* 43 (1989): 125–226.

Thomson, Robert W. "Supplement to A Bibliography of Classical Armenian Literature to 1500 AD: Publications 1993-2005." *Le Muséon* 120 (2007): 207–223.

Tinti, Irene. "On the Chronology and Attribution of the Old Armenian Timaeus: A Status Quaestionis and New Perspectives." *EVO* 35 (2012): 219–282.

Todt, Susanne Regina. "Die syrische und die arabische Weltgeschichte des Bar Hebraeus – Ein Vergleich." *Der Islam* 65 (1988): 60–80.

Tolan, John. *Jews in Early Christian Law: Byzantium and the Latin West, 6th–11th Centuries*, RLMCMS 2. Turnhout: Brepols, 2014.

Tonneau, R.-M. *Sancti Ephraem Syri, In Genesim et in Exodum Commentarii*, CSCO 152–153. Louvain: Peeters, 1955.

Torrance, Alexis. "Precedents for Palamas' Essence-Energies Theology in the Cappadocian Fathers." *VC* 63 (2009): 47–70.

Tottoli, Roberto. *Biblical Prophets in the Qur'ān and Muslim Literature.* London: Routledge, 2002.

Tov, Emanuel. *Textual Criticism of the Hebrew Bible.* Minneapolis: Fortress, 2001.

Treiger, Alexander. "Could Christ's Humanity See His Divinity? An Eighth-Century Controversy Between John of Dalyatha and Timothy I, Catholicos of the Church of the East." *JCSSS* 9 (2009): 3–21.

Treiger, Alexander. "Al-Ghazālī's 'Mirror Christology' and Its Possible East-Syriac Sources." *The Muslim World* 101 (2011): 698–713.

Trimingham, J. Spencer. *Christianity Among the Arabs in Pre-Islamic Times.* Beirut: Librarie du Liban, 1990.

Tubach, Jürgen. "Das Anfänge des Christentums in Südarabien: Eine Christliche Legende Syrischer Herkunft in Ibn Hišām." *PdO* 18 (1993): 101–111.

Ubl, Karl. *Inzestverbot und Gesetzgebung: Die Konstruktion eines Verbrechens (300–1100)*. Berlin: De Gruyter, 2008.

Uitti, Karl. *Story, Myth and Celebration in Old French Narrative Poetry, 1050–1200*. Princeton: Princeton University Press, 1973.

Urbina, Ortiz de. *Patrologia Syriaca*, 2nd ed. Rome: Pont. Institutum Orientalium Studiorum, 1965.

Van Dam, Raymond. *Glory of the Martyrs*, 2nd ed. Liverpool: Liverpool University Press, 2004.

Van Den Hoek, Annewies. *Clément d'Alexandrie. Les Stromates: Stromate* IV, SC 463. Paris: Cerf, 2001.

Van Rompay, Lucas. "Impetuous Martyrs? The Situation of the Persian Christians in the Last Years of Yazdgard I (419–420)." In *Martyrium in multidisciplinary Perspective. Memorial Louis Reekmans*, edited by M. Lamboigts and P. van Deun, 363–375. Louvain: Peeters, 1995.

Van Rompay, Lucas. "La littérature exégétique syriaque et le rapprochement des traditions syrienne-occidentale et syrienne-orientale." *PdO* 20 (1995): 221–235.

Van Rompay, Lucas. "*Mallpânâ dilan Suryâyâ*: Ephrem in the Works of Philoxenus of Mabbog: Respect and Distance." *Hugoye* 7 (2004): 83–105.

Van Rompay, Lucas. "Humanity's Sin in Paradise: Ephrem, Jacob of Sarug, and Narsai in Conversation." In *Jacob of Serugh and His Times: Studies in Sixth-Century Syriac Christianity,* edited by George Anton Kiraz, 199–217. Piscataway: Gorgias Press, 2010.

Van Rompay, Lucas. "Aphrahat, 'A Student of the Holy Scriptures', The Reception of His Biblical Interpretation in Later Syriac Tradition." In *Storia e Pensiero Religioso nel Vicino Oriente: L'età Bagratide – Maimonide – Afraate*, edited by Carmela Baffioni, Rosa Bianca Finazzi, Anna Passoni Dell'Acqua, and Emidio Vergani, 256–270. Bulzoni: Biblioteca Ambrosiana, 2014.

Van Rompay, Lucas and Andrea B. Schmidt. "Takritans in the Egyptian Desert: The Monastery of the Syrians in the Ninth Century." *JCSSS* 1 (2001): 41–60.

VanderKam, J. C. *The Book of Jubilees*, CSCO 510–511. Louvain: Peeters, 1989.

VanderKam, James C. and William Adler, eds. *The Jewish Apocalyptic Heritage in Early Christianity*, CRINT 4. Assen: Van Gorcum, 1996.

Vasiliev, A., ed. *Kitab al-'Unvan. Histoire universelle écrite par Agapius (Mahboub) de Menbidj*, PO 5.4, 7.4, 8.3, 11.1. Paris: Societas Jesu, 1906–1916.

Vendler, Helen. "A Life of Learning: Charles Homer Haskins Lecture for 2001." *American Council of Learned Societies Occasional Paper* 50.4. https://publications.acls.org/OP/Haskins_2001_HelenVendler.pdf.

Vidas, Moulie. "Greek Wisdom in Babylonia." In *Envisioning Judaism*, edited by R. S. Boustan et al., vol. 1, 287–305. Tübingen: Mohr Siebeck, 2013.

Visotzky, Burton L. "Three Syriac Cruxes." *JSS* 42 (1991): 167–175.

Vittorio, Berti. "Le débat sur la vision de Dieu et la condamnation des mystiques par Timothée I: La perspective du patriarche." In *Les Mystiques Syriaques,* edited by Alain Desreumaux, 151–176. Paris: Geuthner, 2011.

Vööbus, Arthur. *Syrische Kanonessammlungen. Ein Beitrag zur Quellenkunde*, vol. 1. *A.–B.*, CSCO 307. Louvain: Peeters, 1970.

Vööbus, Arthur. *The Synodicon in the West Syrian Tradition,* CSCO 368. Louvain: Peeters, 1974.

Vööbus, Arthur. *The Pentateuch in the Version of the Syro-Hexapla: A facsimile edition of a Midyat MS. discovered 1964*, CSCO 369. Louvain: Peeters, 1975.

Vööbus, Arthur. *The Didascalia Apostolorum in Syriac,* CSCO 407–408. Louvain: Peeters, 1979.

Vööbus, Arthur. *The Canons Ascribed to Marutha of Maipherqat and Related Sources*, CSCO 439–440. Louvain: Peeters, 1982.

Vosté, J.-M. *Catalogue de la Bibliothèque Syro-Chaldéenne du Couvent de Notre-Dame des Sémences près d'Alqoš (Iraq).* Rome: Angelicum, 1929.

Vosté, J.-M. *Ordo iudiciorum ecclesiasticorum, ordinatus et compositus a Mar Abdišo. Latine interpretatus est notis illustravit.* Rome: Typis Poliglottis Vaticanis, 1940.

Vosté, J.-M. "Paul Bedjan, le lazarist persan (27. nov. 1838 – 9. juin 1920). Notes bio-bibliographiques." *OCP* 11 (1945): 45–102.

Walford, Edward. *Epitome of the Ecclesiastical History of Philostorgus.* London: Henry G. Bohn, 1855.

Walker, Joel T. *Narrative and Christian Heroism in Late Antique Iraq: The Legend of Mar Qardagh the Assyrian.* Berkeley: University of California Press, 2006.

Walter, Nikolaus. "Jewish-Greek Literature of the Greek Period." In *The Cambridge History of Judaism*, vol. 2. *The Hellenistic Age*, edited by W. D. Davies and L. Finkelstein, 285–408. Cambridge: Cambridge University Press, 1989.

Ward, Rachel. *Islamic Metalwork*. London: British Museum Press, 1993.

Watt, John W. "The Strategy of the Baghdad Philosophers. The Aristotelian Tradition as a Common Motif in Christian and Islamic Thought." In *Redefining Christian Identity. Cultural Interaction in the Middle East since the Rise of Islam*, edited by J. J. van Ginkel, H. L. Murre-van den Berg, and T. M. van Lint, 151–165. Louvain: Peeters, 2005.

Watt, John W. "Christianity in the renaissance of Islam. Abū Bishr Mattā, al-Fārābī and Yaḥyā Ibn ʿAdī." In *Christians and Muslims in dialogue in the Islamic Orient of the Middle Ages*, edited by M. Tamcke, 92–112. Würzburg: Ergon, 2007.

Watt, Montgomery. "The materials used by Ibn Isḥāq." In *Historians of the Middle East*, edited by Bernard Lewis and P. M. Holt, 23–34. Oxford: Oxford University Press, 1962.

Weitzman, Michael P. "The Interpretative Character of the Syriac Old Testament." In *Hebrew Bible / Old Testament: The History of its Interpretation*, vol. 1. *From the Beginnings to the Middle Ages (until 1300)*, pt. 1. *Antiquity*, edited by M. Sæbø, 587–611. Göttingen: Vandenhoeck & Ruprecht, 1996.

Weitzman, Michael P. *From Judaism to Christianity. Studies in the Hebrew and Syriac Bibles*, JSS Supplement 8. Oxford: Oxford University Press, 1999.

Weitzman, Michael P. *The Syriac Version of the Old Testament: An Introduction*. University of Cambridge Oriental Publications 56. Cambridge: Cambridge University Press, 1999.

Weltecke, Dorothea. "Überlegungen zu den Krisen der syrisch-orthodoxen Kirche im 12. Jahrhundert." In *Syriaca. Zur Geschichte, Theologie, Liturgie und Gegewartslage der syrischen Kirchen, 2. Deutsches Syrologen-Symposium (Juli 2000, Wittenberg)*, SOK 17, edited by Martin Tamcke, 125–45. Münster: Lit, 2002.

Weltecke, Dorothea. "Contacts between Syriac Orthodox and Latin Military Orders." In *East and West in the Crusader States. Context - contacts - confrontations, III. Acts of the congress held at Hernen in September 2000*, OLA 125, edited by Krijnie Ciggaar and Herman Teule, 53–77. Louvain: Peeters, 2003.

Weltecke, Dorothea. "60 years after Peter Kawerau. Remarks on the Social and Cultural History of Syriac-Orthodox Christians from the IIth to the XIIIth Century." *Le Muséon* 121 (2008): 311–335.

Weltecke, Dorothea. "Les trois grandes chroniques syro-orthodoxes des XIIe et XIIIe siècles." In *L'historiographie Syriaque*, ÉS 6, edited by Muriel Debié, 107–135. Paris: Geuthner, 2009.

Weltecke, Dorothea. "Michael the Syrian and Syriac Orthodox Identity." In *Religious origins of nations? The Christian communities of the Middle East*, edited by Bas ter Haar Romeny, 115–125. Leiden: Brill, 2010.

Weltecke, Dorothea. "Zum syrisch-orthodoxen Leben in der mittelalterlichen Stadt und zu den Hūddōyē (dem Nomokanon) des Bar 'Ebrōyō." In *Orientalia Christiana. Festschrift für Hubert Kaufhold zum 70. Geburtstag*, edited by Peter Bruns and Heinz Luther, 586–613. Wiesbaden: Harrassowitz, 2013.

Weltecke, Dorothea. "Bar 'Ebroyo on Identity: Remarks on his historical writing." *Hugoye* 19 (2016): 303–332.

West, Martin L. *Textual Criticism and Editorial Technique: Applicable to Greek and Latin Texts*. Stuttgart: Teubner, 1973.

Westermann, C. *Genesis 37–50*, Biblischer Kommentar Altes Testament I, 3. Neukirchen-Vluyn: Neukirchener, 1982.

Westphalen, Stephan. "Deir Mar Musa: Die Malschichten 1–3." *ECA* 4 (2007): 99–126.

Wevers, John William. *Genesis*. Septuaginta: Vetus Testamentum Graecum 1. Göttingen: Vandenhoeck & Ruprecht, 1974.

Wevers, John William. *Notes on the Greek Text of Genesis*. Septuagint and Cognate Studies 35. Atlanta: Scholars Press, 1993.

Wexler, Paul. *Explorations in Judeo-Slavic Linguistics*. Leiden: Brill, 1987.

Wexler, Paul. *Three Heirs to a Judeo-Latin Legacy: Judeo-Iberio-Romance, Yiddish, and Rotwelsch*. Wiesbaden: Harrassowitz, 1988.

Wheatley, Paul. *The Places where Men pray together. Cities in Islamic Lands, Seventh through the Tenth Centuries*. Chicago: University of Chicago Press, 2001.

Whitby, Michael. *Evagrius Scholasticus, The Ecclesiastical History*. Liverpool: Liverpool University Press, 2000.

Wickes, Jeffrey T. "'Borrowed' Speech and the Scriptural Poetics of Ephrem's *Hymns on Faith*," unpublished paper given at the 38th Annual Byzantine Studies Conference, Holy Cross Greek Orthodox Theological Seminary, Boston, MA, Nov. 2012.

Wickes, Jeffrey T. *St. Ephrem the Syrian. The Hymns on Faith*, FOC 130. Washington: The Catholic University of America Press, 2015.

Wickes, Jeffrey T. "The Poetics of Self-Presentation in Ephrem's *Hymns on Faith* 10." In *Syriac Encounters: Papers from the Sixth North American Syriac Symposium at Duke University, 26–29 June 2011*, ECS 20, edited by Maria Doerfler, Kyle Smith, and Emanuel Fiano, 51–64. Louvain: Peeters Publishers, 2015.

Wickes, Jeffrey T. "In Search of Ephrem's Audience." Unpublished paper given at the Sacred Song in the Late Antique & Byzantine East: Comparative Explorations Workshop, Providence, RI, May 2015.

Wiesehöfer, Josef. "'Geteilte Loyalitäten'. Religiöse Minderheiten des 3. und 4. Jahrhunderts n.Chr. im Spannungsfeld zwischen Rom und dem sasanidischen Iran." *Klio* 75 (1993): 362–382.

Wiessner, Gernot. *Untersuchungen zur syrischen Literaturgeschichte: Zur Märtyrerüberlieferung aus der Christenverfolgung Schapurs II*. Göttingen: Vandenhoeck and Ruprecht, 1967.

Williams, A. V. "Zoroastrians and Christians in Sasanian Iran," *Bulletin of the John Rylands University Library of Manchester* 78 (1996): 37–54.

Wilmshurst, David. *Ecclesiastical Organisation of the Church of the East*, CSCO 582. Louvain: Peeters, 2000.

Witakowski, Witold. *Chronicle of Pseudo-Dionysius of Tel-Mahre*. Liverpool: Liverpool University Press, 1996.

Witakowski, Witold. "Elias Barshenaya's Chronicle." In *Syriac Polemics. Studies in honour of Gerrit Jan Reinink*, OLA 170, edited by W. J. van Bekkum, J. W. Drijvers, and A. C. Klugkist, 219–237. Louvain: Peeters, 2007.

Wittreck, Fabian. *Interaktion religiöser Rechtsordnungen. Rezeptions- und Translationsprozesse dargestellt am Beispiel des Zinsverbots in den orientalischen Kirchenrechtssammlungen*. Berlin: Duncker & Humblot, 2009.

Wolter, Eugen. *Der Judenknabe. 5 griechische, 14 lateinische und 8 französische texte*. Halle: M. Niemeyer, 1879.

Wood, Philip. *'We have no king but Christ': Christian Political Thought in Greater Syria on the Eve of the Arab Conquest (c. 400–585)*. Oxford: Oxford University Press, 2010.

Wood, Philip. "The sources of the Chronicle of Seert: Phases in the writing of history and hagiography in late antique Iraq." *OC* 96 (2012): 106–48.

Wood, Philip. *The* Chronicle of Seert: *Christian Historical Imagination in Late Antique Iraq*. Oxford: Oxford University Press, 2013.

Wortley, John. *The Spiritual Meadow*. Kalamazoo: Cistercian Publications, 1992.

Wright, William. *Contributions to the Apocryphal Literature of the New Testament*. London: Williams and Norgate, 1865.

Wright, William. *The Homilies of Aphraates, the Persian Sage, edited from Syriac Manuscripts of the fifth and sixth Century in the British Museum,* vol. 1. *The Syriac Text*. London: Williams and Norgate, 1869.

Wright, William. *Catalogue of the Syriac manuscripts in the British Museum acquired since the year 1838*. London: Trustees of the British Museum, 1870–1872.

Wüstenfeld, Ferdinand. *Yāqūt Ibn-ʿAbdallāh ar-Rūmī. Kitāb Muʿǧam al-Buldān*. Leipzig: F. A. Brockhausin Comm., 1866–1873.

Xačʻikyan, Levon. *Tʻovma Mecopʻecʻi. Patmagrutʻyun*. Yerevan: Magałat, 1999.

Younansardaroud, Helen. "A list of the known Manuscripts of the Syriac Maqāmat of ʿAbdīšōʿ bar Brīkā's († 1318): Paradise of Eden." *JAAS* 20: (2006): 28–41.

Younansardaroud, Helen. "ʿAbdīšōʿ bar Brīkā's († 1318) Book of the Paradise of Eden: A Literary Renaissance?" *ECS* 9 (2010): 195–204.

Younansardaroud, Helen. "Sogenannte Neologismen in ʿAḇdīšōʿs Paradies von Eden." In *Geschichte, Theologie, Liturgie und Gegenwartslage der syrischen Kirchen. Beiträge zum sechsten deutschen Syrologen-Symposium in Konstanz, Juli 2009*, edited by Dorothea Weltecke, 53–58. Wiesbaden: Harrassowitz, 2012.

Zaborowski, Jason R. *The Coptic Martyrdom of John of Phanijōit: Assimilation and Conversion to Islam in Thirteenth-Century Egypt*. Leiden: Brill, 2005.

al-Zāwītī, Muhammad Shukrī. *Tafsīr al-Ḍaḥḥāk*. Cairo: Dār al-Salām, 1999.

Zinger, Oded. *Women, Gender and Law: Marital Disputes According to Documents of the Cairo Geniza*. Ph.D. Diss., Princeton University, 2014.

Zingerle, Pius. *Echte Akten heiliger Märtyrer des Morgenlandes*. Innsbruck: Wagner, 1836.

Վարք եւ վկայաբանութիւնք սրբոց. Հատընտիր քաղեալք ի ճառընտրաց [Lives and Martydoms of the Saints: Collected Selections from Collections of Sermons]. Venice, 1874.

Index

1. Hebrew Bible / Old Testament
2. Apocrypha and Pseudepigrapha
3. New Testament
4. Qur'ān
5. Hellenistic Jewish Authors
6. Rabbinic and Medieval Jewish Authors and Texts
7. Early and Medieval Christian Authors and Texts
8. Muslim Authors and Texts
9. Classical (Greek and Latin) Authors and Texts
10. Subjects

Hebrew Bible / Old Testament

Genesis 19
1–3 68
1:14 46
1:27 249
8 46
19:1 104
22 164–165
22:2 108–109
25:8 103
25:17 103
25:22–29 25
35:29 103
37:12 163
48:2 102
48:12 102
49:33 97–110

Exodus
3:8 109
3:17 109
13:5 109
13:21 185
21:5–6 169–170
24:10 244
32 72
33:20 236

Leviticus
10:1–3 28

Deuteronomy
15:16–17 169

2 Chronicles
3:1 109

Psalms 187
39:6 40
42:21 vi

Isaiah
24:15 244
65:17 240
66:22 240

Ezekiel
16:25 103

Daniel 25, 143
3 155–158, 161
7:5 25

Zechariah
8:7 136

Apocrypha and Pseudepigrapha

Jubilees
18:13 109
23:1 105

4 Maccabees 138

Testaments of the Twelve Patriarchs 105–106

New Testament

Matthew
5:8 236
7:24–30 66
8:5–13 66, 76
9:2 74
12:40 37, 42
15:21–28 31, 66–82
16:21 37
17:23 37
20:19 37
22:30 30
23:37–40 57
26:61 37

Mark
7:24–30 31
7:28 70, 72
9:31 37
10:34 37
14:58 37

Luke
13:32 37
16:19–31 70–71
17:21 237
18:33 37
23:46 161, 164
24:7 37

John
2:19 37
8:33 170

Acts
15:1 35

Romans
1:21 93
8:17 78
13:1–7 23

1 Corinthians
14:33–35, 37 31
15:4 37

2 Corinthians
4:18 236
6:7 35

Galatians
2:20 249
3:29 78
4:1 78

1 Timothy
2:11–12 31

James 100

2 Peter
3:13 240

Revelation
21:1 240

Qurʾān

3:40 191
4:169 191
5:82 196
9:31 196
9:34 196
19:35 191
22:78 194
85:4–8 191–192

Hellenistic Jewish Authors

Philo 109

Rabbinic and Medieval Jewish Authors and Texts

Babylonian Talmud 28

Moed Katan
17b 41
19b 41
20b 41

Pesachim
4a 41

Qiddushin
72a 25–26

Genesis Rabbah 109

Mishnah 8

Targumim 97, 104–105, 108–109, 165

Early and Medieval Christian Authors and Texts

Aba 123, 140
Abba Isaiah 229, 231
Abba Yawnan 143
ʿAbdishoʿ bar Brikha 266–268, 270, 272
Catalogue 223
Nomocanon 229
ʿAbdishoʿ Ḥazzaya *see* Joseph Ḥazzaya
Abraham of Nathpar 60–63
Abraham Qidunaya 131
Abū Makārim 258

Acacius at Byzantium 137
Acts of Matthew and Andrew 137, 143
Acts of Thomas 8, 137, 143
Agapius of Mabbug
Kitāb al-'unwan 213, 215, 217–220
Aḥudemmeh 137
Alexander and Theodulus at Rome 132
Ammonius and others 137
Ammonius
Massacre of Monks of Mt Sinai 137
Pseudo-Amphilochios of Iconium 12
'Amr b. Mattā 214
Aphrahaṭ 34, 36, 39–41, 50–82, 101, 239
Apollonius and Philemon 131
Apophthegmata Patrum 178
Athanasius 26–28, 229
Contra Gentes 236
Life of Antony 173
Awgen 143
Babai the Great 123. *See also* George (63) *under Persian Martyr Acts*
Babylas 137–138, 153, 161–162
Bar 'Ebroyo 205, 210, 266–268, 270–274
Mukhtaṣār fī al-duwal 214
Bardaiṣan 5–6
Barḥadbshabba
Ecclesiastical History 127, 220, 224
On the Cause of the Foundation of the Schools 92–93
Barsamya 128, 137
Basil of Caesarea 4, 12
Behnam Ḥedlaya 142
Book of Steps 236
Charisius and others 137
Christopher and others 138, 143
Chronicle of 724 223
Chronicle of 1234 220, 225, 267–268
Chronicle of Edessa 128
Chronicle of Khuzistan 221
Chronicle of Seert 9, 127, 142, 213–215, 220–221, 224
Chronicle of Zuqnin 220, 223
Clement of Alexandria
Stromateis 86, 89, 236
Commentary on the Diatessaron see under Ephrem
Cosmas and Damianus 131, 138
Crescens 132
Cyprian and Justina 139, 143
Cyriacus and Julitta 143, 155
Cyril of Scythopolis
Life of Sabas 155
Cyrus of Batna 224
Cyrus of Ḥarran 134
Death of the Blessed Mother of God 138
Didascalia 39–41
Dionysius bar Ṣalibi 270
Dionysius of Tel Maḥre 224
Pseudo-Dionysius the Areopagite 226–227, 229–231, 249
Celestial Hierarchy 230
Divine Names 230, 241
Discovery of the Cross 131
Doctrina Addai see Teaching of Addai

Domitius the Physician 137
Eleutherius 132
Eliya of Nisibis 267–268
Chronicle 214–215, 217, 221–222, 224–225
Dictionary 222
Grammar 222
Ephraem Graecus 13–15, 17
Ephrem 3–49, 59, 66–82, 101, 132, 142, 163, 229, 233
Commentary on Genesis 18–19, 46–48, 106
Commentary on the Diatessaron (possibly spurious) 40, 45, 74–78
Hymns against Heresies 23
Hymns against Julian 10–12, 23–24, 26
Hymns on Abraham Kidunaya and Julian Saba 19–21
Hymns on Faith 4, 7, 18, 23–24, 26, 28, 33–34, 69
Hymns on Nisibis 11, 20, 22–24, 28, 36
Hymns on Paradise 10, 21, 33, 68–69, 71, 73
Hymns on the Crucifixion 37–49
Hymns on the Fast 34
Hymns on the Nativity 32, 71, 80
Hymns on the Resurrection 33
Hymns on Virginity 21
Second Discourse to Hypatius 43, 45–48
Sermon on our Lord 24, 71–73
Erasmus vi
Eugenia, Claudia, and others in Egypt 137
Eusebius of Caesarea 21, 116, 118, 220, 222–224
Martyrs of Palestine 128, 133
Praeparatio Evangelica 86, 89
Eustace of Mtskheta 166
Eustratius of Constantinople
Life of Golindouch 141–142
Eutychius of Alexandria
Annals 213–215, 217, 219–220
Evagrius 96, 226–227, 229, 238, 246–247, 249
Evagrius Scholasticus
Ecclesiastical History 154–160
Febronia 139
Gennadius of Marseilles 52–82
George Synkellos
Ecloga chronographica 218
George the Monk
Chronikon syntomon 218
George, bishop of the Arabs 60, 64
Homily on Severus 105
George 143
Gewargis Warda 124, 266. *See also* Tahmazgard (56) *under Persian Martyr Acts*
Gordianus, father of George 143
Gregory of Nazianzus 90
Gregory of Nyssa 4, 16, 226–227, 229, 231–232, 236–237, 249

De tridui spatio 39, 40
Commentary on the Song of Songs 229
Gregory of Palamas 237
Gregory of Tours
Glory of the Martyrs 154–160
Habib 128, 137
Himyarite Martyrs 143
Himyarite Martyrs from Bar Sahde 140
History of Arbela 220
History of the Patriarchs of Alexandria 214
Ḥunayn b. Isḥāq 213
Ignatius of Antioch 139, 143
Image of Christ 137, 143
Invention of the Cross 143
Isaiah of Aleppo 143
Isho' bar Nun 229
Isho'dad of Merv 29
Isho'dnaḥ of Baṣra
Book of Chastity 220, 227–228
Isho'yahb III 123. *See also* Isho'sabran (64) *under Persian Martyr Acts*
Jacob bar Shakko 266
Jacob of Edessa
Chronicle 223–224
Jacob of Serugh 142, 155
History of Ḥannina 137
Homily on Ephrem (B^2 24 = B^1 33) 4, 7, 19–20, 30–31
Homily on Habib the Martyr (B^2 159 = B^1 232) 155
Homily on the Canaanite Woman (B^2 269 = B^1 396) 66–82
Letters 125
Jacob the Egyptian 138
Jerome 12
Illustrious Men 52
John Bar Malke 143
John Chrysostom 13, 75
De sancto Babylas 153
John Moschos
Spiritual Meadow 154–160
John of Apamea 94, 228
John of Dalyatha 226–250
John of Ephesus
Lives of the Eastern Saints 127, 130
John of Phenek 127, 220–221
John Phanijoit 134
John Rufus
Plerophories 155
John the Little of Scetis 137
John, bishop of Alexandria 137
Joseph Ḥazzaya 228, 247, 249
Judas, the Jewish convert 131
Julian Romance 129, 133
Julian Saba 131, 137
Juliane 143
Justin Martyr
Dialogue with Trypho 38
Kitāb al-majdal 214, 217
Leontios
Life of Simeon the Holy Fool 137, 155
Leontius 138, 152
Letter of Mara bar Serapion 89
Life of Ephrem 3–36
Lucian and Marcian 137

Lucius and others 132
Pseudo-Macarius 226–227, 229, 243–244, 249–250
Mamas 137–138
Man of God 131, 177, 179, 184–185, 187–188
Man who robbed a grave 137
Mar Mari 143
Mārī b. Sulaymān 214
Martianius 137
Marutha of Maypherqaṭ 117, 127, 137, 146
Marutha of Takrit 136, 194
Mary the Egyptian 131
Michael the Great 138–139, 220, 267–268, 270–271
Mika 143
Mimes 143
Miracles of Nicolaus 137
Monk and his sister 137
Montanus and Lucius 155
Moses bar Kepha 135
Mukhtaṣār al-akhbār al-bīʿiyya 214–215, 217, 220–221
Narrative of Dionysius the Areopagite 137
Narsai 127, 155
    Homily 32 'On the Canaanite Woman' 66–82
Pseudo-Nonnos
    Mythological Scholia 90–92
Odes of Solomon 34–35
Onesimus 138
Origen
    Commentary on Matthew 38–39
Orosius
    History against the Pagans 214, 217
Pachomius 29
Panegyric of the Martyrs 136, 140
Pantaleon 143
Paphnutius 131, 137
Paul of Qenṭos and John of Edessa 174–197
Persian Martyr Acts 113–173
    10 Martyrs (45) 121, 140
    40 Martyrs (30) 136–137, 140, 143
    111 Men and 9 Women (17) 117, 132–133, 136, 138, 140
    Aba (59) 123, 139–140
    ʿAbda (44) 121, 139
    ʿAbda damšiḥā (43) 123–125, 134, 138, 149–173
    Abraham of Arbela (16) 120, 140
    Adhurhormizd and Anahid (52) 122, 140, 165
    Aitallaha and Hophsai (24) 120, 140
    ʿAqebshma (31) 120, 132–133, 136, 140
    Azad (12) 117
    Baboi 140
    Baday (32) 140
    Badma (33) 132–133, 140
    Barbaʿshmin (18) 117, 132, 136–137, 140
    Barḥadbshabba of Arbela (23) 120, 132–133, 140
    Barshebya (34) 126, 133, 136–137, 140
    Bassus and Susanna (42) 123–125, 167–168

Behnam and Sarah (22) 123–124, 134, 137–139, 142–143, 152
Candida (1) 126, 130
Captives (27) 126, 136, 140
Christina (Yazdoy) (62) 123
Dadu (35) 139
Daniel and Warda (36) 126, 133, 136, 140–141
George (Mihramgushnasp) (63) 123, 139, 165–166
Great Slaughter (10) 117, 140
Gregory (Pir[an]gushnasp) 123, 139–141, 165–167
Gubralaha and Qazo (4) 123–124, 126–127, 140
Ḥnanya (19) 120, 137, 140
Isho'sabran (Mahanosh) (64) 123, 136, 165–166
Jacob and Azad (29) 120, 140
Jacob and Mary (20) 120, 133, 140
Jacob Intercisus (48) 121–122, 124, 128, 130–131, 140, 142–143
Jacob the Notary (49) 121, 139–140
John of Arbela (14) 120, 140
Karka d-Beth Slokh (53) 120, 125–126, 139–140, 143
Ma'in (37) 125, 138
Martha (9) 117, 138, 140
Martyrs of Gilan (21) 140
Martyrs of Karka d-Beth Slokh (39) 120, 126, 140
Martyrs of Tur Ber'ain (2) 123–124, 138, 143, 166
Martyrs outside court (38) 117, 136
Mihrshabur (50) 121, 136
Miles (40) 126, 130–133, 136, 139–140
Narsai (46) 121, 139–140, 161
Peroz (51) 121, 139
Pethion (54) 122, 138, 142, 152, 165
Pinḥas (41) 123–125, 161
Pusai (8) 117, 119, 138, 140
Qardagh (26) 115, 123, 140, 143
Saba (28) 126, 139, 166
Saba (58) 126, 139, 143
Shabur 121, 125, 139
Shabur of Niqator, Isaac of Karka d-Beth Slokh, and their companions (5) 125, 132, 136, 140–141
Shahdost (13) 117, 132, 136–138, 140, 143
Simeon bar Ṣabba'e (martyrdom = A) (6) 117–119, 126, 133–134, 136–137, 140
Simeon bar Ṣabba'e (history = B) (7) 117–119, 126, 138, 140, 143

Tahmazgard (56) 124
Tarbo (11) 117, 132–133, 136–138, 140, 143
Tataq (47) 121, 140
Thecla and her companions (25) 120, 133, 140, 143
Yazdin (55) 122
Yazdpaneh (61) 123, 139–140
Zebina and his companions (3) 125, 132, 136, 140–141
Philoxenos of Mabbug 9, 231
Placidus and others 138, 143
Praepositus Romulus and others 138
Probus, Tarachus, and Andronicus 138
Procopus at Caesarea 137
Protonike Legend 132
Qusṭā b. Lūqā
The Paradise 213
Rabban Hormizd 143
Rabbula 177, 187
Rish Quryān 4
Saba of the Mountain 137
Sabrisho‘ 123, 140
Sa‘īd b. Baṭrīq 215
Ṣalībā b. Yūḥannā 214
Sergius and Bacchus 136, 143
Seven Sleepers 143
Severus of Antioch 9
Sharbel 128, 137
Shmona and Gurya 128
Simeon Barqaya 223
Simeon of Beth Arsham 184
Simeon of Beth Garmai 223
Simeon of Ṭaybutheh 229
Simeon the Stylite, Letters of 133
Simeon the Stylite, Life of 133
Sophia and her daughters, Sophia, Pistis, Elpis, and Agape 131, 137
Sozomen
Ecclesiastical History 118, 127–128
Stephen of Hierapolis 142
Stephen 143
Stratonice and Seleucus at Cyzicus 137–138
Symeon the Logothete
Chronicle 218
Synksar 5–6
T’ovma Mecop’ec’i 202
Ṭalya 138
Tarachus, Probus, and Andronicus 137
Teaching of Addai 10–11, 22, 128, 131–133
Teaching of Peter 131
Teaching of the Apostles 131
Thecla 138, 143
Theodore 138
Theodore bar Koni
Scholion 93
Theodore of Mopsuestia 10, 67, 80
Theodoret of Cyrrhus
De Graecarum affectionum curatione 87, 89
Theonilla 166
Theophanes Confessor
Chronographia 218
Theophilus of Edessa
History 215
Theopompus 137

Timothy I 228, 237, 245
Trypho 139
Virgin of Caesarea 138
Yaḥyā al-Anṭākī 214, 217–218
Yaḥyā b. ʿAdī 205

Muslim Authors and Texts

ʿAbd Allāh b. al-Mubārak
Book of Jihād 196
Anas b. Mālik 179
al-Bukhārī 179
Farīd al-Dīn ʿAttār
Memorial of the Saints 196
Ibn Abī Uṣaybiʿa
History of Physicians 213
Ibn al-Azraq
History of Mayyāfāriqīn 194
Ibn Hishām 174
The Book of the Crowns of the Kings of Himyar 181
Ibn Isḥāq 179
Life of Muhammad 174–197
Ibn al-Nadīm
The Fihrist 213
Ibn Sīrīn 179
Khalīfa ibn Khayyāṭ
History 218
Maʿmar b. Rāshid 179
Masʿūdī
Murūj al-dhahab 218
al-Mughīra 179, 181
al-Ṭabarī
The History of Prophets and Kings 178, 218
Wahb b. Munabbih 180–181
al-Yaʿqūbī
Complete History 218
Yāqūt al-Rūmī 258
al-Zuhrī 179

Classical (Greek and Latin) Authors and Texts

Aristotle 232
De Anima 232
De Sensu 232
Diogenes the Cynic 94
Juvenal
Satire 14
Libanius
Oration 42 "For Thallasius" 14
Pindar 27
Plato 231–232, 234
Republic 85–96
Thaetetus 232
Timaeus 90, 232
Porphyry 232
Socrates 86, 89, 91–92
Tacitus
Annals 14

Subjects

Abraham of Nisibis 24, 35–36
Abu Galib, Monastery of 138
Adiabene 25, 119
Aetian(s) 23
ʿAlī b. Abī Ṭālib 195
Alqosh 143, 208
Amid 11
Antioch 22, 87, 153, 256

Paulinian(s) 23
Photinian(s) 23
Quanzhou 260
Rome 132
Sabellian(s) 23
Sabinianus 14
Samarqand 202
Samosata 259
School of the Persians (Edessa) 10, 130
Sennacherib 124
Serigus *see* Baḥira
Shapur II 11, 113–114, 119, 141, 162
Sinjar 125, 153–154, 158, 163, 171
Sumaysat *see* Samosata
Takrit 131, 135
Tamerlane *see* Tīmūr Lang
Theodosius II 6
Thomas 22. *See also Acts of Thomas under* 7
Tiberias 259
Tīmūr Lang 201
Trajan 128
Ulugh Bey 201
Vahram II 114
Vahram V 114, 120–121
Wadi Murabba'at 108
Walashfarr 122
Yazdgard I 114, 150, 162
Yazdgard II 114, 120–122
Yuḥanon of Mardin 270, 274
Zayton *see* Quanzhou
Zeno 10